Handbook
of
Comparative
Public Budgeting
and
Financial
Management

PUBLIC ADMINISTRATION AND PUBLIC POLICY

A Comprehensive Publication Program

Executive Editor

JACK RABIN
Professor of Public Administration and Public Policy
Division of Public Affairs
The Capital College
The Pennsylvania State University—Harrisburg
Middletown, Pennsylvania

Additional Volumes in Preparation

ANNALS OF PUBLIC ADMINISTRATION

Handbook
of
Comparative
Public Budgeting
and
Financial
Management

edited by

Thomas D. Lynch
Lawrence L. Martin

School of Public Administration
Florida Atlantic University
Fort Lauderdale, Florida

Marcel Dekker, Inc.   **New York • Basel • Hong Kong**

Library of Congress Cataloging-in-Publication Data

Handbook of comparative public budgeting and financial management /
  edited by Thomas D. Lynch and Lawrence L. Martin.
     p.   cm. -- (Public administration and public policy ; 50)
  Includes bibliographical references and index.
  ISBN 0-8247-8773-0 (alk. paper)
  1. Finance, Public. 2. Budget. I. Lynch, Thomas Dexter.
  II. Martin, Lawrence L. III. Series.
HJ236.H26 1993
336--dc20   92-36823
                                                          CIP

This book is printed on acid-free paper.

MARCEL DEKKER, INC.
270 Madison Avenue, New York, New York 10016

Current printing (last digit):
10 9 8 7 6 5 4 3 2 1

PRINTED IN THE UNITED STATES OF AMERICA

Preface

This book breaks new ground by stressing both a comparative and empirical approach to public budgeting and financial management. Although this approach has been used before, especially in recent journal articles, this book significantly furthers that trend. In the history of mankind, the theory that the earth was the center of the universe was supreme for many centuries because it was consistent with religious beliefs and was also quite simple and elegant. With the invention of better telescopes and through careful observation, the scientific community slowly but eventually accepted other theories of the universe. Facts are the basis we must use to judge and revise our "knowledge," which we call theory.

In public budgeting and financial management, we have descriptive and prescriptive theories that serve us, but a better use of the comparative and empirical approach will be our telescope to improve our theories. By looking at such topics as cash management, budget behavior, and capital budgeting, we can use the comparative and empirical approach to better understand each phenomenon and, consequently, to improve our theories. With better theories, we can better shape our public policies and manage more intelligently.

This book is organized into an overview section and three parts. The first part focuses on international comparative subjects, the second part covers comparative national public budgeting, and the third part covers national comparative public financial management topics.

We believe this book serves several purposes. It should help practitioners and academics keep up with developments in this field. It should also serve academics as a textbook or a supplemental reader in public budgeting and financial management courses. It can also be used in a comparative public budgeting course.

An edited book requires the cooperation and goodwill of many people. We thank all the contributors for their time and patience. We thank Rita Kraemer and Ilene Graham for their smiles and professionalism; coordinating various manuscript and reducing them to one style is a challenge that was met with good grace and necessary persistence. We thank Jack Rabin, Marcel Dekker's Public Administration and Public Policy series editor, for his faith in this project and his wonderful positive spirit.

Thomas D. Lynch
Lawrence L. Martin

Contents

Part II.   Subnational Comparative Public Budgeting

Part III.   Subnational Comparative Financial Management

Contributors

Charles K. Coe is an Associate Professor of Political Science and Public Administration at North Carolina State University at Raleigh. He is the author of *Public Financial Management* and numerous articles on budgeting and financial management.

C. Bradley Doss, Jr., D.P.A., is a Research Associate in the Center for Urban Policy Research at Georgia State University. He also teaches budgeting and financial management in Georgia State's MPA program. He is coauthor of *Fiscal Triage for Government* (1989). In addition to budgeting, his academic interests include housing policy and community development.

Marvin J. Druker is an Assistant Professor of Public Affairs in the Department of Management and Organizational Studies at the Lewiston-Auburn College of the University of Southern Maine. His teaching and research interests include interdisciplinary approaches to managing public organizations and public policy. He has co-authored several articles on downsizing in state governments, focusing on the use of innovation and the impact on quality of working life.

John P. Forrester is an Assistant Professor of Public Administration at the University of Missouri—Columbia. His research interests include budgeting and finance. He has published several articles on this topic.

Merl Hackbart, Ph.D., is Professor of Finance and Public Administration and Special Assistant to the Chancellor at the University of Kentucky. He has twice served as State Budget Director for the Commonwealth of Kentucky and was the first Director of the Martin School of Public Administration at the University of Kentucky. His research and publications have focused on public financial management, including state government debt and cash management.

Robert D. Lee, Jr. is a Professor of Public Administration and Head of the Department of Public Administration at Pennsylvania State University, University Park. He is the lead author of *Public Budgeting Systems*, 4th ed. (1989) and author of *Public Personnel Systems* 2nd ed. (1987).

Kuo-Tsai Liou is Assistant Professor of Public Administration at Florida Atlantic University. His research interests are in public management and public policy analysis.

Thomas D. Lynch is Professor at the School of Public Administration, College of Urban and Public Affairs, Florida Atlantic University, Fort Lauderdale. The author or coauthor of over 25 journal articles and book chapters, as well as the author, editor, or coeditor of seven books, including *Handbook on Public Budgeting and Financial Management* (coedited with Jack Rabin) and *Organization Theory and Management* (both titles, Marcel Dekker, Inc.), he is a member of the American Society for Public Administration, the Government Finance Officers Association of the United States and Canada, and the International Institute of Administrative Sciences, among others. Dr. Lynch received the B.A. degree (1964) from the University of Idado, Moscow, and the M.P.A. degree (1966) in public administration and the Ph.D. degree (1974) in political science from the Rockefeller College of Public Affairs and Policy, the State University of New York at Albany.

Lawrence L. Martin is Associate Professor at the School of Public Administration, College of Urban and Public Affairs, Florida Atlantic University, Fort Lauderdale. The author or coauthor of more than 20 journal articles and book chapters and the coauthor of two books, he is a member of the American Society for Public Administration, the Policy Studies Organization, and the International Institute of Administrative Science. Dr. Martin received the B.S. degree (1971) in political science from Arizona State University, Tempe, the M.I.M. degree (1972) in international management from the American Graduate School of International Management, Glendale, Arizona, and the M.S.W. degree (1980) in social work and the Ph.D. degree (1986) in political science from Arizona State University, Tempe.

Clifford P. McCue is currently affiliated with Florida International University Institute of Government as Research Associate. Additionally, he is a Ph.D. candidate in Public Administration specializing in financial and budgetary management. Prior to joining F.I.U., he served as Senior Budget Analyst, Assistant Finance Director, and Finance Director with various local governments throughout the United States. His current research and publication interests include public pension fund management, public accounting, and auditing.

A. Premchand, an Indian national, is an Assistant Director of the Fiscal Affairs Department, International Monetary Fund. He has written extensively on government financial management. His books include *Government Budgeting and Expenditure Controls* (1983).

James R. Ramsey has a Ph.D. in economics from the University of Kentucky. He is currently the Vice President for Administration and a Professor of Economics at Western Kentucky University. Dr. Ramsey has taught economics at Middle Tennessee State University and has been Associate Dean in the College of Business Administration at Loyola University, New Orleans. Dr. Ramsey was an adjunct Professor at the University of Kentucky and has done consulting work and training programs for several states and corporations. He also was the Chief State Economist for the Commonwealth of Kentucky and Executive Director of the state's Office of Financial Management and Economic Analysis. In addition, Dr. Ramsey has served as Director of Investments for Republic Savings Bank, on the Board of Trustees of the Churchill Tax Free Fund, and the Board of Trustees of the Kentucky Retirement System.

Betty D. Robinson is an Assistant Professor of Management and Organizational Studies at Lewiston-Auburn College, University of Southern Maine. Her areas of expertise include labor relations, human services management, and social policy. She serves on the State of Maine Board of Arbitration and Conciliation and has worked both for labor organizations and management in the human services area. She has published articles in the *Employee Responsibilities and Rights Journal, Employment Relations Today, Sociological Practice Review* and the *Journal of Health and Human Resources Administration*.

Charles J. Spindler is an Assistant Professor of Political Science and holds a joint appointment with the Center for Governmental Services as Research Coordinator at Auburn University, Alabama. He has published in *State and Local Government Review, Policy Studies Review, New Directions in Program Evaluation*, as well as participating in grant and contract research. He has 13 years of practitioner experience, serving as city manager, director of economic development, and community organizer for a community action agency. He received a Doctorate of Public Administration from the University of Georgia in 1986.

Keith J Ward is Director of the Center for Governmental Services and Associate Professor of Political Science at Auburn University, Alabama. His applied research in financial administration, intergovernmental relations, and tax reform has been directed toward improving state and local government in Alabama. He received the Ph.D. degree from the University of Tennessee in 1971.

Katherine G. Willoughby is an Assistant Professor in the School of Public Administration and Urban Studies at Georgia State University in Atlanta. She received her D.P.A. from the University of Georgia and is the 1991 recipient of the NASPAA Dissertation Award for her work on the decision making orientations of state government executive budget analysts. She has published articles in *Public Budgeting and Financial Management* and *Review of Public Personnel Administration*.

1

Comparative Perspective

Thomas D. Lynch

Florida Atlantic University, Fort Lauderdale, Florida

The literature on public budgeting and financial management is rich with ideas, prescriptions, and case histories. However, it is weak in empirical comparative information. In Woodrow Wilson's 1887 *The Study of Administration*, he said "...so long as we know only ourselves, we know nothing." The lack of empirical comparative information is understandable because gathering needed data is difficult, especially when grant support for this type of research is rarely available. The literature deficiency is unfortunate because we need to better understand the state of the profession which can often best be accomplished by empirical comparative research. With a better comprehension of where we stand professionally, our prescriptions can be sharper and we can avoid misdirections. This book begins to address this deficiency in the literature. Chapters 2, 3, and 4 focus on international comparative subjects. Chapters 5, 6, 7, and 8 cover national comparative subjects related to public budgeting. Chapters 9, 10, 11, 12, and 13 address comparative public financial management and capital budgeting.

Spindler and Ward contribute the chapter titled "Contemporary Revenue Systems of the OECD Member Countries: Trends and Analysis." They note Western European countries are making remarkable progress in moving toward economic unity. Their chapter examines the broad trends in revenue systems, especially: (a) the ratio of total taxes to gross domestic product, (b) the average ratio of major taxes to gross domestic product, (c) trends in tax revenues in dollars per capita, (d) trends in major tax ratios, (e) tax equity and incidence comparisons, and (f) trends in direct and indirect taxes.

"An Analysis of Budgetary Performance in the G-7 Industrialized Nations, 1980–1989" by Kuo-Tsai (Thomas) Liou examines the seven major industrial counties during the 1980s in an attempt to assess the impact of fiscal restraint policy. All seven attempted to deal with their yearly deficits and some significantly lowered the yearly increase of their deficits. The best performing countries were the United Kingdom, Japan, and Germany. Interestingly, countries with unitary rather than federal systems tended to perform better at deficit reduction.

A. Premchand at the International Monetary Fund provides us with "A Cross-National Analysis of Financial Management Practices." He stresses that national financial management success depends largely on the formulation and implementation of fiscal policy. In turn, fiscal policy depends on the attention devoted to the design and day-to-day operation of governmental financial management systems.

Premchand notes that national financial management systems can be grouped in categories he calls the British-type system, the French system, the European system, the U.S. system, the Latin American system, the Far East system, and centrally planned economies in transition. He notes that economic conditions impact heavily on a country's approach to financial management. He states that many countries have made improvements in their capacity to ensure effective financial management but many more countries still have financial management systems that can be seriously questioned.

Katherine Willoughby's chapter, "Patterns of Behavior: Factors Influencing the Spending Judgments of Public Budgeters," begins the second set of chapters. These chapters focus on comparative studies within the United States. Her chapter looks at budget behavior in several state governments focusing on budget analysts. She concludes that analysts take their cues from two or three contextual factors when making spending recommendations. She identifies gubernatorial direction, efficiency of agency operation, and work load changes as the important determinants. Her chapter deserves careful review because it takes a unique look at budget behavior and serves as a research model for the academic community.

Cliff McCue's "Local Government Revenue Diversification: A Portfolio Analysis and Evaluation" provides an examination of trends in revenue diversification within the United States. He looks at common revenue sources including sales taxes, income taxes, user charges, and property tax. He finds that the most significant trend in local government taxation is the sales tax which is increasing rapidly. He concludes by noting that local governments have become less reliant on the property tax and are turning to special districts as a means of financing certain types of government services.

John Forrester's chapter, "Use of Revenue Forecasting Techniques," provides an empirical look at revenue forecasting. Every budget is always based on often sensitive and important guesses called revenue forecasts. The normative literature tells us how to forecast better, but little empirical data exists on actual forecasting practices. A continuing debate in the prescriptive literature is between the rationalists, who argue for the use of more sophisticated analytical techniques and the incrementalists, who argue that budgetary decisions are a function of politics.

Forrester believes his empirical findings support the arguments of the rationalists over the incrementalists. He notes that over half of his study respondents generate forecasts using sometimes simple, but also complicated, techniques. He also argues that forecasting does not necessarily displace crucial political and organizational values. Forrester believes that budget reforms, such as the use of forecasting techniques, may not be doomed to failure as argued by the incrementalist. He also finds that budget preparation at the local level has matured in spite of theoretical limitations cited in the literature.

In "The Use of Program Information and Analysis in State Budgeting: Trends of Two Decades," Robert Lee explores state budgeting practices during the 1970s and 1980s. This was a period of remarkable change, especially in terms of using program information and analysis. Lee's conclusions support the Forrester chapter as he notes that program analysis is being used increasingly in executive and legislative decision making. He finds a parallel between the normative budget literature and the practice of budgeting at the state level. Lee speculates that a possible plateau has been reached in the use of program information.

In "States' Responses to Budget Shortfalls: Cutback Management Techniques," Marvin Druker and Betty Robinson address the phenomenon known as cutback management. The literature discusses the topic at length. But how do our state governments respond to fiscal crisis and what are the managerial implications of those responses? Druker and Robinson answer those two questions.

The lead offering in Part III, "Government Purchasing: The State of the Practice," is written by Charles Coe. He examines the state of the practice in government purchasing and concludes that the report card is mixed. Coe discusses the improvements and the various aspects of purchasing that still need improvement. He concludes by noting that there are increasing demands being placed on the purchasing profession due to such factors as heightened ethical standards, demand for better and cost efficient services, increased business competition, resistance to tax increases, and an increasingly sophisticated technology.

The next chapter—"Contracting Out: A Comparative Analysis of Local Government Practices"—is written by the co-editor of this volume. Lawrence Martin maintains that privatization has become an integral part of financial management in government and that contracting out is by far the most popular means of privatization. His chapter examines the current state of the profession in contracting out. Although this technique is widely used in local government, it appears more popular in health and human services, general government administration, public works, transportation, and utility services. Martin argues that contracting out does help constrain and lower service costs largely because private contractors (1) often can get more work out of their employees, (2) make better use of part-time employees, and (3) hold their managers more accountable. Martin maintains that the future should show no lessening in the use of contracting out as a viable public financial management technique.

Ramsey and Hackbart write in "Managing State Debt: Issues and Challenges" that state governments are using debt financing increasingly to fund major capital and infrastructure needs. Although long-term capital projects can be funded logically by borrowing, they argue that there are limits and that rating agencies attempt to quantify an issuer's ability to apply debt service. They explain how an estimating model can help calculate an issuers's debt capacity.

Bradley Doss in "Capital Budgeting Practices" discusses local government capital budgeting versus private capital budgeting, with stress placed on how local financial planners and elected decision makers address capital decisions. Doss finds city size is important in estimating the scope and breadth of capital budgeting practices. He discovers that the definition of Capital Improvement Plan found in the professional literature is too limited to accurately reflect current practices. Not withstanding the literature, Doss finds that traditional methods of financing debt are still preferred. Interestingly, Doss finds that many of the same considerations and constraints exist in both public and private capital spending decisions. Nevertheless, there are important differences in the implementation of the practice both between the sectors and within population strata of the public sector.

In the last chapter, "Public Cash Management: Issues and Practices," Hackbart and Ramsey note that the normative theory of cash management has had a significant impact on state and local government during the last decade. This unusual team of authors consists of a professor and a practitioner professionally interested in cash management. Their chapter identifies and discusses cash management beyond investment of public funds. Their discussion includes the receipt and deposit of funds, cash forecasting, and banking relationships. They point out that the goals of cash management are to ensure that public deposits are made in a timely fashion, bills are paid on time, and available funds are invested properly. They identify four major components of cash management and how each can enhance investment earnings.

In conclusion, this book takes a comprehensive comparative look at the practice of public budgeting and financial management. It begins the process of determining where we stand as a profession at the beginning of the 1990s. One overall conclusion drawn from the various chapters is that the normative litera-ture has indeed made an impact on the practice of public budgeting and finan-cial management. The hope of the editors is that more comparative and empiri-cal research will be conducted so that we can increase our understanding of our field beyond what was possible in this volume. Research, as illustrated in this book, sharpens our collective understanding and permits us to improve our normative theories, education, and training.

Part One
National Comparative Administration

2

Contemporary Revenue Systems of the OECD Member Countries: Trends and Analysis

Charles J. Spindler and Keith J Ward

Auburn University, Auburn, Alabama

I. INTRODUCTION

This chapter examines the public revenue systems of 23 industrial countries in a comparative framework. Overall, the discussion incorporates several perspectives: 1) historical trends and recent reforms; 2) identification of specific revenue sources; 3) differences in revenue systems on the basis of the system of government: federal or unitary; 4) tax equity; and 5) direct and indirect taxation. The comparison of revenue systems begins with a presentation of broad trends, followed by a discussion of major taxes. The taxes discussed include personal and corporate income, property and consumption, and social security. The last section presents a brief summary and conclusions.

The raw data presented in the discussion of major taxes is drawn from the Organisation for Economic Co-operation and Development (OECD).[1] OECD publishes annual financial statistics on 23 member countries. While the International Monetary Fund (IMF) publishes annual financial statistics for 137 countries (IMF, 1988), this is an unwieldy number for comparative analysis. The OECD member countries are roughly equivalent to countries the IMF designates as industrial countries. The IMF industrial countries include Australia, Austria, Belgium, Canada, Denmark, Finland, France, Germany, Iceland, Ireland, Japan, Luxembourg, Netherlands, New Zealand, Norway, Spain, Sweden, Switzerland, United Kingdom, and United States (IMF, 1988). The OECD member countries include all the foregoing as well as Greece, Italy, Portugal, and Turkey. While Iceland is an OECD member, it does not report financial data to the OECD. The members of the European Economic Community are a smaller subset of the OECD countries: Belgium, Denmark, France, Germany, Greece, Ireland, Italy, Luxembourg, the Netherlands, Portugal, Spain, and the United Kingdom. The OECD data set permits the reader to analyze subsets of countries in greater detail, including the IMF Industrial Countries and the twelve member countries of the European Community which constitute Europe 1992.

A. Problems Underlying the Analysis of Revenue Systems

One inherent problem in any cross-national comparison of public revenue systems is the variation in each country's historical and political base. Each revenue system is influenced by a unique combination of taxation, fiscal, and expenditure policies based on historical precedence and politics, and is further impacted by broad economic trends. The result is a continual evolution and change in revenue systems which makes synopsis extremely difficult.

A second complication in comparing revenue systems arises from differences in utilization of nontax revenues. Some governments own and operate public utilities such as water, electric power, and telephone enterprises which support government expenditures and offset taxes, while other countries must rely more heavily on tax revenues for services. As a result, countries differ on the use of taxes compared to the use of fees or sale of government services. These differences ultimately impact the types and levels of taxes utilized in a particular revenue system. This discussion is limited to considering tax revenues only. Additionally, tax deductions, credits, and adjustments make determination of tax base and effective tax rates extremely difficult and further complicates comparisons.

B. Establishing a Basis for Comparison

Several measures are used to create a common basis for comparison. These include the ratio of total taxes to gross domestic product (taxes/gdp), the ratio of total taxes to population (taxes per capita), and the ratio of each tax to total taxes collected (tax ratio). In computing total taxes, the taxes of the national and subnational governments are included for unitary countries; for federal countries the taxes of national, state, and local governments are included. A more complete discussion of unitary and federal countries is presented in the following section.

The ratio of total taxes to gross domestic product shows the share of a country's resources devoted to government activities. This ratio permits a comparison of the tax levels among countries, and shows the relative preferences of public goods over private goods (OECD, 1989). The ratio of tax revenues to total population, like the taxes/gdp measure, is used to compare tax levels among countries. The ratios of each of the major taxes to total taxes (tax ratio) indicate the degree to which each country relies on a particular tax. Based on the tax ratios in 1987, each country is assigned a rank for each tax. The rank and the change in the tax ratio by major tax for each country is presented in several tables. In addition, the unweighted overall tax ratio and change in tax ratio for all countries are presented. The average tax ratio change is computed on the tax ratio change for each country by period. In all ratio measures some rounding of data will occur.

These ratios permit analysis of aggregated data, as well as comparisons between individual countries. The ratio measures generally incorporate data for the period 1965–87 in five-year intervals. Data for the period 1955–87 are available (OECD, 1989), however, it is incomplete for several countries in 1955 and 1960; only the more complete time series are presented and analyzed. The presentation of data in five-year intervals can be partially misleading because tax ratios may fluctuate, sometimes widely within the five-year periods.

II.   CONTEMPORARY REVENUE SYSTEMS—ANALYSIS OF BROAD TRENDS

This section considers contemporary public revenue systems in a broad perspective by examining several trends in public revenues. The first trend examined is the changing size of the public sector measured by the ratio of total taxes to gross domestic product (taxes/gdp); a brief discussion of the ratio of each of the five major taxes to gross domestic product is included. Next, a discussion of relative tax burden on the basis of tax revenues per capita is presented. An analysis of taxes for unitary and federal countries then follows. The discussion of broad trends in contemporary revenue systems concludes with a comparison of trends in direct and indirect taxation.

A.   The Size of Government—Ratio of Total Taxes to Gross Domestic Product

The size of government relative to the private sector can be measured by the ratio of total taxes to gross domestic product. An analysis of the ratio over time will indicate if government is growing or shrinking relative to the private sector.

Table 2.1 presents the ratio of total taxes to gross domestic product for each OECD country over the period 1965–87. Several observations can be made based on the table. First, the overall trend in the tax/gdp ratio is increasing; government is growing larger relative to the private sector.

Table 2.1   Ratio of Total Taxes to Gross Domestic Product

	1965	1970	1975	1980	1985	1987
Australia	23.2	24.2	27.6	29.0	30.4	31.3
Austria	34.7	35.7	38.6	41.2	43.1	42.3
Belgium	30.8	35.2	41.1	43.5	46.5	46.1
Canada	25.4	31.3	32.4	31.6	32.9	34.5
Denmark	29.9	40.4	41.4	45.5	49.0	52.0
Finland	29.5	31.4	35.1	33.0	36.8	35.9
France	34.5	35.1	36.9	41.7	44.5	44.8
Germany	31.6	32.9	35.7	38.0	38.0	37.6
Greece	20.6	24.3	24.6	29.4	35.2	37.4
Ireland	26.0	31.2	31.5	34.0	38.4	39.9
Italy	25.5	26.1	26.2	30.2	34.4	36.2
Japan	18.3	19.7	20.9	25.5	28.0	30.2
Luxembourg	30.4	30.2	39.2	40.9	43.6	43.8
Netherlands	33.2	37.6	43.7	45.8	44.9	48.0
New Zealand	24.7	27.4	31.3	33.1	33.9	38.6
Norway	33.3	39.3	44.9	47.1	47.6	48.3
Portugal	18.4	23.1	24.7	28.7	31.6	31.4
Spain	14.5	16.9	19.6	24.1	29.1	33.0
Sweden	35.4	40.2	43.9	49.4	50.6	56.7
Switzerland	20.7	23.8	29.6	30.8	32.0	32.0
Turkey	15.0	17.7	20.7	21.7	19.7	24.1
United Kingdom	30.4	37.0	35.7	35.3	37.8	37.5
United States	25.9	29.2	29.0	29.5	29.2	30.0
AVERAGE	26.6	30.0	32.8	35.2	37.3	38.8
Unitary	26.5	30.2	33.0	35.8	38.3	40.2
Federal	26.9	29.5	32.2	33.4	34.3	34.6

Source: Adapted from Organisation for Economic Co-Operation and Development, 1989,

Rank	Change					
1987	1965 1970	1970 1975	1975 1980	1980 1985	1985 1987	1965 1987
20	1.0	3.4	1.4	1.4	0.9	8.1
8	1.0	2.9	2.6	1.9	-0.8	7.6
5	4.4	5.9	2.4	3.0	-0.4	15.3
16	5.9	1.1	-0.8	1.3	1.6	9.1
2	10.5	1.0	4.1	3.5	3.0	22.1
15	1.9	3.7	-2.1	3.8	-0.9	6.4
6	0.6	1.8	4.8	2.8	0.3	10.3
11	1.3	2.8	2.3	0.0	-0.4	6.0
13	3.7	0.3	4.8	5.8	2.2	16.8
9	5.2	0.3	2.5	4.4	1.5	13.9
14	0.6	0.1	4.0	4.2	1.8	10.7
21	1.4	1.2	4.6	2.5	2.2	11.9
7	-0.2	9.0	1.7	2.7	0.2	13.4
4	4.4	6.1	2.1	-0.9	3.1	14.8
10	2.7	3.9	1.8	0.8	4.7	13.9
3	6.0	5.6	2.2	0.5	0.7	15.0
19	4.7	1.6	4.0	2.9	-0.2	13.0
17	2.4	2.7	4.5	5.0	3.9	18.5
1	4.8	3.7	5.5	1.2	6.1	21.3
18	3.1	5.8	1.2	1.2	0.0	11.3
23	2.7	3.0	1.0	-2.0	4.4	9.1
12	6.6	-1.3	-0.4	2.5	-0.3	7.1
22	3.3	-0.2	0.5	-0.3	0.8	4.1
	3.4	2.8	2.4	2.1	1.5	12.2
	3.7	2.9	2.8	2.5	1.9	13.7
	2.6	2.6	1.2	0.9	0.4	7.7

p. 83.

While tax reform efforts were underway in many countries in the period 1985–87, only six countries decreased their total tax/gdp ratio. The decreases in Austria, Belgium, Finland, Germany, Portugal, and the United Kingdom are very slight, ranging from −.8% to −.2%.

The stability of the tax/gdp ratio between 1965–87 varies among countries. Over the period 1965–87, fluctuations in tax/gdp ratios are most pronounced in Denmark, Sweden, Spain, Greece, and Belgium. The United States, United Kingdom, Germany, Finland, and Canada have the most stable tax/gdp ratios. In light of the debate in the United States on the size of the federal budget, it is interesting to note the United States had the lowest rate of increase in the tax/gdp ratio of all OECD countries, and ranked 22 of 23 countries in tax/gdp ratio in 1987. The United States is a federal country therefore tax/gdp ratio includes all federal, state, and local taxes.

1. *Relationship Between Rates of Change and Total Tax/GDP Ratios*

Of the ten countries with the highest 1987 tax/gdp ratios (Sweden, Denmark, Norway, Netherlands, Belgium, France, Luxembourg, Austria, Ireland, and Germany), six also rank in the top ten countries with the highest increase in tax/gdp ratio over 1965–87. Sweden, with the highest 1987 tax/gdp ratio, has the second largest increase in tax/gdp ratio over 1965–87. Denmark, the second highest 1987 tax/gdp ratio, has the largest tax/gdp ratio increase between 1965–87. Conversely, the United States has the lowest increase in tax/gdp ratio between 1965–87 and the second lowest tax/gdp ratio in 1987. At first glance, Table 2.1 appears to show a relationship between large increases in the tax/gdp ratio between 1965–87 and the final tax/gdp ratio in 1987.

Using regression analysis, the relationship between the tax/gdp ratio and the tax/gdp ratio in 1987 was investigated. Upon examination, a very weak relationship was found between the size of the tax/gdp ratio in 1987 and the ratio increase between 1965–87: an R^2 value of .36 was obtained. The 1987 tax/gdp ratio is not significantly related to increases in tax/gdp ratio between 1965–87. The level of government revenues in OECD countries was not statistically related to increases in the ratio of taxes to gross domestic product; some countries with a relatively stable tax/gdp ratio between 1965–87 retain a high tax/gdp ratio in 1987.

B. The Average Ratio of Major Taxes to Gross Domestic Product

In Table 2.2, the average ratio of each of the major taxes to gross domestic product is presented for all OECD countries. On average, the ratio of taxes to gross domestic product increased over the study period. The property tax ratio and corporate income tax ratio were smaller and grew more slowly between 1965–87 relative to the other major taxes. The growth rate in the proportion of personal income taxes and social security taxes to gross domestic product was

Table 2.2   Ratios of Major Taxes to Gross Domestic Product

	1965	1970	1975	1980	1985	1987
Taxes on Personal Income	7.3	8.9	10.7	11.6	11.6	12
Taxes on Corporate Income	2.4	2.6	2.4	2.7	3	3
Taxes on Property	2	2	1.9	1.7	1.8	2.1
Consumption Taxes	9.2	9.8	9.2	9.7	10.5	11.2
Social Security	4.9	5.9	7.7	8.6	9.2	9.5
TOTAL	25.8	29.2	31.9	34.3	36.1	37.8

Source: Computed from data from Organisation for Economic Co-Operation and Development, 1989.

more rapid, indicating increasing reliance on these two taxes. Consumption taxes increased more rapidly than property taxes and corporate income taxes, but more slowly than personal income taxes and social security taxes.

C.   Trends in Tax Revenues in Dollars Per Capita

The ratio of tax revenues per capita, like the ratio of total taxes to gross domestic product, permits comparison of tax levels among countries. The average ratio of taxes per capita increased from 1965 to 1980; the rate of increase slowed between 1980–85 for most OECD countries as indicated in Table 2.3. Increases in per capita taxes occurred in 1985–87 in counties which experienced a decrease in 1980–85; these increases are higher, often substantially higher, than previous increases. For countries which increased taxes per capita in 1985–87, the amount of increase generally compensates for the loss or slowdown in 1980–85. By comparison, only Canada and the United States have a smaller increase in per capita taxes in 1987, compared to 1985.

For all countries studied, the per capita tax burden in 1987 was higher than in 1985. Tax reform, where it is occurring, is not reducing the per capita tax burden. Sweden has the highest tax revenue per capita in 1987, followed by Denmark, Norway, Switzerland, and Luxembourg. Turkey has the lowest tax revenue per capita preceded by Portugal, Greece, Spain, and Ireland. The United States ranked 14 in 1987 for total taxes per capita.

D.   Trends in Major Tax Ratios—Overall Average, Federal and Unitary Countries

Six countries in the OECD have a federal system of government: Australia, Austria, Canada, Germany, Switzerland, and the United States. The primary difference between a unitary and federal system is one of a constitutional divi-

Table 2.3   Total Taxes per Capita

	1965	1970	1975	1980	1985	1987
Australia	483	743	1990	3091	3184	3978
Austria	452	691	1920	4193	3712	6550
Belgium	547	935	2636	5326	3851	6665
Canada	707	1264	2490	3589	4673	5710
Denmark	640	1296	3076	5885	5565	10257
Finland	539	743	2110	3564	4080	6515
France	702	987	2398	5145	4215	7099
Germany	619	1002	2412	5022	3867	6880
Greece	144	275	571	1223	1185	1764
Ireland	243	411	833	1925	2020	3307
Italy	328	523	1004	2421	2565	4778
Japan	175	397	964	2358	3111	5959
Luxembourg	646	1001	2815	5743	4747	8084
Netherlands	538	965	2779	5484	3901	7012
New Zealand	528	623	1343	2353	2294	4076
Norway	633	1132	3186	6649	6664	9546
Portugal	81	169	418	775	678	1185
Spain	107	187	579	1366	1239	2459
Sweden	1000	1665	3880	7373	6060	10707
Switzerland	485	788	2511	4899	4544	8267
Turkey	40	63	185	276	208	315
United Kingdom	564	823	1477	3354	3028	4451
United States	892	1404	2029	3399	4740	5396
AVERAGE	482	786	1896	3714	3484	5694
Unitary	439	717	1780	3601	3259	5540
Federal	606	982	2225	4032	4120	6130

Source: Adapted from Organisation for Economic Co-Operation and Development, 1989,

Rank	Change					
1987	1965 1970	1970 1975	1975 1980	1980 1985	1985 1987	1965 1987
18	260	1247	1101	93	794	3495
10	239	1229	2273	-481	2838	6098
9	388	1701	2690	-1475	2814	6118
13	557	1226	1099	1084	1037	5003
2	656	1780	2809	-320	4692	9617
11	204	1367	1454	516	2435	5976
6	285	1411	2747	-930	2884	6397
8	383	1410	2610	-1155	3013	6261
21	131	296	652	-38	579	1620
19	168	422	1092	95	1287	3064
15	195	481	1417	144	2213	4450
12	222	567	1394	753	2848	5784
5	355	1814	2928	-996	3337	7438
7	427	1814	2705	-1583	3111	6474
17	95	720	1010	-59	1782	3548
3	499	2054	3463	15	2882	8913
22	88	249	357	-97	507	1104
20	80	392	787	-127	1220	2352
1	665	2215	3493	-1313	4647	9707
4	303	1723	2388	-355	3723	7782
23	23	122	91	-68	107	275
16	259	654	1877	-326	1423	3887
14	512	625	1370	1341	656	4504
	304	1110	1818	-230	2210	5212
	279	1062	1822	-342	2280	5101
	376	1243	1807	88	2010	5524

p. 99, Table 34.

sion of authority between the central government and regional governments. In a federal system there is a regional level of government, in addition to the national and local levels, with legally constituted and protected powers. In a unitary system there is one central locus of power and weak, if any, regional government. While some authority may be devolved in unitary states to the regional level, the regional governments depend entirely upon the central government for their power which may be withdrawn at any time. Tax data reported by OECD for unitary countries combines the national and subnational taxes; for federal countries the taxes of national, state, and local governments are included in computing total taxes.

As indicated in Table 2.1, the total tax/gdp ratio for all countries increased over the period 1965–87. The rate of increase in the total tax/gdp ratio was slower for federal countries than for unitary countries for each period. The rate of increase slowed in the 1980s, but this appears more the result of the twin pressures of inflation and recession brought about by the oil embargoes than political will.

Table 2.4 presents the average ratio of major taxes to total taxes collected for all OECD countries and by system of government—federal or unitary. For purposes of comparison, tax revenues are aggregated for all levels of government, and revenues for federal and unitary countries are shown separately.

Changes in the tax ratios are summarized as follows:

1. The ratio of personal income taxes to total taxes increased overall.
2. The corporate income tax decreased from 1965 to 1987; the corporate income tax ratio in federal countries fell more than in unitary countries.
3. Social security contributions increased overall.
4. Property taxes declined overall and for unitary and federal countries.
5. Taxes on goods and services declined overall and in unitary and federal countries. The decline of relative share was marginally greater in unitary countries on average than in federal countries.

The personal income tax grew in importance for OECD countries overall between 1965–87 as shown in Table 2.4. The relative share of the personal income tax for OECD countries increased from an average 26.3 in 1965 to 30.1 in 1987, a gain of 3.8 percent. The average personal income tax ratio was higher in federal than unitary countries for each period under discussion. The relative share of the personal income tax increased 2.6 percent in unitary countries and 6.8 percent in federal countries.

The corporate income tax remained stable over the period 1965–87, declining in the overall average from a 9.2 percent share in 1965 to an 8.3 percent share in 1987. For federal countries over this period, the corporate income tax declined in importance, with a fall of 4.5 percent of total share. For unitary countries the average corporate income tax declined from 1965–75, then

Table 2.4 Unweighted Averages of Major Taxes as a Percentage of Total Taxes for all OECD Countries, and by System of Government—Unitary or Federal[a]

Personal Income Tax	1965	1970	1975	1980	1985	1987
AVERAGE	26.3	27.0	31.4	32.7	31.1	30.1
Unitary	25.9	25.7	30.9	32.2	30.0	28.5
Federal	27.5	30.9	32.9	33.9	33.8	34.3

Corporate income tax	1965	1970	1975	1980	1985	1987
AVERAGE	9.2	9.0	7.7	7.7	8.1	8.3
Unitary	8.5	8.7	7.3	7.5	8.6	8.9
Federal	11.3	9.8	8.9	8.1	6.7	6.8

Social Security Contributions	1965	1970	1975	1980	1985	1987
AVERAGE	19.9	21.7	25.9	26.5	26.8	26.6
Unitary	20.1	21.7	26.2	26.5	26.2	25.9
Federal	19.3	21.6	25.0	26.6	28.6	28.8

Property Taxes	1965	1970	1975	1980	1985	1987
AVERAGE	7.9	7.1	6.1	5.2	5.0	5.5
Unitary	7.3	6.4	5.5	4.6	4.4	4.9
Federal	9.8	9.2	7.6	6.8	6.8	7.1

Taxes on goods and services	1965	1970	1975	1980	1985	1987
AVERAGE	37.1	34.8	30.1	29.1	29.8	30.3
Unitary	38.6	36.6	31.3	30.0	31.0	32.0
Federal	33.1	29.8	26.9	26.5	26.6	25.4

[a] For purposes of comparison, tax revenues from all levels of government are combined for federal countries.
Source: Computed from data from Organisation for Economic Co-Operation and Development, 1989.

increases slightly between 1980–87. Between 1965–80, the average corporate income tax ratio is larger in federal countries; between 1985–87 the ratio is larger in unitary countries.

Social security contributions grew from an average 19.9 percent of all taxes collected in 1965 to 26.6 percent share of total taxes collected in 1987. The increase in social security contributions was larger in federal than unitary countries on average.

Property taxes varied slightly over the period 1965–87, with an overall average share of 7.9 percent in 1965 falling to 5.5 percent in 1987. The average share for unitary and federal countries declined nearly equally.

Taxes on goods and services exhibit a declining trend as well. The overall average share of taxes on goods and services declined from 37.1 in 1965 to 30.3 in 1987. The average relative share in unitary countries fell 6.6 percent over the period 1965–87, from 38.6 to 32. The decline was more pronounced in federal countries, a reduction of 7.7 percent of relative share. However, for unitary countries the downward trend appears to reverse, beginning in 1985.

Trends in overall average tax/gdp ratios for all countries are graphically displayed in Figure 2.1.

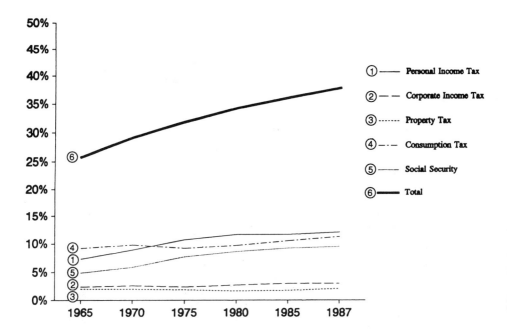

Figure 2.1   Ratio of major taxes to gross domestic product.

E. Revenue Structure—Tax Equity and Incidence

To discuss direct and indirect taxation, two related measures of taxes will be considered: tax equity and tax incidence.

1. *Tax Equity*

Tax equity is described in terms of horizontal and vertical equity. A tax with vertical equity will tax higher incomes at a higher marginal rate than lower incomes. A tax with horizontal equity will tax similar incomes equally. A tax is considered regressive if the amount of tax paid as a percentage of income is negatively related to income; a tax is more progressive if the tax increases as income increases. Consumption taxes, basically taxes on goods and services, are generally regressive because they are inversely related to income. When levied on necessity goods they are especially regressive. Taxes on income, both corporate and personal, offer greater potential for tax equity because the tax can be positively related to income; this potential is not always realized.

2. *Tax Incidence—Direct and Indirect Taxes*

Taxes are additionally categorized as direct or indirect on the basis of tax shifting and incidence. A direct tax, such as the individual income tax, has several distinctive characteristics:

1. Direct taxes are related to income and therefore to the individual.
2. Direct taxes are not subject to market transactions; they can not be shifted through changes in the price of goods and services.
3. Direct taxes, because they are based on income, have greater potential for tax equity than indirect taxes.

Indirect taxes are subject to tax shifting away from the original statutory point of impact because they adapt to market transactions (Herber, 1983). For example, an excise tax will be shifted from the point of levy (the retailer) to the point of incidence (the consumer). Indirect taxes tend to be more regressive because they are not related to income, and because they are subject to shifting.

Property taxes may be considered a special class of direct tax. Two arguments are made to classify property taxes as direct taxes. First, property represents an income stream over time. A tax on property can be construed as a tax on income from this perspective. Second, as income of the taxpayer increases, the value of taxpayer's property tends to be larger, thus meeting the requirement that a direct tax be related to income. Three arguments may be made against classifying the property tax as a direct tax. First, in the case of rental property, property taxes are subject to shifting as the owner of rental property includes the cost of the property tax in the rental price, market conditions permitting. Second, lower income persons are likely to bear a greater burden of property tax in relation to their income. Third, the property tax bears no direct relationship to current income. For consistency with previous studies (Davis, 1976), however, the property tax is classified as a direct tax.

F. Trends in Direct and Indirect Taxes

In Table 2.5, direct taxes include the personal income tax, corporate income tax and property taxes. Indirect taxes include consumption taxes such as general sales taxes, value added taxes, and excise taxes. Social security contributions are excluded from direct and indirect tax comparisons; the sum of direct, indirect, and social security contributions may add up to more than 100 percent in some years, due to rounding. The average direct tax ratio for all OECD countries is nearly constant between 1965–87. The average direct tax ratio reaches a peak of 45.6 percent of total taxes collected in 1980 then falls between 1980–87 to 43.9 percent in 1987. The change in the overall average tax ratio is not explained by the changes in the ratio for unitary and federal countries. In four of the five periods, the changes in direct tax ratios move in opposite directions for unitary and federal countries.

Table 2.5 Unweighted Averages for Direct and Indirect Taxes as a Percentage of Total Taxes for all OECD Countries, and by System of Government—Unitary or Federal[a]

Direct Taxes	1965	1970	1975	1980	1985	1987
AVERAGE	43.5	43.2	45.2	45.6	44.1	43.9
Unitary	41.6	40.8	43.7	44.4	43.0	42.3
Federal	48.5	49.9	49.3	48.8	47.3	48.3

Indirect Taxes	1965	1970	1975	1980	1985	1987
AVERAGE	37.1	34.8	30.1	29.1	29.8	30.3
Unitary	38.6	36.6	31.3	30.0	31.0	32.0
Federal	33.1	29.8	26.9	26.5	26.6	25.4

[a] For purposes of comparison, tax revenues from all levels of government are combined for federal countries. Social security contributions are excluded from indirect and direct comparisons. Property taxes are classified as a direct tax.
Source: Computed from data from Organisation for Economic Co-Operation and Development, 1989.

The overall average for indirect taxes declined steadily from a 37.1 share in 1965 to a low of 29.1 in 1980, then grew slightly to 30.3 in 1987. From 1965–87 indirect taxes lost a 6.6 share in unitary countries and a 7.7 share in federal countries. Direct taxes were more important than indirect taxes for both unitary and federal countries on average.

III.   TAXATION IN CONTEMPORARY REVENUE SYSTEMS

This section examines recent trends in the major taxes comprising the revenue systems of OECD countries. The discussion of different taxes is presented in the following order:

Direct Taxes	Personal Income Tax
	Corporate Income Tax
	Property Tax
Indirect	Taxes on Goods and Services
Taxes	Value Added Tax
	Social Security Contributions

In general, the personal income tax remains the preoccupation of tax policy in most countries. Some reforms are also taking place in corporate income tax systems including reductions in the number and extent of tax allowances, credits and reliefs, the reduction of tax rates and some integration of corporate and personal income tax systems. Consumption taxes are beginning to emerge as an alternative and potentially superior base to direct taxes (Musgrave, 1987). Social security contributions are likely to remain higher in Europe than in the United States as they support a more developed social welfare system. Recent reform efforts are discussed for each type of tax.

A.   Taxes on Personal Income

All revenue systems are the result of political decisions, and personal income taxes are no exception. The personal income tax system secures certain relative contributions from various family groupings at different income levels in each country. The amount of the tax, tax bracket, deductions, allowances, and credits are ultimately decided in the political arena. The choice of tax unit (individual, joint, or family), the definition of income, type and amount of allowances (family/children, quotient system, schedules, and credits) the practice of indexing exemptions and rate brackets to compensate for inflation, and the range and steepness of the rate schedule (zero rated first bracket, progressive, proportional or regressive), can produce comparable after-tax income under systems which seem to be built upon different principles (OECD, 1977).

1. Defining Income, Tax Reflief, and Tax Units

Some commonalities emerge between personal income tax systems in OECD countries. First, some consistency exists in the definition of income between countries. A study of 17 OECD countries (OECD, 1990) found the types of incomes most frequently subject to tax includes employment income, net business income, rent, and public pensions. These sources of income represented the major share of the personal income tax base in the countries studied. Other sources of income, including fringe benefits, interest and dividend income, social transfers, alimony, and capital gains showed more variation (OECD, 1990).

A second similarity is the time period used to compute taxable income. The income tax is generally levied on the basis of income in a 12-month period; this may be a calendar year, a 12-month period, or an average of two or more years. The exact time period varies among countries, and sometimes within the same country (OECD, 1986).

Third, allowances such as deductions from income, termed standard tax reliefs and non-standard reliefs, are found in all countries. Standard tax reliefs, unrelated to specific expenditures, are available to all taxpayers who meet the eligibility requirements. Standard tax reliefs may be made available 1) without regard to family status, 2) on the basis of marital status, and 3) on the basis of dependent children or other taxes paid, including social security. Non-standard reliefs, based on specific expenditures may be provided for insurance premiums, pension contributions, interest payments, medical expenses, alimony, and travel expenses.

Tax reliefs include tax allowances, tax credits, and zero-rated first brackets. Tax allowances provide a deduction from income to determine taxable income; a deduction for each dependent child is an example of such an allowance. Tax credits are computed not to exceed a fixed amount or as a percentage for particular income or expenses; for example, a credit of 12.5 percent of the value of the property is deducted from rental income in Belgium. With a zero-rated first bracket, income tax is eliminated for persons earning income within the first tax bracket.

In the 1970s and 1980s inflation in many countries caused citizens to experience increases in their taxable income without increases in real income. Beginning in the 1970s, many OECD countries provided additional exemptions and indexed rate brackets for wage income to compensate for the effects of inflation.

2. *Reform of Personal Income Taxes*

Revenue collection systems define the tax unit for the payment of personal income taxes in one of three ways: individual, joint, or family. Under "individual taxation," earned income is taxed on the basis of the individual earning the income. Under a system of "joint taxation," the earned income of the spouses are combined for the purpose of determining taxable income. Joint taxation may be compulsory or optional, and may or may not include splitting provisions. In a system of "family taxation," the earned income of spouses and dependent children are aggregated (OECD, 1977).

A trend away from compulsory joint or family taxation to individual taxation began in the 1970s. This trend reflects larger societal changes, in particular the changing role of women, the emergence of two-earner high income households, and a changing family structure. Despite this trend, eight OECD countries continued to use joint or family taxation in 1990. The move from joint to individual taxation tends to give the greatest benefit to high-income two earner households. The move from family or joint taxation to individual taxation produces varying results for different countries due to the interaction of tax units, tax rates, income brackets and tax allowances.

Table 2.6 identifies the tax unit for each OECD country in 1990. If the tax system is either compulsory or optional individual taxation, then the tax unit in that country is classified as individual.

The goals of the personal income tax system are shifting in some countries from a system based on and supportive of traditional attitudes toward the role of men and women, the family, and the responsibility of spouses for children (OECD, 1977). The movement toward individual taxation, different income intervals for families, and cash transfers for dependents tends to promote the goals of tax equality between men and women and greater participation by women in the workforce. These changes often conflict with a more traditional tax philosophy.

Reform of the personal income tax became an issue in the 1980s in many OECD countries due to the complexity of compliance, perceived unfairness, and the adverse effects of the tax on economic growth, savings, and work decisions (OECD, 1986). While proposals for radical tax reform have been advanced, changes to income tax systems tend to be gradual. A survey of OECD countries conducted on reform in the personal income tax systems (OECD, 1986) reached two major conclusions. The first conclusion was that inflationary fiscal drag was the main cause of upward pressure on income tax rates. Inflationary fiscal drag is the change in income due to inflation only. When tax rates are not indexed to inflation, real taxes can increase without an increase in real income. The second conclusion was that successful reform of

Table 2.6   Tax Units for Earned Income in OECD Member Countries, 1990

Individual Taxation	Joint Taxation	Family Taxation
Austria	Belgium	Luxembourg
Canada	France	Turkey
Finland	Germany	
Ireland	Greece [a]	
Italy	Portugal	
Japan	Switzerland	
Netherlands		
New Zealand		
Norway [b]		
Spain [c]		
Sweden [d]		
United Kingdom [e]		
United States		

[a] Husband and wife must file a joint tax return, but the income of each spouse is taxed separately.

[b] If both spourses have earned income each individual is taxed separately. With only one income a joint filing is required.

[c] The family unit remains the basic system for taxation in Spain but the system is no longer compulsory.

[d] Spouses are taxed separately except on wealth.

[e] In the United Kingdom prior to April 6, 1990, husbands and wives are considered the tax unit unless they elect for separate taxation of the wife's earnings. After that date husband and wife will be taxed independently on all their income.
Source: Price Waterhouse, 1990.

tax legislation, including both informal and formal indexation, to offset inflationary fiscal drag was not universally achieved in OECD countries.

3.   *Progressivity or Regressivity of Personal Income Tax System*

The progressivity of different personal income tax systems is difficult to measure. The tax unit, definition of income, and the type and amount of allowances and exclusions can offset a rate schedule with progressive marginal rates. An OECD report (OECD, 1990) concluded that progressivity in the personal income tax system is primarily determined by 1) the definition of taxable income, and 2) the application of a progressive rate structure to taxable income. Taxable income is differentiated from broader concepts of income through the use of allowances and credits. In addition, the OECD found that the method used to measure progressivity determined in large measure, the progressivity of each income tax system. For example, the ranking of countries will be different when the measure of tax progressivity is determined by the percentage distribution of taxes across deciles compared to the impact of the tax on income distribution. For example, the United Kingdom has a more progressive income tax structure when using the first measure, Sweden is more progressive based on the second measure (OECD, 1990).

Different countries utilize different means to achieve progressivity in their personal income tax system. In Ireland and Sweden the definition of taxable income contributes most to the progressivity of the system. A progressive rate schedule plays a more substantial part in creating a progressive system in Austria, France, Greece, the Netherlands, and the United States (OECD, 1990).

Comparisons between countries are substantially complicated by the range of variations in definitions of income and taxable income, the use and size of allowances and credits, the definition of tax unit, size of zero-rate bracket (if any), the range of tax rates, and bands of income. Frequent changes can and do occur in many provisions of the personal income tax system, further complicating analysis. Detailed data and analyses to compare personal income tax systems among countries are available (Price Waterhouse, 1990b; OECD, 1981, 1984, 1986, 1988a, 1988b, 1990). Due to the difficulty of generalizing the data, and the level of detail the comparisons entail, the reader should refer to the cited works.

4. *Personal Income Tax Trends*

Personal income taxes gained in relative importance among most OECD countries between 1965 and 1987. Taxes on personal income as reported in this section include levies on both income and profits. As Table 2.7 illustrates, the overall average personal income tax ratio increased steadily over the period 1965–80. Increased real income, a result of rapid growth, and a growing welfare state made higher income taxation acceptable in many countries during this period.

The affects of decreasing real income, inflation, and public resistance to higher taxes precipitated declines in personal income tax ratios beginning in the 1980–85 period; the downward trend continued in 1985–87. Despite a decline in the income tax ratio between 1980 and 1987, most countries had a higher personal income tax ratio in 1987 than in 1965; the exceptions are the Netherlands, Norway, Sweden, and the United Kingdom. Ireland, Italy, and Greece approximately doubled this tax ratio between 1965 and 1987.

Among the countries reporting personal income tax data, New Zealand ranks near the top in personal income tax ratio for every interval. New Zealand has the highest reliance on the personal income tax of any country for all periods, reaching a high in the personal income tax ratio of 61.6 in 1980. Denmark, with a declining income tax ratio since 1975, ranks second in personal income tax ratio in 1987. However, a portion of the personal income in Denmark includes social security contributions which could contribute to the high ratio. Greece, France, and the Netherlands demonstrate consistently low rank-

Table 2.7   Ratio of Personal Income Taxes to Total Taxes

	1965	1970	1975	1980	1985	1987
Australia	34.4	37.3	43.6	44.0	45.5	45.4
Austria	20.0	20.7	21.6	23.2	22.9	22.7
Belgium	20.5	24.4	31.9	35.2	34.2	32.7
Canada	23.0	32.4	32.8	34.1	35.2	38.7
Denmark	41.4	48.6	55.9	51.8	50.2	49.2
Finland	35.8	42.0	48.5	44.7	47.0	45.6
France	10.6	12.0	12.3	12.9	12.8	12.7
Germany	26.0	26.7	30.2	29.6	28.7	29.0
Greece	7.3	10.1	9.2	14.9	13.8	12.3
Ireland	16.7	18.3	25.2	32.0	31.3	34.6
Italy	10.9	10.9	15.2	23.1	26.7	26.3
Japan	21.7	21.5	23.9	24.3	24.7	24.0
Luxembourg	24.9	24.1	27.8	26.8	26.3	25.3
Netherlands	27.7	26.8	27.1	26.3	19.4	7.0
New Zealand	39.4	42.7	54.3	61.6	59.8	49.9
Norway	39.6	35.2	31.5	28.0	22.3	26.4
Portugal						
Spain	14.3	11.5	14.5	20.4	19.7	21.3
Sweden	48.7	49.8	46.1	41.0	38.6	37.2
Switzerland	31.2	33.2	36.1	35.6	34.9	34.0
Turkey	24.8	27.0	32.9	43.5	27.5	24.9
United Kingdom	29.8	31.4	37.9	29.4	26.0	26.6
United States	30.5	35.2	32.8	36.9	35.7	36.2
AVERAGE	26.3	27.0	31.4	32.7	31.1	30.1
Unitary	25.5	25.4	30.3	31.7	29.6	28.2
Federal	29.0	33.0	35.1	36.0	36.0	36.7

Rank	Change					
1987	1965 1970	1970 1975	1975 1980	1980 1985	1985 1987	1965 1987
4	2.9	6.3	0.4	1.5	-0.1	11.0
18	0.7	0.9	1.6	-0.3	-0.2	2.7
10	3.9	7.5	3.3	-1.0	-1.5	12.2
5	9.4	0.4	1.3	1.1	3.5	15.7
2	7.2	7.3	-4.1	-1.6	-1.0	7.8
3	6.2	6.5	-3.8	2.3	-1.4	9.8
20	1.4	0.3	0.6	-0.1	-0.1	2.1
11	0.7	3.5	-0.6	-0.9	0.3	3.0
21	2.8	-0.9	5.7	-1.1	-1.5	5.0
8	1.6	6.9	6.8	-0.7	3.3	17.9
14	0.0	4.3	7.9	3.6	-0.4	15.4
17	-0.2	2.4	0.4	0.4	-0.7	2.3
15	-0.8	3.7	-1.0	-0.5	-1.0	0.4
22	-0.9	0.3	-0.8	-6.9	-12.4	-20.7
1	3.3	11.6	7.3	-1.8	-9.9	10.5
13	-4.4	-3.7	-3.5	-5.7	4.1	-13.2
23						
19	-2.8	3.0	5.9	-0.7	1.6	7.0
6	1.1	-3.7	-5.1	-2.4	-1.4	-11.5
9	2.0	2.9	-0.5	-0.7	-0.9	2.8
16	2.2	5.9	10.6	-16.0	-2.6	0.1
12	1.6	6.5	-8.5	-3.4	0.6	-3.2
7	4.7	-2.4	4.1	-1.2	0.5	5.7
	1.9	3.2	1.3	-1.6	-1.0	3.8
	1.3	3.5	1.4	-2.1	-1.4	2.6
	3.9	2.1	0.9	0.0	0.7	7.6

ings for this tax ratio. In Luxembourg and Norway, the personal income tax ratio declines over four of the five periods. In the United States, the personal income tax ratio declines in 1970–75 and 1980–85 but increases between 1985–87. For 1970–75, only three other countries experienced a decline in the income tax ratio. For 1980–85, the downward shift in the United States was below the OECD average for that period. While the personal income tax ratio declined under the Reagan administration, it did not decline as much as the OECD average during that period.

The convergence of income tax ratios among countries: Some studies suggest that a convergence in the income tax ratios of most OECD countries occurred between 1975 and 1983 with income tax ratios rising in low income tax countries and falling in high income tax countries (OECD, 1986). This observation, and variations were examined as follows. First, the variance in the personal income tax ratio over time was examined using the standard deviation of the tax ratios. If the standard deviation becomes less with each period, this would suggest less variance from the mean, and therefore convergence in tax ratios. The standard deviation of the income tax ratio was computed for all countries for each period. Convergence was not confirmed; the standard deviation was approximately 10.6 in 1965, 11.5 in 1970, 12.6 in 1975, 11.5 in 1980, 11.6 in 1985 and 10.5 in 1987.

The second task was to determine if the ratio varied as much in high income tax ratio countries as in low income tax countries. Countries were ranked on the basis of personal income tax ratios for each period and divided into an upper and lower half based on rank. The standard deviation in the tax ratio for high tax countries was computed and compared to the standard deviation for low tax countries for each period. Countries with a high income tax ratio have greater variance in tax ratios as shown by the standard deviation than do low ratio countries for every period. The differences in standard deviations are the greatest in 1985: approximately 9.0 for high ratio countries and 4.9 for low ratio countries. Any convergence taking place in income tax ratios is occurring in low income tax ratio countries, not between low and high ratio countries.

B. Taxes on Corporate Income

Corporate income taxes include taxes based on profits and capital gains (OECD, 1989). This section begins with a discussion of two important issues relevant to corporate taxation: 1) reforming corporate tax relief, and 2) the integration of the personal and corporate tax systems.

Several general observations can be made about corporate taxes in the 1970s and 1980s (OECD, 1987):

Tax reliefs permit government to directly intervene in selected sectors of the economy.

Corporate tax relief accelerated during the 1970s and early 1980s to compen-
sate for the effects of inflation.
Tax reliefs were designed to foster new/growth industries.
Tax reliefs were more politically feasible than direct subsidies.
The adoption of tax reliefs in one country leads to pressure for equivalent tax
reliefs in other countries.

1. Reforming Corporate Tax Relief

Corporate tax policy began in most OECD countries as a broad based tax with
relatively few tax reliefs (OECD, 1987). Corporate taxation has since evolved
with the development of special tax reliefs. Tax reliefs are typically provided
to attract corporate investment. There are two basic types of corporate tax
relief: 1) tax allowances, exemptions, and deductions which reduce the tax
base on which the tax is levied; and 2) tax credits which are deductible from
the tax payable.

Reform of corporate tax reliefs was considered in many OECD countries
throughout the 1980s. Several factors contributed to the erosion of support for
corporate tax relief:

A trend toward greater acceptance of a "free-market" approach to the economy and less support for government intervention.
Concern over the tradeoffs between tax relief and marginal rates; recognition
that greater tax relief led to higher marginal tax rates.
The effectiveness and efficiency of tax relief was questioned: Were reliefs
effective in increasing investment? Were alternate means to increasing
investment more efficient?
Tax reliefs were exploited by corporations to avoid taxes.
Tax reliefs complicated the revenue system.

Since the 1980s, lower taxes and greater tax neutrality has been advanced
by many countries over tax relief. By 1990, many tax reliefs had been phased
out by OECD countries. The most prominent forms of corporate tax relief still
in use in 1990 include development zones, accelerated depreciation, investment tax credits, tax credits for reserves, and tax credits for employment
(Price Waterhouse, 1990a). These are discussed below.

Regional development zones: Regional development zones, also known
as employment zones or enterprise zones are formed for the purpose of attract-
ing corporate investment into a specific area or region. Qualifying enterprises
locating in designated zones are exempted from certain taxes, most frequently
the corporate income tax, for a set period of time; other exemptions may
include taxes on interest, dividends, and real estate.

Accelerated depreciation: Accelerated depreciation of eligible buildings, machinery and equipment can be used to offset corporate taxes. In some

countries, the availability of the accelerated depreciation credit is restricted to development zones.

Investment tax credit: An investment tax credit against corporate income tax can be earned on investment in eligible items, typically buildings, machinery, and equipment. Countries frequently limit the application of tax credits in any one year to a maximum level, some countries permit unused credit to be carried back and forward. Occasionally, an investment tax credit is given for expenditures for the development of export markets and tourism promotion (New Zealand) or for research (Japan).

Tax credit for reserves: Some countries permit the deferral of taxes on amounts appropriated by the corporation for different types of reserves, including a reserve for inventory or payroll (Sweden, Finland), operating reserve (Finland), and a doubtful debt reserve (Finland).

Tax credit for employment: A tax credit may be earned in some countries for the employment of persons in a designated group such as handicapped, youth, minorities, or low income.

2. *Integrating Personal and Corporate Income Taxes*

In addition to reform of corporate tax relief, the integration of personal and corporate income tax systems has become a goal in many countries. For the 12 European Common Market countries which will constitute Europe 1992, the harmonization of corporate and personal taxes has taken on a greater urgency. In general, there has been more progress in harmonizing indirect taxes than direct taxes. Agreement has been reached in value-added tax rates. The critical task remaining in the effort to coordinate taxes in the EEC is the harmonization of corporate taxes (Musgrave, 1987: 220–223).

The harmonization of corporate tax systems and the integration of corporate and individual tax systems in the EEC will remain difficult. Corporate tax allowances, credits, reliefs, incentives, inventory taxes, and effective tax rates impose major obstacles to harmonization. A major issue in the integration of corporate and personal income taxes is the treatment of corporate dividends.

Taxing distributed corporate profits: Corporate income taxes are levied on the corporation as an entity, and not the individuals who own the company's shares. Technically, corporate taxes are not subject to tax shifting. In some countries there is double taxation of dividends; corporations pay taxes on distributed income (dividends) and shareholders are also liable for dividend income.

Considerable variation exists between countries in the treatment of distributed corporate profits (dividends). Under a classical or unintegrated system of corporate taxation, the corporation is considered independent of the shareholder. The corporation pays tax on distributed profits independent of the shareholders; the shareholders must pay a tax on any dividend income. In an integrated system of corporate and personal taxation, the corporation's payment of tax on distributed profit is credited as a prepayment of the shareholder's personal income tax. Between these two extremes lie the two-rate system and the imputation system. The two-rate system provides a lower corporate tax rate on distributed profits. The imputation system allows a credit against personal income tax up to a certain amount of corporate dividend. A reduction of corporate taxes or a credit on personal taxes will reduce overall tax revenues.

3.   *Trends in the Corporate Income Tax Ratio*

The average corporate income tax ratio for OECD countries declined between 1965 and 1987 as illustrated in Table 2.8. The corporate income tax ratio is lower in thirteen countries in 1987 compared to 1965, higher for eight and the same for one. In 1987, the corporate income tax ratio exceeded 10 percent of total taxes collected in only six countries including Japan, Turkey, Luxembourg, United Kingdom, Italy, and Australia.

In 1965, the average corporate income tax ratio for federal countries was higher than unitary countries. By 1987, the positions were reversed. Unitary countries had a higher average corporate income tax ratio in 1987 at 8.9 percent of total taxes than in any preceding period. The average corporate income tax ratio for federal countries fell steadily from 11.3 in 1965 to 6.8 in 1987.

Japan maintained the highest corporate income tax ratio for all periods considered. Corporate tax rates in Japan have been raised several times since 1970, mainly to finance reductions in the individual income tax for middle-class tax payers (Nagano, 1988). Corporate tax preferences designed to encourage exports, savings, and investments were reduced in Japan in the 1980s.

The corporate income tax ratio in the United States fell steadily for each period from 1965 to 1985. There was a marginal increase in the corporate income tax ratio in 1985–87.

C.   Property Taxes

Property taxes are levied on the use, ownership, or transfer of property. Property taxes include taxes on real property, inheritance or gift taxes, and taxes on financial and capital transactions.

The property tax represents a relatively minor source of revenue for most OECD countries as shown in Table 2.9 below. Ten countries including Australia, Canada, Denmark, Japan, Luxembourg, New Zealand, Sweden, Switzerland, the United Kingdom, and the United States collected more than 5 percent of tax revenues from the property tax in 1987. Only three countries collected more than 10 percent of tax revenues from the property tax (Japan,

Table 2.8 Ratio of Corporate Income Taxes to Total Taxes

	1965	1970	1975	1980	1985	1987
Australia	16.3	17.0	12.4	12.2	9.3	10.3
Austria	5.4	4.4	4.3	3.5	3.4	3.3
Belgium	6.2	6.8	7.2	5.7	6.4	6.6
Canada	15.1	11.3	13.6	11.6	8.2	8.0
Denmark	4.5	2.6	3.1	3.2	4.9	4.5
Finland	8.3	5.5	4.3	4.5	4.0	3.9
France	5.3	6.3	5.2	5.1	4.5	5.2
Germany	7.8	5.7	4.5	5.5	6.1	5.0
Greece	1.9	1.7	3.5	3.8	2.7	4.4
Ireland	9.1	8.8	4.8	4.5	3.2	3.2
Italy	6.9	6.5	6.3	7.8	9.2	10.5
Japan	22.2	26.3	20.6	21.8	21.0	22.9
Luxembourg	11.0	19.3	15.7	16.5	18.2	17.1
Netherlands	8.1	6.7	7.7	6.6	7.0	7.7
New Zealand	20.7	17.8	11.8	7.8	8.3	8.9
Norway	3.8	3.3	2.8	13.3	17.0	6.7
Portugal						
Spain	9.2	8.2	6.9	5.1	5.2	6.7
Sweden	6.1	4.4	4.3	2.5	3.5	4.1
Switzerland	7.1	7.6	7.7	5.8	6.0	6.2
Turkey	4.8	6.4	5.1	4.1	9.5	19.7
United Kingdom	7.1	9.1	6.7	8.4	12.7	10.6
United States	15.8	12.7	10.8	10.2	7.1	8.1
AVERAGE	9.2	9.0	7.7	7.7	8.1	8.3
Unitary	8.5	8.7	7.3	7.5	8.6	8.9
Federal	11.3	9.8	8.9	8.1	6.7	6.8

Source: Computed and adapted from data from Organisation of Economic Co-Op-

Rank	Change					
1987	1965 1970	1970 1975	1975 1980	1980 1985	1985 1987	1965 1987
6	0.7	-4.6	-0.2	-2.9	1.0	-6.0
21	-1.0	-0.1	-0.8	-0.1	-0.1	-2.1
13	0.6	0.4	-1.5	0.7	0.2	0.4
9	-3.8	2.3	-2.0	-3.4	-0.2	-7.1
17	-1.9	0.5	0.1	1.7	-0.4	0.0
20	-2.8	-1.2	0.2	-0.5	-0.1	-4.4
15	1.0	-1.1	-0.1	-0.6	0.7	-0.1
16	-2.1	-1.2	1.0	0.6	-1.1	-2.8
18	-0.2	1.8	0.3	-1.1	1.7	2.5
22	-0.3	-4.0	-0.3	-1.3	0.0	-5.9
5	-0.4	-0.2	1.5	1.4	1.3	3.6
1	4.1	-5.7	1.2	-0.8	1.9	0.7
3	8.3	-3.6	0.8	1.7	-1.1	6.1
10	-1.4	1.0	-1.1	0.4	0.7	-0.4
7	-2.9	-6.0	-4.0	0.5	0.6	-11.8
11	-0.5	-0.5	10.5	3.7	-10.3	2.9
23						
12	-1.0	-1.3	-1.8	0.1	1.5	-2.5
19	-1.7	-0.1	-1.8	1.0	0.6	-2.0
14	0.5	0.1	-1.9	0.2	0.2	-0.9
2	1.6	-1.3	-1.0	5.4	10.2	14.9
4	2.0	-2.4	1.7	4.3	-2.1	3.5
8	-3.1	-1.9	-0.6	-3.1	1.0	-7.7
	-0.2	-1.3	0.0	0.4	0.3	-0.9
	0.2	-1.4	0.2	1.0	0.3	0.3
	-1.6	-1.1	-0.7	-1.7	0.2	-4.9

eration and Development, 1989, p. 88, Table 12.

Table 2.9   Ratio of Property Taxes to Total Taxes

	1965	1970	1975	1980	1985	1987
Australia	11.4	11.0	8.8	7.8	7.8	9.2
Austria	4.0	3.7	3.1	2.9	2.5	2.3
Belgium	3.7	3.0	2.3	2.4	1.7	2.1
Canada	13.2	13.0	9.4	9.1	9.3	9.2
Denmark	8.0	6.0	5.9	5.7	4.2	5.1
Finland	4.1	2.3	2.1	2.1	3.0	3.2
France	4.3	3.5	3.4	3.5	4.4	4.7
Germany	5.8	4.9	3.9	3.3	3.0	3.2
Greece	10.3	9.7	10.0	4.6	2.7	2.5
Ireland	15.1	12.2	9.7	5.3	4.0	4.4
Italy	7.2	6.0	3.3	3.7	2.5	2.6
Japan	8.1	7.6	9.1	8.2	9.7	11.2
Luxembourg	6.2	6.6	5.1	5.7	5.6	6.8
Netherlands	4.4	3.3	2.4	3.6	3.5	3.6
New Zealand	11.5	10.4	9.2	7.9	7.4	7.0
Norway	3.1	2.4	2.3	1.7	1.9	2.5
Portugal	5.1	4.2	2.5	1.4	1.9	2.0
Spain	6.4	6.5	6.3	4.6	3.5	3.7
Sweden	1.8	1.5	1.1	0.9	2.3	5.7
Switzerland	8.8	8.8	7.1	7.3	8.2	8.5
Turkey	10.5	10.8	6.9	5.4	4.6	3.2
United Kingdom	14.5	12.4	12.7	12.0	11.9	13.2
United States	15.3	13.6	13.2	10.1	10.1	10.2
AVERAGE	7.9	7.1	6.1	5.2	5.0	5.5
Unitary	7.3	6.4	5.5	4.6	4.4	4.9
Federal	9.8	9.2	7.6	6.8	6.8	7.1

Source: Adapted from data from Organisation for Economic Co-Operation and De-

Rank	Change					
1987	1965 1970	1970 1975	1975 1980	1980 1985	1985 1987	1965 1987
4	-0.4	-2.2	-1.0	0.0	1.4	-2.2
21	-0.3	-0.6	-0.2	-0.4	-0.2	-1.7
22	-0.7	-0.7	0.1	-0.7	0.4	-1.6
5	-0.2	-3.6	-0.3	0.2	-0.1	-4.0
10	-2.0	-0.1	-0.2	-1.5	0.9	-2.9
15	-1.8	-0.2	0.0	0.9	0.2	-0.9
11	-0.8	-0.1	0.1	0.9	0.3	0.4
17	-0.9	-1.0	-0.6	-0.3	0.2	-2.6
20	-0.6	0.3	-5.4	-1.9	-0.2	-7.8
12	-2.9	-2.5	-4.4	-1.3	0.4	-10.7
18	-1.2	-2.7	0.4	-1.2	0.1	-4.6
2	-0.5	1.5	-0.9	1.5	1.5	3.1
8	0.4	-1.5	0.6	-0.1	1.2	0.6
14	-1.1	-0.9	1.2	-0.1	0.1	-0.8
7	-1.1	-1.2	-1.3	-0.5	-0.4	-4.5
19	-0.7	-0.1	-0.6	0.2	0.6	-0.6
23	-0.9	-1.7	-1.1	0.5	0.1	-3.1
13	0.1	-0.2	-1.7	-1.1	0.2	-2.7
9	-0.3	-0.4	-0.2	1.4	3.4	3.9
6	0.0	-1.7	0.2	0.9	0.3	-0.3
16	0.3	-3.9	-1.5	-0.8	-1.4	-7.3
1	-2.1	0.3	-0.7	-0.1	1.3	-1.3
3	-1.7	-0.4	-3.1	0.0	0.1	-5.1
	-0.8	-1.0	-0.9	-0.2	0.5	-2.5
	-0.9	-0.8	-0.9	-0.2	0.5	-2.4
	-0.6	-1.6	-0.8	0.1	0.3	-2.7

velopment, 1989, p. 93, Table 23.

the United Kingdom, and the United States). The property tax ratio in unitary countries fell as a proportion of total taxes from 7.3 percent in 1965 to 4.9 percent in 1987. The property tax ratio was relatively stable in federal countries with the ratio in 1987 (7.1) marginally lower than 1965 (9.8).

1. Types of Property Taxes

Six property taxes are included in the classification of property tax (OECD, 1989): 1) recurrent taxes on immovable property (real property); 2) net wealth taxes; 3) taxes on estates and inheritances and taxes on gifts; 4) taxes on financial and capital transactions; 5) nonrecurrent taxes on property; and 6) other recurrent taxes on property. Property taxes may further be classified in terms of how often they are levied: recurrent or nonrecurrent.

Recurrent taxes on immovable property: Recurrent taxes on immovable property are levied on land and buildings on the basis of a percentage of an assessed property value. The assessed value may be determined on the basis of 1) real or potential rental income, sales price, capitalized yield, or "best use," or 2) size, location, construction, and improvements. Recurrent taxes on immovable property are utilized in 21 OECD countries. The tax is so small in Italy as to be insignificant; it generated only one million lire in 1987 (OECD, 1989). Portugal does not report a recurrent tax on real property. The tax was discontinued in Turkey in 1986.

Net wealth taxes: Recurrent taxes on net wealth are levied in most cases on both personal and real property. Net wealth taxes can be levied on individuals and corporations. The countries of Austria, Canada, Denmark, Finland, Germany, Luxembourg, the Netherlands, Norway, Spain, Sweden, and Switzerland all had net wealth taxes in 1987. With the exception of France, which adopted a net wealth tax in 1982, and Spain (adopted in 1978), net wealth taxes on individuals are at least 60 years old among the OECD countries which use the tax (OECD, 1988b:31).

Canada does not tax individual net wealth; the Netherlands does not tax corporate net wealth. Ireland had a net wealth tax from 1975 to 1986, but dropped the tax in 1987; the tax was not attributed to either individual or corporate collections. Spain dropped its corporate net wealth tax in 1986 (OECD, 1989). France adopted an individual net wealth tax on "impot sur les grandes fortunes" (tax on great fortunes) in 1982, but abolished it in 1987 following a change in government. Japan abolished the tax shortly after the Second World War. Where the wealth tax is utilized, analysis indicates that it does not radically redistribute wealth (OECD, 1988b:17).

(1) The Tax Unit for Personal Net Worth Tax. In all OECD countries with a personal net wealth tax, the wealth of both husband and wife is combined for tax purposes. The wealth of dependent children is aggregated with

the parents in all countries except Denmark and the Netherlands (OECD, 1988b:39).

(2) Tax Exemptions and Deductions. Outstanding tax debts are generally deductible from the base of the net wealth tax. Pension rights are exempted in all OECD countries, and most countries exempt household and personal effects with the exception of Norway, Spain, and half of the 26 Swiss cantons (OECD, 1988b:46). Jewelry is usually included in the tax base, with the exception of Denmark; some countries grant an exemption where the total value does not exceed a set amount. Cars and boats are included in the tax base in most countries.

Taxation of other items of personal net worth vary considerably among countries. For example, there is no standard pattern of taxation or relief on the treatment of savings, with some countries taxing small amounts and others taxing amounts above a set level. Taxation of works of art also vary considerably among countries. No standard pattern of relief for owner-occupied houses emerges.

Taxes on estates and inheritances and taxes on gifts: Estate taxes are levied on the value of the total estate. The tax rate and base are determined by the amount transferred by the donor. Inheritance taxes are based on the shares the beneficiary receives from the estate (OECD, 1988b, 1989). Individual inheritance taxes may be adjusted on the basis of the relationship of the individuals to the deceased. In most OECD countries the individual, not the aggregated family, is the tax unit. In the Netherlands and Denmark, however, a married couple is treated as the tax unit in the case of gifts.

Most OECD countries levied estate, inheritance, and gift taxes in 1987; 20 of the 23 countries had death and gift taxes at the federal or central level. Canada discontinued the gift tax in 1972 as part of a tax reform package which introduced a capital gains tax. Denmark, Italy, Luxembourg, Norway, and Switzerland do not have a gift tax. In Switzerland most of the cantons levy gift and death taxes. Austria, Japan, Portugal, and Turkey report combined estate, inheritance, and gift taxes to OECD. Australia discontinued the estate tax in 1977, and Australia and Spain discontinued the gift tax in 1984.

Most countries included in this study have inheritance-type taxes. New Zealand, the United Kingdom, and the United States have estate-type taxes. Italy has both estate and inheritance taxes. Australia, Canada, and Switzerland do not have federal or central government transfer taxes. The remaining 16 OECD countries utilize inheritance type taxes (OECD, 1988b:78).

Taxes on financial and capital transactions: Typically, taxation of financial and capital transactions include stamp duties, registration duties for securities and property transfers, duties on land registration and transfers, and taxation of specific legal transactions such as validation of contracts and the sale of immovable property (OECD, 1989). Canada is the only OECD country that does not impose some form of tax on financial and capital transactions.

Non-recurrent taxes on property: Non-recurrent property taxes are a one-time only levy on net wealth or property. Examples include taxes on the revaluation of capital or taxes levied to meet emergency expenditures (OECD, 1989). In 1987, non-recurrent property taxes were levied by Canada, Greece, Portugal, Spain, Sweden (new in 1987), and the United Kingdom.

Other recurrent taxes on property: This classification includes taxes on wealth such as livestock, and jewelry, and external signs of wealth. It is rare in OECD countries; only Greece and Spain had this type of tax in 1987.

2. *Trends in the Property Tax Ratio*

As illustrated in Table 2.9, average property tax ratios have declined overall from 1965 to 1987; unitary countries are slightly below, and federal countries are slightly above the average.

The United States had the highest property tax ratio in 1965 followed closely by Ireland and the United Kingdom and more distantly by Canada and Australia. The United Kingdom, Japan, the United States, Australia, and Canada had the highest property tax ratios in 1987.

Most countries experienced an overall decline in the property tax ratio between 1965 and 1987. Ireland had the largest decline in property tax ratio of all OECD countries (− 10.7) for the period 1965–87. Three other countries, Greece, Turkey, and the United States, show a decline in the property tax ratio of more than 5 percent between 1965 and 1987. Despite the decline, the United States still ranks third in property tax ratio in 1987; possibly the result of continued reliance on property taxes by local governments.

The property tax ratio increased overall in only a few countries during the period under consideration. The countries with the largest overall increase in property tax ratio are Sweden (3.9) and Japan (3.1).

D. Consumption Taxes

Taxes on consumption are levied indirectly on the consumer in contrast to taxes on property and income which are levied directly.

1. *Defining Consumption Taxes*

Consumption taxes can be defined in several ways: as taxes "paid on the enjoyment of goods and services" (OECD, 1988c:25); as taxes on goods on the way to the consumer; or, as taxes on the consumer paid indirectly through one or more installments by the manufacturer, wholesaler, and/or retailer.

The application of consumption taxes is limited only by imagination and good sense. Consumption taxes may be levied on the creation, removal, sale, transfer, lease, or delivery of goods and services, on the use of goods, or on *permission* to use goods, or to perform activities (OECD, 1989:44). In principle, consumption taxes are levied on goods in the country in which they are consumed (OECD, 1988c:25); however, certain taxes such as export taxes are classified as consumption taxes by OECD.

Consumption taxes include two categories of taxes: 1) general consumption taxes, and 2) excise taxes. The general consumption tax category includes the value added tax (VAT). General consumption taxes are levied on a broad base of goods and/or services in comparison to excise taxes which are levied on a more narrow base.

The horizontal and vertical base of consumption taxes, tax administration, and methods of calculation are discussed first in this section. Reforms of consumption taxes are discussed next, followed by an examination of consumption tax incidence and progressivity. The section concludes with a presentation of consumption taxes trends.

Horizontal base—narrow or broad: The horizontal base of consumption taxes is defined as either broad or narrow, determined by the number of items included in the tax base. If the tax is levied on a small number of items, the horizontal base is narrow; if the tax applies to a wide range of goods and services, the horizontal base is broad.

There are two categories of consumption taxes, determined by the base the tax covers: 1) general taxes on consumption (sales taxes), and 2) selective taxes on consumption (excise taxes). General sales taxes have a broad horizontal base since they are designed to tax all or almost all consumption; a retail tax on sales is an example of a general tax. Selective taxes by definition have a more narrow base because they target a certain good; significant sources of revenues are selective excise taxes on alcohol, tobacco, and motoring—both oil products and vehicles. Excise taxes imposed for the purpose of reducing consumption of a certain good, such as alcohol or tobacco, are known as sumptuary excise taxes.

Vertical base—single- or multi-stage levies: The vertical base of consumption taxes potentially includes manufacturers, distributors, and retailers. Each represents a different stage in the process of moving goods to the consumer. Consumption taxes are levied in either a single-stage or multi-stage at these levels. A single-stage tax is levied once on sales from the manufacturer, or wholesaler, or retailer. Multiple stage-taxes are levied at more than one point in the sequence of sales from manufacturer to retailer. If the tax is restricted to two stages, it a *dual-stage* tax; if three stages are taxed it is an *all-stage* tax.

Administration: Consumption taxes may be levied on the monetary value of goods purchased (i.e., retail sales tax), or on the purchase of number of units of a particular commodity (i.e., gasoline sales tax) (Herber, 1983:244). Taxes levied on units, rather than price, do not keep pace with inflation unless adjustments are made to the base rate.

Consumption taxes may be levied in a cumulative or non-cumulative manner. Cumulative taxes, or cascade taxes, are levied at the same rate at each point of collection. In an all-stage system with a cumulative tax, the manufacturer, distributor, and retailer pay the same percentage of sales in tax each time a good is sold. The final price of the good reflects the accumulation of taxes levied at each stage. A tax is cumulative if no credit is given to purchasers for tax paid on the purchase of inputs (OECD, 1988c).

A tax is non-cumulative if a portion of the tax is refunded or credited at each stage of collection so that a net tax is paid only on the value added at each stage. A non-cumulative consumption tax may be implemented with one of three methods: 1) subtraction (direct, intermediate, and indirect); 2) addition; and 3) tax credit. In Europe, the tax credit method is applied almost universally in the value added tax. Under the tax credit method, each firm is allowed to take a credit of the consumption tax paid at the previous stage against the tax owed. The tax does not accumulate on the price of the good with each succeeding stage. Theoretically, a seller has no economic burden on his purchases because he is able to take credit for the VAT paid. The two other methods of achieving a non-cumulative tax, the subtraction and addition methods, are limited in use (Terra, 1988:32–34; for discussion of these methods see OECD, 1988c:80–83).

The major advantage of the cumulative tax is that it is relatively easy to administer and each stage shares a similar burden. There are two major disadvantages. The price of a good rises with each successive stage, producing distortions in competition. Integrated manufacturers/wholesalers have a lower tax burden per good sold than non-integrated manufacturers who must sell to wholesalers.

2. *Reform of Consumption Taxes*

The European Economic Community (EEC) has played a major role in the reform of consumption taxes in Europe. The first EEC effort to reform consumption taxes was the introduction of the value added tax. The European Community made a second effort to harmonize the VAT in anticipation of a single market under Europe 1992.

Introduction and adoption of the VAT: Until the adoption of standardized value added taxes, most European countries utilized multi-stage, cumulative general consumption taxes. Prior to adoption of a generalized VAT in 1968, France continued to utilize forms of cumulative general consumption tax. Prior to adoption of the VAT, cumulative consumption taxes were also utilized in Austria, Belgium, Germany, Greece, Italy, Luxembourg, the Netherlands, and Spain. Variations in exemptions from the base, tax rates, and net taxes on different goods were widespread.

The impetus for widespread adoption of the value added tax in Europe came from different sources. One source of change was the formation and development of the European Economic Community.[2] In 1962, adoption of a standard form of the VAT became mandatory for membership in the EEC (OECD, 1988c). The First and Second Directives of the European Community called for the replacement of existing "turnover" (cumulative) taxes by a common system of value added tax in member countries (Wheatcroft, 1973; OECD, 1988c:275).

Another factor contributing to the adoption of the value added tax was criticism of existing consumption taxes. In Denmark and Sweden growing demands for revenues and opposition to higher income taxes in the late 1960s created dissatisfaction with single-stage taxes (OECD, 1988c). The value added tax offered a source of revenue to fund higher social benefits without increasing income taxes.

France was the first European country to adopt a partial form of the value added tax in 1948 (OECD, 1988c:79), prior to formation of the European Community. Denmark introduced the VAT July 3, 1967, followed by Germany and Sweden on January 1, 1968; France extended the limited VAT to a general VAT covering services and retail sales on that date also. The Netherlands adopted the VAT January 1, 1969, followed by Luxembourg and Norway, January 1, 1970, and Belgium on January 1, 1971. Ireland adopted the VAT November 1, 1972, followed by Austria and Italy on January 1, 1973, and the United Kingdom on April 1 of 1973 (Price Waterhouse, 1989). It was another 12 years before the VAT was adopted in Turkey (1985), Portugal, Spain, and New Zealand (1986), and Greece (1987). By 1987, the VAT had replaced all multi-stage cumulative taxes in the OECD countries.

Leaders of the European Community realized by the mid-1980s that the goal of a single common market was not fully accomplished (Cecchini, 1988:3). In response, the *White Paper on Completing the Internal Market* was released and endorsed at the European Community summit in 1985. The legislative program set the framework for Europe 1992 by eliminating remaining trade barriers, and ensuring the free movement of goods, persons, services, and capital by 1992.

Reforms of the VAT include a new two-rate system with a standard rate of between 14 and 20 percent and a reduced rate of between 4 and 9 percent for certain goods and services (OECD, 1988c: 92). The standard VAT rate varied in 1987, from 12 percent in Luxembourg and Spain to 25 percent in Ireland. The spread of rates created substantial price differences between countries. The countries of Denmark, Finland, Norway, and Sweden have a single-rate system with a relatively high rate of more than 17 percent; New

Zealand has a single-rate system with a rate of less than 13 percent. Austria, Belgium, France, Greece, Ireland, Italy, the Netherlands, and Portugal have multi-rate systems with standard rates over 17 percent. Germany, Luxembourg, Spain, Turkey, and the United Kingdom have multi-rate systems with rates of less than 17 percent (OECD, 1988c).

Single-stage taxes still exist in the federal countries of Australia, Canada, Switzerland, and the United States, and in Iceland (OECD, 1988c). Australia and Switzerland levy single-stage consumption taxes exclusively at the federal level, Canada at the federal and provincial levels, and the United States at the federal, state and local levels.

3. Incidence and Progressivity of Consumption Taxes

Consumption taxes of any variety, general or excise, single- or multi-stage, cumulative or non-cumulative, are by definition indirect taxes. The tax is generally added to the price of the good unless supply is inelastic in relation to price. With this exception, the incidence of a consumption tax eventually falls on the consumer.

Consumption taxes are based on the value or amount of a good or service purchased, not the consumer's income or ability to pay. Consumption taxes are inherently regressive in their relation to income and place a greater marginal tax burden on the poor than the wealthy.

In addition to income, analysis of progressivity may be based on consumption. Some studies indicate that consumption taxes, and the VAT in particular, are roughly proportional when related to consumption (OECD, 1988c:123). In the United States, some necessity goods such as food and prescription medicine have been exempted from some states' sales taxes to reduce regressivity. In some European countries, a lower VAT rate may be applied to essential goods or services, or to a higher rate to luxuries in order to increase progressivity.

4. Major Trends in Consumption Taxes

Overall, consumption taxes declined in importance relative to other taxes during the period 1965–87 as illustrated in Table 2.10. There was a decline in the average consumption tax ratio for OECD countries, which includes general and excise taxes, from 1965 to 1987. The decline was the consequence of two factors. First, both the personal income tax and social security taxes increased in most countries during this period. Second, there was a real decline in the excise tax, which accounted for a substantial portion of the overall consumption tax ratio in 1965. From 1965 to 1987, a loss of 6.2 percent in the proportion of consumption taxation to total taxation occurred. However, consumption taxes started to regain some lost ground beginning in 1980, due to increased revenues from the VAT. Increases in consumption taxes occurred in half the

OECD countries in 1985 and 1987. Figure 2.2 illustrates the trend of the ratio of total consumption taxes to all revenues between 1965–87, as well as the trends of the separate consumption taxes.

General consumption taxes: The ratio of general consumption taxes to total taxes grew over the period 1965 to 1987 as shown in Figure 2.2 above. This trend is especially pronounced as VAT was introduced. There was continued expansion of the general consumption tax ratio in both federal and unitary countries.

The VAT assumed increasing importance in European countries; by 1975, it surpassed the excise tax ratio. Greece had the highest VAT ratio in 1987, followed by Finland, Turkey, Portugal, and Austria as shown in Table 2.11. Among countries with a VAT, Sweden, Luxembourg, Italy, Belgium, and Germany had the lowest ratio (see Table 2.12). Comparisons between federal and unitary VAT ratios are difficult to draw because only two federal countries (Austria and Germany) have the VAT which exaggerates the federal average. In addition, the difference in time of VAT adoption among countries makes comparisons of VAT ratios over time extremely difficult.

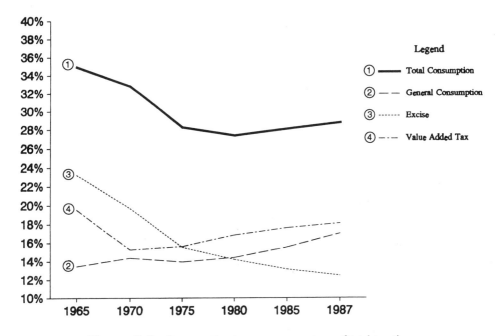

Figure 2.2 Consumption taxes as a percentage of total taxation.

Table 2.10   Ratio of Consumption Taxes to Total Taxes

	1965	1970	1975	1980	1985	1987
Australia	30.0	27.8	25.8	27.8	28.4	25.8
Austria	36.6	36.6	33.9	30.6	31.5	31.2
Belgium	34.1	32.7	24.6	24.6	22.7	22.8
Canada	35.3	27.6	26.0	24.5	26.1	25.3
Denmark	38.3	36.6	31.6	35.6	32.9	32.8
Finland	42.5	40.0	33.5	38.5	35.7	37.7
France	37.5	37.1	32.4	29.5	28.7	28.4
Germany	31.1	30.0	25.6	25.9	24.6	24.3
Greece	47.1	46.1	43.6	38.2	39.9	44.7
Ireland	49.1	49.5	44.4	43.0	42.6	40.7
Italy	37.0	36.3	28.3	25.2	23.6	25.0
Japan	25.0	20.9	15.1	14.1	12.1	11.1
Luxembourg	23.5	19.4	20.0	20.5	23.3	23.8
Netherlands	27.1	26.2	22.5	23.1	23.4	23.8
New Zealand	26.2	25.2	22.8	21.4	22.0	31.8
Norway	39.9	41.6	36.6	34.4	36.3	38.7
Portugal	41.5	42.2	38.1	43.4	41.3	48.3
Spain	40.6	35.8	24.0	20.7	27.7	29.3
Sweden	29.5	26.5	22.7	22.6	25.3	23.2
Switzerland	28.4	24.9	18.3	18.8	17.5	17.8
Turkey	53.5	48.8	40.9	25.2	35.7	31.6
United Kingdom	30.8	26.5	23.5	27.7	29.7	29.7
United States	19.2	16.9	16.2	14.4	15.4	14.5
AVERAGE	34.9	32.8	28.3	27.4	28.1	28.8
Unitary	38.6	36.6	31.3	30.0	31.0	32.0
Federal	33.1	29.8	26.9	26.5	26.6	25.4

Source: Computed from data from Organisation for Economic Co-Operation and De-

Rank	Change					
1987	1965 1970	1970 1975	1975 1980	1980 1985	1985 1987	1965 1987
13	-2.2	-2.0	2.0	0.6	-2.6	-4.2
9	0.0	-2.7	-3.3	0.9	-0.3	-5.4
20	-1.4	-8.1	0.0	-1.9	0.1	-11.3
14	-7.7	-1.6	-1.5	1.6	-0.8	-10.0
6	-1.7	-5.0	4.0	-2.7	-0.1	-5.5
5	-2.5	-6.5	5.0	-2.8	2.0	-4.8
12	-0.4	-4.7	-2.9	-0.8	-0.3	-9.1
16	-1.1	-4.4	0.3	-1.3	-0.3	-6.8
2	-1.0	-2.5	-5.4	1.7	4.8	-2.4
3	0.4	-5.1	-1.4	-0.4	-1.9	-8.4
15	-0.7	-8.0	-3.1	-1.6	1.4	-12.0
23	-4.1	-5.8	-1.0	-2.0	-1.0	-13.9
17	-4.1	0.6	0.5	2.8	0.5	0.3
18	-0.9	-3.7	0.6	0.3	0.4	-3.3
7	-1.0	-2.4	-1.4	0.6	9.8	5.6
4	1.7	-5.0	-2.2	1.9	2.4	-1.2
1	0.7	-4.1	5.3	-2.1	7.0	6.8
11	-4.8	-11.8	-3.3	7.0	1.6	-11.3
19	-3.0	-3.8	-0.1	2.7	-2.1	-6.3
21	-3.5	-6.6	0.5	-1.3	0.3	-10.6
8	-4.7	-7.9	-15.7	10.5	-4.1	-21.9
10	-4.3	-3.0	4.2	2.0	0.0	-1.1
22	-2.3	-0.7	-1.8	1.0	-0.9	-4.7
	-2.1	-4.6	-0.9	0.7	0.7	-6.2
	-2.0	-5.3	-1.3	1.0	1.1	-6.5
	-3.3	-2.9	-0.4	0.0	-1.2	-7.8

velopment, 1989, p. 95, Table 27.

Table 2.11   Ratio of General Consumption Taxes to Total Taxes

	1965	1970	1975	1980	1985	1987
Australia	7.4	7.4	6.7	5.3	8.0	8.2
Austria	18.7	18.5	19.8	20.1	21.0	20.9
Belgium	21.1	21.0	15.9	16.8	15.7	15.7
Canada	18.2	14.4	12.5	11.5	13.1	14.1
Denmark	9.1	18.8	16.9	22.2	20.0	18.9
Finland	19.0	20.0	17.9	20.8	21.4	24.6
France	23.3	25.5	23.4	21.1	20.0	19.5
Germany	16.5	17.1	14.7	16.6	15.8	15.7
Greece	11.0	17.5	18.9	13.2	17.1	26.9
Ireland	5.7	13.1	14.7	14.8	20.6	20.2
Italy	12.9	13.2	14.3	15.6	14.5	14.6
Japan						
Luxembourg	12.4	10.3	12.0	10.8	12.8	13.5
Netherlands	12.4	14.6	14.4	15.8	16.2	16.4
New Zealand	7.7	8.0	9.0	10.2	10.4	16.7
Norway	21.5	23.8	20.5	18.1	18.2	20.8
Portugal		8.4	11.2	16.2	12.6	21.0
Spain	22.2	20.3	15.3	10.2	14.7	16.9
Sweden	10.4	10.3	12.0	13.4	13.9	13.3
Switzerland	9.4	7.8	7.7	9.1	9.3	9.7
Turkey					23.3	23.4
United Kingdom	5.9	6.5	8.8	14.5	15.9	16.1
United States	4.6	5.6	6.7	6.6	7.4	7.4
AVERAGE	13.5	14.4	14.0	14.4	15.5	17.0
Unitary	13.9	15.4	15.0	15.6	16.7	18.7
Federal	12.5	11.8	11.4	11.5	12.4	12.7

Source: Computed from data from Organisation for Economic Co-Operation and De-

Rank	Change					
1987	1965 1970	1970 1975	1975 1980	1980 1985	1985 1987	1965 1987
21	0.0	-0.7	-1.4	2.7	0.2	0.8
5	-0.2	1.3	0.3	0.9	-0.1	2.2
14	-0.1	-5.1	0.9	-1.1	0.0	-5.4
17	-3.8	-1.9	-1.0	1.6	1.0	-4.1
9	9.7	-1.9	5.3	-2.2	-1.1	9.8
2	1.0	-2.1	2.9	0.6	3.2	5.6
8	2.2	-2.1	-2.3	-1.1	-0.5	-3.8
15	0.6	-2.4	1.9	-0.8	-0.1	-0.8
1	6.5	1.4	-5.7	3.9	9.8	15.9
7	7.4	1.6	0.1	5.8	-0.4	14.5
16	0.3	1.1	1.3	-1.1	0.1	1.7
18	-2.1	1.7	-1.2	2.0	0.7	1.1
12	2.2	-0.2	1.4	0.4	0.2	4.0
11	0.3	1.0	1.2	0.2	6.3	9.0
6	2.3	-3.3	-2.4	0.1	2.6	-0.7
4	8.4	2.8	5.0	-3.6	8.4	21.0
10	-1.9	-5.0	-5.1	4.5	2.2	-5.3
19	-0.1	1.7	1.4	0.5	-0.6	2.9
20	-1.6	-0.1	1.4	0.2	0.4	0.3
3					0.1	23.4
13	0.6	2.3	5.7	1.4	0.2	10.2
22	1.0	1.1	-0.1	0.8	0.0	2.8
	1.6	-0.4	0.5	0.7	1.5	4.8
	1.5	-0.4	0.6	1.1	2.0	4.8
	-0.7	-0.5	0.2	0.9	0.2	0.2

velopment, 1989, p. 96, Table 29.

Table 2.12   Ratio of Value Added Tax to Total Taxes

	1965	1970	1975	1980	1985
Australia					
Austria			19.8	20.1	21.0
Belgium		1.0	15.9	16.8	15.7
Canada					
Denmark		18.8	16.9	22.2	20.0
Finland	19.0	19.6	16.7	19.3	20.0
France	20.1	25.5	23.1	20.9	19.7
Germany		17.1	14.7	16.6	15.8
Greece					
Ireland			14.7	14.8	20.6
Italy			13.7	15.6	14.5
Japan					
Luxembourg		6.9	12.0	10.8	12.8
Netherlands		14.6	14.4	15.8	16.2
New Zealand					
Norway		23.8	20.5	18.1	18.2
Portugal					
Spain					
Sweden		10.3	12.0	13.4	13.9
Switzerland					
Turkey					22.3
United Kingdom			8.8	14.5	15.9
United States					
AVERAGE	19.5	15.3	15.6	16.8	17.6
Unitary	19.5	15.0	15.3	16.6	17.5
Federal		17.1	17.3	18.4	18.4

Source: Computed from data from Organisation for Economic Co-Opera-

1987	Rank 1987	Change				
		1965 1970	1970 1975	1975 1980	1980 1985	1985 1987
20.9	5			0.3	0.9	-0.1
15.7	15		14.9	0.9	-1.1	0.0
18.9	9		-1.9	5.3	-2.1	-1.1
23.3	1	0.6	-2.9	2.5	0.7	3.3
19.2	8	5.4	-2.4	-2.2	-1.2	-0.4
15.7	14		-2.4	1.9	-0.8	-0.1
20.9	4					
20.2	7			0.1	5.8	-0.4
14.6	16			1.9	-1.1	0.1
13.5	17		5.1	-1.2	2.1	0.7
16.4	11		-0.3	1.5	0.4	0.2
16.7	10					
20.8	6		-3.3	-2.4	0.1	2.5
20.9	3					
16.0	13					
13.3	18		1.7	1.4	0.5	-0.6
22.8	2					0.5
16.1	12			5.7	1.4	0.2
18.1			0.3	1.2	0.8	0.5
18.1			0.3	1.2	0.9	0.6
18.3			0.1	1.1	0.0	-0.1

tion and Development, 1989, p. 102–153, Tables 38–60.

Table 2.13   Ratio of Excise Taxes to Total Taxes

	1965	1970	1975	1980	1985	1987
Australia	22.7	20.3	19.1	22.6	20.5	17.6
Austria	18.0	18.0	14.0	10.4	10.4	10.2
Belgium	13.0	11.8	8.7	7.8	7.0	7.1
Canada	17.1	13.2	13.6	13.0	13.0	11.2
Denmark	29.2	17.9	14.7	13.4	12.9	13.8
Finland	23.5	20.0	15.6	17.7	14.4	13.1
France	14.3	11.6	9.0	8.4	8.7	8.9
Germany	14.6	12.9	10.9	9.3	8.7	8.6
Greece	36.1	28.5	24.7	25.1	20.8	16.8
Ireland	43.4	36.4	29.7	28.3	22.0	20.5
Italy	24.1	23.2	14.0	9.7	9.1	10.3
Japan	25.0	20.9	15.1	14.1	12.1	11.1
Luxembourg	11.1	9.0	8.0	9.7	10.5	10.3
Netherlands	14.7	11.6	8.1	7.3	7.2	7.4
New Zealand	18.5	17.2	13.8	11.2	11.7	15.1
Norway	18.4	17.8	16.1	16.3	18.1	18.0
Portugal	41.5	33.8	27.0	27.2	28.7	27.3
Spain	18.4	15.5	8.7	10.5	13.0	12.4
Sweden	19.2	16.3	10.7	9.2	11.4	9.8
Switzerland	19.0	17.1	10.6	9.7	8.2	8.1
Turkey	53.5	48.8	40.9	25.2	12.4	8.2
United Kingdom	24.9	19.9	14.8	13.2	13.9	13.6
United States	14.6	11.3	9.5	7.8	7.9	7.2
AVERAGE	23.3	19.7	15.5	14.2	13.2	12.5
Unitary	23.8	20.0	15.8	15.3	14.8	14.1
Federal	21.6	18.9	14.8	11.2	8.6	7.8

Source: Computed from data from Organisation for Economic Co-Operation and De-

Rank	Change					
1987	1965 1970	1970 1975	1975 1980	1980 1985	1985 1987	1965 1987
4	-2.4	-1.2	3.5	-2.1	-2.9	-5.1
15	0.0	-4.0	-3.6	0.0	-0.2	-7.8
23	-1.2	-3.1	-0.9	-0.8	0.1	-5.9
11	-3.9	0.4	-0.6	0.0	-1.8	-5.9
7	-11.3	-3.2	-1.3	-0.5	0.9	-15.4
9	-3.5	-4.4	2.1	-3.3	-1.3	-10.4
17	-2.7	-2.6	-0.6	0.3	0.2	-5.4
18	-1.7	-2.0	-1.6	-0.6	-0.1	-6.0
5	-7.6	-3.8	0.4	-4.3	-4.0	-19.3
2	-7.0	-6.7	-1.4	-6.3	-1.5	-22.9
14	-0.9	-9.2	-4.3	-0.6	1.2	-13.8
12	-4.1	-5.8	-1.0	-2.0	-1.0	-13.9
13	-2.1	-1.0	1.7	0.8	-0.2	-0.8
21	-3.1	-3.5	-0.8	-0.1	0.2	-7.3
6	-1.3	-3.4	-2.6	0.5	3.4	-3.4
3	-0.6	-1.7	0.2	1.8	-0.1	-0.4
1	-7.7	-6.8	0.2	1.5	-1.4	-14.2
10	-2.9	-6.8	1.8	2.5	-0.6	-6.0
16	-2.9	-5.6	-1.5	2.2	-1.6	-9.4
20	-1.9	-6.5	-0.9	-1.5	-0.1	-10.9
19	-4.7	-7.9	-15.7	-12.8	-4.2	-45.3
8	-5.0	-5.1	-1.6	0.7	-0.3	-11.3
22	-3.3	-1.8	-1.7	0.1	-0.7	-7.4
	-3.6	-4.2	-1.3	-1.1	-0.7	-10.8
	-3.9	-4.2	-0.5	-0.5	-0.7	-9.7
	-2.7	-4.1	-3.6	-2.6	-0.8	-13.8

velopment, 1989, p. 102–153, Tables 38–60.

Excise taxes: The average excise tax ratio in 1965 was larger than the general consumption tax ratio, however, there is continual decline in the average excise tax ratio from 1965 to 1987 as shown in Figure 2.2. Excise tax ratios declined in all countries between 1965 and 1987 as illustrated in Table 2.13.

Portugal, Ireland, Norway, Australia, and Greece had the highest excise tax ratios in 1987; Belgium, the United States, the Netherlands, Switzerland, and Turkey had the lowest ratios. The average excise tax ratio in federal countries was approximately half the ratio in unitary countries 1987.

The most significant excise taxes levied in OECD countries in 1985 was on motoring, which includes mineral oils (gasoline, oil), as well as vehicles and licenses. The United States, Canada, Luxembourg, and Turkey did not collect revenues from motoring excise taxes.

E.   Social Security/Welfare

Despite differences among countries, several general observations on European social policy can be made. First, protection of the disabled, children, families, and the elderly is a broadly supported public policy in Europe in contrast to the United States where those in need are labeled as deprived or disadvantaged in need of "special services." Most OECD countries have social policies which affect families and children, whether or not they are explicit policies. Second, national pension systems have been adopted by all European countries and have achieved a high standard of provision (International Labour Office 1989:78). Third, national health services are widespread in contrast to optional health insurance as utilized in the United States; while most OECD countries had free access to hospital care by 1960, the major exception was the United States. Fourth, social policies in Europe are moving toward means-tested benefits.

Due to the variations among countries in the level of benefits, beneficiaries, administration, and financing, a full description of the nature and scope of social welfare systems is beyond the scope of this chapter. The discussion begins with a general description of social welfare policy including definitions of social security, the provision of benefits, and financing methods. Next, family welfare policy, pensions, and health care policy are discussed. Major trends in social security contributions are presented next, followed by a discussion of the regressivity and incidence of contributions. Last, future trends in social policy are examined.

1.   *Social Welfare/Social Security Policy*

A distinction is often made between *social security* and *social welfare*. The basis of the distinction is the connection between a payment or contribution and entitlement to benefits. This distinction, while tenuous at times, is the basis for social security programs. Social security programs link payment and benefit, while under social welfare programs there is no connection between payment and benefits. This distinction has less practical application to social policy in Europe due to the adoption of entitlements for pensions, health care, and family benefits.

Five types of programs are generally included in social security benefits: 1) old age pensions, disability and death benefits; 2) health care including sickness and maternity benefits; 3) support during work injury; 4) unemployment; and 5) family allowances (U.S. Department of Health and Human Services, 1989:vi). The broader category of social welfare includes education, and family assistance but may also include health care and pensions if universal entitlement to these programs is adopted (for a discussion on the nuances of the different social welfare systems, see U.S. Department of Health and Human Services 1989 and International Labour Office, 1989).

Provision of benefits: There are three general methods of providing social benefits in OECD countries: social insurance, universal systems, and means-tested systems. The social insurance approach relates benefit payments directly or indirectly to one or more factors: length of employment, earnings or, in the case of family allowances, to employment itself. Universal systems provide benefits without consideration of income, employment, or means; this is the basis of social welfare rather than social security. Means-tested programs use a standard level of income to determine eligibility for benefits.

Administration varies between programs and among OECD countries. Some programs are administered solely by the national government, or by the national government with state/provincial governments, or are administered in whole or in part by private insurers.

Financing social benefits: Financing social benefits vary in terms of revenue source, level of contribution from each source, and the base and rate of taxation. To meet the OECD classification of *social security contributions*, contributions must satisfy all of the following criteria: 1) they must be compulsory; 2) levied on earnings or as a function of the number of employees; 3) made by insured persons or their employees; 4) paid to the general government which provides social security benefits; and 5) earmarked to provide social security benefits (OECD, 1989:42).

Different programs may operate as social welfare or social security depending on the country. Systems can be financed in part by mandatory contributions, voluntary contributions, and by taxes levied on income or goods and services. Taxes earmarked for social benefits are accounted for on the basis of the separate tax base (i.e., income tax, tax on goods and services, etc.) and not as social security contributions. This may skew analysis of social security contributions.

Universal benefits may exist side by side with earnings-related benefits, and each may be financed differently. A worker may pay a flat rate for basic universal pension insurance and voluntarily make employee contributions, based on wage or taxable income, for a social insurance pension with additional benefits. The flat rate contribution is mandatory and goes to the national government; the voluntary contribution may be to a private insurer.

The national government may directly finance some, all, or none of the system, and may supplement funds when contributions are less than requirements. In the United States the social security contribution is evenly divided between the employer and the employee; this is frequently not the case in OECD countries (International Labour Office, 1989:77–115.)

Government financing may be through general revenues, or through earmarked taxes. The employer may be required to contribute to the system, generally based on a percentage of payroll, or employer contributions may not be required. Finally, the base and rate of contribution may vary by program. The financing of pension benefits may be different from the financing of health benefits within the same country, as well as between countries.

Table 2.14 illustrates the different financing administration for social security systems in OECD countries. There are five different financing sources: 1) general government revenues; 2) social security contributions; 3) voluntary contributions; 4) compulsory contributions to the private sector; and 5) other taxes.

2. *Family Policy, Pensions and Health Policy*

Family policy, pensions and health policy represent substantial expenditures by the different OECD countries. The following discussion, while brief, provides information on these policies.

Family policy: Families in Europe are viewed as a part of public life. Explicit family welfare policy avoids stigmatizing certain families as deprived or disadvantaged by making benefits available to all families. There are three classifications of family policies: 1) explicit, comprehensive family policy found in countries such as France, Norway, and Sweden; 2) an explicit but narrowly focused family policy found in countries such as Austria, Denmark, and Finland; and 3) no explicit family policy—in countries such as the United Kingdom, the United States, and Canada.

As noted in the introduction to the section on social welfare policy, all OECD countries have a range of policies that affect families with children. In the EEC, family policies have four common objectives: 1) to increase population growth by providing incentives for families; 2) to protect children from poverty through the redistribution of income towards those with family responsibilities; 3) to promote freedom of choice for the family unit with recognition that the role of the State is to reduce differences in the standard of living of families, particularly of children; and 4) to promote the perceived interests of the labor market by providing incentives for women to enter or leave the labor market. "The commitment to family policy is based on the recognition of two facts. First, there is agreement that the young and the elderly require care and protection, and that it is a legitimate objective of societies and of governments to facilitate that care" (International Labour Office, 1989:70).

Pensions: The modern pension systems of European members of the OECD produce a high standard of pension provision in all European countries, with similarities in the scope of coverage and program objectives. Differences in the provision of pension benefits are found in the extent of coverage, mix between public and private provision, the functions assigned to various tiers of pension coverage (basic protection, complementary benefits, etc.), and the source of funds. In many countries there is debate over *guaranteed minimum pension*, where the link between benefits and contributions is non-existent (International Labour Office, 1989).

Broad-based national programs which cover all residents (universal) are in place in the Netherlands, Switzerland, and the United Kingdom. Pension systems organized more narrowly for various socio-occupational groups are in place in the countries of Austria, France, Germany, Italy, and Spain. In these countries one major "general" state pension scheme for employees covers a large proportion of the working population (the first tier) and a "special" pension program (the second tier) is provided for specific occupational groups such as persons employed in agriculture, miners, railway workers, etc. Second-tier programs may be compulsory for specific occupational groups, as in France, or negotiated between employers and workers under guidelines set forth by the state as in Germany, the Netherlands, the United Kingdom, and Sweden.

There is no uniformity among OECD countries in the financing of public pensions. There are three general types of pension financing systems in OECD countries: the flat-rate system; mixed system which adds a pension based on earnings to a basic pension amount; and an earnings-related pension system. Some countries finance pensions solely from worker contributions with no subsidies or transfers from the general fund. Some countries combine taxes and contributions to pay for pensions. Others use only taxes.

Financing may include a flat rate or a contribution based on income. Regardless of where responsibility for financing the system lies, all pension systems in OECD countries, including the United States, are effectively pay-as-you-go schemes. The current generation of workers provides the revenues for those who have retired (OECD, 1988d:33). As a result, declines in the ratio of beneficiaries to contributors will have an effect on the financial status of the system (OECD, 1988e; International Labour Office, 1989).

Table 2.14 Financing Social Security Systems—Total Contribution by Source in Percentage

	1965	1970	1975	1980	1985	1987
Australia						
Financed entirely from general revenues	100.0	100.0	100.0	100.0	100.0	100.0
Austria						
Social security contributions	98.0	98.4	98.8	98.5	99.5	99.3
Voluntary contributions	2.0	1.6	1.2	1.5	0.5	0.7
Belgium						
Social security contributions	100.0	100.0	100.0	100.0	100.0	100.0
Canada						
Social security contributions	41.6	58.7	87.9	100.0	100.0	100.0
Other taxes	58.4	41.3	12.1			
Denmark						
Social security contributions	44.6	49.5	19.8	27.7	41.7	90.3
Other taxes	49.6	42.8	73.7	65.9	54.4	
Voluntary contributions	0.2		1.1	1.4	1.1	3.1
Compulsory contributions to private sector	5.7	7.7	5.5	5.0	2.7	6.6
Finland						
Social security contributions	26.9	33.2	38.8	35.6	36.1	34.3
Voluntary contributions	30.0	28.5	22.1	15.1	19.1	17.7
Compulsory contributions to private sector	43.1	38.3	39.1	49.3	44.7	48.1
France						
Social security contributions	100.0	100.0	98.8	98.8	98.2	98.3
Other taxes			1.2	1.2	1.8	1.7
Germany						
Social security contributions	90.6	91.8	90.3	91.5	91.6	91.9
Voluntary contributions	8.9	7.6	9.0	7.8	7.6	7.3
Compulsory contributions to private sector	0.5	0.6	0.7	0.7	0.7	0.8
Greece						
Social security contributions	79.3	85.3	88.0	100.0	100.0	100.0
Other taxes	20.7	14.7	12.0			
Ireland						
Social security contributions	100.0	100.0	100.0	100.0	100.0	100.0
Italy						
Social security contributions	100.0	100.0	100.0	100.0	100.0	100.0
Japan						
Social security contributions	100.0	100.0	100.0	100.0	100.0	100.0

	1965	1970	1975	1980	1985	1987
Luxembourg						
Social security contributions	100.0	100.0	100.0	100.0	100.0	100.0
Netherlands						
Social security contributions	40.3	41.1	41.4	42.1	44.2	46.0
Voluntary contributions	2.0	2.1	2.0	1.9	1.6	0.2
Compulsory contributions to private sector	57.6	56.9	56.5	56.0	54.1	53.9
New Zealand						
Financed entirely from general revenues	100.0	100.0	100.0	100.0	100.0	100.0
Norway						
Social security contributions	60.6	68.2	85.9	86.4	86.9	83.3
Other taxes	39.4	31.8	14.1	13.3	12.7	16.3
Compulsory contributions to private sector				0.3	0.4	0.4
Portugal						
Social security contributions	100.0	100.0	100.0	99.7	99.3	99.2
Other taxes				0.3	0.7	0.8
Spain						
Social security contributions	100.0	100.0	100.0	99.5	99.4	100.0
Other taxes				0.5	0.6	
Sweden						
Social security contributions	77.5	79.5	100.0	100.0	100.0	100.0
Other taxes	22.5	20.5				
Switzerland						
Social security contributions	49.1	53.9	62.5	59.8	63.4	96.1
Other taxes	5.8	7.6	3.7	2.9	2.9	3.9
Voluntary contributions	1.6	1.7	1.5	1.6	1.6	
Compulsory contributions to private sector	43.4	36.8	32.4	35.7	32.0	
Turkey						
Social security contributions	100.0	100.0	100.0	100.0	100.0	100.0
United Kingdom						
Social security contributions	59.5	58.4	54.5	50.3	56.2	59.5
Voluntary contributions		0.2	0.1		0.1	0.1
Compulsory contributions to private sector	40.5	41.4	45.3	49.7	43.7	40.4
United States						
Social security contributions	98.3	97.5	97.8	98.3	98.2	98.2
Voluntary contributions	1.7	2.5	2.2	1.7	1.8	1.8

Source: Computed from data from Organisation for Economic Co-Operation and Development, 1989, p. 156–159, Tables 61–83.

Health care: Health-care coverage can be provided in four ways: 1) optional health insurance, 2) compulsory health insurance, 3) national health insurance, and 4) national health service.

With optional health insurance the individual decides whether or not to take health insurance. This system is very rare in Europe, except in Switzerland, and in the United States.

Compulsory health insurance links entitlement to medical care conditional on the payment of contributions by the insured person, and in some cases by the employers. Austria, Belgium, France, and Germany have compulsory health insurance, although this type of scheme has been losing ground recently.

National health *insurance* does not make entitlement to benefits subject to the payment of contributions. National health insurance may be financed in different ways: by state subsidies, employers, and/or wage earner's contributions.

National health *services* are also universal schemes which cover the full range of preventive and corrective care, at least in principle. Under national health service, the public authority which finances health services also delivers health services. National health services vary depending upon the country and may or may not co-exist with private health care or with one or several different health insurance schemes. National health services are very widespread in Europe including the United Kingdom, Greece, Iceland, Italy, and Portugal.

Collective coverage for health benefits has become the rule in Europe. Collective coverage provides equal access to medical care in principle and it spreads the financial risks associated with illness over a greater number of people.

3. *Major Trends in Social Security Contributions*

Social security contributions are classified separately from taxes and voluntary contributions, even though all may pay for benefits. Social security benefits are based on contribution, social welfare benefits are universal. The following discussion concerns social security contributions only.

As illustrated in Table 2.15, OECD social security contributions increased on average from 19.9 percent of total tax revenues in 1965 to 26.6 percent in 1987. The average social security contributions for unitary countries grew at a slower rate than federal countries over this time period. The average social security tax ratio for unitary countries was 20.1 percent in 1965, growing to 25.9 percent in 1987; for federal countries the ratio was 19.3 percent in 1965 and 28.8 percent in 1987.

While most OECD countries experienced an increase in the proportion of social security taxes to total taxes collected during 1965–1970 and 1970–1975, both the base and rate of increase varied widely. The average increase for 1965–70 was 1.7 percent; unitary countries were slightly below the overall average at 1.6 percent; federal countries were slightly above at 2.3 percent.

The most significant increases in social security contributions occur between 1970 and 1975 with a smaller increase between 1975 and 1980. Social security contributions averaged .2 percent increase in 1980–85 and −.2 percent 1985–87. The social security tax ratio in unitary countries declined −.3 percent during both periods; federal countries experienced a small average increase of 2.1 percent over 1980–85 and a smaller increase of .1 percent over 1985–87 as shown in Table 2.15.

General trends in social expenditures: Over the period 1960–81, social expenditures were the fastest growing component of total public expenditures in OECD countries (OECD, 1985:19). The relative share between major programs was not constant, however. A shift in overall expenditures for education, health, and pension expenditures occurred between 1960 and 1980. In 1960, approximately 27 percent of social expenditures went to education, approximately 19 percent was allocated to health care and 32 percent to pensions. By 1980, education share dropped to a 23 percent share, health care increased to approximately 23 percent and pensions increased only marginally (OECD, 1985:24).

The rate of increase in social expenditures slowed in the 1980s. One perspective suggests that it was "inevitable that such rapid growth should eventually have been called into question" (OECD, 1985:9). Another perspective places more emphasis on world events for the slowdown in the rate of growth.

As a result of the oil shocks of 1973–74 and 1979–80, a downturn in economic growth was accompanied by a rapid increase in inflation This combination brought economic and social policies into conflict (OECD, 1985:9). Efforts to control inflation through reductions of public expenditures and deficits, contrasted sharply with the expansionary momentum of social programs established in the 1960s and reinforced by growing unemployment in the 1970s. An enlarged commitment to social policy benefiting the elderly and the disabled during the first half of the 1970s produced rapid growth in pension expenditures in the majority of European countries. The growth of pension expenditures slowed during the second half of the decade due to inflation, which prompted cost-cutting strategies. The growth in European health care policy slowed in the 1970s as most countries approached almost universal coverage and private sector insurance was more available (OECD, 1985:42). Since 1981, the rate of growth in social expenditures has slowed in most OECD countries; this decline is paralleled in similar reductions in social security contributions.

Pension reform: Pension reform has taken two directions in OECD countries and debate continues on another potential reform. In most OECD

Table 2.15 Ratio of Social Security Contributions to Total Taxes

	1965	1970	1975	1980	1985	1987
Australia						
Austria	24.9	25.4	27.6	30.9	31.8	32.3
Belgium	31.4	30.5	31.9	30.4	33.1	33.9
Canada	5.7	9.6	10.1	10.5	13.5	13.3
Denmark	5.4	4.0	1.3	1.8	3.8	3.7
Finland	3.2	4.8	8.7	9.5	9.1	9.0
France	34.2	36.3	40.6	42.7	43.3	43.0
Germany	26.8	30.3	33.5	34.4	36.5	37.3
Greece	26.9	27.1	27.2	32.9	35.7	32.6
Ireland	6.5	8.2	13.8	14.3	14.8	14.0
Italy	34.2	37.8	45.9	38.0	34.7	34.3
Japan	21.8	22.3	29.0	29.1	30.3	28.6
Luxembourg	32.3	28.6	29.5	29.3	25.5	26.4
Netherlands	30.8	35.1	38.4	38.1	44.3	42.7
New Zealand						
Norway	11.9	16.1	24.8	21.0	20.6	23.7
Portugal	21.9	23.9	34.6	29.5	25.9	28.2
Spain	28.3	37.4	47.5	48.6	41.3	36.2
Sweden	12.1	14.9	19.5	28.8	24.8	24.2
Switzerland	22.5	23.4	29.2	30.9	32.0	32.1
Turkey	5.9	6.3	9.5	14.0	14.3	15.9
United Kingdom	15.4	13.9	17.4	16.6	17.8	18.1
United States	16.4	19.3	24.6	26.2	29.4	28.8
AVERAGE	19.9	21.7	25.9	26.5	26.8	26.6
Unitary	20.1	21.7	26.2	26.5	26.2	25.9
Federal	19.3	21.6	25.0	26.6	28.6	28.8

Source: Computed from data from Organisation for Economic Co-Operation and De

Rank	Change					
1987	1965 1970	1970 1975	1975 1980	1980 1985	1985 1987	1965 1987
22						
8	0.5	2.2	3.3	0.9	0.5	7.4
6	-0.9	1.4	-1.5	2.7	0.8	2.5
19	3.9	0.5	0.4	3.0	-0.2	7.6
21	-1.4	-2.7	0.5	2.0	-0.1	-1.7
20	1.6	3.9	0.8	-0.4	-0.1	5.8
1	2.1	4.3	2.1	0.6	-0.3	8.8
3	3.5	3.2	0.9	2.1	0.8	10.5
7	0.2	0.1	5.7	2.8	-3.1	5.7
18	1.7	5.6	0.5	0.5	-0.8	7.5
5	3.6	8.1	-7.9	-3.3	-0.4	0.1
11	0.5	6.7	0.1	1.2	-1.7	6.8
13	-3.7	0.9	-0.2	-3.8	0.9	-5.9
2	4.3	3.3	-0.3	6.2	-1.6	11.9
23						
15	4.2	8.7	-3.8	-0.4	3.1	11.8
12	2.0	10.7	-5.1	-3.6	2.3	6.3
4	9.1	10.1	1.1	-7.3	-5.1	7.9
14	2.8	4.6	9.3	-4.0	-0.6	12.1
9	0.9	5.8	1.7	1.1	0.1	9.6
17	0.4	3.2	4.5	0.3	1.6	10.0
16	-1.5	3.5	-0.8	1.2	0.3	2.7
10	2.9	5.3	1.6	3.2	-0.6	12.4
	1.7	4.3	0.6	0.2	-0.2	6.7
	1.6	4.5	0.3	-0.3	-0.3	5.8
	2.3	3.4	1.6	2.1	0.1	9.5

velopment, 1989, p. 89, Table 15.

countries, public pensions have been indexed to inflation since the 1970s, a reaction to high inflation during that period. Benefit levels have been increased to keep pace with increased earnings, as well as on an ad hoc basis. Finally, both "the number and size of various allowances and supplements have increased in most systems" (OECD, 1988e:48).

The second reform, occurring in the 1980s, is the equalization of husbands' and wives' rights to benefits. The equalization of benefits is another step away from traditional concepts of the role of women and the family. Austria, Denmark, and Sweden have revised pension benefits to make them equally available, and other countries are following suit. There is debate on the subject of the relationship between contributions and pensions centers. The debate between a contribution-based pension system and one based on entitlements centers around the fixing of a minimum pension. With a guaranteed minimum pension the link between contributions and pensions vanishes.

Benefits and expenditures: Countries may spend significant amounts for social welfare benefits, yet have a less developed system in terms of benefits and beneficiaries. The United States spends more for health care as a percentage of gross domestic product, as well as on a per capita basis, than other OECD countries. The high level of health expenditures in the United States has often been directed toward a specific population. The United States spends significantly more on elderly health care than for persons aged 0–64 in comparison to other OECD countries (OECD, 1988e). This policy excludes large numbers from health care in the United States because they lack private health insurance.

Universal health care in most OECD countries has had several notable effects, including a reduction in infant mortality. The United States, the only major OECD country without universal health care, had the fourth highest infant mortality rate in 1988 at 1.04 deaths per hundred, a rate surpassed only by Turkey with 6.5 deaths per hundred, Portugal at 1.59 per hundred, and Greece at 1.22 per hundred (OECD, 1988e:42).

4. *Regressivity and Incidence of Social Security Contributions*

Contribution schemes may be progressive or regressive in design: there may be a flat rate or the contribution may be based on income. In either a flat rate or a contribution based on income an upper limit may be established as the maximum amount of contribution. The upper limit may be set based on the amount of the contribution or on the level of salary. In either case, if the upper limit is low then higher income persons will contribute less to the system in proportion to their total income. Low limits will contribute to regressivity.

5. *Future Developments in Social Protection*

The social welfare/security system is far from constant. However, there is a general trend which seems to be a move away from means-tested benefits ("social assistance") to universal benefits. The recent growth in social expenditures appears to be primarily the result of broadening policy beneficiaries and benefits (OECD, 1985:10). Future increases in the proportion of elderly to the total population, the result of increasing life spans and declining birth rates, will produce a decline in the proportion of the working population in the early part of the next century. In the near future, the growth of the elderly population will exert a growing demand on social expenditures *given the same level of benefits*. The increase in elderly population will continue to erode the economic base of public pensions and place greater fiscal demands on the working population. Demographic changes will have far less impact on the health sector than on retirement pensions (International Labour Office, 1989:153).

IV. SUMMARY AND CONCLUSIONS

In most OECD countries there was an observable increase in income tax and/ or social security contributions over the period 1965–75, while the consumption tax ratio scarcely changed (Messere and Owens, 1989). After the mid-seventies the consumption tax ratio grew at an increasing rate. The trend between 1965 and 1975 can be explained by public acceptance of higher personal taxes at a time when personal incomes were increasing. The general increase in consumption taxes in the mid-seventies is explained by greater public resistance to personal taxes, the result of inflation driven wage increases and consequently higher taxes. The increase of VAT actually began in 1970, with general consumption taxes increasing in 1975. By the mid-seventies, the VAT had been widely adopted in the European Economic Community.

The property tax ratio and corporate income tax ratio were smaller and grew more slowly between 1965–87 relative to the other major taxes. The growth rate in the proportion of personal income taxes and social security taxes to gross domestic product was more rapid, indicating increasing reliance on these two taxes. Consumption taxes increased more rapidly than property taxes and corporate income taxes, but more slowly than personal income taxes and social security taxes.

During the period 1965–75, a period of sustained economic growth, increasing social expenditures was met with little resistance and found general support. Worsening economic conditions following the oil crises, and increased unemployment made it difficult to finance rising costs of social programs in the late 1970s and 1980s. Despite efforts to increase compulsory contributions and limit the growth of expenditures, an aging population in most countries will continue to increase demands on age-related benefit programs such as pensions, as well as medical consumption with pensions.

In conclusion, revenue policy is determined by the historical interaction of a number of social, political, technical, and economic factors on both the national and international level. The first three factors frame the set of permissible policy options allowable within each country's current economic constraints. The forces of solidarity and special interests also frame the policy debate. In many countries, the solidarity of labor is reflected in the support of universal health care, guaranteed pensions and benefits, and family support. While in the United States, where measures of health care, economic productivity, and education continue to slip, Congress is unable or unwilling to shift the debate from one of keeping taxes low to that of mobilizing society's resources to benefit all of society, and not just the special interests with powerful lobbies.

NOTES

1. The OECD was established in Paris in 1960 for the purpose of fostering economic development and world trade. Original members of OECD include the developed nations of Austria, Belgium, Canada, Denmark, France, the Federal Republic of Germany, Greece, Iceland, Ireland, Italy, Luxembourg, the Netherlands, Norway, Portugal, Spain, Sweden, Switzerland, Turkey, the United Kingdom, and the United States. The following countries were accepted into the OECD on the date shown: Japan (1964), Finland (1969), Australia (1971), and New Zealand (1973).
2. On March 25, 1957, Belgium, France, Germany, Italy, Luxembourg, and the Netherlands signed the Treaty of Rome creating the European Economic Community. The primary goal was the creation of a common market among member countries. Denmark, Ireland, and the United Kingdom joined the European Community January 1, 1973, followed by Greece in 1981, and Portugal and Spain in January 1986.

REFERENCES

Altenstetter, Crista (1986). German social security programs: An interpretation of their development. *Nationalizing Social Security in Europe and America* (Douglas E. Ashford and E. W. Kelley, ed.). JAI Press, Greenwich, Connecticut, pp. 73–97.

Bird, Richard M. (1987). Corporate-personal tax integration. *Tax Coordination in the European Community* (Sijbren Cnossen, ed.). Series on International Taxation, No. 7, Kluwer Law and Taxation Publishers, New York. pp. 227–51.

Cayley, Michael (1989). Recent trends in company taxation. *Changes in Revenue Structures* (Aldo Chiancone and Ken Messere, ed.). Wayne State University Press, Detroit, pp. 103–12.

Cecchini, Paolo, with Michel Catinat and Alexis Jacquemin (1988). *The European Challenge 1992: The Benefits of a Single Market* (by John Robinson). Grower, Brookfield, Vermont.

Davies, David G. (1976). *International Comparisons of Tax Structures in Federal and Unitary Countries.* Research monograph 16. Center for Research on Federal Financial Relations, The Australian National University, Canberra.

Egret, Georges (1973). The value added tax in France. *Value Added Tax in the Enlarged Common Market* (G.S.A. Wheatcroft, ed.). John Wiley & Sons, New York, pp. 41–55.

Herber, Bernard P. (1983). *Modern Public Finance*. Fifth Edition, Richard D. Irwin, Inc., Homewood, Illinois, p. 147.

International Labour Office (1989). *From Pyramid to Pillar*. International Labour Office, Geneva, Switzerland.

International Monetary Fund (1988). *Government Finances Statistical Yearbook*. Series, International Monetary Fund, Washington, D.C.

Lund, Michael S. (1986). The politics of a national minimum income: The Poor Law coalition in postwar Britain. *Nationalizing Social Security in Europe and America* (Douglas E. Ashford and E. W. Kelley, ed.). JAI Press, Greenwich, Connecticut, pp. 25–58.

Messere, Ken C. and Owens, Jeffrey P. (1989). Long-term revenue trends and current tax reform issues in OECD countries. *Changes in Revenue Structures* (Aldo Chiancone and Ken Messere, ed.). Wayne State University Press, Detroit, pp. 21–35.

Musgrave, Peggy (1987). Interjurisdictional coordination of taxes on capital income. *Tax Coordination in the European Community* (Sijbren Cnossen, ed.). Series on International Taxation, No. 7 Kluwer Law and Taxation Publishers, New York. pp. 197–223.

Musgrave, Richard A. (1987). Fifty years of public finance. *International Institute of Public Finance Semicentennial 1937 to 1987* (K. W. Roskamp, ed.). Wayne State University Press, Detroit, p. 32.

Nagano, Atushi (1988). Japan. *World Tax Reform: A Progress Report* (Joseph A. Pechman, ed.). The Brookings Institution, Washington, D.C., pp. 155–169.

Organisation for Economic Co-Operation and Development (1977). *The Treatment of Family Units in OECD Member Countries Under Tax and Transfer Systems*. Organisation for Economic Co-Operation and Development, Paris, France.

Organisation for Economic Co-Operation and Development (1981). *Income Tax Schedules Distribution of Taxpayers and Revenues*. Organisation for Economic Co-Operation and Development, Paris, France.

Organisation for Economic Co-Operation and Development (1984). *Tax Elasticities of Central Government Personal Income Tax Systems*. Organisation for Economic Co-Operation and Development, Paris, France.

Organisation for Economic Co-Operation and Development (1985). *Social Expenditure 1960–1990; Problems of Growth and Control*. Organisation for Economic Co-Operation and Development, Paris, France.

Organisation for Economic Co-Operation and Development (1986). *Personal Income Tax Systems under Changing Economic Conditions*. Organisation for Economic Co-Operation and Development, Paris, France.

Organisation for Economic Co-Operation and Development (1987). *Taxation in Developed Countries*. Organisation for Economic Co-Operation and Development, Paris, France.

Organisation for Economic Co-Operation and Development (1988a). *The Taxation of Fringe Benefits*. Organisation for Economic Co-Operation and Development, Paris, France.

Organisation for Economic Co-Operation and Development (1988b). *Taxation of Net Wealth, Capital Transfers and Capital Gains of Individuals.* Organisation for Economic Co-Operation and Development, Paris, France.

Organisation for Economic Co-Operation and Development (1988c). *Taxing Consumption.* Organisation for Economic Co-Operation and Development, Paris, France.

Organisation for Economic Co-Operation and Development (1988d). *The Future of Social Protection.* Organisation for Economic Co-Operation and Development, Paris, France.

Organisation for Economic Co-Operation and Development (1988e). *Reforming Public Pensions.* Organisation for Economic Co-Operation and Development, Paris, France.

Organisation for Economic Co-Operation and Development (1989). *Revenue Statistics of OECD Member Countries, 1965-1988.* Organisation for Economic Co-Operation and Development, Paris, France.

Organisation for Economic Co-Operation and Development (1990). *The Personal Income Tax Base: A Comparative Survey.* Organisation for Economic Co-Operation and Development, Paris, France.

Pechman, Joseph A. (1988). Introduction. *World Tax Reform: A Progress Report* (J. A. Pechman, ed.). The Brookings Institution, Washington, D.C., pp. 1-13.

Price Waterhouse (1989). *Guide to VAT in Europe.* Graham & Trotnam, London.

Price Waterhouse (1990a). *Corporate Taxes, a Worldwide Summary.* Price Waterhouse Center for Transnational Taxation, New York, New York.

Price Waterhouse (1990b). *Individual Taxes, a Worldwide Summary.* Price Waterhouse Center for Transnational Taxation, New York, New York.

Terra, Ben J. M. (1988). *Sales Taxation: The Case of Value Added Tax in the European Community.* Series on International Taxation, No. 8, Kluwer Law and Taxation Publishers, Boston.

Teune, Henry (1986). The political development of the welfare state in the United States. *Nationalizing Social Security in Europe and America* (Douglas E. Ashford and E. W. Kelley, ed.). JAI Press, Greenwich, Connecticut, pp. 7-24.

U.S. Department of Health and Human Services, Social Security Administration (1989). *Social Security Programs Throughout the World—1989.* Office of International Policy, Office of Research and Statistics, Washington, D.C., Research Report No. 62.

Wheatcroft, G. S. A. (1973). Appendix II—Second Directive of the Council of 11 April 1967 (1973). *Value Added Tax in the Enlarged Common Market* (G. S. A. Wheatcroft, ed.). John Wiley & Sons, New York, pp. 123-36.

3

An Analysis of Budgetary Performance in the G-7 Industrialized Nations, 1980–1989

Kuo-Tsai Liou

Florida Atlantic University, Fort Lauderdale, Florida

I. INTRODUCTION

Starting in the mid-1970s and continuing through the 1980s, most industrialized nations considered fiscal restriction as the major goal of their budgetary policy. The fiscal restraint policy was derived from the anti-government movement, the argument of "government being too big," and became the major campaign issue in the late 1970s because of these governments' inability to solve the economic crisis of that time. Key issues emphasized in the policy included controlling governmental spending, balancing governmental budgets, deregulation, decentralization, and privatization.

The fiscal restraint policy became the top priority of newly elected chief executives and cabinets in the major industrialized nations. For example, the fiscal restraint policy was implemented by the Thatcher government in the United Kingdom, the Reagan administration in the United States, the Suzuke and Nakasoni cabinets in Japan, the Clark and Trudeau governments in Canada, and the Mitterrand government in France. While facing similar budget scarcity problems and adopting similar policies, these nations achieved varying results in the control of public expenditures and the reduction of budget deficits.

This chapter examines budget performance in seven major industrialized nations (i.e., the G-7 nations, including Canada, France, Germany, Italy, Japan, the United Kingdom, and the United States) during the 1980s to evaluate the impact of fiscal restraint policy. The examination stresses the comparison of the overall budgetary performance among these nations and does not examine factors affecting each nation's performance. The chapter begins with a general review of budgetary issues in the United States and in the other six nations during the 1980s. Next, the economic conditions and budgetary performances of these nations is examined to see the impact of fiscal restriction. Finally, the impact of the political system on budgetary performance is examined by comparing budgetary performance between nations with federal systems and those with unitary systems.

II.   BUDGETARY CONTROL IN THE G-7 NATIONS

All seven major industrialized nations entered the 1980s with serious fiscal problems resulting from: rising oil costs, low growth, high inflation and high unemployment in the late 1970s. The economic conditions of the 1970s brought to an end the use of conventional countercyclical prescriptions to solve fiscal problems. The new fiscal and budgetary orientation developed by the G-7 nations was that of fiscal restraint (e.g., Schick, 1986; Tarschys, 1986; Campbell, 1985a). The major policy options were alterations to expenditure plans, tax rate changes, and changes in central government budget balances (OECD, 1980: 35). The nature of the specific actions taken by these nations, however, differed.

A.   Budgetary Issues in the United States

Caiden (1985:495) suggests that three major issues have affected the development of public budgeting in the United States since the late 1970s. These three issues are: (1) the turbulence of the budgetary environment, (2) the emphasis on financial management, and (3) the politicization of the budget process. First, the environment of public budgeting was characterized by fiscal stress. Starting with the local "tax revolt" of the late 1970s and continuing through large federal budget deficits of the 1980s, American governments faced such challenges as citizen-imposed taxing and spending limits, political oriented deregulation and the privatization movement. The consequences of these challenges were the development of some retrenchment strategies in terms of revenues, expenditures, and borrowing, actions which fragmented public officials' authority (e.g., MacManus et al., 1989; Sharp and Elkins, 1987; Hamilton, 1983; Danziger and Ring, 1982).

Second, the turbulent environment and the development of retrenchment strategies brought additional complexity to financial management practices in the public sector. Budgeters realized that traditional public budgeting topics, such as the budget cycle, institutional analysis, and budgeting behavior were inadequate to prepare them to practice in the current budget environment. To deal with the new environment, budgeters suggested reforms in government financial management structures and systems (e.g., General Accounting Office, 1985; Bowsher, 1985; Hildreth, 1987), and enhanced training and teaching of financial management skills to practitioners (e.g., Thai, 1982; Berne, 1982; Alexander, 1984; Grizzle, 1985).

Finally, reacting to the turbulent environment, budgeters noticed the significant role of the budgetary process and recognized new rules in the political game (e.g., Caiden, 1984; McCaffery, 1985). For example, the Reagan administration adopted a supply-side economic policy of tax reduction and budget cuts. Without successfully cutting non-defense spending, the Reagan administration's tax reduction programs and the increase in defense spending resulted in a huge increase in the federal deficit (e.g., Miner, 1989). Several studies have attempted to explain methods and remedies to deal with the huge deficit (e.g., Thai, 1987; Eisner, 1986). The Congress of the United States passed the Gramm-Rudman-Hollings law (GRH) in 1985 and attempted to balance the budget through the political process and the establishment of annual deficit targets. While there have been different arguments about the effect of GRH, the deficit targets of the law were not met (e.g., Leloup et al., 1987). The unsuccessful experience of GRH brought another political solution, the Budget Reconciliation Act of 1990. Nevertheless, the deficit will not be lowered soon because of the cost of the savings and loan crisis and the 1990–91 economic recession.

B. Budgetary Control in Other G-7 Nations

The economic crisis of the late 1970s and early 1980s also brought various changes in the budgetary practices of the other six major industrialized nations (e.g., Schick, 1990a, 1988, 1986; Tarschys, 1986). The changes involved both macro- and micro-level practices. The macro-budgetary changes introduced included: fiscal norms and targets to restrain agency budget requests, the conversion of multi-year budgeting from a planning to a control process, the use of baseline data to compute cutback objectives, and prepreparation techniques to strengthen the conversation function of budgeting (Schick, 1986:124). The micro-budgetary changes made included: cutback budgeting, a renewed emphasis on cash budgeting, new efforts to stimulate reallocations in resources, increased use of program evaluation, closer monitoring of budget execution, and the strengthening of financial management practices in general (Schick, 1988:523). These changes not only affect overall budgetary practices but also provide an opportunity to change the culture of public management from traditional compliance to incentives for managerial flexibility (Schick, 1990a:26).

In addition to the changes in budgetary practices noted above, the other six G-7 nations also adopted many conservative policy actions to deal with the fiscal restraint issue of the 1980s. In the United Kingdom, for example, the policy actions of the Thatcher government included 1) reduced taxes, 2) reduced public expenditures and debts, 3) increased competition, 4) reduced subsidies to government corporations, and 5) the privatizing of public sector firms (Mountfield, 1983; King, 1985).

The policy of fiscal restraint also brought reforms to Japan and Canada. In Japan, the Suzuke and Nakasoni cabinets carried out restraint policy through their administrative reform movement. The goal of reform was "fiscal reconstruction without a tax hike" (Campbell, 1985b; Tashiro, 1988). In Canada, the budgetary dilemma led to the adoption of the "envelope system." The envelope system attempts to limit spending increases to the level of the rate of real growth in the GNP and to change some tax reform measures (Doern, 1983).

The remaining three G-7 nations (Germany, France, and Italy) tied the implementation of fiscal restraint policy to their specific political and economic environments. In the Federal Republic of Germany, for example, the primary goal was the reduction of budget deficits because of the commandment of article 115 of the Basic Law (German Constitution) requiring that borrowing be limited to the sum of appropriations earmarked for investments (Korff, 1983). Despite its socialistic nature, the Mitterrand government of France instituted structure changes that placed constraints on government deficits and tax burdens (Ashford, 1985). Finally, the Italian government found fiscal restraint significant but difficult to implement because of massive budget deficits and the general political environment (Buglione and France, 1983). To better control government deficits, the Italian government stressed public sector borrowing requirements and revised its budgetary procedures. The new procedures specify that all new proposed expenditures must be submitted within the framework of a multi-year plan. Any new measures, involving new expenditures, must include provisions for funding (OECD, 1990b:26).

C. Cross-National Comparison Studies

Realizing the importance of budgetary control, researchers have conducted several cross-national comparative studies of budgetary control since the early 1980s. The topics of these studies include: fiscal and expenditure trend analysis (Wolfe and Burkhead, 1983; Madhusudham and Burkhead, 1987), intergovernmental transfers and grants (Bahl, 1986; Wolman and Page, 1987), decentralization (Wasylenko, 1987), and budget deficits (Schick, 1990b). Two international financial organizations, the International Monetary Fund (IMF) and the Organization for Economic Co-operation and Development (OECD), also published general reports on the condition and progress of fiscal performance in the major industrialized countries (e.g., IMF, 1986; OECD, 1990b).

Most of the research reported at least some positive findings regarding budgetary control. The studies noted that the seven major industrialized nations experienced a period of sustained economic growth during the 1980s. The governments of these nations reduced their budget deficits from the peaks occurring earlier in the decade (Schick, 1990b:38). In fact, some countries even reported budget surpluses by the end of the 1980s.[1]

Several findings revealed in these studies are of particular note. For example, Schick (1990b:38) points out that the progress of deficit reduction was accomplished during a period of economic growth. He believes that the true test of maintaining a fiscal balance will occur when these countries' economies undergo cyclical weakness. Some researchers (e.g., Schick, 1990b; Cao and Thai, 1986; Korff, 1983) also note the impact of political capacity on budgetary performance. They argue that in federal systems, with their separation of power principle, governments are less effective in terms of budgetary control.

Notwithstanding their contributions, several weaknesses exist in the studies cited. First, most of the research was conducted during the early to mid 1980s. Thus, we have only a partial picture of what occurred during the decade of the 1980s. Second, some of the research (e.g., Wolfe and Burkhead 1983; Madhusudham and Burkhead, 1987) did not include Japan. Considering Japan's economic power and recent important Japanese administrative reform, it is essential to include Japan in the evaluation of budgetary performance at the international level. Third, the impact of political system was addressed normatively rather than empirically. Little data exists comparing budgetary performance between federal systems and unitary systems.

The above review of research on budgetary control issues indicates the importance placed on fiscal restraint policy by the G-7 nations during the 1980s. The purpose of the following sections is to examine the impact of this fiscal restraint policy through a cross-national comparison of major economic and financial indicators.

III. RESEARCH METHODS

A. Research Questions

To evaluate the budgetary performance of the seven major industrialized nations during the 1980s, this section focuses on the following research questions: What was the overall economic performance of these nations during the 1980s? Did they achieve their stated goals of constraining public expenditures and reducing budget deficits? On a comparative basis, which nations performed better than others? Finally, did nations with a federal system perform better or worse than nations with a unitary system?

B.   Research Variables and Data

Eight indicators of budgetary performance were selected to answer the above questions. They are: economic growth rate, unemployment rate, inflation rate, outlays of government, general government and central government budget deficits, net public debt, and interest payments. The first three indicators provide background information on the general economic performance of the G-7 nations during the 1980s. The next three indicators are measures of national performance in terms of expenditure control and deficit reduction. The last two indicators assess the impact of budget deficits. Most of the data are mainly from *Economic Outlook*, published by the Organization for Economic Co-Operation and Development (OECD, 1990a). Additional data are taken from *International Financial Statistics Yearbook*, published by the International Monetary Fund (IMF, 1990).

IV.   ANALYSIS AND RESULTS

To examine the budgetary performance of the G-7 nations, this study used the simple descriptive statistics of mean measure, standard deviation, and percentage difference. The means and standard deviations of the selected financial indicators provide a summary picture of the economic and budgetary performance of these nations during the 1980s. The percentage differences calculated between the beginning and the end of the 1980s show the change in budgetary conditions and the effects of restrictive policies (e.g., Wolfe and Burkhead, 1983; Madhusudham and Burkhead, 1987; Schick, 1990b).

The overall analysis includes three stages. The first stage examines general economic performance of the G-7 nations. The second stage focuses on major budgetary indicators of the seven nations. Here, the analysis addresses both budgetary conditions and budgetary improvement in the seven nations during the 1980s. The last part of the analysis compares budgetary performance between federal-systems and unitary-systems. Again, the comparison shows both the budgetary condition and the budgetary improvement of these nations during the 1980s.

A.   General Economic Performance

To measure general economic performance of the G-7 nations during the 1980s, the average economic growth rate, the average unemployment rate, and the average inflation rate are first calculated. Then, an economic performance index is developed to measure the overall economic performance of these countries. The Economic Performance Index (EPI) is calculated according to the following formula:

$$EPI = \frac{\text{Economic growth rate}}{\text{Unemployment rate + Inflation rate}} \times 100$$

This index offers a more sophisticated measure of the overall economic behavior than the commonly used misery index, i.e., the sum of unemployment and inflation rates (McKay and Grant, 1983:2). The overall economic performance of the G-7 nations in the 1980s is presented in Table 3.1.

Table 3.1 shows that during the 1980s, the G-7 nations had average rates of 2.7 percent in growth, 7.7 percent in unemployment, 6.0 percent in inflation, and an average score of 29.4 on the Economic Performance Index.[2] From a comparative perspective, Japan and the United States performed the best among the G-7 nations, with growth rates above the average and unemployment and inflation rates below the average. Germany and Canada were in

Table 3.1 Economic Performance in the G-7 Nations, 1980–1989

	Economic growth rate[a]	Unemployment rate[b]	Inflation rate[c]	Economic performance score[d]
United States	2.7	7.3	4.9	22.1
Japan	4.2	2.5	1.6	102.4
Germany	1.9	5.6	3.0	22.1
France	2.1	9.1	7.2	12.9
Italy	2.5	10.3	11.7	11.4
United Kingdom	2.3	9.6	7.6	13.4
Canada	3.2	9.3	5.7	21.3
(Average)	(2.7)	(7.7)	(6.0)	(29.4)

[a] Economic growth rate is the average growth of real GNP/GDP rate.

[b] Unemployment rate is the average unemployment rate.

[c] Inflation rate is the average GDP deflators.

[d] The economic performance index (EPI) is calculated as follows:

$$EPI = \frac{\text{real rate of GNP/GDP growth}}{\text{unemployment rate + inflation rate}} \times 100$$

Source: Calculated from OECD, *Economic Outlook* 47 (Paris: OECD 1990), IMF, *International Financial Statistics Yearbook* (Washington D.C.: IMF, 1990).

the second group and also did relatively well during this period. Germany's unemployment and inflation rates were below average but its growth rate was also low. Canada, on the other hand, had a high growth rate as well as high unemployment and high inflation rates. France, Italy, and the United Kingdom were in the last group, with growth rates below average and unemployment and inflation rates above average.

The national scores on the Economic Performance Index show similar results about the overall economic performance of the G-7 nations. Japan has the highest index score (102.4) because its economic growth rate exceeds the sum of its unemployment and inflation rates. Next to Japan, comes the United States, Germany, and Canada with scores above 20. France, Italy, and the United Kingdom, all had index scores below 20.

B. Budgetary Performance

The budgetary performance of the G-7 nations during the 1980s consists of both budgetary condition and budgetary improvement of these countries during this period. Results of the budgetary condition are summarized in Table 3.2.

The G-7 nations averaged 43.9 percent of government outlays to GDP, 3.7 percent of general government deficit to GNP, 4.2 percent of central government deficit to GNP, 33.7 percent of net public debt to GNP, and 6.6 percent of interest payments to total expenditures.[3] All the G-7 nations showed some strengths and weaknesses in their budgetary conditions. Germany and France had low percentages of general and central government deficits, public debt and interest payment. However, they had high percentages of government outlays. Japan and the United States had low percentages of government outlays, general government deficits, public debt and interest payments but a high percentage of central government deficits. The United Kingdom showed low percentages of government deficits but high percentages of government outlays, public debt and interest payments. Canada had large percentages of government deficits and medium level of the outlays, debt, and interest payments. Italy's budgetary condition ranked last among the G-7 nations, with the largest percentages of government deficits, public debt and interest payment.

While showing the budgetary condition of the G-7 countries in the 1980s, Table 3.2 does not provide us with the necessary information to evaluate the improvement of their budgetary conditions during this period. To accomplish this, the percentage differences on all the budgetary indicators between 1980 and 1989 for the G-7 nations was calculated. The results are presented in Table 3.3.

During the 1980s the G-7 nations experienced an average of: a 2.4 percent increase of government outlays to GDP, a 1.5 percent decrease in general and central government deficits to GNP, an 11.1 percent increase in net public debt

Table 3.2 Budgetary Performance in the G-7 Nations, Mean Measures During the 1980s

	Outlays of government[a]		Budget deficit general[b]		Budget deficit central[c]		Net public debt[d]		Interest payment[e]	
	Mean	S.D.	Mean	S.D.	Mean	S.D.	Mean	S.D.	Mean	S.D.
United States	36.0	1.2	−2.6	0.9	−3.9	1.0	25.3	4.2	5.8	0.9
Japan	33.2	0.5	−1.4	2.4	−3.1	1.6	22.1	4.3	4.3	0.9
Germany	47.9	0.9	−2.0	1.1	−1.5	0.5	20.6	2.7	4.4	0.8
France	50.4	1.8	−2.1	0.9	−2.3	0.8	21.2	4.3	3.4	0.8
Italy	48.4	2.9	−11.0	1.0	−11.5	0.9	76.2	14.0	14.1	1.5
United Kingdom	46.1	1.4	−2.0	1.7	−2.1	2.0	43.8	4.6	7.1	0.4
Canada	45.1	2.4	−4.6	1.9	−4.7	1.5	27.0	10.6	8.0	1.8
(Average)	(43.9)	(6.1)	(−3.7)	(3.1)	(−4.2)	(3.2)	(33.7)	(18.9)	(6.7)	(3.3)

[a] Outlays of government as percentage of GDP from 1980 to 1988.

[b] General government budget deficit (−) as percentage of nominal GNP/GDP from 1980 to 1989.

[c] Central government budget deficit (−) as percentage of nominal GNP/GDP from 1980 to 1989; the data for Japan were from 1982 to 1989.

[d] Net public debt as percentage of nominal GNP/GDP from 1980 to 1989.

[e] Net public debt interest payment as percentage of total expenditures from 1980 to 1989.

Source: Calculated from OECD, *Economic Outlook* 47 (Paris: OECD, 1990), OECD, *Economic Outlook* 44 (Paris: OECD, 1988), OECD, *Economic Outlook* 42 (Paris: OECD, 1987), IMF, *International Financial Statistics Yearbook* (Washington, D.C.: IMF, 1990).

Table 3.3 Budgetary Improvement in the G-7 Nations, Percentage Differences Between 1980 and 1989

	Outlays of government[a]	Budget deficit general[b]	Budget deficit central[c]	Net public debt[d]	Interest payment[e]
United States	2.6	0.7	−1.0	10.1	2.8
Japan	0.3	−7.1*	−4.4*	−3.2	−0.5
Germany	−1.7	−3.1*	−1.4*	7.6	2.3
France	4.2	1.4	1.6	11.1	2.2
Italy	9.1	1.60	.03	40.7	5.0
United Kingdom	−1.7	−4.7*	−6.0*	−14.6	−1.1
Canada	3.9	0.6	0.3	26.2	5.9
(Average)	(2.4)	(−1.5)*	(−1.5)*	(11.1)	(2.4)

See Table 3.2.

*Negative sign indicates a reduction of the budget deficit.

Source: Calculated from OECD, *Economic Outlook 47* (Paris: OECD, 1990), OECD, *Economic Outlook 44* (Paris: OECD, 1988), OECD, *Economic Outlook 42* (Paris: OECD, 1987), IMF, *International Financial Statistics Yearbook* (Washington, D.C.: IMF, 1990).

to GNP, and a 2.4 percent increase of interest payments to total expenditures. Table 3.3 also shows each nation's budgetary improvement during the eighties. The United Kingdom ranked at the top of the G-7 nations in terms of budgetary improvement with: a decrease of 1.7 percent in government outlays to GDP, a 4.7 percent decrease in general government deficits, a 6.0 percent decrease in central government deficits, a 14.6 percent decrease in net public debt to GNP, and a 1.1 percent decrease in interest payments to total expenditures.

Japan and Germany also performed better than the mean percentages of the G-7 nations on those major budgetary indicators. They reduced their budgetary deficits at both the general and central government levels. Japan reduced its public debt and interest payments despite a small increase in governmental outlays. Germany's public debt and interest payments increased, although government outlays decreased.

The performance of the other four G-7 nations (the United State, France, Italy, and Canada) was below average. All the nations managed to keep their deficit increases below two percent of GNP. The United States even reduced its central government deficit despite a small increase in governmental outlays and interest payments, as well as a medium increase in public debt. France had a large percentage increase in governmental outlays but this was offset by a small increase in interest payments and a medium increase in public debt. Canada and Italy had large percentage increases in governmental outlays, public debt, and interest payments despite their low percentage increases in budget deficits. Italy's increase in government outlays and net public debt was extremely high, more than 3.5 times the average increase.

C. Federal System vs. Unitary System

To examine the impact of political system on fiscal restriction, the G-7 nations are divided into two groups: federal system nations and unitary system nations. Federal system G-7 nations include the United States, Germany, and Canada. Unitary system G-7 nations are Japan, France, the United Kingdom, and Italy. The comparison between the two groups focuses on both the average budgetary performance of these nations in the 1980s and the average budgetary improvement of these nations between 1980 and 1989. The results of the comparison are presented in Table 3.4 and Table 3.5. Table 3.4 reveals that during the 1980s unitary system G-7 nations had higher mean scores in all budgetary indicators than did federal system G-7 nations. In other words, the unitary systems had larger percentages of government outlays, general and central government budget deficits, public debt, and interest payments.

Examining budgetary improvement in the G-7 nations between 1980 and 1989, Table 3.5 exhibits somewhat different results. As Table 3.5 shows,

Table 3.4 Budgetary Performance: Federal System versus Unitary System, Mean Score in the 1980s

Indicators	Federal system[a]		Unitary system[b]	
	Mean	S.D.	Mean	S.D.
Outlays of government (as a percentage of GDP)	43.0	5.1	44.5	6.7
General government budget deficit (as a percentage of nominal GNP/GDP)	3.1	1.1	4.1	4.0
Central government budget deficit (as a percentage of nominal GNP/GDP)	3.4	1.4	4.8	3.9
Net public debt of general government (as a percentage of nominal GNP/GDP)	24.3	2.7	40.8	22.3
Net public debt interest payments (as a percentage of total expenditures)	6.1	1.5	7.2	4.2

[a] Federal system G-7 nations consist of the United States, Germany, and Canada.

[b] Unitary system G-7 nations consist of the United Kingdom, Japan, Italy, and France.

Source: Calculated from OECD, *Economic Outlook 47* (Paris: OECD, 1990), OECD, *Economic Outlook 44* (Paris: OECD, 1988), OECD, *Economic Outlook 42* (Paris: OECD, 1987), IMF, *International Financial Statistics Yearbook* (Washington, D.C.: IMF, 1990).

Table 3.5 Budgetary Improvement: Federal System versus Unitary System, Percentage Differences Between 1980 and 1989

Indicators	Federal system[a]		Unitary system[b]	
	Mean	S.D.	Mean	S.D.
Outlays of government (as a percentage of GDP)	1.6	2.4	3.0	4.1
General government budget deficit (as a percentage of nominal GNP/GDP)	−0.6*	1.8	−2.2*	3.8
Central government budget deficit (as a percentage of nominal GNP/GDP)	−0.7*	0.7	−2.1*	3.2
Net public debt of general government (as a percentage of nominal GNP/GDP)	14.6	8.4	8.5	20.7
Net public debt interest payments (as a percentage of total expenditures)	3.7	1.6	1.4	2.4

a, b See Table 3.4.
*Negative sign indicates a reduction of the budget deficits.
Source: Calculated from OECD, *Economic Outlook 47* (Paris: OECD, 1990), OECD, *Economic Outlook 44* (Paris: OECD, 1988), OECD, *Economic Outlook 42* (Paris: OECD, 1987), IMF, *International Financial Statistics Yearbook* (Washington, D.C.: IMF, 1990).

despite higher increases in government outlays, the G-7 unitary system nations had larger reductions in their general and central government budget deficits, and smaller increases in public debt and debt interest payments.

V. DISCUSSION AND CONCLUSION

This chapter analyzed the budgetary performance of the seven major industrialized nations during the 1980s to examine the impact of fiscal restraint policy. Several important observations can be made based on the analysis. First, concerning the general economic environment, all G-7 nations experienced sustained economic growth during the 1980s although some countries had relatively high unemployment and inflation rates. The overall economic index shows that Japan, the United Sates, and Germany lead the other G-7 nations demonstrating high economic growth rates and low inflation and unemployment rates.

Second, the G-7 nations showed various strengths and weaknesses in terms of general budgetary performance. The results may be partially reflective of these countries traditional political and economic conditions. For example, France had the largest percentage of government outlays to GDP, which may be accounted for by the nature of its socialist government. The small percentage of national budget deficits to GNP/GDP in Germany may also reflect its constitutional provisions. Italy's historic economic problems are evident in its large budget deficits, public debt and interest payments relative to GNP/GDP.

Third, when focusing on budgetary improvement between 1980 and 1989, the G-7 nations did achieve some success in their restraint actions, although the success was uneven. All G-7 nations either reduced their budget deficits or had only small increases. The United Kingdom, Japan, and Germany lead the G-7 nations in reducing or controlling government outlays, general and central government deficits, public debt, and interest payments. Unlike Japan and Germany, however, the United Kingdom's successes were accompanied by high unemployment and inflation rates. In comparison to the other G-7 nations, the United States did well in terms of fiscal restraint and ranked in the middle of the G-7 nations.

Fourth, regarding the comparison between federal systems and unitary systems, the analysis provided some mixed results. On the one hand, unitary system G-7 nations performed better than federal system G-7 nations in reducing budget deficits, public debt and interest payments. On the other hand, unitary system G-7 nations had larger increases in government outlays and higher scores on all budgetary condition indicators. The results seem to suggest that: 1) there may be some differences in budgetary performance between unitary systems and federal systems, and 2) to measure the difference may depend on the definition of budgetary performance. In this study, for example, we can argue that unitary systems may be better than federal systems in terms of budgetary improvement and that they are inferior to federal systems in measures of government growth and general budgetary conditions.

Finally, the analysis provides answers to the research questions raised earlier. Under the sustained economic growth environment of the 1980s, most of the G-7 nations achieved their stated goals of controlling public expenditures and reducing budget deficits. On a comparative basis, Japan, Germany, and the United Kingdom performed better than other G-7 nations. When focusing on the difference between federal systems and unitary systems, the study showed that unitary system G-7 nations performed better than federal system G-7 nations in reducing budget deficits, public debt, and interest payments but not in controlling government expenditures.

NOTES

1. Japan ran budget surpluses in the level of general government in the years 1987, 1988, and 1989. The United Kingdom had budget surpluses in both levels of general and central government in the years 1988 and 1989. Germany experienced budget surplus in the general government level in 1989. For further information, see OECD, *Economic Outlook*, 47 (Paris: OECD, June 1990), p. 15.
2. The average score of Economic Performance Index of the G-7 nations is skewed and inflated because of Japan's high score of 102.4.
3. The average percentages of general and central government deficits, net public debt, and interest payments are skewed due to Italy's larger percentages.

REFERENCES

Alexander, James R. (1984). Curriculum reform in budgeting and financial management: Preliminary thoughts on the dimensions of the field. *Public Budgeting & Finance. 4*:91–96.

Ashford, Douglas E. (1985). Governmental responses to budget scarcity: France. *Policy Studies Journal 13, 3*:517–524.

Bahl, Roy (1986). The design of intergovernmental transfers in industrialized countries. *Public Budgeting & Finance 6, 4*: 3–22.

Berne, Robert (1982). A basic course in public sector financial management. *Public Budgeting & Finance. 2*:111–122.

Bowsher, Charles A. (1985). Sound financial management: A federal manager's perspective. *Public Administration Review. 45*:176–184.

Buglione, Enrico and George France (1983). Skewed fiscal federalism in Italy: Implications for public expenditure control. *Public Budgeting & Finance 3, 3*:43–63.

Caiden, Naomi (1984). The new rules of the federal budget game. *Public Administration Review. 44*:109–118.

Caiden, Naomi (1985). The boundaries of public budgeting: Issues for education in tumultuous times. *Public Administration Review.* *45*:495–502.

Campbell, John C. (1985a). Research roundtable: Governmental responses to budget scarcity. *Policy Studies Journal* 13, *3*:471–477.

Campbell, John C. (1985b). Governmental responses to budget scarcity: Japan. *Policy Studies Journal*, Vol. 13, No. 3 (March), pp. 506–516.

Cao, Le T. and Khi V. Thai (1986). Structural budget deficits in the federal government: A theoretical perspective. *International Journal of Public Administration* 8, *1*:33–55.

Danziger, James N. and Peter S. Ring (1982). Fiscal limitations: A selective review of recent research. *Public Administration Review.* *42*:47–55.

Doern, C. Bruce (1983). Canada's budgetary dilemmas: Tax and expenditure reform. *Public Budgeting & Finance* 3, 2: 28–46.

Eisner, Robert (1986). *How Real Is the Federal Deficit.* New York: The Free Press.

General Accounting Office (1985). *Managing the Cost of Government: Building An Effective Financial Management Structure.* Volume 2, Government Printing Office, Washington, D.C.

Grizzle, Gloria A. (1985). Essential skills for financial management: Are MPA students acquiring the necessary competencies? *Public Administration Review.* *45*:840–844.

Hamilton, Randy (1983). The world turned upside down: The contemporary revolution in state and local government capital financing. *Public Administration Review.* *43*:22–31.

Hildreth, W. Bartley (1987). Financial management in government: A symposium. *Public Administration Quarterly.* *11*:241–245.

International Monetary Fund (1986). *International Financial Statistics, Supplement on Government Finance*, supplement series, No. 11, Washington, D.C.: IMF.

International Monetary Fund (1990). *International Financial Statistics Yearbook.* Washington, D.C.: IMF.

King, Anthony (1985). Governmental responses to budget scarcity: Great Britain. *Policy Studies Journal* 13, *3*:476–493.

Korff, Hans Clausen (1983). Planning and budgeting in the Federal Republic of Germany. *Public Budgeting & Finance* 3, *4*:57–70.

Leloup, Lance T., Barbara Luck Graham, and Stacey Barwick (1987). Deficit politics and constitutional government: The impact of Gramm-Rudman-Hollings. *Public Budgeting & Finance* 7, *1*:83–103.

MacManus, Susan A., Jessie M. Rattley, Patrick J. Ungaro, William R. Brown, Scott O'Donnell, Donald L. "Pat" Shalmy, Norm Hickey, and Denies Jubell (1989). A decade of decline: A longitudinal look at big city and big county strategies to cope with declining revenues. *International Journal of Public Administration* 12, *5*:749–796.

Madhusudham, Ranjana G. and Jesse Burkhead (1987). Expenditure trends in selected industrialized countries. *Public Budgeting & Finance* 3, *4*:97–102.

McCaffery, Jerry (1985). Budget reform: The path to reform of process. *International Journal of Public Administration* 7, *4*:403–423.

McKay, David and Wyn Grant (1983). Industrial policies in OECD countries: An overview. *Journal of Public Policy* 3, *1*:1–11.

Miner, Jerry (1989). The Reagan deficit. *Public Budgeting & Finance* 9, *1*:15–32.

Mountfield, Peter (1983). Recent developments in the control of public expenditure in the United Kingdom. *Public Budgeting & Finance* 3, *3*:81–102.

Organization for Economic Co-operation and Development (1980). *OECD Economic Outlook* 28, Paris:OECD.

Organization for Economic Cooperation and Development (1990a). *OECD Economic Outlook* 47, Paris:OECD.

Organization for Economic Cooperation and Development (1990b). *Progress in Structural Reform*, supplement to *OECD Economic Outlook* 47, Paris:OECD.

Schick, Allen (1986). Macro-budgetary adaptations to fiscal stress in industrialized democracies. *Public Administration Review* 46, 2:124–134.

Schick, Allen (1988). Micro-budgetary adaptations to fiscal stress in industrialized democracies. *Public Administration Review.* 48:523–533.

Schick, Allen (1990a). Budgeting for results: Recent developments in five industrialized countries. *Public Administration Review.* 50:26–34.

Schick, Allen (1990b). Why the deficit persists as a budget problem: Role of political institutions. In A. Prenchand (ed.), *Government Financial Management: Issues and Country Studies*. Washington, D.C., IMF, pp. 38–52.

Sharp, Elane B. and David Elkins (1987). The impact of fiscal limitation: A tale of seven cities. *Public Administration Review.* 47:385–392.

Tarschys, Daniel (1986). From expansion to restraint: Recent developments in budgeting. *Public Budgeting & Finance* 6, *3*:25–37.

Tashiro, Ku (1988). Japan. In Donald C. Rowat (ed.), *Public Administration in Developed Democracies: A Comparative Study*. NY:Marcel Dekker, Inc., pp. 375–394.

Thai, Khi V. (1982). Teaching public budgeting and financial management: A symposium. *Southern Review of Public Administration.* 6:263–271.

Thai, Khi V. (ed.) (1987). *Structural Budget Deficits in the Federal Government: Causes, Consequences, and Remedies*. Lanham, MD:University Press of America.

Wasylenko, Michael (1987). Fiscal decentralization and economic development. *Public Budgeting & Finance* 7, *4*:57–71.

Wolfe, C. Stephen, and Jesse Burkhead (1983). Fiscal trends in selected industrialized countries. *Public Budgeting & Finance* 3, *4*:97–102.

Wolman, Harold and Edward Page (1987). The impact of intergovernmental grants on subnational resource disparities: A cross-national comparison. *Public Budgeting and Finance* 7, *3*:82–98

4

A Cross-National Analysis of Financial Management Practices

A. Premchand

International Monetary Fund, Washington, D.C.

I. INTRODUCTION

The success achieved in the formulation and implementation of fiscal policy is dependent, to a very large extent, on the attention devoted to the design and day-to-day operations of the Financial Management System by the public authorities. These operations, which deal with the various technical aspects of the system, are a detail whose neglect can have far-reaching implications for the management of public money. As Stendhal remarked, "all the truth, and all the pleasure, lies in the details." But these details, as well as the way in which they are addressed, differ from country to country, and also vary depending on the economic conditions. Inasmuch as these details have a profound and enduring effect on the system of values that govern public financial management, they need to be analyzed.[1] Not all the values may be explicit or may manifest themselves in the financial management of government. But the organizational culture and the approaches to management are affected by the values. There is a reciprocity between systems and structures and values and this affects the financial management system as well.

Procedures, systems, and institutions and their operations constitute tangible instruments, while values are soft and less tangible. Ironically, however, the softer ones often tend to dominate the harder ones and influence the out-

The views expressed are personal and do not in any way represent those of the International Monetary Fund.

come. The attempt here, however, is a relatively narrow one, more concerned with the hard and tangible parts while recognizing that, although managers tend to give more attention to systems and structures, attention also needs to be given to the role of values.

The core of financial management has, like the perennial attributes of good literature, revolved round the basic pursuit of economy, efficiency, and effectiveness[2] in the mobilization, allocation, and utilization of monetary resources that form the public purse. But each country pursues these goals in its own way. While there are many areas of convergence in the practices, there are also areas where there are substantial divergences. It is not the intent here, however, to provide a comparative history of the practices, their antecedents, and current implications.[3] Rather, the limited purpose here is to provide a comparative perspective on the practices, and how such practices facilitate or, alternatively, hinder the pursuit of the goals of financial management. A caveat should be noted at the outset. The practices that are now found have evolved over a long period and what is observed in some countries may not be comparable to the previous practices in the same country. There have been several discontinuities, but these discontinuities will be noted in the following discussion, in broad terms, rather than in specific terms of a country's experience.

II.   TYPOLOGIES AND THEIR VIABILITY

The analysis of country practices has so far largely been in terms of typologies based on legal and constitutional traditions, political traditions, economic philosophies of governments, economic conditions, and the relative stages of prosperity, industrial and commodity orientations, and in terms of the administrative and political legacies. For example, the legal typology envisaged the analysis in terms of Roman-Germanic law or English law. In countries with a Roman-Germanic legal tradition (also called civil law countries), there is well developed comprehensive legislation governing all aspects of financial management, while in countries with an English legal tradition (also called common-law countries), the extent of legislation or specification in law is relatively limited.

Similarly, distinctions were sought in terms of political orientation or the role of the legislature or its corresponding entity (which in socialist regimes, may be a People's Congress) in financial management. As will be illustrated further on, the respective roles of the legislature and the executive in the macro- and micro-management of the finances of the country differ from one type of country to another. Typologies were also envisaged in terms of the economic philosophies or the degree of market orientation found in the economic management of the country. Thus, countries are divided into those that have mixed economies, market economies, and centrally planned economies. In a variation on this theme, countries were divided into industrial and developing countries. In yet another variation, countries were also divided into rich and poor. Another approach has been to group countries in terms of their administrative and legal legacy and tradition. Each of these approaches has some limitations in that it provides only a partial glimpse into the intricacies of the systems. Further, a system may have some features of each of the preceding approaches. It has to be recognized however, that each offers a framework of analysis for specific purposes.

In describing the unique features of the national practices, it has to be noted that most practices are drawn from colonial legacies, or the constitutional and legal traditions of countries. Some colonies, however, made efforts to distance themselves from the colonial traditions and evolved their own systems, which in turn became models for other countries. This chapter adopts an eclectic combination of the administrative tradition approaches, regional approaches, and market orientation to examine the features of the systems.

A. Systems Groups

In terms of general traditions and administrative legacies, seven broad and illustrative types of systems can be identified. These groups and their broad features are described below.[4]

1.   The British-type budgetary system: This system is primarily drawn from the United Kingdom, which has evolved its own approaches to financial management over an extended period, and is to be found in British commonwealth countries in Africa, Asia, and the Caribbean. Although the United Kingdom itself had few budgetary laws, the former colonies have a well developed legal charter governing financial management. The system in these countries largely revolves around a consolidated fund, which is cash based, and into which all revenues and expenditures flow. Legislative approval is needed for all appropriations except for some items (called "charged expenditure") which continue regardless of the nature of the government in power. Revenue proposals to the legislature are usually shrouded in secrecy, and budgeting of resources follows parallel paths from expenditure budgets that converge only at the penultimate stage of budget formulation. Operations of spending agencies are subjected to different degrees of control during the resource management stage (discussed further on).

2.   The French system, which is also found in its former colonies (and variants are found in Latin American and the Middle Eastern countries), is distinguished by two features: a highly centralized financial control system and a central treasury. The control system has three operational levels:

a. comptrollers attached to spending ministries and overseeing their transactions;

b. a cadre of public accountants responsible for the collection and disbursement of public monies; and

c. inspectors of finance representing, as it were, a staff function, and embodying the financial conscience of the government. The treasury functions both as a cashier and a banker. Although the number of funds that form the essential nucleus of the financial system have been only a few initially, they tended to grow in number as a result of "debudgetization." The incidence of the special funds outside the purview of the budget is higher in some French-speaking African countries.

3.   A third type may be identified as the European system. Included in this group are Germany, Italy, the Netherlands, Portugal, and the Nordic countries. Of these, the Dutch, Italian, and Portuguese systems are to be found in their former colonies, such as Indonesia and Somalia. The Dutch system shows greater adaptation of the practices of the commercial world, including double-entry bookkeeping, provision for depreciation, and, until recently, accrual-based accounting. The Italian system, until the changes in mid-1970 when cash-based systems were introduced, had provisions for continuation of funds beyond the fiscal year and there was a parallel operation of the preceding and current years' budgets controlled by the Comptroller General.

4.   The fourth type is the U.S. system, which is largely centered around a general budget and several trust funds. A main feature of this system, as distinct from others (who also have a general fund and several trust funds), is the role of the legislature, which, in the final analysis, prepares its own budget.

5.   A somewhat more amorphous category is what may be broadly called the Latin American type. These countries, which initially adopted procedures that had a strong Spanish influence, developed their own hybrid systems as a byproduct of their administrative experience.[5] The main features of this system are extensive earmarking of funds, decentralization of government activities into autonomous agencies, reliance on modified accrual or noncash basis, and, in some countries, combined accounting and audit machinery. Within these broad types of systems, various financial management practices have evolved, and there are now several common and dissimilar features.

6.   Another distinct variety is the Far Eastern budgetary system, which would appear to have been influenced, both in terms of organization and in terms of approaches to budgeting, by the United States and Japan. This system usually comprises a general account, several special accounts dealing with specialized or quasi-trading activities, and extra budgetary accounts of which the most important is the Fiscal Investment and Loan Programs, largely financed by borrowing. Practices of this type are found in Korea, the Philippines, and Thailand.

7.   The final group comprises those countries that now constitute centrally planned economies in transition. Included in this category are countries

from Eastern Europe (excluding Yugoslavia, which has a unique system), Algeria (which had an additional layer of central planning over and above the traditional French type system), China, Myanmar (formerly Burma), and Vietnam. The budgetary and accounting systems in these countries have significant common features, all of which have been heavily influenced by the central planning system that evolved in the Soviet Union.[6] The budgets in these countries follow the framework indicated in their development plans. Their coverage is frequently the same as that of the national government in that the budgets of provinces, municipalities, and communes are included in the national budget. Also, in view of the preponderance of public enterprises, the transactions between government and enterprises (taxes paid, depreciation resources transferred to the government budget, subsidies to enterprises, and investment transfers, among others) dominate the budget. In recent years, this factor has also contributed to the emergence of a large variety of extrabudgetary accounts comprising enterprise and administrative activities, as a result of the general change in the approach toward a market-oriented management. Yet another feature of these economies is the extent of dependence of the government on its central bank for managing its liquidity and maintaining its accounts.

B.   Other Approaches

The economic conditions of a country impact heavily on the country's approach to financial management. The case of what started as "undeveloped" and later became "underdeveloped," only to be called at still a later stage "less developed" or "developing," illustrates this. These countries, which gained independence during a two-decade period after the Second World War, resorted to development planning on a significant scale. Development planning, in turn, revealed the limitations of traditional budget systems. The traditional systems, which were primarily input oriented and which had legal accountability as their primary source, proved to be inadequate to meet the emerging needs of investment budgets. Investment appraisal was introduced as a consequence, and a number of countries also took the opportunity to usher in development budgets as a variation of traditional capital budgets. This, in turn, contributed, over the years, to a whole set of new practices, as well as to a multitude of issues in the relations between ministries of finance and ministries of planning and to the relative primacy of each in the overall process of government financial management. Years of planning experience contributed to a general acceptance of this element as an essential part and a standard fixture of government financial management which, since the late 1970s and early 1980s, took the form of rolling expenditure planning and multiyear estimates that are now common in a number of industrial countries.[7]

Another response in financial management practices to changing economic conditions relates to the impact of inflation. Countries with high rates of inflation had to devise new methods to examine the implications of monetary expansion for expenditure estimates. This, in turn, contributed to a more in-depth examination of the mix of labor and capital in the expenditure profiles of each agency, and to the development as well as the use of indices that would reflect the unique features of each spending agency. Moreover, inflation neces-sitated the introduction of a system of cash limits to ensure that government expenditures are maintained at stipulated levels rather than increased through the automatic application of various types of indices.

The events since the early 1970s such as stagflation and the high level of budget deficits, demonstrated the umbilical linkages between the economy and the budget and their mutual impact on each other. This contributed over the years to a greater integration of economic analysis with budget making so that the resource constraints could be explicitly recognized in the process. Such integration is, however, more common in the industrial countries where National Income Accounts data are available on a regular basis. Although a growing trend toward such integration is also discernible in developing coun-tries, data limitations would appear to stand in the way of full utilization of the potential benefits.

The fiscal stress—in terms of the structural imbalance between receipts and expenditures of government as well as the short term imbalances—has contributed to a common experience in several countries regardless of their economic philosophy and market orientation. Further, it also gave rise to several issues on the adequacy of the instruments that are a part of the tradi-tional arsenal of financial management. Although these issues cover a very wide area, the more important ones may be noted. First, the conflict between conservers and claimants of resources became more acute during conditions of fiscal stringency. The experience gained from years of relying heavily on claiming more resources for existing policy expansion and pursuing new growth policies was less useful in a context where the leading issues were how much should be cut and whose budget should be reduced. Second, this conflict sheds new light on the limitations of process or compliance controls which emphasized adherence to regulations. While such compliance is undoubtedly important, the pursuit of economy, efficiency, and effectiveness is less well served by such controls. More significantly, such controls tended to be viewed as contributing to organizational rigidities and, over a period, to a kind of ossification. Third, this recognition contributed to an approach that envisioned a mixture of policy, process, and efficiency controls rather than the customary excessive dependence on process controls. It was realized that controls should have a strategy and should have a flexibility to permit a differentiated applica-tion in response to the changing situations. Fourth, the experience in the management of fiscal stress also revealed the need for a balanced approach in choosing control strategies that take into account immediate benefits as well as medium-term costs.

The above developments and their enduring impact on financial management sets the stage for an informed assessment of the practices found in various countries.

III. CURRENT PRACTICES

Some of the structural features of different systems need to be noted at the outset. Generally, all countries have an annual budget system. In Bahrain, the budget is on a biennial basis. In Uruguay, a five-year budget is formulated in real terms and the annual budget is updated in nominal or monetary terms using a complex vector of prices. In Sweden, effective from 1990, a triennial budget is prepared within the overall framework of multi-year estimates. Each year about one-third of the budget is subjected to intensive scrutiny. Thus, the activities of each agency are reviewed in detail once every three years. In most cases, funds lapse at the end of the fiscal year. There are exceptions to this, however. In some countries, although annual budgets are formulated on a cash basis, the appropriations are on the basis of obligation authority (e.g., in the United States) which permits the agencies to spend amounts for as long as such authority is valid. In some countries (e.g., in the Middle East) appropriations for the development budget are done on an extended basis and funds are available until projects are completed.[8] In Sweden, there is a system of extended grants where funds can be spent over a period of years. In a number of Central and South American countries, there is a complementary period that may well extend to about six months beyond the fiscal year that permits funds to be spent during the extended period.[9]

Budget offices are mostly located in ministries of finance. In a number of developing countries, the purview of ministries of finance has tended to be limited to revenues and current budgets, while foreign aid (which is substantial in several countries) and related external resources as well as developmental outlays undertaken as part of a plan are within the responsibilities of the ministries of planning. In some countries, budget offices are located in the office of the president (e.g., in the United States), in the office of prime minister (e.g., in Thailand), in the planning bureau (e.g., in Korea), organized as a separate department (e.g., in Australia), or as a separate ministry (e.g., in France—until recently). The functions of the budget office, however, have extensive commonality even though locations differ.

In some systems, the role of the legislature or its equivalent (such as a People's Congress in China and the Soviet Union) is more pronounced than in others, as noted previously. The legislature may formulate its own budget, substantially modify the proposals of the executive, or may merely acquiesce to the proposals of the executive. The approval of the legislature may be restricted in some cases to the increments proposed in the budget, while in some others it may be required to approve both continuing and new outlays. In some countries, there are legislature-imposed ceilings on the level of budget deficit (e.g., in the United States) while in some others there is a requirement of a balanced budget (e.g., in Japan, Indonesia, and others). Such a requirement is more in the nature of an accounting balance in that receipts (which include, in some cases, proceeds from domestic and external borrowing) are to be equal to outlays. In some countries, there are legal limits on domestic borrowing (e.g., in the Netherlands and the United States), while in some others such borrowing cannot be undertaken without the approval of the legislature (e.g., in Canada). These legal aspects cover, in some cases, the minutiae of financial management, including restrictions on creation of posts in government, reappropriation from one program to another or within a program (virement), and excess of expenditure over and above those that are approved by the legislature.

The budget coverage varies from one country to another. In general, however, there has been a gradual tendency to create autonomous funds, generally financed by earmarked revenues, to carry out activities that have been traditionally carried out as a part of the budget. The incidence of such autonomous entities is relatively high in Central and South American countries. A related aspect is the existence and operation of what are known as quasi-fiscal accounts operated by the central bank. These comprise selected lending activities, losses on public debt servicing arising from exchange rate changes, and other activities which would have been normally carried out from the budget but are administered by the central bank from its finances. Both these practices suggest that in determining the goals of fiscal policy, the total transactions—budget and outside the budget—need to be taken into account.

Normally, the classification of the budget follows a functional and program approach. There are, however, two countries—Chile and New Zealand—which follow a kind of modified balance sheet approach for the presentation of receipts and outlays of each agency. A number of countries in the industrial and developing categories have the practice of providing multi-year estimates, usually ranging to three years. In some countries (e.g., in Australia and the United Kingdom), these multi-year estimates are of considerable importance and usually provide the framework within which annual budgets are made.

The other features may be examined in terms of resource management and information systems needed for resource planning and management. Resource management involves the application of three basic principles: propriety, accountability, and adequacy of systems for the delivery of services to the community. Propriety refers to the application of funds for the purposes approved by the legislature. Accountability refers to the implementation of policy in a prudent and transparent manner, and for producing results commensurate with outlays. A wide variety of practices are found in this stage, particularly in regard to the payment process. In most countries, the spending agencies are empowered to authorize payments against their budgetary provisions and apportionments. In the British-type systems, there is really no organized system of apportionments that facilitates a time-slice based release of funds. However, certain specified transactions usually above some monetary ceilings require the prior approval of the ministry of finance. In the French type and associated systems, a visa has to be obtained from the relevant authorized officials before making commitments.[10] In some countries, however, the spending departments and agencies are free to make commitments and process payment authorizations within approved budget estimates. In most countries, the final issue of checks, however, is done by the ministry of finance and its agencies. In the British-type system, they are issued on the basis of the review of vouchers and related documentation, by the pay and accounts officers or accountants general who serve under the ministry of finance. In the French-type system, they are issued by the treasury, which is also responsible for the management of all financial resources. In the United States, checks are issued by the disbursing officers who are the specified agents of the treasury.

In the centrally planned economies, spending agencies are free to spend (authorize and pay) the budgetary allocations after the approval of the budget. In most cases, the productive or developmental departments (a classification that has been traditionally urged by economists but applied so far only in centrally planned economies) are even assigned a government-owned development bank which acts as a payment agency. The bank is also responsible, in some cases, for the compilation of the accounts of the agency for which it is acting as a banker.

In some countries, payment authorizations are subjected to internal audit by the general accounting office or similar organizations and checks are issued only after their clearance. Notwithstanding these elaborate designs of checks and balances, excess expenditures over and above approved amounts do occur but the process of dealing with them differs among systems. In the British-type systems, excess expenditures, while not encouraged, are legalized on the basis of the recommendations of legislative committees. In the U.S.-type systems, excesses are not permitted. In others, excesses are, in principle, subject to the imposition of penalties. In practice, however, these penalties are rarely invoked. Failures in the resource management process contribute to over- and underpayment and to fraud in the handling of government monies.

The practices also need to be seen in terms of the design of the information systems, which play a supporting role and are intended primarily to produce data for the use of decision makers inside government and, to an extent, outside government. In this regard, during recent years, there has been a greater commonality among countries, largely reflecting the availability of computer technology. The introduction of the technology has facilitated the operation of payrolls, recording of commitments and payment lags, recording of the availability of goods and services, maintenance of inventory of assets, and compilation of domestic and external debt transactions. In a number of countries budget requests and data on monthly financial transactions are normally processed in the form of diskettes, effectively replacing the traditional pen. In some countries, project accounting has made significant strides (e.g., in Chile) through the introduction of electronic data processing. In Middle Eastern countries, where the problem of trained manpower has become particularly acute in the context of massive development plans, timely investment in the introduction and use of computer technology has paid handsome dividends. The differences in this regard are now largely in terms of the capacity of the computer and end use of the information produced. Practices in industrial and developing countries show that there are a number of common problems. First, accounting statements are often not useful for purposes of expenditure control and would appear to be primarily geared for legal compliance. Enormous delays and reconciliation of different transactions continue to be major sources of frustration. Second, the accounting statements continue to be inadequate for the evaluation of programs and for the assessment of performance in terms of costs and effectiveness. Third, the statements' utility in aiding decisions through the provision of adequate cost information on whether services should be performed by government or be contracted out remains to be demonstrated. Fourth, the statements continue to be less than helpful in indicating the magnitude of post-employment benefits or the current status of assets.

IV. RECENT ADVANCES

During the 1960s and 1970s many governments attempted to introduce variants of planning, programming, and budgeting systems. Although most of these were tentative and even half-hearted, the systems proved to be less than adequate to meet the fiscal stress that characterized much of the late 1970s and 1980s. High inflation, high unemployment, difficulty in sustaining expenditure programs initiated during periods when resource position was more comfortable, problems of control of entitlements, and the burgeoning size of the public sector have all contributed to this fiscal stress. This time, governments would appear to have made more selective improvements in preference to packaged systems that attempted an overhaul of decision making in financial management matters.

Although these developments cover a wide area, two aspects deserve particular recognition. These relate to 1) budget review, and 2) strengthening management flexibility and introduction of incentives. During the 1970s, the annual budget process was recognized as offering few opportunities to review programs in detail. The processes also did not permit an explicit recognition of resource constraints. The maximum that could be changed in the annual budget was, it was averred, less than 3 percent of the total outlays. This appeared only natural, given that most of the outlays were legacies from past decisions. To address this problem, medium term financial plans were, as noted earlier, introduced in several countries. Sweden, however, went a step further by introducing a triennial budget system within the framework of multi-year estimates. A notable development in terms of the recognition of the resource constraint was the Canadian experiment, since abandoned, with an envelope budgeting system. As a part of this system, government departments were divided into several envelopes and each envelope was given a ceiling of resources (on the basis of medium-term planning) within which the departments had to consider the trade offs between old and new expenditures. From 1990, the Canadian Government reverted to the traditional approach of cabinet decision making on budget allocation.

The overall success of a financial management system in large organizations, such as governments, depends on the participation and contribution of the spending agencies. While central controls continue to have a role, alone they would not be in a position to discharge the complex tasks of government. This requires the strengthening of the financial management capability in spending agencies through the provision of management flexibility and incentives for securing economies in expenditure. In Australia and New Zealand managers have been given, in lieu of the traditional manpower ceilings, monetary ceilings within which they could determine the mix of manpower and materials reflecting their needs. Effectively, thus, central manpower controls have yielded to decentralized and flexible controls. In the United Kingdom, control on manpower has yielded to control of operational or running costs (including manpower). Further, a program of incentives was introduced in Australia under which about half of the economies procured in expenditures could be retained by the agencies for spending on approved programs and the other half returned to the national exchequer for general use. It is likely that these practices would have an extended application in the future.

It would appear, however, that on the whole there are a number of common features, although nuances are bound to differ. This is not surprising given that responses tend to be similar in certain economic situations. But the apparent commonness in institutions, systems, and, to a lesser extent, in operational procedures should not obscure the fact that the problems as well as their magnitude are different in each case. It is appropriate to recall Tolstoy's opening lines in *Anna Karenina*, "All happy families are alike; unhappy families are unhappy for their own reasons." This is equally applicable to governments.

V. CONCLUSIONS

The financial management systems now in operation in several countries have evolved over the years and bear the imprint of a variety of factors ranging from colonial inheritance and legislative influence to the economic philosophy of government. While each system endeavors in its own way to pursue the perennial themes of economy, efficiency and effectiveness of public moneys, the systems differ in terms of the details of institutions, systems, and operational practices. These details can be (and have been) examined in terms of several typologies, but each typology has some limitations as it provides only a narrow perspective on the working of a system. A more useful approach is to analyze the systems through an eclectic combination of administrative legacy and economic philosophy of governments.

Although the systems have been in operation for several decades, and have over the years absorbed a number of improvements, their capacity to ensure an effective management has come to be seriously questioned during recent years. The systems would appear to be under severe stress reflecting in major part the growing disparity between resources and expenditures. Thus, several deficiencies have been recognized in resource allocation planning and resource use management. Some of these problems are being addressed through improved budget review, strengthening of financial management capability in agencies and through appropriate provision of incentives for enhancing efficiency. More, however, remains to be done.

NOTES

1. These aspects have not received any major consideration in the literature. However, three studies undertaken by the Auditor General of Canada are relevant. See references at the end of the chapter.
2. Given the generic use of these themes, it is appropriate that they be defined here. Economy refers to the actual use of resources in relation to planned levels. Efficiency refers to the use of resources in relation to outputs and effectiveness refers to the impact on the fulfillment of program objectives.
3. Some ideas about the comparative recent experiences can be formed from the country studies included in Premchand and Burkhead (1984), and Premchand (1990).
4. A discussion of the first six groups is to be found in greater detail in Premchand (1983).

5. For a fuller discussion of these developments, see James P. Wesberry Jr., "Government Accounting and Financial Management in Latin American Countries," in Premchand (1990).

6. For a discussion of the features of these systems, see the country studies on China and Poland in Premchand (1990).

7. A more detailed discussion of these aspects is provided in Premchand (1983).

8. In general, budgets can be formulated with reference to two approaches—funding and limiting. Under the former, funds are made available for the completion of a project regardless of its time profile. The latter aims at restricting the funds available to specified levels within a fiscal year.

9. During recent years, several countries of the British commonwealth type, which had observed the annual lapseability procedure, have taken to extending the unspent outlays (through supplementary provision in the following year) to avoid excessive rush of expenditure at the end of the fiscal year, e.g., Australia and the United Kingdom.

10. See the case studies, in particular on Turkey, included in Premchand (1990).

REFERENCES

Auditor General of Canada, *Constraints to Productive Management in the Public Service* (1983); *Well-Performing Organizations* (1988); and, *Values, Service and Performance* (1990); Ottawa, Canada.

Premchand, A. (1983). *Government Budgeting and Expenditure Controls* (International Monetary Fund, Washington, D.C.).

Premchand, A. (ed) (1990). *Government Financial Management* (International Monetary Fund, Washington, D.C.).

Premchand, A., and Burkhead, Jesse (eds.) (1984). *Comparative International Budgeting and Financing* (Transaction Books, New Brunswick, New Jersey).

Part Two
Subnational Comparative Public Budgeting

5

Patterns of Behavior: Factors Influencing the Spending Judgments of Public Budgeters

Katherine G. Willoughby

Georgia State University, Atlanta, Georgia

I. INTRODUCTION

The sheer magnitude of public budgets today as well as the many purposes they serve necessitate an understanding of how they are developed. Inherent in such an understanding is the distinction between content and process. While the contents of budgeting—revenues, appropriations, and program expenditures—are relatively simple to quantify and analyze, the process of budgeting is much more difficult to operationalize and, hence, examine empirically. The process of budgeting involves both the uniqueness and commonness of human behavior in a certain context (Golembiewski and Rabin, 1983:91). In a most elemental sense, budgets are the result of the spending judgments of those legally responsible for requesting, recommending, and appropriating public money.

Not surprisingly, the difficulty in identifying decision typologies of budgeters has hampered research efforts concerning their spending behavior (Duncombe, Duncombe, and Kinney, 1989:49–50). Typically, research on this topic has been confined to aggregate analyses of financial data or anecdotal case analyses of specific budgetary circumstances (Clynch and Lauth, 1990:3–4). Very little budgeting research is both behavioral and empirical: behavioral meaning the direct observation of budgeters engaged in a decision-making task, and empirical implying the rigor associated with true experimental design.

A review of the literature of this flavor does provide a few postulates about budget process, and particularly, individual decision strategy in a budgetary context. First, the repetitive nature of the budget cycle fosters routine activities and budget roles which can be measured substantively and quantitatively (Crecine, 1967; Willoughby, 1991). Second, while budgeters utilize a few familiar cues when involved in routine budgetary decision making, most 1) remain unclear regarding an understanding of their own decision strategies, and 2) incorrectly assess the budgeting strategies of their counterparts in the process (Barber, 1966; Stedry, 1960; Stewart and Gelberd, 1976). And third, certain factors, particularly revenue availability (or the lack thereof), can disrupt and/or alter these routines and roles (Bretschneider, Straussman, and Mullins, 1988; McCaffery and Baker, 1990). For instance, fiscal stress fosters more conservative behavior concerning the development of revenue estimates, yet requires budgeters to consider a broader spectrum of criteria when developing spending plans (Straussman, 1979).

These postulates are insightful, yet most of the studies mentioned above remain limited in scope and generalizability of results (due to deficient sample size, representativeness, and/or stringency of statistical tests employed). This chapter addresses such inadequacies by presenting research which uses advanced methodological techniques to analyze the actual decision behavior of a relatively large sample of public budgeters. Specifically, this chapter examines factors which influence the decision orientations of 131 state government budget analysts from the central budget offices of ten Southern states.[1] This research takes advantage of survey data from a study by Willoughby (1992) to analyze the relationships between analysts' spending judgments regarding agency budget requests, and their financial, organizational, technical, and personal environments.

The first part of this chapter explains the external setting of the state government budget analyst in terms of fiscal climate, budget office strength, and technological sophistication. The next section describes discriminant analysis and operationalizes the dependent variable, the analyst's judgment policy. A third section defines a research model symbolic of the relationship between the independent and dependent variables. The fourth section presents research results. Finally, the conclusion considers the strengths and weaknesses of the model, and discusses the contribution of this study to understanding public budgeting behavior.

II. THE EXTERNAL ENVIRONMENT: FACTORS INFLUENCING ANALYSTS' DECISION TYPOLOGIES

This section assesses the financial, organizational, and technical environments of the participating budgeters for fiscal year 1989. Individual state data are preceded by a comparison of the Southern region's average general revenues and expenditures, and long-term debt to the rest of the nation. Portraits of the organizational setting and mission of each budget office are surveyed, and the technological capabilities afforded analysts are presented as well.

A. Fiscal Climate

The past decade has been a period of great financial and operational transition for most state governments. The federal government's retreat from the provision of many service and support systems has further burdened state governments with additional administrative and financial responsibilities. Most states have met the challenge through traditional as well as nontraditional methods of budget balancing (Hackbart and Leigland, 1990).[2] However, while many state governments maintained balanced budgets throughout the 1980s, they did so at the expense of savings, rainy day funds, and/or year-end balances (Carnevale, 1988; see also, Leigland, 1988:222).

To get a picture of the financial condition of the state governments included in this research, it is necessary to summarize that of the rest of the United States.[3] From 1982 to 1988, general revenues (taxes, intergovernmental revenues [federal aid], charges, and miscellaneous revenues), general expenditures (including education, welfare and social services, transportation, and hospitals), and long-term debt increased, on average, across the nation, as measured by percent change in constant dollars. For instance, for all states other than those included in this survey, general revenues increased by 24 percent; general expenditures increased by 23 percent; and long-term debt increased by 44 percent.[4] The dramatic growth in long-term debt is indicative of the increasing emphasis placed on debt financing for state government operations.

The same figures for the Southern region alone are only marginally different from those above. From 1982 to 1988, general revenues increased by 29 percent; general expenditures increased by 25 percent; and long-term debt increased by 39 percent. The slightly higher increases in revenues and expenditures for this ten state region compared to the rest of the nation are attributable, in part, to demographic shifts. This region experienced a 9 percent increase in population from 1982 to 1988; the rest of the nation experienced a 5 percent increase for the same period.

While the Southern region of the United States has experienced slightly greater financial growth than the rest of the nation (from 1982 to 1988), it is evident that the region's fiscal capacity is less than that of the other states. Comparison of per capita general revenues and per capita general expenditures for the Southern region to the rest of the states demonstrates this point. For the period from 1978 to 1988, on average, per capita revenues for the Southern states are 72 percent of the rest of the nation, and per capita expenditures are

76 percent of the rest of the nation. Ultimately, the financial growth of the region does not signify parity with averages (per capita and total) for the rest of the nation.

Ending balance as a percent of total (1989) estimated expenditures also provides evidence of fiscal stress being experienced by this region. Of the ten states included in this study, only one (South Carolina) approaches the 5 percent threshold recommended by analysts for healthy financial operation with an ending balance as a percent of expenditures of 4.46 (Colby, 1989:11). The aggregate 1989 estimated ending balance for this region is 1.08 percent of the aggregate 1989 spending estimate—a balance far below the 5 percent recommendation.[5]

The financial data collected from the state governments included in this research are confirmed by that provided in *City and State*'s (1989) Fourth Annual State Financial Report for the 50 states. Table 5.1 provides the mea-

Table 5.1   Financial Variables by State (1989 Estimates)[a]

State	REVSPC: General Fund Revenue ($/capita)	LTDPC: Long Term Debt ($/capita)	Bond Ratings (Moody/S&P)	Bond Score[b]
Alabama	727.89	144.61	Aa/AA	75
Florida	760.03	308.81	Aa/AA	75
Georgia	977.04	315.39	Aaa/AA+	90
Kentucky	886.46	768.20	Aa/AA	75
Louisiana	914.25	692.00	Baa1/BBB+	50
Mississippi	663.28	196.24	Aa/AA-	70
North Carolina	945.20	102.53	Aaa/AAA	100
South Carolina	885.71	198.00	Aaa/AAA	100
Tennessee	690.18	221.60	Aaa/AA+	90
Virginia	899.92	55.00	Aaa/AAA	100

[a] Estimated general fund revenues per capita were calculated using the figure for 1989 estimated general fund revenues provided by financial officers in each participating state government divided by the 1988 population figure provided by *City and State*'s (1989) Fourth Annual State Financial Report. Estimated long term debt per capita is the figure provided by financial officers in each state. Bond ratings provided by the financial officers were checked against those indicated for each state in *City and State*'s report.

[b] This score is based on a judgmental, interval scale developed by the researcher which establishes 100 as the strongest/best quality rating and 50 as the weakest/poorest quality rating. This score is the variable, BOND, used along with REVSPC and LTDPC as predictor variables in the discriminant model.

sures of fiscal capacity gathered for each state, including: 1989 estimated general fund revenues per capita, 1989 estimated long-term debt per capita, and bond ratings (both Moody's and Standard and Poor's).

The averages presented earlier for the Southern region indicate similar growth yet less capacity when compared to the rest of the nation. Additionally, the 1989 estimates in Table 5.1 illustrate some diversity of fiscal situation among the states in this region. For instance, Mississippi's 1989 estimated general fund revenues per capita are 68 percent of Georgia's; and Kentucky's projected long-term debt per capita is almost 14 times that of Virginia's.

The states can be compared according to their bond rating as well. In this case, an interval scale from 50 points (weakest rating) to 100 points (strongest rating) was developed by the researcher to indicate the strength of the bond rating. The final column in Table 5.1 represents the score assigned to each state government based on this judgmental scale. The three financial variables (REVSPC, LTDPC, and BOND) presented in this table are considered independent variables in the research model explained later in this chapter.

B. Budget Office Strength

Five variables are used to measure budget office strength in terms of organizational setting, analyst allegiance and focus, and budget mission and format. These variables include organizational location of the budget office, method of appointment of the budget office director, size of the office, budget format, and primary mission of the office. Each of these variables is weighted equally at 20 points;[6] therefore, the highest possible composite score that an office could receive is 100.

Organizational location of the budget office and the method of appointment of the director are two variables which measure allegiance of budget staff to the governor. Location of the budget office within the executive office of the governor and gubernatorial appointment of the budget director strengthen the chief executive's budget powers, and foster a strong allegiance on the part of budget staff to their governor (Abney and Lauth, 1989:830). In this case, budget offices located within the governor's executive office receive 20 points; those located outside of the executive office receive no points. Offices employing directors appointed by the governor receive 20 points; those with directors appointed by the governor with consent of one or both houses of the legislature receive 15 points; those with directors appointed by a department head with approval of the governor receive 10 points; and those with directors appointed by a department or division head receive 5 points.

Scoring for the organizational variables based on survey results are presented in Table 5.2. Four of the participating offices are located within the executive offices of the governor (Florida, Georgia, Kentucky, and North

Table 5.2   Assessment of Budget Office Strength: Organizational Setting, Analyst
Focus, and Budget Mission

| State | Variable Name | | | | | Total Score[a] |
	LOCATION	DIRECTOR	SIZE	FORMAT	MISSION	
Alabama	0	10	5.6 (18)	20	10	45.6
Florida	20	20	10.7 (118)	0	20	70.7
Georgia	20	20	12.0 (74)	0	10	62.0
Kentucky	20	20	9.2 (30)	20	20	89.2
Louisiana	0	5	8.0 (41)	0	10	23.0
Mississippi	10	15	3.0 (9)	0	10	38.0
North Carolina	20	20	5.4 (58)	20	10	75.4
South Carolina	0	5	5.1 (25)	0	10	20.1
Tennessee	0	20	8.3 (31)	20	10	58.3
Virginia	0	20	20.0 (104)	20	15	75.0

[a] Total Score is a composite score of the values for each of the scores on the variables from
LOCATION to MISSION. Total score is the variable, ORGSCORE, an interval level
measurement of budget office strength.

Carolina). In all of these states, the budget director is appointed by the governor and serves at the pleasure of the chief executive. Each of these states
receives 20 points for the variable, LOCATION, and 20 points for the variable, DIRECTOR.

On the other hand, four state governments have their budget offices
located in separate departments or divisions of administration and/or finance
(Alabama, Louisiana, Tennessee, and Virginia). These states did not receive
any points for the location variable. Nevertheless, Tennessee and Virginia
have budget staff whose allegiance to the governor is strengthened by virtue of
the appointment of their director by the chief executive. And, each director's
term of office is determined by the governor. Thus, these two states receive 20
points each for the variable, DIRECTOR.

In Alabama, the State Budget Officer is appointed by the head of the Department of Finance, subject to gubernatorial approval. This officer serves at the pleasure of the department head. Louisiana's Budget and Management Director is a civil service employee, appointed by the Commissioner of the State's Division of Administration. The appointment strategies for Alabama and Louisiana are indicated by the scores for the variable, DIRECTOR, of 10 and 5, respectively.

Two states have rather unusual arrangements concerning the placement of a central budget office. Mississippi's budget office is not within the executive office of the governor, yet is closely aligned with the chief executive by virtue of its independence from other departments.[7] This state's budget office is a division of the Financial Management Board (FMB) which is chaired by the governor. This office is directly responsible to the governor for provision of the budget document to be presented to the legislature; it is a counterpart to the Joint Legislative Budget Committee's Legislative Budget Office (Clynch, 1988). In this case, the budget director is appointed by the governor, with advice and consent from the Senate; this officer serves at the pleasure of the governor. Because of the relationship between the FMB and the governor, this budget office receives 10 points for the location variable. The appointment of the head of the budget division within the FMB warranted 15 points for the variable, DIRECTOR.[8]

South Carolina's central budget office is placed within the state's Budget and Control Board (BCB), another unique setting. This is an executive/legislative body of which the governor is chairman. While the power of the BCB in budget development is acknowledged (Whicker, 1986), for the purposes of this study, the score for the location variable is related solely to allegiance to the governor. In South Carolina, those who staff the budget division hold an allegiance to the BCB, and not specifically to the governor. Therefore, South Carolina receives a score of zero for this variable. Concerning appointment of the budget director, this is the responsibility of the BCB Commissioner. The director's term of office is indefinite. Because of this, South Carolina's budget office receives a score of 5 for the variable, DIRECTOR.

The size of the budget office also contributes to the resources and influence of those employed within it (Lee, 1981). The score which measures office size considers a ratio of the number of employees within the budget office (line and staff, 1988) to the total number of state government employees (1988). This ratio provides a relative measure of size and allows for comparability across the ten participating state governments. The state with the largest budget office compared to the other nine offices receives 100 percent of 20 points possible. The score for every other office is determined by multiplying the ratio of percentages by 20 points. For instance, Georgia's budget office employs .12 percent of total state employees. This number is divided by .20 percent (percent of total state employees in Virginia's budget office—the state with the largest budget office, according to this measure). The result is then multiplied by 20 to provide a score indicative of size. For Georgia, the score for the variable, SIZE, is 12.0.

Table 5.2 indicates the calculated score for the variable, SIZE, as well as the actual number of employees (line and staff) working in each budget office in 1988. Alabama, Mississippi, and South Carolina have relatively small budget shops (25 employees or less). Medium-sized operations (from 26 to 50 employees) are found in Kentucky, Louisiana, and Tennessee. Considerably larger offices are found in North Carolina, Georgia, and especially, Florida and Virginia.

Concerning the fourth organizational variable, budget format, all state budget officers interviewed acknowledged a tendency toward hybridization, if not in form, at least in thought. Generally, the line-item format serves as a starting point for budgetary negotiations between analysts and agency personnel, particularly for budgeters in states where the line-item format is legally required for submission to the legislature.

In answer to the question, Which one of the following best characterizes the budget format used in your state?, five budget officers checked, "traditional, line-item budget." Mississippi's budget director noted, however, movement toward program budgeting. In fact, Mississippi law requires the submission of the budget to the legislature in program budget format, even though control of appropriations by the budget office remains at the line-item level.[9] Similarly, South Carolina's budget director pointed out that their 1988 budget cycle included a pilot study in the use of program-performance budgeting. Nevertheless, these five states receive no points for the variable, FORMAT.

North Carolina was the only state to indicate that two budget formats were applicable—both line-item and program. This state receives 20 points for the variable, FORMAT, because of the complete integration of the program format in their budget process. The following explanation of narrative and statistical data included in the general instructions to agency personnel regarding budget preparation emphasizes the program format required in North Carolina:

> For a number of years, narrative and statistical data—departmental goal statements, program purpose statements, program objective statements, and statistical measures of program activity—have been a part of the recommended state budget. Since the last biennium, the Office of State Budget and Management has worked closely with departments to make program statistical measures more meaningful. The current budget preparation cycle continues this emphasis on quantifiable program data which will indicate the impact and outcomes of programs in addition to measuring activities. This effort is intended to supplement narrative descriptions with program statistical data which identify the target populations or environmental conditions, the specific relationships of the programs to these populations or conditions, and intended outcomes (Cameron, 1988:1).

Also included in North Carolina's budget instructions is a request that program managers provide information which relates program objectives to the goals of the department as well as "providing quantifiable program data to support budget requests" (Cameron, 1988:v).

Alabama, Kentucky, and Virginia checked program budget as the appropriate categorization of their format. Virginia's deputy budget officer added that their format, "includes elements of all theory." Finally, Tennessee was the only state with a format signified as a "modified zero base approach." Each of these states, along with North Carolina, receives 20 points for the variable, FORMAT.

A question related to budget office mission required the budget officer completing the survey instrument to rank functions in terms of their importance to the role of the budget office in their state. The missions included, in random order: controlling agency expenditures; evaluating the efficiency of agency performance; serving as policy and planning staff to the governor; and evaluating the effectiveness of agency performance. Average ranking for the ten states substantiates the predominance of the control function of most budget offices. That is, average rank for the control mission is first (1.3); for the policy mission, second (2.2); for the efficiency mission, third (3.0); and for the effectiveness mission, fourth (3.4).

Seven budget officers ranked the control mission as the primary one required of their office, while three ranked it as the second most important function of their office. Two budget officers (Florida's and Kentucky's) ranked the policy mission as primary, while five ranked it second. Finally, one officer (Virginia's) ranked the efficiency mission as the most important function of that state's budget office. The budget officers in Mississippi and Tennessee ranked this mission as the second most important function of their office. Scores for the variable, MISSION, indicate the primary function as control (10 points), efficiency (15 points), or policy development (20 points).

A total score, ORGSCORE, for each state government budget office is calculated by adding the points received by each office for the individual organizational variables. According to the values for ORGSCORE provided in the last column of Table 5.2, Kentucky is an example of a state with a strong budget office in terms of staff allegiance to the governor, coupled with a program budget format, and a primary mission of policy development and planning. It is expected that analysts in this type of setting would be more inclined to display spending orientations which ascribe predominant weight to gubernatorial direction. Other state government budget offices which can be considered powerful, in this sense, are those in Florida, Virginia, North Carolina, and Georgia.

Not surprisingly, Table 5.2 suggests the less powerful offices to be found in Alabama, Mississippi, Louisiana, and particularly, South Carolina—a state with an especially weak governor (from a budgetary perspective). It is expected that analysts in these budget offices will exhibit traditional, incremental behavior regarding the review of agency spending plans. Gubernatorial direction should be less important to these analysts as a decision cue than it would be to those employed in offices more closely aligned with the governor.

C. Technological Setting

A related aspect of the influence of organizational setting and budget office mission to decision strategy of the budgeter is the technological sophistication of the office (Botner, 1985 and 1987; see also, Cope, 1987, Grizzle, 1987; Poister and McGowan, 1984; Poister and Streib, 1989). The score measuring technological sophistication is comprised of two equivalent parts of 50 points each. The range of scores for each part of the variable, TECSCORE, is a judgmental scale developed by the researcher. The first part of the TECSCORE measures access of microcomputers to analysts within their office. Question nine of the computer section of the 1988 State Government Budget Analysts Project questionnaire determines if each analyst is provided a microcomputer upon entry into their respective budget office (Willoughby, 1991). Scores for the variable, ACCESS, range from zero points for no access, to 25 points for limited access, and 50 points for complete access (every analyst is provided with a microcomputer upon entry into the office). Table 5.3 indicates that in 1988 half of the budget offices provided complete access to the hardware in question, while half provided limited access to their analysts.

A second part of the composite score measuring technological sophistication measures software and peripheral amenities provided by each office. Question three of the above questionnaire provides a checklist of peripherals available in each budget office, while question four provides a checklist of available software packages. The variable, SOFTWARE, is measured in a similar manner as the variable, SIZE, is measured in Table 5.2. That is, the budget office with the greatest number of peripherals and software capabilities receives 100 percent of 50 points possible. The score of every other office is determined by dividing the number of capabilities from the largest office into the number for the office of interest, and then multiplying by 50. The resulting scores for all offices indicate the relative capabilities of the offices. For instance, Tennessee's budget office offered the largest array of peripheral and software capabilities to their analysts in 1988, while Louisiana's office afforded the least amount of peripheral and software capability to their analysts.

Total scores measuring technological sophistication of budget offices (TECSCORE) are determined by adding the points received for the variables, ACCESS and SOFTWARE, together. Values for TECSCORE indicate that six of the budget offices surveyed are rather sophisticated in terms of hardware

Table 5.3 Assessment of Budget Office Sophistication: Access and Availability of
Computer Technology

| | Variable name | | Total |
State	ACCESS	SOFTWARE	Score[a]
Alabama	50	22.7	72.7
Florida	25	25	50
Georgia	50	22.7	72.7
Kentucky	50	18.2	68.2
Louisiana	25	11.4	36.4
Mississippi	25	15.9	40.9
North Carolina	50	22.7	72.7
South Carolina	25	18.2	43.2
Tennessee	25	50	75
Virginia	50	25	75

[a] Total score is a composite score of the values for the variables, ACCESS and SOFTWARE. This score is the variable, TECSCORE, an interval level measurement of the technological sophistication of the budget office.

access and software/peripheral availability (scores from 68 to 75). Three offices (Louisiana's, Mississippi's, and South Carolina's) illustrate environments with rather rudimentary technological capabilities, compared to their neighbors in the region. Florida's budget office falls closer to these states, although complete access to microcomputers for their analysts was established in November of 1988—a date following the researcher's visit to that office.

The composite scores developed which measure budget office strength (ORGSCORE) and technological sophistication (TECSCORE) are interval level variables used as predictors in discriminant analysis. The following section explains this analytical procedure and measurement of the dependent and independent variables.

III.   THE DISCRIMINANT MODEL

A.   A Description of Discriminant

Discriminant analysis provides a means of classifying subjects into groups according to predictor variables. In this case, group membership or decision typology is the dependent variable. This variable is a qualitative, nominally measured one. The independent or discriminating variables are quantitative, interval level measurements.

According to Kachigan (1986:357–358), "discriminant analysis identifies boundaries between groups; the boundaries are defined in terms of variable characteristics which discriminate objects into criterion groups." Likewise, Klecka (1980) suggests the primary objectives of using the discriminant procedure. One objective is explanation—to learn which variables are related to the criterion variable (group membership). Another objective is prediction—to classify subjects into groups according to their known values on the independent (predictor) variables. Ultimately, the purpose of the discriminant procedure is to develop mathematical functions which optimally separate subjects according to their group membership based on their values for the independent variables.[10] "Ideally, the resulting function scores within a particular group will be quite similar. The closer the scores, the more homogeneous the individual groups will be internally, and the more distinct each group will be from the others" (Legge and Ziegler, 1979:28).

In this case, discriminant analysis will be used to answer the following questions:

1. Which variable(s) is(are) the best predictor(s) of an analyst's spending policy?
2. In what manner do predictor variables influence an analyst's consideration of criteria concerning agency budget requests for the purpose of making spending recommendations to the governor?
3. If the values of the predictor variables are known, how much is prediction of analysts' spending policies improved over chance alone by using the discriminant model?

B. The Dependent Variable: Group Membership

The first step in utilizing the discriminant procedure requires consideration of the criterion variable, group membership. As noted earlier, the data for this research takes advantage of work by Willoughby (1991 and 1992) which examines the spending policies of 131 executive budget analysts from ten Southern states. Social judgment analysis was used to mathematically and graphically portray these budgeters' spending strategies. This method of analysis necessitated development of a simulation; prototypes of the decision task presented to analysts described hypothetical state agency budget requests. Each request was comprised of seven cues most often used by these budgeters when reviewing agency spending plans.[11] Subjects provided their judgments for each of 40 randomly generated requests in the form of strength of recommendation to their governor concerning the inclusion of the request in the total budget package.[12] Multiple regression of each analyst's recommendations provided an arithmetic model of individual spending policy. Grouping the policies of the analysts yielded 11 clusters of decision typologies.

These groups, while relevant, are sometimes only minimally distinctive. Therefore, for present research purposes, it was determined that the 11 groups could be categorized into 4 general types of spending orientation or policy. These types are classified as Politico, Mixed-Value, Rationalist, or Incrementalist.

Analysts are classified as Politico if they apply predominant weight to one or more of the political criteria included in the hypothetical budget requests (governor's agenda, legislative agenda, agency head reputation for trustworthiness, and/or public support). Of the 131 analysts included in 3 of the 11 clusters, 35 can be categorized as Politicos. Those labeled Mixed-Value include analysts who ascribe almost equal consideration to the cue, governor's agenda, and to one or both of the rational cues, workload and efficiency. The Mixed-Value category includes the largest number of analysts (83) from 4 of the 11 clusters. Two very small groups, Rationalists (with five analysts) and Incrementalists (with eight analysts), are those who ascribe predominant weight to either one or both of the rational cues (workload and efficiency), or to agency acquisitiveness, respectively. Table 5.4 lists the four policy types, the predominant use of budget cues by analysts characterized by each orientation, and total number of analysts in each group. These four groups will serve as the dependent variable in the analysis to be presented.

Figure 1 illustrates function forms of average judgment policy by type. Function forms graphically represent the way in which analysts interpret each cue when reviewing agency budget requests. In this case, the vertical axis

Table 5.4 Analysts Grouped According to Policy Type

Group	Policy Type	Predominant use of budget cues	Total number of Analysts in group
1	Politico	Gubernatorial agenda, legislative agenda, agency head reputation, and/or public support	35
2	Mixed-Value	Gubernatorial agenda and agency workload and/or agency efficiency	83
3	Rationalist	Agency workload and/or agency efficiency	5
4	Incrementalist	Agency acquisitiveness	8
		Total:	131

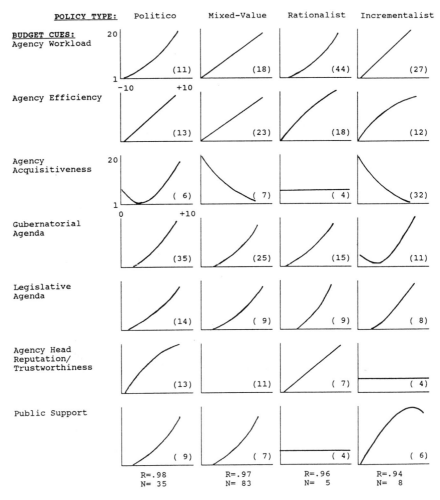

Figure 5.1 Function forms by policy type.

represents analysts' recommendation for each of the 40 profiles, scored on a scale from 1 to 20. The horizontal axis represents the scores applied to specific cues within each profile on a scale from -10 to $+10$, or 0 to $+10$ in the case of the cue, agency acquisitiveness.[13] A predictability score (multiple R) is printed below the function forms for each average policy type. This score or multiple correlation coefficient indicates both goodness of fit of the model and the consistency with which analysts adhere to a particular policy type when making decisions about agency spending plans (Willoughby, 1991). A predictability score of .80 or above is considered good (Stewart, 1988:41–74). Relative weights are found in the lower right corner of the function forms. These are standardized beta weights which result from multiple regression. These weights measure percent of variability in an analyst's judgment policy that is explained by each cue. Relative weights for each typology sum to 100.

Consideration of function forms with the weights illustrates the distinctiveness of the four policy types. That is, while analysts may interpret cues similarly, they can weigh them differently. Alternatively, they may weigh cues similarly, yet interpret them differently. For instance, analysts characterized as Politicos consider gubernatorial agenda most heavily compared to the other cues. Also, approximately 71 percent of the variability in these analysts' judgments can be attributed to their consideration of political factors alone (including governor's agenda, legislative agenda, agency head reputation, and public support). Politicos consider each of these cues in a positive, slightly curvilinear fashion. The more positively the agency's budget is endorsed by the governor and the legislature, the more trustworthy the agency head in terms of equating requests with actual spending practice, and the more positive and vocal public support for the agency's programs and/or services, the stronger the analyst's recommendation to include the request in the total budget package.

Alternatively, for analysts characterized as Mixed-Value, gubernatorial agenda and efficiency of operation are considered equally in determining spending plans (weights of 25 and 23, respectively). And together, the rational cues (workload and efficiency), account for 41 percent of the variability in these analysts' judgment policies. While cue weights are different, the manner in which these factors are considered by analysts in these first two groups are similar. Like the Politicos, Mixed-Values utilize workload, efficiency, and governor's agenda in a positive, linear or slightly curvilinear fashion.

Analysts characterized as Rationalists ascribe predominant weight to the cue, workload, followed by efficiency. Sixty-two percent of the variability in these analysts judgments can be attributed to their consideration of the rational cues alone. Gubernatorial direction serves as the third most important cue to these analysts, while the other political factors, and agency acquisitiveness are of little significance. Finally, Figure 1 illustrates that Incrementalists consider agency acquisitiveness most heavily in determining spending plans. The function form for this cue shows the guardianship role typical of the traditional executive budget analyst (Meltsner and Wildavsky, 1970). As agency acquisitiveness increases, analysts' recommendations to include such requests in the total budget package weaken.

C.   The Independent Variable

`. second step to prepare for discriminant requires the definition and measurement of the independent variables. The present model includes nine predictor variables. Five of these include the financial, organizational, and technical variables described in the first part of the chapter. Four variables quantify the personal characteristics of the analysts.

Specifically, the financial climate of the state is measured by 1989 estimated general revenues per capita (REVSPC), long term debt per capita (LTDPC), and bond score (BOND). Strength of the budget office in terms of organizational setting, analyst focus, and budget mission, as measured by the composite score, ORGSCORE, is a fourth predictor variable. The technological sophistication of the budget office, as measured by TECSCORE, is a fifth one. These variables are measured at the interval level.

Several variables measure the educational background, work experience, and other personal characteristics of analysts. These include: SCHOOL, SEX, YEARS, and AGE. SCHOOL and SEX are dummy variables coded 0 or 1 (college graduate or advanced degree (master's or doctoral), and female or male, respectively). YEARS is the number of years an analyst had served in the position at the time of administration of the survey. AGE is analyst's age in years. These variables are interval level measurements.

Table 5.5 provides the means for each of the predictor variables by policy type and for all analysts included in this research.

Results indicate distinctions across all or some of the policy types for each of the independent variables. For instance, analysts in the Mixed-Value category are in a financial, organizational, and technological environment somewhat different from those in the other three categories. These analysts are employed in environments characterized as less fiscally secure, less powerful (from an organizational and mission standpoint) and less sophisticated concerning technical capabilities than the environments of analysts who exhibit the other decision making orientations.

Distinctions across the personal characteristics of analysts as grouped are evident as well. Looking at the averages for the four categories across these variables it is possible to develop a profile of the analyst most likely to exhibit each type of decision making orientation. In general, analysts exhibiting the spending behavior of the Politico or the Rationalist are male, middle-aged, probably the recipient of an advanced degree, and with over five years experience in the position. Rationalists have more experience in the position, on average, than Politicos. Analysts in the Mixed-Value category are similar to Politicos and Rationalists, yet younger and less experienced, on average.

The profile of the Incrementalist is quite different from that of the other three profiles. Analysts in this category are predominantly female, middle-aged, and less experienced in the position than either the Politicos or the Rationalists. Also, these analysts are less likely than those in other groups to have an advanced degree (master's or doctoral).

Table 5.5 Means of Predictor Variables by Policy Type

Variable	Policy Type Group Number[a]				All Analysts
	1	2	3	4	
REVSPC	$857	$848	$855	$925	$856
(N=)	(35)	(83)	(5)	(8)	(131)
LTDPC	$248	$354	$231	$318	$319
(N=)	(35)	(83)	(5)	(8)	(131)
BOND	89	78	93	88	82
(N=)	(35)	(83)	(5)	(8)	(131)
ORGSCORE	63	56	75	65	59
(N=)	(35)	(83)	(5)	(8)	(131)
TECSCORE	61	59	74	72	61
(N=)	(35)	(83)	(5)	(8)	(131)
SEX	.71	.66	1.0	.37	.67
(N=)	(34)	(83)	(5)	(8)	(130)
AGE	42	37	42	39	39
(N=)	(34)	(83)	(5)	(8)	(130)
SCHOOL	.55	.58	.60	.25	.55
(N=)	(33)	(81)	(5)	(8)	(127)
YEARS	5.6	4.4	6.9	4.9	4.8
(N=)	(33)	(77)	(5)	(8)	(123)

[a] Group numbers correspond to the following policy types: 1 = Politico, 2 = Mixed-Value, 3 = Rationalist, and 4 = Incrementalist.

Consideration of means of the independent variables across groups is a first step in the distinction of analysts' spending policies. However, such analysis does not provide statistical confirmation of the discriminating power of these variables or evidence that they serve to facilitate the correct classification of analysts according to policy type. The following section addresses this issue by presenting the results from discriminant analysis.

IV. ANALYSIS AND RESULTS

The first part of this analysis is exploratory; to determine which variables are the best predictors of decision typology. This analysis uses a forward stepwise discriminant procedure to select the variable which provides the greatest univariate discrimination of subjects. This variable is then paired with the next most discriminating variable until all relevant predictors are included in the model. The stepwise procedure is a "logical and efficient way to seek the best combination [of predictor variables]" (Klecka, 1980:53). The selection criterion used as a measure of discrimination for the present model is Rao's V. This measures the separation of group centroids (group means of discriminant scores for functions).

Variables which generate a statistically significant change in Rao's V are the most influential in terms of aiding prediction of group membership. Results from discriminant analysis indicate that BOND, a measure of state government bond rating, provides the greatest discriminating power, followed by AGE (analyst's age in years), and then TECSCORE (measure of technological sophistication of the budget office). While the addition of the other variables does not generate a statistically significant change in Rao's V, they contribute enough to classification to be included in the discriminant model. YEARS (number of years in the analyst position) and LTDPC (long term debt per capita) are the only variables not included in this model.

These results suggest that the best predictors of analysts' spending orientations are not confined to one type of variable. That is, a mix of financial, personal, technical, and organizational characteristics serve to distinguish analysts' decision typologies. Specifically, the historical fiscal health of a state government, the age of the analyst, and the technological sophistication of the budget office serve as the best determinants of an analyst's consideration of budget cues when making spending recommendations to the chief executive officer. Also, by virtue of their inclusion in the final discriminant model, other variables (namely, SCHOOL, SEX, ORGSCORE, and REVSPC) cannot be summarily ruled out as influential to the classification of analysts according to policy type.

A second discriminant analysis was conducted using only the predictor variables included in the initial model. The results from this analysis are presented in Table 5.6. This model produces results similar to the first one. Again, the variables, BOND, AGE, and TECSCORE, provide the most discriminating power. Education level (SCHOOL) indicates more discriminating power than the previous model. The contributions of budget office strength, sex of the analyst, and estimated revenue climate provide only limited contribution to the classification of analysts.

The bottom half of this table provides information concerning the functions derived from the discriminant procedure. Interpretation of eigenvalues allows for the comparison of the relative discriminating power of functions. The value for the first function (.28) indicates that it is twice as powerful as the second function, and more than four times as powerful as the third function concerning discriminating ability.

Conversion of eigenvalues to relative percentages provides a better measure of the discriminating power of each function. In this case, the first func-

Table 5.6 Discriminant Analysis: Key Variables Entered

Variable	F to enter/ remove	Number included	Rao's V	Change in Rao's V	Sig. of Change
BOND	3.6	1	16.82	16.82	.0008
AGE	3.0	2	27.98	11.15	.0109
TECSCORE	2.8	3	36.44	8.46	.0374
SCHOOL	2.0	4	43.22	6.78	.0792
ORGSCORE	1.2	5	48.35	5.13	.1629
SEX	1.7	6	53.28	4.94	.1765
REVSPC	1.3	7	57.80	4.52	.2104

Discriminant function	Eigenvalue	Relative percentage	Canonical correlation	χ^2	DF	Sig
1	.28	59.3	.47	21.8	12	.0396
2	.14	28.9	.35	6.5	5	.2637
3	.06	11.7	.23			

tion contains 59.3 percent "of the total discriminating power in this system of equations" (Klecka, 1980:36). The relative percentages of the second and third functions (28.9 percent and 11.7 percent, respectively) indicate moderate/weak to weak discriminatory power.

The canonical correlation coefficient provides another statistical avenue to determine the importance of discriminant functions. The square of the canonical correlation provides a measure of "the amount of variance in the discriminant function explained by the groups" (Legge and Ziegler, 1979:31). According to the present model, group membership explains 22 percent of the variance in the first function, 12 percent of the variance in the second function, and 5 percent of the variance in the third function.

Chi-square values and significance levels are presented in the bottom, right of Table 5.6. This information is used to determine the necessity of including all derived functions in a final model.[14] As the results show, after deriving the first function, the remaining discrimination is significant at the .04 level. However, following the derivation and inclusion of the second function, "all significant information about group differences has been absorbed" (Klecka, 1980:41). Therefore, the remainder of the analysis will consider the first two functions only.

Analysis of centroids provides a clearer understanding of the separation of policy types according to the predictor variables. As mentioned earlier, centroids are mean discriminant scores for functions by group. Table 5.7 presents

Table 5.7   Centroids for Functions by Policy Type

Policy type	Group mean for function 1	Group mean for function 2
Politico	0.74	0.23
Mixed-Value	− 0.39	0.04
Rationalist	0.81	0.10
Incrementalist	0.44	− 1.36

the centroids for the first and second discriminant functions by spending policy. The discrepancy of mean scores across policy types for each function is evident. Concerning the first function, analysts characterized as Mixed-Value generate the lowest scores, on average, compared to their counterparts in the other groups. For the second function, Incrementalists generate the lowest scores compared to the other analysts.

The separation among decision making orientations can be displayed graphically using a plot. Figure 5.2 presents the plot of centroids for both functions. The horizontal axis represents values for discriminant scores for the first function; the vertical axis represents values for discriminant scores for the second function. Comparing centroids according to the first function (horizontally), the most dramatic separation occurs between the Politicos and Rationalists, and Mixed-Values. Comparing centroids according to the second function, the greatest separation exists between the Politicos and the Incrementalists. Mixed-Values and Rationalists have almost identical centroid values (.04 and .10, respectively) on this function. Given these results, it is expected that the first function will be most helpful in distinguishing Mixed-Values from all others, while the second function will be most helpful in distinguishing Incrementalists from all others, particularly Politicos.

To assess the relative contribution of each independent variable to the derived functions, standardized discriminant function coefficients are generated. These coefficients are standardized to account for the different units in which each of the variables is measured. Table 5.8 presents the standardized function coefficients for the first two functions by policy type. Results show that BOND, and then AGE, are the strongest contributers to the discriminatory power of the first function (.75 and .62, respectively). Substantively, as fiscal climate of a state government improves, and as the analyst ages, the score of an analyst on this function increases. Alternatively, as the fiscal climate deteriorates (reflected in a poorer bond rating), and for younger analysts, the score on the first function should be lower. This information corresponds to that presented in Table 5.5. Specifically, Mixed-Values are younger, on aver-

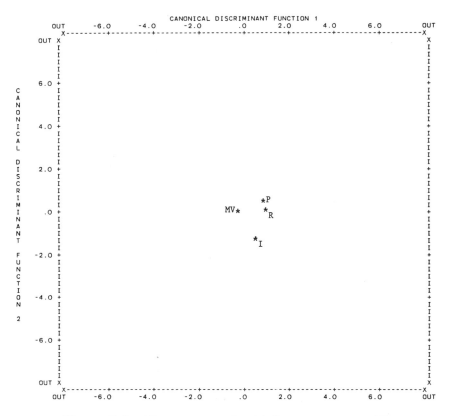

Figure 5.2   All groups scatterplot (* indicates a group centroid).

Table 5.8   Standardized Discriminant Function Coefficients

Variable	Function 1 coefficients	Function 2 coefficients
BOND	0.75	0.50
AGE	0.62	−0.003
ORGSCORE	0.40	0.43
SCHOOL	−0.37	0.43
TECSCORE	−0.25	−0.99
SEX	−0.06	0.37
REVSPC	0.02	−0.52

age, than analysts in other categories. Also, their environment is less stable, financially, than those of analysts exhibiting the other spending orientations.

Turning to the second function, the technological sophistication of the budget office is the predominant factor contributing to this function's discriminatory power. In this case, higher values for TECSCORE would generate lower scores for this function. Alternatively, lower values for TECSCORE would generate high scores for this function. Politicos represent a group whose technical environment is less sophisticated when compared to that of the other policy types, particularly Incrementalists. For this function, it is expected that Politicos would generate the highest scores, while Incrementalists would generate the lowest scores.

Finally, a classification matrix is derived using the second, two-function discriminant model. Table 5.9 presents a crosstabulation of actual (rows) with predicted (columns) group membership. The "agreement diagonal" shows the number of correctly classified cases (Legge and Ziegler, 1979:29). Based on the information from analysis of centroids, it has been determined that the discriminant model is most powerful in terms of separating Mixed-Values on function one and Incrementalists on function two. Therefore, it is expected that the greatest percent of correct classifications would occur in these cells. In fact, classifications are correct 62 percent of the time for the Mixed-Values, and 75 percent of the time for the Incrementalists. These two cells have the greatest percent of correct classifications, although Rationalists are close behind (correctly classified 60 percent of the time).

The percentage of known cases correctly classified (56 percent) provides a measure of the predictive accuracy of the model (Klecka, 1980:50). With four groups, it would be expected that classification would be correct 25 percent of the time by chance alone (a one in four chance of correctly classifying sub-

Table 5.9 Classification Matrix: Two Function Model (Percent of "Grouped" Cases Correctly Classified: 56%)[a]

Policy type	No. of cases	Politico	Mixed-Value	Rational.	Incrmntl.
Politico	32	11 (34%)	8 (25%)	10 (31%)	3 (9%)
Mixed-Value	81	14 (17%)	50 (62%)	4 (5%)	13 (16%)
Rational.	5	1 (20%)	1 (20%)	3 (60%)	0 (0%)
Incrmntl.	8	1 (13%)	0 (0%)	1 (13%)	6 (75%)
Total	126	27	59	18	22

[a] Classification Processing Summary: 131 cases were processed, 0 cases were excluded for missing codes or out-of-range group codes, 5 cases had at least one missing discriminating variable, 126 cases were used for classification matrix output.

jects). That the model would generate correct classification 56 percent of the time indicates the helpfulness of the model in distinguishing analysts by policy type.

A standardized measure of improvement in prediction by using the model can be calculated using tau, a proportionate reduction in error measure.[15] The tau value indicates that the prediction of decision making orientation among analysts can be improved by 41 percent by knowing the values for the financial, organizational, technical, and personal variables included in the model. Another way of interpreting this value is to note that classification of analysts based on the predictor variables included in this model made 41 percent fewer errors than would be expected by chance alone.

V.   CONCLUSIONS

A.   The Usefulness of Discriminant Analysis

Bibb and Roncek (1976:356) suggest that the greatest difficulty to using discriminant analysis is the initial differentiation of subjects into groups. In other words, once group membership is defined, discriminant provides a powerful means of analyzing the variables which best predict such membership. Ultimately, the strength of the procedure lies in its ability to discriminate according to the qualitative nature of the dependent variable. So often in the social sciences, the dependent variable is unable to be measured at more than the nominal level. Thus, traditional multiple regression is not an analytical option to the researcher.

In the present study, discriminant offers the key to determining both the statistical and substantive relationships between analysts' spending policies and traditional factors related to their external and personal decision environments. The strength of the model lies in the variables considered. Development of groups required extensive preliminary analysis to generate legitimate policy types which actually characterize and separate analysts according to their spending strategies (Willoughby, 1991 and 1992). Consideration of the nine initial independent variables necessitated the collection of financial, organizational, technical, and personal data, development of composite scores, judgmental scales, and in some instances, dummy measurement. The validity and reliability of these measures can only be substantiated by collaboration with past literature and perhaps by the consideration of future researchers.

In this case, use of discriminant is appropriate. The model assumes the following structure: (1) the number of discriminating variables is less than the number of cases by at least two; (2) all variables are measured at the interval level; (3) no variable is a linear combination of other discriminating variables; (4) no two predictor variables are perfectly correlated; (5) the population covariance matrices are equal for each group; and (6) each group is drawn from a population that has a multivariate normal distribution.

The fifth and sixth assumptions are somewhat problematic for this data, primarily due to the variability in group size. Concerning the equality of group covariance matrices, Bibb and Romcek (1976:364) concede that unequal matrices can bias the discriminant weights toward the group having the largest variance, thereby distorting the predictive power of the model. On the other hand, "precisely how crucial equality of dispersion matrices is remains subject to dispute" (Bibb and Romcek, 1976:364). And, the authors emphasize that the conventional discriminant function can adequately substitute for an optimally refined quadratic form when the number of independent variables is limited, as in this instance.

Concerning group size, Kachigan (1986:359) notes that equality of subjects across groups is not essential for the correct application of discriminant. The shortcomings of the present data to these last two assumptions are noted but are not deemed extreme enough to preclude use of a discriminant model (see also, Klecka, 1980; Lachenbruch, Sneeringer, and Revo, 1973; and Melton, 1963).

B. The Case of the State Government Budget Analyst

Results from this research produce new information about a little known budget player—some facts coincide with the findings of past studies, yet some generate questions about budget behavior and practice. Related to the decision making behavior of executive budget analysts, evidence shows that, on average, these budgeters take advantage of two or three cues predominantly when making spending recommendations. In this sample, most adhere to gubernatorial direction, and then efficiency of operation of the agency, and/or changes in workload when determining spending plans. The influence of agency heads and the legislative agenda are not as important as these first three cues to analysts when making spending recommendations. Acquisitiveness of the agency head and public support for agency services and/or programs are considered only slightly by analysts, on average, when reviewing budget requests.

Analyses of decision patterns involve both the types of criteria considered by analysts to be important, and the manner of their influence. For example, relatively few analysts (six percent) consider the acquisitiveness of the agency head as important when developing spending recommendations. Of those who weigh this cue heavily, most exhibit traditional "guardian" behavior—that is, the more acquisitive the agency head (request compared to current budget), the more negatively the analyst interprets the request. For these analysts, the more a director asks for, the more he or she gets cut.

Concerning manner of influence, most of the other cues are utilized by analysts in a positive linear, or slightly curvilinear, fashion. For instance, the more positively a request is endorsed by the governor, the stronger the recommendation by the analyst to include it in the total budget package. Such behavior is to be expected. These analysts naturally consider the congruence of their chief executive's policy agenda with program objectives, weighing gubernatorial direction rather heavily when reviewing agency budget requests. It is interesting, however, that distinctions in the manner in which cues are interpreted by analysts do exist, particularly for those considering acquisitiveness most heavily. While the predominant number of these analysts exhibit traditional behavior, some do interpret the cue differently—greater acquisitiveness generating stronger recommendations. These results signify that even if budgeters weigh cues similarly, they may interpret them differently.

Grouping analysts according to decision orientation results in four typologies or policy types. Sixty-three percent of the analysts can be categorized as Mixed-Value—indicating that a strong majority utilize at least two types of cues (in this case, rational or analytical, and intuitive or political). Alternatively, only 37 percent of the sample ascribe predominant weight to just one type of cue, be it rational, quasi-rational, or intuitive. Of these analysts, 73 percent are categorized as Politico, with relatively few confining their consideration to either rational or incremental cues only.

Perhaps the most interesting aspect of this work is the statistical reiteration of the role of fiscal climate and personal characteristics on budget behavior. While technical and organizational factors cannot be discounted in the determination of analysts' decision making orientations, fiscal stability of the state, along with the age of the analyst, provide the greatest influence on these budgeters when engaged in the activity of budgeting. Results indicate that rational decision tools can be expected to play the greatest role in budgetary decisions in less fiscally stable environments and for younger analysts. These results substantiate much of the the work mentioned in the introduction—that as "decisional leeway" becomes limited, decision makers search for more objective, technical methods of solving problems.

The relationship between age and analytical thinking on the part of analysts may be more complex. It may be that younger analysts are more familiar than older analysts with such decision tools, and so, are more comfortable with their use. Or, perhaps they are just less familiar with the politics of budgeting. Younger analysts may be less confident concerning their recommendation strategy and, therefore, rely on a combination of analytical and intuitive cues when determining spending plans.

C.   Contribution to Public Budgeting Theory

Mathematics aside, what do these results tell us about public budgeting today? Clearly, budgeters tend to rely on a few preferred or comfortable cues when making spending decisions. However, as fiscal stringency increases, such budgeters are likely to take advantage of a wider range of criteria in making their decisions, and specifically to consider objective measures of performance along with political factors when budgeting. It is logical then, that governments be advised not to wait until periods of fiscal stress to incorporate rational decisions tools into their budget process. While they may be ignored in surplus and stable times, they are a necessary component of decision making in periods of fiscal decline. If such aids are not incorporated into the budget process before periods of fiscal stringency, they cannot be properly accessed in time of need.

Also, given the relationship between an analyst's age and spending orientation, governments should understand the necessity of proper training of budgeters in the use of such tools. Older analysts may need special training and/or continuing education concerning the use of analysis in developing spending plans. In other words, the existence of rational decision tools, and fiscal environment alone, do not guarantee their use in budget process.

From a practical standpoint regarding the quality of public spending decisions today, practitioners and scholars alike may breathe easier. For the results of this project suggest that a majority of modern budgeters maintain a mixed-value orientation. It is difficult to interpret most subjects of this study as strictly technicians or politicos—given the mix of criteria considered most heavily by these experts when making budgetary recommendations. And, this orientation is expected, given the financial climate of most of the states visited. In this environment and for this group of budgeters, traditional incremental behavior does not prevail. Rather, these subjects characterize budgeters who acknowledge and weigh both analytical and intuitive guidance when determining spending plans. Given the conclusions of Hammond et al. (1987) concerning error-free judgment and the usefulness of both types of guidance when making choices, such an orientation among public budgeters may be the best that reformers and citizens can hope for.

NOTES

1. Executive budget analysts from the following states participated in this research project: Alabama, Florida, Georgia, Kentucky, Louisiana, Mississippi, North Carolina, South Carolina, Tennessee, and Virginia. See Willoughby (1991 and 1992) for an explanation of sampling, survey instrument development and administration, and response rate.
2. Traditional strategies of budget balancing include cutting spending and raising taxes. Non-traditional methods include tapping new revenue sources and developing new debt strategies.
3. All information presented in this section takes advantage of financial and population data from *State Government Finances* of the Government Finance Series

developed by the U.S. Bureau of the Census, for 1978 through 1988. Data from Table 3 (Summary of State Government Finances, by State) and Table 22 (Population and Personal Income) provided the information for this section, specifically.

4. Constant dollars are determined using the implicit price deflator for GNP related to state and local government purchases of goods and services, 1982 = 100, base year; 1988 = 130.8. The fourth quarter figure from Table 7.4 in *Survey of Current Business* (1989:16–17) is used.

5. Eight of the ten states in this survey estimate revenue shortfalls in 1989. Hackbart (1988) points out that state governments have little experience with such shortfalls. He adds that "revenue shortfalls are a novelty of the 1980s. They are reflective of an economic downfall [particular to the Southern region of the United States]" (Hackbart, 1988).

6. The literature assessing the influence of each of these variables on an analyst's decision making orientation provides no empirical work which ranks the variables as to their relative importance to a budgeter. Therefore, each variable is afforded equal weight in the development of an overall score related to the influence of the budget office, organizationally, on the spending policies of analysts.

7. The organizational setting of Mississippi's budget office has changed since 1988. Currently, the Office of Budget and Fund Management is located within the Division of Budget and Policy, which is housed in the Department of Finance and Administration.

8. Since its inception, the Joint Legislative Budget Committee's budget has served as the starting point for budgetary negotiations in the legislature, while the executive budget is usually ignored. However, greater impetus on the part of Governor Ray Mabus has fostered more consideration by the legislature of gubernatorial priorities. Clynch (1988:18–19) is cautiously optimistic about the movement away from "politics as usual" in Mississippi to the executive-centered budget system characteristic of most states.

9. Clynch (1988) substantiates this "nudging" toward program budgeting in Mississippi and suggests recent gubernatorial influence to be partially responsible.

10. Discriminant analysis uses the information known for each subject (group membership, and values for each of the predictor variables) to develop functions. A discriminant function is a weighted, linear combination of the values on the independent variables. Discriminant scores are calculated for each subject using a function equation.

11. The cues included: rational measures of program workload and efficiency; a heuristic cue, acquisitiveness of the agency head; and, several political or intuitive criteria, namely, gubernatorial and legislative agendas, trustworthiness of the agency head in terms of past requests compared to actual spending, and degree of public support for or against agency programs or services (GOVSAGENDA, LEGISLATURE, AGHEADREP, and SUPPORT). See Willoughby (1991 and 1992) for a detailed explanation of profile development, criteria definition, and scaling.

12. Recommendations were provided by subjects on a scale from 1 (very weak recommendation for inclusion) to 20 (very strong recommendation for inclusion).

13. In developing hypothetical agency budget requests, it was determined that an agency head asking for less than current budget was atypical. Therefore, possible scores for this cue ranged from 0 (no change from current budget) to +10 (significant increase in funding from current budget).

14. The number of functions used in a discriminant model depends on the number of groups. Generally, the number of functions is equal to the number of groups less one (Kachigan, 1986:361). However, this rule of thumb can change. It is incumbent upon the researcher to determine the efficiency of including all functions in a final discriminant model regardless of their statistical significance.

15. This measure is generated by subtracting the summation of prior probability of group membership from the number of cases correctly classified using the model, and dividing this value by that obtained by subtracting the summation of prior probability of group membership from the total number of cases (Klecka, 1980:50–51). The following represents the calculation of tau for this data:

$$\tau = \frac{(11+50+3+6)}{126} - \frac{[(.25\times32)+(.25\times81)+(.25\times5)+(.25\times8)]}{[(.25\times32)+(.25\times81)+(.25\times5)+(.25\times8)]}$$

REFERENCES

Abney, Glenn, and Lauth, Thomas P. (1989). The executive budget in the states: Normative idea and empirical observation. *Policy Studies Journal. 17*:829–840.

Barber, James D. (1966). *Power in Committees*. Rand McNally and Company, Chicago, Illinois.

Bibb, Robert, and Roncek, Dennis W. (1976). Investigating group differences: An explanation of the sociological potential of discriminant analysis. *Sociological Methods and Research. 4*:349–379.

Botner, Stanley B. (1987). Utilization and impact of microcomputers in state central budget offices. *Public Budgeting and Finance. 7*:99–108.

Botner, Stanley B. (1985). The use of budgeting/management tools by state governments. *Public Administration Review. 45*:616–620.

Bretschneider, Stuart, Straussman, Jeffrey J., and Mullins, Daniel (1988). Do revenue forecasts influence budget setting? A small group experiment. *Policy Sciences. 21*:305–325.

Cameron, C.C. (1988). Memorandum: Instructions for preparation of the 1989–1991 recommended state budget, from the Executive Assistant to the Governor for Budgeting and Management, Office of State Budget and Management, Raleigh, North Carolina, March 30: Introduction and Page 1 of General Instructions.

Carnevale, John T. (1988). Recent trends in the finances of the state and local sector. *Public Budgeting and Finance. 8*:33–48.

City and State (1989). The 50 states: Fourth annual state financial report, April 24–May 7.

Clynch, Edward J. (1988). Budgeting in Mississippi: Does the Governor really count? Paper presented at the Annual Southeastern Conference for the American Society of Public Administration, October 12–14, Birmingham, Alabama.

Clynch, Edward J., and Lauth, Thomas P., eds. (1990). *Governors, Legislatures, and Budgets*. Greenwood Press, Westport, Connecticut.

Colby, Mary. (1988). States reporting stable finances. *City and State*, April 11:13-41.

Cope, Glen Hahn. (1987). Local government budgeting and productivity: Friends or foes? *Public Productivity Review*. 41:45-57.

Crecine, John P. (1967). A computer simulation model of municipal budgeting. *Management Science*. 13:786-815.

Duncombe, Sydney, Duncombe, William, and Kinney, Richard. (1989). New directions in budget theory since Key. *New Directions in Public Administration Research*. 2:41-58.

Golembiewski, Robert T., and Rabin, J., eds. (1983). *Public Budgeting and Finance: Behavioral, Theoretical, and Technical Perspectives*, 3rd ed, Marcel Dekker, Inc., New York, New York.

Grizzle, Gloria A. (1987). Linking performance to funding decisions: What is the budgeter's role? *Public Productivity Review*. 41:33-44.

Hackbart, Merlin M. (1988). Discussant on panel entitled, Budgeting in the Southern States, at the Annual Southeastern Conference of the American Society of Public Adminstration, Thursday, October 13, Birmingham, Alabama.

Hackbart, Merlin M., and Leigland, James. (1990). State debt management policy: A national survey. *Public Budgeting and Finance*. 10:37-54.

Hammond, Kenneth R., Hamm, Robert M., Grassia, Janet, and Pearson, Tamra. (1987). Direct comparison of the efficacy of intuitive and analytical cognition in expert judgment. *IEEE Transactions on Systems, Man, and Cybernetics*. 17:753-770.

Kachigan, Sam Kash (1986). *Statistical Analysis*, Radius Press, New York, New York.

Klecka, William R. (1980). *Discriminant Analysis*, Sage Publications, Beverly Hills, California.

Lachenbruch, Peter, Sneeringer, Cheryl, and Revo, Lawrence T. (1973). Robustness of the linear and quadratic discriminant function to certain types of non- normality. *Communications in Statistics*. 1:39-56.

Lee, Robert D., Jr. (1981). Centralization/decentralization in state government budgeting. *Public Budgeting and Finance*. 1:76-79.

Legge, Jerome S., and Ziegler, Herbert F. (1979). Utilizing discriminant analysis in social research: An explanation and illustration. *Journal of Public Data Use*. 7:27-35.

Leigland, James. (1988). State government finances. In *The Book of the States*, The Council of State Governments, 27:222-224.

McCaffery, Jerry, and Baker, Keith G. (1990). Optimizing choice in resource decisions: Staying within the boundary of the comprehensive-rational method. *Public Administration Quarterly*. 14:142-172.

Melton, R.S. (1963). Some remarks on the failure to meet assumptions in discriminant analysis. *Psychometrika*. 28:49-53.

Meltsner, Arnold J., and Wildavsky, Aaron. (1970). Leave city budgeting alone: A survey, case study and recommendations for reform. In *Financing the Metropolis— Public Policy in Urban Economics*, by John Crecine, ed., Sage Publishing, Beverly Hills, California, 311-355.

Poister, Theodore H., and McGowan, Robert P. (1984). The use of management tools in municipal government: A national survey. *Public Administration Review.* 43:215–223.

Poister, Theodore H., and Streib, Gregory. (1989). Management tools in municipal government: Trends over the past decade. *Public Administration Review.* 49:240–248.

Stedry, A.D. (1960). *Budget Control and Cost Behavior.* Prentice-Hall, Inc. Englewood Cliffs, New Jersey.

Stewart, Thomas R. (1988). Judgment analysis: Procedures. In *Human Judgment: The Social Judgment Theory View*, by Berndt Brehmer and C.R.B. Joyce, eds., Elsevier Science Publishers B.V., North-Holland, pp. 41–74.

Stewart, Thomas R., and Gelberd, Linda. (1976). Analysis of judgment policy: A new approach for citizen participation in planning. *American Institute of Planners Journal.* 42:33–41.

Straussman, Jeffrey D. (1979). A typology of budgetary environments. *Administration and Society.* 11:216–226.

Survey of Current Business (1989). 69:December, 16–17.

Whicker, Marcia Lynn (1986). Legislative budgeting in South Carolina. *State and Local Government Review.* 18:65–70.

Willoughby, Katherine G. (1992). Decision making orientations of state government budget analysts: Rationalists or incrementalists? *Public Budgeting and Financial Management.* 3:forthcoming.

Willoughby, Katherine G. (1992). Decision making orientations of state government budget analysts: Rational or intuitive thinkers? DPA dissertation, University of Georgia, Athens.

6

Local Government Revenue Diversification: A Portfolio Analysis and Evaluation

Clifford P. McCue

Florida International University, Miami, Florida

I. INTRODUCTION

Generating enough money to provide, maintain, and expand essential services is a challenge to all local governments throughout the nation. In the aftermath of the elimination of federal revenue sharing, a historical overreliance on inelastic revenue sources, increasing debt burdens, and various property tax limitation movements which have either been enacted into law, or are currently being proposed, local governments are facing severe difficulty in raising sufficient resources. Given these constraints, a diversified revenue portfolio is needed for continued provision of vital public services. The options available to local governments can be generally classified as: developing new revenue sources, broadening existing sources through rate increases, or reducing service levels (Advisory Commission on Intergovernmental Relations, 1989). The methods and techniques currently in practice tend towards greater use of nonproperty taxes, and in a selective few municipalities development of creative techniques for generating additional revenue (Governmental Accounting Office, 1988). The purpose of this chapter is to provide a descriptive look at the practice of revenue diversification in local government fiscal administration.

II. TRENDS IN REVENUE DIVERSIFICATION

Between 1957 and 1987 reliance on revenues other than the traditional property tax witnessed rapid increases. For example, the property tax, as a source of locally generated revenue, declined from 69 percent in 1957 to 47 percent in 1987. Charges for services and miscellaneous revenues rose from 20 percent to 36 percent, intergovernmental revenues increased from 30 percent to 37 percent, and dependency on income taxes increased from 1 percent to 6 percent. Local sales and gross receipt taxes also increased slightly: from 6 percent in 1957 to 10 percent in 1987, while dependency on licenses and permits declined from 4 percent to 3 percent. Although the percentage change in local government portfolios identified above represent current dollars rather than constant dollars, the relative diversification in the composition of local revenues is still apparent. The techniques used by local governments to decrease their dependency on property taxes is discussed below.

A. The Sales Tax

Local governments seeking alternative revenue sources to decrease dependency on property taxes have increasingly turned to the sales tax. One of the primary reasons for this development is citizen tax preferences (Schroeder and Sjoquist, 1975). In 1971, an urban observatory study polled citizens attitudes to alternative revenue sources and concluded that the sales tax was preferred by a wide margin over increasing property taxes, individual and corporate income taxes, utility taxes, or taxes on automobile owners.

Surveys of citizen's attitudes toward government and taxes conducted by the Advisory Commission on Intergovernmental Relations (ACIR) during the 1980s found similar results. In 1987, respondents were asked: If their local

Table 6.1   Composition of Local Government Revenues, 1957 and 1987 (Millions)

	1957	1987	Percentage own-source 1957	Percentage own-source 1987
TOTAL GENERAL REVENUE	$25,531	$433,977	100%	100%
Total own-source	17,866	271,263	70	63
Taxes:				
Property tax	12,385	127,191	69	47
Sales & gross receipts tax	1,031	26,122	6	10
Income tax	191	10,272	1	4
Licenses and other tax	679	8,010	4	3
Current charges and miscellaneous	3,580	99,668	20	36
Intergovernmental	7,664	162,713	30	37

Source: U.S. Department of Commerce, Bureau of the Census, *Government Finances in [year]*, Table 19.

government decided to raise a small amount of additional revenue to help meet costs and improve services, which type of tax would citizens prefer? Twenty percent of survey respondents preferred the local sales tax, and 33 percent preferred increasing user charges. The property tax as an alternative revenue source received only a 9 percent approval rating and was the least favored means of generating additional revenue among all alternatives presented.

As a fiscal entity of the state, most local governments must receive explicit or implicit approval from the state legislature to impose a sales tax, and local referenda are typically required. Authority to levy sales tax on the local level can take various forms, such as home rule charter authority, specific provisions from the state legislature, or powers implied through statutory regulations granting authority to use this form of taxation. In 1987, some 6,800 local governments nationally used the sales tax as part of their revenue portfolios.

National totals, however, disguise major differences between local governments reliance on the sales tax. In 1987, only 29 states granted their local governments the ability to levy some form of sales tax. Generally, local governments are granted authority to levy either a sales tax or an income tax as a local revenue option (only five states allow both: Alabama, Iowa, Missouri, New York, and Ohio). Of the 29 states which permit local sales taxes, Illinois has the largest number of taxing authorities using this source (1,375), followed by Texas (1,029), Missouri (657), Oklahoma (473), and California (445). The five states cited above account for roughly 58 percent of all taxing jurisdictions using this source and 34 percent of total sales tax revenue collected.

In addition to an increasing reliance on sales taxes among specific states, the most prominent trend in local taxation is the use of selective sales taxes (Rodgers, 1987). This form of taxation imposes an additional levy on the sale of certain commodities or services of particular industries separately and apart from the application of the general sales and gross receipts taxes. The most common forms of selective sales taxes are the tourist development tax, the gas tax, the transit tax, the documentary tax, and the indigent health care tax (U.S. Census Bureau, 1987).

B. The Income Tax

In 1987, there were a total of 16 states with 3,550 local governments levying some form of income tax. Of the 16 states allowing local governments to use this instrument, roughly 80 percent of total revenue came from 4 states (Maryland, New York, Pennsylvania, and Ohio). Additionally, the State of New York accounts for 26 percent of aggregate revenues collected from local income taxes nationwide, while Pennsylvania accounts for 21 percent. Further-

Table 6.2   Number and Percentage of Local Jurisdictions Using Sales Tax, 1987, by State and Type of Jurisdiction

State	Cities and townships Number	Percent	Counties Number	Percent	Special districts Number	Percent	Local governments Number	Percent
U.S. Total	5,488	15%	1,243	41%	158	<1%	6,889	8%
Alabama	326	75	56	84	0	0	382	36
Alaska	87	58	6	67	0	0	93	54
Arizona	75	93	2	13	0	0	77	13
Arkansas	76	16	35	47	0	0	111	8
California	380	86	58	100	7	<1	445	10
Colorado	193	73	31	50	1	<1	225	14
Georgia	0	0	143	91	1	<1	144	11
Illinois	1,271	47	102	100	2	0	1,375	21
Iowa	23	2	0	0	0	0	23	1
Kansas	108	5	60	57	0	0	168	4
Louisiana	192	64	63	100	70	78	325	72
Minnesota	3	<1	0	0	0	0	3	<1
Missouri	474	38	114	100	69	4	657	21
Nebraska	22	2	0	0	0	0	22	1
Nevada	0	0	7	44	0	0	7	4
New Mexico	100	100	28	85	0	0	128	39
New York	26	2	58	100	0	0	84	3
North Carolina	0	0	100	100	0	0	100	11
North Dakato	3	<1	0	0	0	0	3	<1
Ohio	0	0	79	90	2	<1	81	2
Oklahoma	457	77	16	21	0	0	473	26
South Dakota	111	9	0	0	0	0	111	6
Tennessee	10	3	95	100	0	0	105	12
Texas	1,023	88	0	0	6	<1	1,029	23
Utah	219	97	29	100	0	0	248	47
Virginia	41	18	95	100	0	0	136	32
Washington	268	100	39	100	0	0	307	17
Wisconsin	0	0	12	17	00	0	12	<1
Wyoming	0	0	15	65	0	0	15	4

Source: ACIR, *Local Revenue Diversification: Local Sales Tax,* September 1989, Table 2.

more, New York is the only state which allows a municipality, the City of New York, to levy both an individual and corporate income tax.

Basically, there are three categories in which income taxes can be classified on a local level: 1) wage or payroll tax systems, 2) piggyback tax systems, and 3) the locally designed tax systems (Deran, 1968). The most common form, without question, is the wage or payroll tax system (sometimes referred to as the earned income tax). The local payroll tax is typically levied at a flat rate, and is calculated based on the total dollar value of all payrolls for businesses residing within the jurisdiction's boundaries.

Different from federal and state income tax structures, the payroll tax on the local level normally has no deductions, exemptions, nor does it require the filing of separate tax returns. Since it is collected by payroll withholdings it is considered a tax on salaries and wages rather than on total income. Administration of the tax is typically provided by the locality levying the tax, and therefore, the costs of administration and enforcement are borne entirely by the local government.

The second most common form of local government income tax is the piggyback tax. From the first adoption of a local income tax in Philadelphia (1939) until 1962, all local income taxes imposed were payroll taxes (Choi, 1986). In 1962 the first piggybacked local income tax was adopted in Detroit, Michigan.

Currently the piggybacked income tax is used in Indiana, Iowa, Maryland, and in the cities of Detroit, Michigan, and Yonkers, New York. Typically, this form of tax is levied against either state or federal income taxes filed, hence the name piggyback. Some local income taxes are collected by the local government itself; however, most of the more recently adopted taxes are collected on the state level. The major impetus behind this movement is to realize economies of scale and to provide uniformity between jurisdictions using this form of taxation (ACIR, 1989). As a result, states handle the administration and collection of income taxes for local governments and return the amount generated back to the locality levying the tax, minus a minor administration charge.

The final type of local income tax is that employed in New York City. This tax is extremely similar in structure to the New York State personal income tax, using the same standard deductions and exemptions, but applies differing rates. Therefore, it is not piggybacked on New York state taxes, but is treated differently. In fact, prior to 1976, New York City residents had to file two state income tax returns. The income tax rate imposed in New York City is considered one of a few progressive tax structures in the country because the tax rates have ranged from 1.5 percent to 3.5 percent of income for residents, and a single flat rate of 0.45 percent for nonresidents.

In fiscal year 1987, local income taxes generated $9.7 billion in revenues (see Table 6.3). However, the aggregate national figures disguise the relative importance of local income taxes because of the limited number of local governments using this form of taxation. In the three states where the local income tax is most widely used, Ohio, Pennsylvania, and Maryland, it is a sizeable portion of locally generated revenues. Furthermore, in some cities it is the most significant form of locally generated revenues. Cleveland, Ohio, for example, derives more than half of its locally generated own-source reve-

Table 6.3   Local Income Taxes, Selected Years, 1957–1987

Year	Income taxes (millions)	Percentage of total revenue
1957	$ 191	0.0%
1967	916	0.9
1977	3,754	1.5
1982	6,105	1.5
1987	9,663	1.7

Source: ACIR, *Significant Features of Fiscal Federalism,* August 1990, Tables 60 and 61.

nue from this tax, while in Philadelphia, the local income tax accounted for 49.2 percent of local revenues.

C.   User Charges

The point is made that the purpose of user charges is to apportion what is available in limited supply or to regulate certain products and services, thus influencing the way people utilize these resources (Bell and Levitan, 1990). The ultimate goal of user charges, it is asserted, is to limit consumption (Gitajn, 1984). Local governments currently use two types of user charges: consumption based user charges and regulatory based user charges.

Consumption based user charges such as sewerage, hospitals, airports, water transportation, sanitation, parking facilities, and water supply typically are levied against the amount consumed by individuals or groups of individuals. Benefits from consumption based services can be directly inferred (so many tons of sewage produced) and costs of producing these services are definable and measurable. Therefore, in theory at least, charges are based on the economic costs of production and the quantity demanded (Bird, 1976).

Regulatory based user charges in the form of licenses and permits, are directed towards insuring certain levels of quality in production or regulating certain activities, such as those designed to protect consumers (building permits, zoning fees, certificates of occupancy, and construction plan approval fees). Others attempt to enforce professional standards by excluding unqualified individuals from the right to participate in certain activities, such as professional licenses for auto mechanics, beauticians, and medical doctors. And others attempt to regulate the quantity of services provided (they restrict the number of participants who may engage in the activity) like taxicabs, and privately owned and operated school bus systems.

Regulatory user charges are typically much harder to cost than consumption charges (Kelly, 1984). There may be direct benefits received, like certificates of occupancy which insure that the construction of habitats meet certain prescribed building standards, but determining monetary values for these benefits is difficult. Regulatory levies are normally located in a local government's general fund operations where rates are determined more on custom then equilibrium pricing (Arthur Young and Company, 1987).

Distinguishing between charges based on consumption and those based on regulation is important because the trend in local governments is toward consumption based user charges (ACIR, 1987).

D. The Property Tax

Although the relative dependency on property tax, as a percentage of total local revenues, has declined over the last 30 years, it still plays a major role in the composition of local revenues (Kramer, 1982). Furthermore, aggregating property taxes without considering how various forms of local government depend on this source mask many important facts. In 1987, county governments generated 74 percent of their total revenue from property taxes, municipalities 49 percent, townships 92 percent, school districts 98 percent, and special districts 72 percent. As Table 6.4 shows, from 1957 to 1987 county, municipal, and special districts showed the largest decline in property taxes as a portion of own source revenues (decreasing from 20 percent, 24 percent, and 29 percent, respectively), while townships, and school districts remained relatively reliant on this form of revenue (a decrease of around 6 percent for townships and a 1 percent decrease for school districts).

Another major trend in property taxes as a source of local revenues is the differences in regional reliance on property taxes. As Table 6.5 denotes, New England states are far more dependent on this form of revenue than other regions (98 percent of total local tax revenues were collected from property

Table 6.4 Property Taxes, Percentage Distribution by Type of Government, Selected Years, 1957–1987

Years	Total (millions)	County	Municipal	Township	School District	Special District
1957	$ 14,286	93.7%	72.7%	98.6%	98.6%	100.0%
1967	29,074	92.1	70.0	92.8	98.4	100.0
1977	74,852	81.2	60.0	91.7	97.5	91.2
1979	80,606	77.1	55.8	90.7	96.7	89.6
1981	94,776	76.4	53.6	93.7	96.1	80.4
1983	113,145	77.8	51.5	94.0	96.9	74.0
1985	134,473	75.1	49.2	93.2	97.3	74.0
1987	158,216	73.5	49.1	92.3	97.5	72.4

Source: Advisory Commision on Intergovernmental Relations (ACIR), *Significant Features of Fiscal Federalism*, 1990 Edition, Volume II, August 1990, Table 62.

Table 6.5   Local Property Taxes as a Percentage of Total Local Tax Revenues, Selected Years, 1957–1987

Region	1987	1985	1984	1981	1977	1972	1967	1957
United States	73.7%	74.2%	75.0%	76.6%	80.6%	83.7%	86.6%	86.7%
New England	97.9	98.4	98.6	99.1	98.9	98.6	98.6	97.6
Mideast	63.9	64.9	65.8	68.8	75.0	77.1	84.1	84.9
Great Lakes	80.9	82.6	83.1	82.9	89.4	91.4	93.8	93.6
Plains	83.3	83.6	84.4	85.5	91.0	93.1	94.5	93.3
Southeast	68.8	68.8	70.4	70.7	75.1	78.0	81.0	82.7
Southwest	79.6	78.5	78.7	79.7	79.6	84.0	86.2	88.6
Rocky Mountain	77.4	76.2	76.6	78.1	88.5	92.0	93.3	93.9
Far West	70.3	69.4	70.1	71.0	78.6	84.0	87.8	85.5

Source: ACIR, *Significant Features of Fiscal Federalism,* Volume 2, Table 84.

taxes in 1987), while Southeastern states had the least reliance on property taxes as a contributing source of local revenues (69 percent in 1987).

Current techniques employed by local governments to intensify revenue yields from property taxes can be classified as: 1) decreasing the differential between assessed value and true market value, 2) employing mid-year reassessments, and perhaps the most noteworthy, 3) creating special taxing districts to finance certain "off-budget" activities of government (Porter, 1987).

One approach for dealing with the growing discomfort of property taxes, and an effective means of generating additional revenue, is to decrease the differential between assessed value and true market value (Fisher, 1989). This change has been aided by the advent of micro computers, as well as the development of digital geographical programs which let users automatically adjust land values when properties are sold. However, since many local governments have become more sophisticated in assessing property the possibility of this method to sustain revenue increases in the future is questionable. Therefore this method is considered a one-time revenue adjustment which may or may not provide continued yield for periods greater then three years.

That is, since property assessments must eventually reach an asymptotic point, where assessed value truly equals market value, revenue diversification is limited. Fundamental to this concern is that revenues derived are still predicated on property assessments regardless of market value. Reducing the differential between assessed value and market value should be viewed as a "good government" move which may actually foster hostility in jurisdictions which had assessment values well below market value due to the rapid increase in property taxes paid. As a potential successful source of revenue diversification, this form is extremely limited and is better classified as a short-term revenue diversification technique.

Again, current practices have considered the use of mid-year reassessments as an effective means of generating additional revenue. Rather then assessing property on a yearly basis, many localities are moving towards mid-year assessments. The intent behind this movement is to lessen the effects of paying property taxes in one lump sum, as well as creating opportunities to increase yield (ACIR, 1989). But, again, this form of additional revenue is extremely limited as a continued source of revenue diversification. The use of mid-year assessments can also be considered a one-time revenue adjustment, as well as a means of fine tuning property taxes, but not as a method of diversifying revenues over the long run.

The most significant and effective technique for diversifying local property taxes has been the increased utilization and creation of special districts. Fundamentally, there are two categories of special districts: independent and dependent. Independent special districts are defined according to the U.S. Census Bureau (1988) as "All organized local entities (other than counties, municipalities, townships, or school districts) authorized by State law to provide only one or a limited number of designated functions, and with sufficient administrative and fiscal autonomy to qualify as separate governments; known by a variety of titles, including districts, authorities, boards, and commissions" (p. XII). Dependent special districts are defined as creations of the local authority through which financial and administrative decisions are primarily controlled through the local legislative process (Falconer, 1989).

As a group, special districts are by far the most rapidly increasing form of government. This increase reflects the demand for the provision of specialized services either not offered by a governmental unit, or if offered is not performed to a satisfactory level (MacManus, 1982). Since most special districts perform only one function, or a limited amount of functions, their creation furnishes local governments with viable alternatives to increasing tax yields on existing sources. California, for instance, with the passage of Proposition 13, still found special taxing districts an important vehicle for generating additional property tax revenue. In 1978 there were roughly 2,227 special districts in California. By 1987 this number had risen to 2,774, an increase of 547 special districts in less then ten years. Although Proposition 13 effectively addressed the issue of restricting the amount of overlapping debt which could be imposed, local governments in California still found special districts an attractive means for diversifying their revenue portfolios (Barber, 1984).

Areas served by special districts show that about three-fourths of all districts serve an area within the same boundaries as those of some other local government (county, city, or township). Although a large majority of all special districts are located within the confines of a county government, about 9

Table 6.6 Growth in Special Taxing Districts, Selected Years, 1957–1987
(Millions)

Years	Total units	Total tax	Property taxes	General and selective sales and gross receipts	Other taxes
1957	14,424	$ 283	$ 283	$ —	$ —
1967	21,264	589	589	—	—
1977	25,962	1,743	1,590	133	20
1982	28,078	2,774	2,189	539	46
1987	29,427	5,687	4,116	1,366	205

Source: Computation based on U.S. Department of Commerce, Bureau of the Census, *Government Finances in [year]*, Table 57.

percent (or 263 districts) have jurisdictions which extend into two or more county areas.

As Table 6.6 demonstrates, the growth in special districts has increased dramatically over the last 30 years. In 1957 there were 14,424 special taxing districts; in 1987 there were 29,427. Furthermore, over 90 percent of the special taxing districts serve single purpose functions (natural resources, public safety, transportation, social services, and utilities). The largest number of these functions are in the natural resource category which includes flood control, drainage, irrigation, and soil and water conservation districts (in 1987 there were 6,321 such districts). The next most common form of special taxing district is fire protection (5,063).

The states experiencing the greatest increase in the number of special districts between 1977 and 1982 were Oklahoma (510), California (279), and Texas (256). Even though multiple function special districts constitute a small portion of all special districts (less than 10 percent), the housing and community development districts which have multiple functions experienced the largest increase between 1977 and 1982. Not only have the quantity of special taxing districts increased over this period, the value and types of funding activities have changed. Special districts generated $283 million in revenues in 1957, rising to $5.7 billion in 1987. Furthermore, in 1957, 100 percent of revenues were derived from property taxes, while in 1987, 72 percent was collected from ad valorem taxes (24 percent was from sales and gross receipts and 4 percent was generated from other taxes, such as special assessments, debt, and user charges).

E. Other Revenues

Through a grant from the California Intergovernmental Personnel Act, the Center for Public Policy and Administration and California State University, under the direction of Daniel Barber, examined 105 local governments in Los Angeles and Orange counties to determine which strategies in revenue diversification were most frequently used (1981). The study intended to examine the effects of Proposition 13 on the composition of local government revenues in California. Conclusions drawn from the study were that local governments have diversified their portfolios by developing various revenue alternatives coupled with employing expenditure reducing activities to provide a balanced budget. The findings of the study can be classified into five general categories:

Joint venturing and resource development
Private philanthropy
Traditional volunteering
Management consolidation or retrenchment, and
Contracting out service delivery.

In addition to the categories defined by the Center for Public Policy and Administration, there are other techniques used in local government revenue diversification worth noting. These can be added to the previous list as:

Debt issuance and management
Utilizing reserves and fund balances, and
Other alternatives.

The list provided is not intended to be an exhaustive categorization of all alternatives used on the local level to raise additional revenues, but it does provide an accurate assessment of the major trends experienced in the quest to diversify portfolios. The options cited can be classified into two types: 1) one-time revenue enhancers, and 2) expenditure reduction activities. The one-time revenue enhancers are private philanthropy, debt issuance and management, and the utilization of unencumbered fund balances. The expenditure reducing activities of local governments, such as joint venturing and resource development, voluntarism, management consolidation, and contracting out for service delivery will not be discussed since their primary purpose is to reduce expenditures.

1. *Issuance and Management of Debt*
One of the most prominent revenue diversification techniques used by local governments over the last 30 years has been the issuance and management of debt. From the period 1957 to 1987 debt outstanding at the end of the fiscal year for all local governments escalated from $39,301 million to $461,580 million, representing a 1,075 percent increase (see Table 6.7). Of the debt outstanding at the end of fiscal year 1987, 97 percent was for long-term debt and 3 percent was for short-term debt. Additionally, of the long-term debt, 30 percent was secured by the full faith and credit of the governing body, and 70

Table 6.7   Local Government Indebtness and Debt Transactions, 1987 (Millions)

Function	Total	County	Municipal	Township	School District	Special District
Debt outstanding	$461,580	$99,749	$ 181,634	$ 7,926	$35,248	$137,023
Long-term	447,273	97,460	177,070	6,790	33,527	132,427
Full faith and credit	134,819	27,162	56,574	4,753	33,399	12,931
Nonguaranteed	312,455	70,298	120,496	2,037	128	119,496
Short-term	14,307	2,289	4,564	1,137	1,722	4,596
Long-term debt by purpose						
Education	43,781	3,346	3,969	539	33,527	2,400
Utilities	108,618	4,039	40,735	653	-	63,190
Other	294,875	90,075	132,365	5,598	-	66,837
Long-term debt issued	84,132	18,344	35,910	1,254	6,016	22,609
Long-term debt retired	49,778	9,979	20,785	659	4,308	14,675
Exhibit:						
Long-term debt outstanding	374,997	74,814	144,743	6,739	30,949	117,752
Offsets to long-term debt	72,267	22,646	32,327	51	2,578	14,675

Source: U.S. Department of Cmmmerce, Bureau of the Census, *Goverment Finances*, Volume 4, 1987, Table 13.

percent was nonguaranteed. The dramatic increase in the use of nonguaranteed debt is a prominent trend in local government utilization of one-time revenue enhancers.

An additional trend in the issuance and management of debt is the one-time revenue enhancer of refinancing outstanding debt. This generally occurs when debt which was previously issued at a higher interest rate is refinanced at a current lower rate. When the difference between the two rates is substantial enough to cover the costs of reissuance, and to maintain the life cycle of the instrument, then many local governments turn to this source as an additional revenue. However, there are many new legislative activities aimed at addressing the ability of local governments to issue and refinance debt.

2.   *Fund Balances and Encumbrances*

Another major trend in local government revenue enhancement is the use of fund balances to maintain current service levels. During the 1960s and 1970s local governments were able to secure sizeable unencumbered fund balances (the rainy day account) as a result of strong economic conditions, large increases in intergovernmental funding, and limited service demands. With these reserves local governments were able to leverage debt at low rates, invest idle cash in longer term instruments to increase yields, and provide for one-time expenditures such as equipment purchases and capital improvements. In many jurisdictions these same fund balances are currently at an all-time low. Many local governments have been forced to use these reserves to meet increasing service demands. Lack of sensitivity on behalf of policymakers towards the need for additional revenues in the form of higher tax rates or alternative funding mechanisms have depleted many local governments reserves.

3. *Private Donations*

Once it was unthinkable for any local government to solicit private donations for special projects that could otherwise be financed with public funding. However, in the last 10 to 15 years local government policymakers have realized that private sources could and would support public projects; the unthinkable is now thinkable (Paul, 1988). The first major solicitation of private funds came from state universities, through alumni associations, foundations, and other private sources. Public libraries soon followed suit, by initiating campaigns aimed at raising funds for books, equipment, and capital improvements. However, it was not until the late 1970s that local governments began to pursue private funds for other public projects (Taft, 1986).

J. Richard Taft (1986) states that charitable donations is an $80 billion a year industry. Of that figure, "approximately $10 billion come from corporations and foundations while roughly $70 billion come from individuals. The bulk of individual giving comes in small gifts. But significant billions also come from large, major gifts from individuals, and from wills and bequests" (p. 18).

III. SUMMARY AND DISCUSSION

In general local governments have become less reliant on property taxes as a percentage of own source revenues. What has become apparent from this analysis is that local governments are increasingly turning to the use of special districts as a method for financing certain governmental goods and services. This conclusion is supported when revenues received from general property taxes and ad valorem taxes derived from special districts are added together local governments can be said to have maintained or marginally reduced their relative reliance on property taxes. When 1987 revenues derived from general property taxes and those generated from special districts are combined they account for roughly 59 percent of locally generated revenues. This represents a decrease, as a percentage of own source revenues, from 1957 to 1987 of 10 percent rather than the suggested 22 percent.

Perhaps the most significant trend in local government revenue diversification is experienced in the area of sales tax. This is by far the most rapidly increasing area of local government finances. Not only has the number of jurisdictions using the sales tax increased, revenues as a percentage of own source has increased dramatically. In addition, another trend in sales taxation is the utilization of selective sales and gross receipts tax, normally on items such as tourism, gas consumption, transit, and hospitals. However, as more and more local governments turn to selective sales taxes, caution must be taken in order to avoid the negative effects of tax pyramiding. Tax pyramiding occurs when the cost of an intermediate good or service is taxed when sold, and when the final product, the intermediate input, is used to produce is also taxed. Since the cost of the intermediate input is embodied in the cost of the final product, the intermediate input is effectively taxed twice. This process of taxing intermediate goods and services can occur many times over in intricate chains of economic links.

User charges have also experienced a rather sharp increase as a locally generated revenue source over the past 30 years. It is important to remember, however, that the trend in user charges is towards consumption based activities rather then regulatory based activities. In addition, the relative dependency on income taxes has not received much attention on the local level, but has shown a marginal increase in usage over the last 30 years.

This capsule summary provides some idea as to the magnitude and diversity of revenue options utilized by local governments in America. The process of determining which revenue alternatives to use on the local level involves some very basic, but extremely difficult, choices, both political and economic. Few taxes are strictly neutral, and some tax payers will have to bear an additional burden. Moreover, taxes influence a wide range of individual and organizational behaviors, such as how much to consume, where to invest resources, types of economic growth in a locality, where to locate businesses, whether to purchase a home in a jurisdiction or live in outlying areas, and finally election outcomes. Economists cannot always agree on what the impact or revenue productivity of a particular tax instrument will be. Ultimately, questions of "Who will pay the tax?" and "Who will benefit from the expenditure?" must be decided by elected officials, who want to avoid adverse voter reaction resulting from unpopular and burdensome taxes.

Much work is needed to be accomplished, both on the revenue and expenditure side of local governments. If the composition of tax structures are not projected to change in the near future, then local governments must consider further reductions in the quantity and quality of services provided, or face financial bankruptcy. The bottom line is, local governments are continually facing the fiscal paradox, increasing demands for more and better services coupled with a high propensity to resist tax initiatives on behalf of the voting public. Strong leadership, a willing public, and capable administrators will be needed to solve this dilemma and provide local governments the flexibility they so desperately need as we approach the 21st century.

REFERENCES

Aaron, Henry J. (1975). *Who Pays the Property Tax?* The Brookings Institution, Washington, D.C.

Advisory Commission on Intergovernmental Relations. (1990). *Significant Features of Fiscal Federalism, 1990 Edition.* ACIR, Washington, D.C.

Advisory Commission on Intergovernmental Relations. (1989). *Local Revenue Diversification: Local Sales Taxes.* ACIR, Washington, D.C.

Advisory Commission on Intergovernmental Relations. (1987). *Local Revenue Diversification: User Charges.* ACIR, Washington, D.C.

Advisory Commission on Intergovernmental Relations. (1987). *Changing Attitudes on Government and Taxes 1987.* ACIR, Washington, D.C.

Advisory Commission on Intergovernmental Relations. (1974). Local Revenue Diversification: Income, Sales Taxes and User Charges. ACIR, Washington, D.C.

Barber, Daniel M. (1981). *Alternative Revenue Raising Strategies for Human Service Agencies.* Center for Public Policy and Administration, California State University, California.

Barber, Daniel M. (1984). Alternative revenue raising: A post Proposition 13 retrospective. *National Civic Review.* 73:549–555.

Bell, William J. and Levitan, D. (1990). Money doesn't grow on trees: The search for additional municipal revenues. *Municipal Finance Journal.* 11:205–216.

Bird, Richard M. (1976). *Charging for Public Services: A New Look at an Old Idea.* Canadian Tax Foundation, Toronto.

Choi, Yearn H. (1986) The local income tax as a new revenue? An assessment. *Planning and Administration.* 2:48–52.

Deran, Elizabeth (1968). Tax structure of cities using the income tax. *National Tax Journal.* 21:147–152.

Falconer, Mary Kay (1989). Special districts: The "other" local governments—definition, creation, and dissolution. *Stetson Law Review.* 18:583–613.

Gitajn, Arthur (1984). *Creating and Financing Public Enterprises.* Government Finance Research Center, Washington, D.C.

Kelly, Joseph T. (1984). *Costing Government Services: A Guide for Decision Making.* Government Finance Research Center, Washington, D.C.

Kramer, Bruce M. (1982). The Texas tax relief amendment: Much ado about nothing. In *Tax and Expenditure Limitations: How to Implement and Live Within Them,* Jerome G. Rose (Ed.). Center for Urban Policy Research, New Jersey.

MacManus, Susan A. (1982). Special districts: A common solution to political pressures stemming from city- county fiscal inequalities. *Journal of Urban Affairs.* 4:1–10.

National League of Cities (1971). City taxes and services: Citizens speak out. *Nation's Cities.* 12:4–10.

Paul, Amy Cohen (1988). Private funds: Public projects. *Baseline Data Report.* 20:234–246.

Porter, Douglas R. (1987). Financing infrastructure with special districts. *Urban Land.* 46:9–13.

Rodgers, James D. (1987). Sales taxes, income taxes, and other nonproperty revenues.

In *Management Policies in Local Government Finances,* J. Richard Aronson and
Eli Schwartz (Eds.), 3rd Edition. International City Managers Association, Washington, D.C.

Schroeder, Larry D. and Sjoquist, David L. (1975). The *Property Tax and Alternative
Local Taxes: An Economic Analysis.* Praeger Publishers, New York.

Taft, Richard J. (1986). *Private Dollars for Public Projects: Exploding the Myths.* The
Taft Group, Washington, D.C.

U.S. Department of Commerce, Bureau of the Census. (1988). Local Government
Finances. 1987. Census Bureau, Washington, D.C.

U.S. Department of Commerce, Bureau of the Census. (1988). *Government Finances in
1986–1987, Finances of Special Districts.* Census Bureau, Washington, D.C.

U.S. General Accounting Office. (1988). *Revenue Options.* GAO, Washington, D.C.

Arthur Young and Company (1987). *User Charges: Towards Better Usage.* Arthur
Young and Company, Washington, D.C.

7
Use of Revenue Forecasting Techniques

John P. Forrester

University of Missouri—Columbia, Columbia, Missouri

I. INTRODUCTION

Budget preparation, still the black hole of budget theory, may at last be coming to the forefront of municipal budget practice. The impetus for this appears rooted in both economic and political developments. A ten-year legacy of fend for yourself federalism and federal efforts (rhetoric or not) to decrease the national deficit have pressured local governments to expand their services, while pervasive operating deficits and oscillating citizen concerns over taxation have sensitized governments to restrained revenue growth. Possible solutions may also be rooted in economics and politics. One option is budgetary forecasting. This process is promising since the forecast model can incorporate key economic assumptions while simultaneously reflecting, and responding to, political realities.

Reforming budget preparation in ways that reflect economic values, however, has historically been plagued with failure. Wildavsky (1979) argued that budget reforms were too concerned with economic values and technical rationality, and Schick (1971:44–85) saw performance measures as unreliable and irrelevant to most budgetary decision making. And relying on traditional reforms (PPBS, ZBB, . . .), or otherwise turning over budgetary problems to technicians, may have provided good technical solutions but they also yielded undesirable organizational solutions (see Gurwitt, 1989). Current research, however, shows that local governments are trying to reconcile the demands of a complex political budgetary environment by constructing alternatives that also reflect economic values and technological growth.

This chapter will explore the state of the art of revenue forecasting as used by municipal governments. Specifically, the chapter will focus on answering two related questions. First, is forecasting a tool governments can use to manage and plan their revenue needs, or is it, as others have suggested, beyond the cognitive limits of man and machinery, too demanding, thereby rendering it useless to budget preparation? Second, can revenue forecasting be grounded in the political, economic, and organizational history of a government and its city, or must it be ignorant of the past and thus irrelevant to budgeting? These two questions will be addressed by exploring conditions of effective forecasting and the degree to which budget officers believe forecasting affects budgetary decision-making.

Data for this discussion of municipal revenue forecasting is based on findings from a mail survey sent to budget directors of municipal governments having a city population of 50,000 or more. Such a broad target population is diverse enough to indicate the extent to which revenue forecasting is used by many municipalities. There were 180 respondents, constituting a response rate of about 38 percent. The survey was conducted in May 1989.

II.   CONDITIONS FOR EFFECTIVE REVENUE FORECASTING

Contrary to incrementalists, budget reformers suggest that man can improve the budgetary process by using technology, such as forecasting, to supplement his cognitive limitations. Forecasting can incorporate many techniques of varying sophistication (see Makridakis and Wheelwright 1982:6) depending upon the capabilities and needs of the users. Consequently, the number and variety of techniques cities can use to estimate revenues is quite vast. A municipality can rely on estimates provided by the state and federal governments and economic think tanks, as might be done in forecasting state aid and sales tax revenue. It might instead rely on forecasting done internally in conjunction with estimates provided by others. Or it could simply use in-house forecasting procedures and estimates.

For this study we will classify forecasting techniques into four broad categories, becoming progressively more sophisticated and demanding, although not necessarily more appropriate:

Expert forecasting—a means of predicting a revenue by a person who is very familiar with the particular source of revenue. For example, the police chief who relies on his/her experience to estimate the Police Department's parking ticket revenues for the next fiscal year.

Trend forecasting—a way of predicting a revenue based on prior changes in that revenue. For instance, in Figure 7.1, sales tax revenue for FY1988 could be a linear extrapolation of the sales tax trend since 1979.

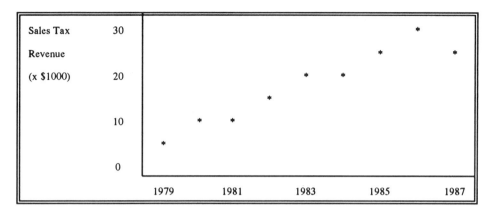

Figure 7.1   An example of trend forecasting.

Deterministic forecasting—future revenues are estimated based upon a percentage change in social, economic or other variables that directly affect the revenue. If a city receives $50 each time it processes a particular application, then total application revenues will be $50 times the number of applications.

Econometrics—relies on statistically estimated coefficients of one or more economic predictor variables. For instance, sales tax revenue for an area might be $9.1 + (0.1 \times$ personal income$) + (1.6 \times$ Consumer Price Index$) + \epsilon$, where ϵ is an error term.

If revenue forecasting models are to be valuable to a local government, they need to reflect significant and relevant economic, political, and budgetary conditions. At first glance, the criteria would suggest that an appropriate model would be complex. However, complex models may not be the best (Henderson, 1978). More specifically, recent research suggests that results from complex models are not necessarily more accurate than results from simpler models (see Frank, 1988). For instance, future tax revenues might be best estimated by deterministic methods (with predictors including income, population, prices, and local building activity); non-tax revenues could be estimated by a variety of techniques: user fees would be estimated by econometric techniques; debt and capital purchases would be estimated by experts; and intergovernmental revenue (IGR) should be assumed constant (see Schroeder, 1981). As another example, Downs and Rocke (1983) found little advantage to using multivariate ARMA (autoregressive moving average) models as opposed to other models (naive, univariate, MA(1)) to predict property tax revenues; a little improvement was found regarding other revenues. However, others have found complex models to be more robust. According to

Lorek (1982), financing private sector earnings was more accurately estimated using ARIMA (autoregressive integrated moving average) models as opposed to using Moving Average, Auto Regressive, weighting schemes, and exponential smoothing.

Sophisticated models do not unconditionally out perform simpler models, ironically, because of the complex nature of government revenues and expenditures. According to Makridakis and Wheelwright, forecasting "is not just a statistical area, but the domain of psychology, sociology, politics, management science, economics, and other related disciplines" (1982:3). If this is true, then we have little reason to expect, at this time, more than a handful of local governments understand the changing relationship of their revenues in a dynamic and diverse local, state, national, and international economy. Yet Makridakis and Wheelwright's description of forecasting indicates that forecasting may be useful to the budget process to the extent the forecast can be managed, it can incorporate assumptions about economic performance, and it can be sensitive to the needs of the organization. In short, effective forecasting must thoroughly consider the locus of responsibility for generating the forecasts (Schroeder, 1982), that which is to be forecasted (Mabert and Showalter, 1982), and the adaptability of the forecasting process to a changing environment (see Lewis, 1982; Beckenstein, 1982).

A. Loci Of Responsibility

Respondents were asked, "Who is (are) responsible for producing the multi-year projections of revenues?" and "Who actually produces the multi-year projections of revenues?" They were also asked the same questions with regard to expenditures. Nearly two-thirds identified the budget officer as the person responsible for producing both revenue and expenditure projections. While 47 percent of finance officers were responsible for projecting revenues, only 34.3 percent had the same responsibility for expenditures (see Table 7.1). This finding reflects the broader responsibility budget officers tend to have in developing resources, as well as in managing resource consumption.

While most cities relied on budget or finance officers to generate the projections, many cities also relied on departments to supply the estimates. Just under one-fifth of the respondents indicated that departments, which have responsibility for providing services, projected their expenditures; about 11 percent projected revenues. Finally, only one respondent reported bringing in an expert to produce projections. Minimal reliance on outside expertise may indicate that external experts are no better at forecasting than are internal budget and finance personnel. It may also indicate that experts were used initially to set up the forecasting process, but have since outlived their usefulness. Or perhaps many cities use relatively simple techniques that require minimal, if any, outside expertise.

Table 7.1   Multi-Year Forecasts: Who Produces Them?

Responsibility for producing:	Budget officer	Finance officer	Departments	External experts	Other
MY revenue projections	62.0%	47.2%	11.1%	0.9%	5.6%
MY expenditure projections	63.9%	34.3%	18.5%	0.0%	1.9%

Actual producer of:	Party responsible for producing projections			Responsible party's staff	Other
MY revenue projections		55.6%		48.1%	4.6%
MY expenditure projections		54.6%		46.3%	3.7%

Note: Multiple parties may be responsible for and may actually produce the projections.

Respondents were also asked to identify the producer of the projections. While budget and finance officers are most often responsible for making the projections, many of these officers delegate this responsibility to their budget staff. The findings in Table 7.1 show that projections were actually produced by the party responsible (usually the budget and finance officer) in about 55 percent of the respondent cities, and by their staff in just under half of the cities. Delegation is a reasonable way for budget and finance officers to manage their broadening budgetary responsibilities. Clearly, the short-term budgetary responsibilities of budget and finance directors did not preclude them from producing forecasts.

B.   Revenues That Are Forecasted and How They Are Forecasted

1.   *The Revenues and the Techniques*

The responses to this survey suggest that of the major revenue sources cities forecast, those that are forecasted most frequently are property taxes and fees and charges (see Table 7.2). For example, by themselves and in combination with other techniques, respondents indicate that trend models are used in forecasting property tax revenues by nearly 60 percent of the cities, expert models by 48.2 percent and deterministic models by 43.6 percent. Also, fees and charges are estimated by over 96 percent of the respondents that forecast, however, the methods most commonly used include expert and trend techniques, not econometrics as experts have recommended. There are at least

Table 7.2 Percent of Cities and the Techniques, Computers, and Software Used to Project Revenues ($n = 108$)

Forecasting techniques	Taxes(%)			Fees and charges(%)	Revenue from	
	Property	Sales	Utility		State(%)	Federal(%)
None	2.8	18.5	25.0	3.7	5.6	18.5
Expert	5.6	2.8	5.0	10.2	15.7	25.9
Trend	12.0	14.8	17.6	11.1	10.2	6.5
Deterministic	9.3	0.9	2.8	4.6	7.4	7.4
Econometric	3.7	11.1	5.6	2.8	3.7	1.9
Expert and others	42.6	31.5	25.0	43.5	29.6	21.3
Trend and others	47.2	37.0	30.6	50.9	35.2	20.4
Deterministic and others	34.3	18.5	19.4	32.4	14.8	9.3
Econometric and others	17.6	24.1	16.7	24.1	12.0	8.3
State and others	6.5	10.2	6.5	4.6	16.7	1.9
Computer						
None	8.3	22.2	29.6	12.0	17.0	27.8
Micro	56.5	47.2	42.6	55.6	50.0	44.4
Micro and mainframe	10.2	12.0	9.3	9.3	6.5	4.6
Other	24.0	21.3	18.6	22.2	19.4	15.7
Unspecified	10.2	9.3	9.3	8.3	12.0	12.0
Software						
None	16.7	30.6	37.0	20.4	24.0	35.2
Lotus and others	60.2	49.1	37.0	59.3	51.3	46.3
Other	12.9	12.0	16.7	12.0	12.7	6.5
Unspecified	10.2	8.3	9.3	8.3	12.0	12.0

three reasons that may account for the methods cities use to forecast these revenues, and the large number of cities that forecast them. First, cities have historically relied heavily on these revenues to meet their expenditure requirements. Second, as a result of their traditional popularity, cities may have an extensive and reliable data base on these sources. This is indicated by the frequency with which trend analysis is used to estimate taxes and fees. Finally, cities may have more autonomy over the fate of revenue flows from these sources than from other sources since they fall almost exclusively within the authoritative and political domain of the municipal government.

Instead of assuming future state and federal aid will remain constant, most cities try to estimate them, especially state aid. The reasons for this may stem from the reasons that taxes and fees are commonly forecasted. First, as creatures of the state, most cities have historically relied more on the state for financial assistance than on the federal government. Second, consequently, the historical data cities keep on state aid may be more complete and reliable than that kept on federal assistance. Finally, although cities have little autonomy over state and federal aid, the era of fend for yourself federalism has clearly indicated that more cities are receiving increasing amounts of revenue from the state and less revenue from the federal government. And the political popularity of a "smaller" federal government reinforces the pervasiveness of this trend.

Along with federal aid, cities are also not as likely to forecast revenues from sales taxes and utility taxes. The reason appears to be related to the complex nature of estimating sales and utility revenues, which tend to vary with economic activity and with time (seasonality). For instance, when these resources are forecasted, trend, econometric, and to a lesser degree, deterministic means tend to be employed, however simple or in error they may be. Also, 11.1 percent assert to depend upon information provided by the state, which is also reasonable given the historical experiences most states have with sales taxes. Fewer cities tend to use expert recommendations.

2. *Computer Technology*

If the forecast is estimated from budgetary and other data, the process may be more easily managed if the forecast is generated from a computer. This may lead to a quicker forecast but not necessarily to a better forecast. On the one hand, advancements in technology may have met the requirements of forecasting (see Nickell, 1983). On the other hand, "the use of computers ... may change the appearance of what is going on, but does little to change the reliance upon judgments of which trends are worth analyzing and which are trivial, and which relationships merit most scrutiny" (Page, 1982). While we cannot resolve this controversy here, recent research has found that advances in computer technology provide a vehicle for expanding the use of multi-year financial forecasting for both state (Grafton and Permaloff, 1985; Ostrowski, Gardner and Motawi, 1986; Botner, 1987) and local governments (Darocoa and Darocoa, 1986; Mallory, 1986).

For the respondents who indicated they forecast revenues, many reported to rely on a computer to generate the estimates. Over half rely on microcomputers, and about one in ten depend on a mainframe. Very few rely on a minicomputer. Regardless of the revenue, most cities rely on Lotus 1-2-3 in conjunction with the city's own algorithms or SMART. Very few cities report using other packages such as Symphony, EXCEL, Quatro, MegaCalc, Statplan, Multiplan, Supercalc, SAS, SPSS, and RevEx.

C. Adaptability of Forecasting to a Changing Budgetary Environment

A third factor that will determine the usefulness of forecasting to local governments is the degree to which the forecasting effort reflects the dynamics of the budgetary environment. In particular, reactiveness of forecasting to the environment will tend to be greatest where 1) the government is familiar with forecasting, 2) information used to generate the forecast comes not only from previous budgets, but from previous audits and budget actors, and 3) information used to generate the forecast and results of the forecast reflect political realities.

1. Municipal Experience with Forecasting

Both an individual's and a government's experience with forecasting may indicate whether or not forecasting is realistically promising or is too cognitively demanding. With experience forecasters may grasp "what needs to be forecast" (see Kappauf and Talbott, 1982) and they may have a better feel for the technical skills and the data needed to forecast (see Davidson and Ayers, 1982). Experience may also allow for refining organizational and communication skills, which can be major roadblocks to reliable forecasting (Boswell and Carpenter, 1986). The amount of experience that municipal governments have had with generating forecasts with various methods is given in Table 7.3.

Results from the survey indicate that trend and expert techniques, which tend to be the least mathematically sophisticated, are most commonly used. Less than 10 percent of the respondents said they did not use these techniques.

Table 7.3 Municipal Experiences with Various Forecasting Techniques

| | p-value[a] | | Average experience[b] | | | |
	Revenue	Expenditure	Revenue projections	Expenditure projections	Average year[c]	Not sure[d]
Technique						
Trend	0.58(0.00)	−0.06(0.04)	9.2	8.6	1979/80	19.4
Expert	0.61(0.00)	−0.07(0.47)	9.1	8.5	1978	14.8
Deterministic	0.72(0.00)	0.04(0.68)	6.3	5.3	1980	16.7
Econometric	0.16(0.12)	0.02(0.88)	4.1	3.5	1983/84	9.3

[a] Pearson correlation of city size with forecaster's experience in forecasting revenues and expenditures, by technique.

[b] In years, reflects the average experience present forecasters have with producing both types of projections.

[c] Reflects average year in which projection techniques were first used by cities.

[d] Reflects the percent of respondents who do not know when their city first used the forecasting techniques.

Deterministic forecasting, which tends to be more demanding, is not used by 24.1 percent of the cities, and even fewer use econometric forecasting in any form.

Large governments are likely to have more experienced revenue forecasters, regardless of the procedure used. This may suggest that either larger governments have more experience and have more resources than smaller governments for forecasting revenues, or that smaller cities see less of a need to generate forecasts (especially since larger cities are more experienced with the simpler noneconometric methods). Small cities, however, are likely to have greater experience with expert and trend techniques (especially expert) when forecasting expenditures. Large cities tend to have slightly more (but statistically insignificant) experience with the more sophisticated techniques. Together these findings indicate that large governments are attempting sophisticated forecasting of expenditures, but only to a very limited extent.

When asked to identify the years in which the projection techniques were first used by their city, the least rigorous and demanding techniques tended to be adopted first. On average, cities began experimenting with expert forecasting around 1978 and trend forecasting a year and a half later. Deterministic methods tended to be used first in 1980 and econometric methods in 1983–84. And perhaps because cities began using the less sophisticated techniques so "long" ago, of the technique adoption dates that could not be recalled by respondents, most could not recall when they adopted expert techniques and very few could not recall when they adopted econometric forecasting. The same held true for the current forecasters.

2. *Where the Information Comes From*

According to incrementalism budget requests are based on the current year's budget base (see Davis, Dempster and Wildavsky, 1966). While as a current theory of budgeting incrementalism is dead,[1] in the past proponents saw much value in incremental-based budgetary decisions. First, an incremental process would structurally limit the possibility of resurrecting old battles or of entertaining volatile new ones. Second, it would assure interested parties that the adopted budget would be grounded in history. In contrast, forecasting calls for budget projections and requests to be based on a process that may question fundamental assumptions about previous revenue decisions. Furthermore, it may be grounded not simply in the recent past but on a reconciliation of the past (perhaps beyond the previous fiscal year) with the present and expectations about the future. The informational demands of the two approaches are distinct: to make decisions incrementally, last year's budget would be the primary source of information; to make decisions based on forecast estimates, last year's budget could be much less important. Revenue forecasting information may come from budget related documents (prior budgets and audits), units from within the government (finance department, operating departments, and the CEO), and others.

Regardless of what is being projected, finance/budgeting departments may be the most important sources for data, simply because of their mission. Prior budgets also may be very important since together they present a catalogue of critical trends in revenues and expenditures. They may also indicate the economic assumptions on which past budgets and future programs are based.

Operating departments may be relied on less frequently since not all departments support revenue generating functions (compared to expenditures, where departmental expertise might play a more critical role). Henderson (1978) argues that forecasts of revenues associated with city departments should depend upon data obtained from those departments since they may be most knowledgeable about the market producing the revenue and the department has information pertinent to its programs. Schroeder (1982) argues that departments are much more likely to be involved in forecasting expenditures,

Table 7.4 Mean Responses of Types of Forecasting Data Gathered from Various Sources ($n = 106$)

Type of data	Organizational units			Budget Documents		
	Operating departments	Finance department	CEO	Prior budgets	Prior audits	Other
Economic data for projecting *revenues* derived from department operations	1.91	2.36	0.98	1.62	0.97	0.53
Revenue data for projecting *revenues* derived from department operations	2.41	2.67[a]	0.80	2.11	1.17	0.25
Economic data for projecting *tax* revenue[b]	0.95	2.53	0.93	1.58	0.74	0.93
Revenue data for projecting *tax* revenue	1.11	2.91	0.80	2.26	1.23	0.70
Economic data for projecting *expenditures*	1.62	2.49	0.94	1.58	0.71	0.62
Expenditure data for projecting *expenditures*	2.38	2.72	0.98	2.42	1.28	0.24

0:source is not used; 1:source is used a little; 2:source is used some; 3:source is used a lot; 4:source is always used

[a]$n = 107$

[b]$n = 105$

especially if the forecasting process is decentralized. In this case, departmental personnel would be expected to compile all the necessary data. Such efforts, however, may be time consuming and costly.

Prior year audits may provide reliable trends on revenues and expenditures, as well as feedback on the efficiency and problems of programs. Finally, the chief executive officer (CEO) generally coordinates the administration of government policy, but is expected to be a weak source of information.

Respondents were asked to identify the sources they relied on for supplying data to be used in the forecast. The results are found in Table 7.4. Regardless of the data being sought, most municipal governments relied on their finance departments to provide data, and few relied on the CEO. This suggests that forecasters are prudent, relying on the skills of finance staff to supplement other data, provide calculations, and put data in a form usable for forecasting.

Departments tend to be used more than prior budgets as sources of both economic and revenue data to project revenues derived from department operations. Prior budgets, however, are used by more municipalities to provide the data to project tax revenues. Both operating departments and prior budgets are used as data for projecting expenditures.

Finally, the findings suggest that the four major sources of information—operating departments, finance department, prior budgets and prior audits—are more commonly used to provide revenue and expenditure data than economic data. This indicates that regardless of the projections being made, cities are more likely to use nonrigorous techniques (expert and trend) as opposed to more information demanding techniques (deterministic and econometric) of forecasting.

3. *Forecasting and Political Realities*

Politics and the basis of forecasting: The broad base of information on which forecasting depends reflects not only decisions incorporated in the previous budget but broader organizational concerns as well. Yet budget reform efforts have been criticized for their singular orientation towards the future, paying little heed to past agreements and decisions (see Mabert and Showalter, 1982; Wildavsky, 1988:416–418). Today budgeters realize that forecasting must have a broad historical base if it is to be a useful analytical tool (see Page, 1982). Historical data can be used to explore the influence of past and current policies and programs on future revenues and expenditures (for example, see the Financial Trend Monitoring System, Groves and Godsey, 1981). The hard part for the forecaster is to decide exactly how historical the data need to be.

Henderson (1978) argues that a five to ten year historical record should be used to forecast annual revenues, while Schroeder (1981) suggests a time frame between ten and 15 years. Downs and Rocke (1983) contend that the number of observations is dependent upon the model that is selected; for the multivariate ARMA model they tested, they recommend about 30 usable annual observations. Similarly, the time series model used by Box and Jenkins (1976) requires about 50 observations. In addition to such rules of thumb, the frequency of observations may depend upon the economic nature of financial data, at least in private corporations. Collecting data on a quarterly (as opposed to annual earnings data) basis allows the forecaster to control for the effects of seasonality and statistical dependencies between adjacent quarters in the same year (see Lorek, 1982).

The findings (see Table 7.5) show that multi-year forecasting tends to be at least as historical as traditional budgeting. The data, however, do not appear to be as historical as recommended. Less than 10 percent of the cities use more than ten years of prior data to generate projections of general fund revenues, and less than 5 percent do so to forecast general fund expenditures. Much more emphasis is given to recent history (ten years or less), yet this should not be disconcerting. Most cities have had little experience with forecasting and have not needed to keep prior data in a form compatible with the needs of forecasting. Consequently, as governments gain experience with forecasting, the data base used to make the projections may continue to grow. This would explain why cities have more experience forecasting revenues than expenditures (see Table 7.5).

Politics and reporting the forecast: Since proposed revenues and expenditures for the current year are subject to political and public debate, for forecasting to impact the budgetary process the Council should bring estimated future revenues and expenditures into their budgetary decisions. This calls for forecasting to be more than an internal tool for planning. According to our findings, most cities submit their forecasts to political evaluation; over 85 percent of the respondents report forecasting results to the City Council. If the Council witnesses the report, then forecasting has an opportunity to affect the Council's decisions.

Table 7.5 Percent of Cities that Use Prior Data in Making Multi-Year Projections of the General Fund

What is projected from the general fund	Historical data				
	Not used	<5 years	5–10 years	>10 years	Not specified
Revenues	0.0%	46.3%	42.6%	9.3%	1.9%
Expenditures	0.9%	64.8%	29.6%	3.7%	0.9%

For forecasting to be useful to decision makers, however, they must contain pertinent budgetary information. Unfortunately, there is little evidence to suggest what should be included in local government budgetary and financial documents (if there is an exception, that would be accounting reports). At the state level, a qualitative analysis of budget formats in North Carolina and Florida led Gloria Grizzle (1986) to conclude that "format did influence 'what the conversation was about' during the legislatures' review of the states' proposed budgets." At the local level, the importance of budget documents (for a sample of various documents however, see Miller, 1982 and 1984) and forecast documents has not been tested. Nevertheless, some research indicates that a presentation of the annual forecast should include statements on the future of the economy, the revenue structure, cost of services, service levels, proxy variables used, rationale and assumptions, implications for public policy, and strategies to avoid predictions (Schroeder, 1981). Boswell and Carpenter (1986) suggest further that it should include a city's economic and demographic outlook, trend indicators of the city's financial condition, critical issues anticipated by each department during the forecast period, and a comprehensive summary of the city's operating funds.

From Table 7.6, we see that reports of forecasts to the city council tended to include a variety of elements. First, more than 90 percent of the respondents indicated that the revenue structure was included in the presentation of the forecast to the council. This is exceptionally encouraging, given the pressure

Table 7.6 Elements Most Commonly Included in the Presentation[a] of the Multi-Year Forecast to the City Council

Elements of the forecast presentation	Percent included[b]
The revenue structure	91
Assumptions guiding the forecast	86
Costs of city services	83
Future of the economy	70
Forecast's implications for policy	68
Level of services produced	62
Strategies to avoid predictions	42

[a] These percentages tend to hold whether the forecast is presented prior to, or along with, the executive budget. Two cities indicated that they presented discussion on various revenue or expenditure limitations or history. One clearly recognized that the presentation includes an open forum discussion.

[b] Percent of cities that include above elements in their presentations.

on local government revenues over the past decade. Second, over 80 percent indicated that their presentations identified assumptions used to guide the forecast, and the costs of city services. Both of these elements are fairly straight forward, not likely requiring much time and effort to determine.

Third, about two-thirds said that their presentations included implications the forecast might have on policy, the future of the economy, and the level of services being produced. Estimating these elements may involve more speculation, effort, and resources compared to the previous three. Some cities may not have included these because of their relative inexperience in using forecasting. Still others may not view them as being important. Finally, some governments may intend for the forecasts to be true estimates of future revenues and expenditures rather than as a means for diagnosing current policies, politics, and environment. This is very significant since it may indicate that municipal governments are drastically underutilizing forecasting.

III.   IS FORECASTING USED TO AFFECT BUDGETARY DECISIONS?

Clearly, municipal governments produce forecasts. But to date there is little evidence to suggest that forecasting actually impacts on the budgetary process. In fact, the demise of early reforms provides little hope that forecasts can affect budgets. In this section we will present data which suggests a more optimistic outlook. According to budget directors, numerous budgetary actors find forecasting information useful to their decision making processes. Yet, the actual impact of forecasting on budgetary decisions is often limited because the results tend to be used more for internal analysis rather than as information to be analyzed by the council. But in cities that give the forecast to the council for deliberation, usually there is opportunity for the forecast to indeed affect the budget: the results of the forecasts are usually presented along with, or before, the budget presentation.

A.   Usefulness of Projections to Decision-makers

The findings in Table 7.7 indicate that players are most likely to use short- and medium-term forecasts as inputs to their decision making processes. This suggests that forecasting is much more likely to be used as a tool for short-term budgeting than long-term planning; long-term projections are rarely used by any party. Regardless of the time frame of the projections, the players most responsible for coordinating budget preparation and execution, the city manager and budget/finance director, tend to use the short-term forecasts *some* or *a lot* when making decisions. This runs counter to what traditional budgeters would expect, and indicates that reforming budget preparation may be within reach.

Table 7.7 Do Budget Officers Think Forecasts Affect the Annual Budget?

	0 Never	1 Rarely	2 Sometimes	3 Usually	4 Always	a	Mean
The forecast is presented:							
Before the budget is presented	25.0%	12.0%	10.2%	25.0%	25.9%	1.9%	2.15
Along with the budget presentation	21.3	10.2	17.6	17.6	31.5	1.9	2.28
After the budget is presented	50.0	19.4	15.7	2.8	10.2	1.9	1.02
The forecast is used:							
As an internal document	1.9	1.9	13.9	38.9	40.7	2.8	3.18
To help the Council	2.8	15.7	32.4	20.4	26.9	1.9	2.54
Forecast estimates are included in the budget:							
Revenues estimates	29.6	9.3	18.5	11.1	29.6	1.9	2.02
Expenditure estimates	26.9	10.2	17.6	13.0	30.6	1.9	2.10

a Results not specified.

The findings also indicate that city managers and departments are a little more likely to use expenditure forecasts than revenue forecasts when making decisions. On the one hand, this is quite reasonable. Departments are responsible for providing specific services and the city manager is responsible for overseeing and coordinating the administration of the services. On the other hand, cities and their forecasters tend to have less experience forecasting expenditures than revenues.

Other actors, according to the budget/finance director, are a little more likely to use revenue projections than expenditure projections. For all users this may be partly a function of the experience and expertise cities have with projecting revenues; it may also be a function of their responsibilities. Budget and finance directors are responsible for assuring that resources are available to provide services. The explanation for the council and the mayor is less clear.

Because of the fiscal stress cities have undertaken in recent years (see Levine, Rubin, and Wolohojian, 1981) and cuts in federal grants in aid to local governments (see Forrester and Spindler, 1990), we would expect them to value revenue projections quite highly, much more so than expenditure projections. Indeed, budget directors indicate that the legislative side is most interested in revenue projections. This suggests that cities are seeking ways to expand their budgetary constraint, which may be used to maintain current service levels or program expansion, not cutbacks.

B. Impact of Producing Projections on the Budget

Other evidence suggests that cities have designed the forecasting process to affect, with mixed success, budget preparation and budget adoption. Over 50 percent of the respondents indicated that they *usually* or *always* present the multi-year forecast before they present the budget or along with their budget presentation (see Table 7.7). Moreover, nearly 70 percent contend that they *never* or *rarely* present the forecast after the budget is presented. If respondents had been more inclined to present the forecast results after the budget then the potential impact on the current year estimates would have been lessened.

That forecasting is used to affect the annual budgetary process is evidenced by two other findings. First, while nearly 80 percent of the cities intend for the forecast to be used for internal (managerial) purposes, many of the same cities state that forecasting is used to help the council make decisions. Just under half of the budget directors indicated that forecasting results are usually or always used by the council; another 32.4 percent said that the results are used sometimes. Only three cities, 2.8 percent of the respondents, said that results were never used by the council. Second, 60 percent said that revenue and expenditures estimates generated from forecasts are at least some-times included in the actual budget. This would indicate that budgetary actors see forecasts as pertinent to the budget process.

IV. CONCLUSION

Since the 1960s, incrementalists have seen budget reform as an unreachable dream, perhaps even a nightmare. For them, integrating planning and budget-ing was a marriage grounded in divorce. The findings here suggest otherwise. Describing and prescribing the budgetary process as incremental undermines advancements in budgetary practices.

Preliminary evidence indicates that municipal governments are budgeting beyond incrementalism. One part of this budget outgrowth assumes that expec-tations about the future should affect decisions in the here and now. Over half of the respondents reportedly generate forecasts. They use techniques that range from the most simple to the most complicated, with assistance provided by computers and a variety of software.

The findings also indicate that using forecasting to affect budget will not necessarily displace crucial political and organizational values. First, future projections are based on past budgetary decisions, as well as current organiza-tional demands. Second, forecasting tends to be the responsibility of budget and finance officers (not planning departments), allowing the objectives of budgeting and forecasting to be easily coordinated. Finally, while many cities use forecasts internally, some cities present their forecasts to the city council (usually before or along with the budget presentation).

Budget reform may not be doomed to failure; in fact, expanding cognitive boundaries and appreciating the complex logical bases of budgeting may point away from traditional budgeting. Budgetary preparation has continued to mature in spite of theoretical limitations. Perhaps cognitive bounds and various logics will determine the future for budget reform—its possibilities.

NOTE

1. For example, even Aaron Wildavsky, in *The New Politics of the Budgetary Pro-cess*, stated "When there was (mostly) agreement on the base, the old Politics stressed conflict over the increments. The new Politics stresses the base because it is often disagreed. Conflict is now about fundamentals." (p. xiv).

REFERENCES

Beckenstein, Alan R. (1982). Forecasting and the environment: The challenges of rapid change. In *The Handbook of Forecasting*, Spyros Makridakis and Steven C. Wheelwright (Eds.), pp. 259–272.

Boswell, Charles R. and Carpenter, J. Mark (1986). Long-range financial forecasting in Fort Worth. *Government Finance Review.* 2 (6):7–10.

Botner, Stanley B. (1987). Microcomputers in state central budget offices. *Public Budgeting & Finance.* 7 (3):99–108.

Box, G.E.P. and Jenkins, G.M. (1976). *Time-Series Analysis: Forecasting and Control, revised edition. San Francisco: Holden-Day.*

Daroca, Andrea and Daroca, Frank P. (1986). Budgeting with microcomputers for smaller cities. *Government Finance Review.* 2 (5):32–34.

Davidson, Timothy A. and Ayers, Jeanne L. (1982). Selecting and using external data sources and forecasting services to support a forecasting strategy. In *The Handbook of Forecasting, Spyros Makridakis and Steven C. Wheelwright (Eds.), pp. 469–483.*

Davis, Otto A., Dempster, M. A. H., and Wildavsky, Aaron (1966). A theory of the budgetary process. *The American Political Science Review.* 60 (September):529–547.

Downs, G.W. and Rocke, D.M. (1983). Municipal budget forecasting with multivariate ARMA models. *Journal of Forecasting.* 2:377–387.

Frank, Howard A. (1988). "Close Enough for Government Work: Thoughts on Local Government Forecasting in Florida." A paper delivered at the 1988 Annual Meeting of the Southeast Conference of Public Administration, October 12–14, Birmingham, Alabama.

Forrester, John P. and Spindler, Charles J. (1990). Assessing the impact of the elimination of GRS on municipal revenues. *State and Local Government Review.* 22 (2):73–83.

Grafton, Carl and Permaloff, Anne (1985). Budget implementation with microcomputers. *Public Productivity Review.* 9 (2–3):202–212.

Grizzle, Gloria (1986). Does budget format really govern the actions of budgetmakers? *Public Budgeting & Finance.* 6 (1):60–70.

Groves, Sandord M. and Godsey, W. Maureen (1981). Managing financial condition. In *Management Policies in Local Government Finance, J. Richard Aronson and Eli Schwartz (Eds.). Washington, D.C.: ICMA, pp. 277–301.*

Gurwitt, Rob (1989). Happy machines, unhappy people: How to ease the pain of the computer transition. *Governing.* May: 63–66, 68.

Henderson, Harry H. (1978). Revenue forecasting in a working perspective. *Governmental Finance.* 7 (4):11–15.

Kappauf, Charles H. and Talbott, J. Robert (1982). Forecasting, planning and strategy: What needs to be forecast. In *The Handbook of Forecasting, Spyros Makridakis and Steven C. Wheelwright (Eds.), pp. 487–502.*

Levine, Charles H., Rubin, Irene S., and Wolojohian, George G. (1981). *The Politics of Retrenchment: How Local Governments Manage Fiscal Stress. Beverly Hills: Sage.*

Lewis, C.D. (1982). Monitoring and adjusting forecasts. In *The Handbook of Forecasting, Spyros Makridakis and Steven C. Wheelwright (Eds.), pp. 225–243.*

Lorek, Kenneth S. (1982). Financial forecasting: requirements and issues. In *The Handbook of Forecasting, Spyros Makridakis and Steven C. Wheelwright (Eds.), pp. 53–67.*

Mabert, Vincent A. and Showalter, Michael J. (1982). Forecasting for service products. In *The Handbook of Forecasting, Spyros Makridakis and Steven C. Wheelwright (Eds.), pp. 429–448.*

Makridakis, Spyros and Wheelwright, Steven C. (1982). Introduction to management forecasting: status and needs. In *The Handbook of Forecasting, Spyros Makridakis and Steven C. Wheelwright (Eds.), pp. 3–12.*

Mallory, Jim (1986). Budget projection software for Canadian localities. *Government Finance Review. 2 (4):30.*

Miller, Girard. (1982). *Effective Budgetary Presentations: The Cutting Edge.* Chicago, IL: Municipal Finance Officers Association.

Miller, Girard. (1984). *Capital Budgeting: Blueprints for Change.* Chicago, IL: Government Finance Officers Association.

Nickell, Daniel B. (1983). *Forecasting on Your Microcomputer. Blue Ridge Summit: Tab Books, Inc.*

Ostrowski, John W., Gardner, Ella P., and Motawi, Magda H. (1986). Microcomputers in public finance organizations: A survey of uses and trends. *Government Finance Review. 2 (1):23–29.*

Page, William (1982). Long-term forecasts and why you will probably get it wrong. In *The Handbook of Forecasting, Spyros Makridakis and Steven C. Wheelwright (Eds.), pp. 449–456.*

Schroeder, Larry (1981). Forecasting local revenues and expenditures. In *Management Policies in Local Government Finance, J. Richard Aronson and Eli Schwartz (Eds.). Washington, D.C.: ICMA, pp. 66–90.*

Schroeder, Larry (1982). Local government multi-year budgetary forecasting: Some administrative and political issues. *Public Administration Review. 42 (2):121–127.*

Schick, Allen (1971). *Budgetary Innovations in the States. Washington, D.C.: The Brookings Institution.*

Wildavsky, Aaron (1988). *The New Politics of the Budgetary Process. Glenview, Il: Scott, Foresman and Company.*

Wildavsky, Aaron (1979). *The Politics of the Budgetary Process, third edition. Boston: Little, Brown.*

8

The Use of Program Information and Analysis in State Budgeting: Trends of Two Decades

Robert D. Lee, Jr.

The Pennsylvania State University, University Park, Pennsylvania

I. INTRODUCTION

The period from 1970 to 1990 was a tumultuous one for state governments. In the early part of the period, state programs expanded as part of the legacy of the 1960s. Budgetary and other administrative reforms were attempted, including program budgeting systems, zero base budgeting, management by objectives, productivity improvement, strategic planning, and the like. The 1970s brought spending and taxing limitations, such as Proposition 13 in California. The recession of the early 1980s was particularly hard on state governments as were federal aid cutbacks throughout the decade. Northeastern and midwestern states suffered major losses in industrial production, while oil producing states saw their revenues decline as the price of oil declined. Other states encountered major growth that challenged both state and local governments in delivering and financing essential services. How states dealt with these challenging situations from a budgetary standpoint has been explored by numerous authors, including Schick (1971), Howard (1973), and Kee (1987).

This chapter explores the changes in state budgeting practices during the 1970s and 1980s. Specifically, the chapter is concerned with trends in the use of program information and program analysis in budgetary deliberations. Was there a marked increase in the use of such information or have state capitals largely ignored the prevailing literature that emphasizes the need for such information? The chapter also explores the extent to which different components of the budget process may be related to one another in the use of program information. For example, what are the relationships between the executive and legislative branches regarding the conduct of analysis and its use in decision making? Another consideration in this discussion is whether state characteristics are related to budgetary practices. Are states with large populations more likely to use program information in budgeting than smaller states?

The discussion is based on surveys conducted of state budget offices in 1975, 1980, 1985, and 1990. Since the 1975 survey asked states not only about their current practices but also about practices in 1970, information is available for two decades. All of the surveys were conducted by the Department of Public Administration at The Pennsylvania State University, with some of the surveys being endorsed by the National Association of State Budget Officers and/or the Pennsylvania Budget Office. All 50 states plus the District of Columbia were surveyed and responses were 50, 48, 43, and 47 for the 4 respective surveys (see Lee, 1976, 1977, 1989, 1991; Stevens, 1981). Given that states had four successive opportunities to report on their budgetary practices, the results of the surveys collectively constitute one of the best available sources of longitudinal information about state budgeting.

II. TRENDS

A. Expected Trends

A dominant theme in budgetary literature, at least since the 1950s, is that budgetary decision making can be improved by incorporating program information and analysis into deliberations; such information is in addition to familiar resource data about dollars and personnel (Lee, 1989; Rubin, 1990; Schick, 1966). There seemingly is a consensus among budgeting scholars that measuring the accomplishments (or failures) of governmental programs can provide important insights when scarce resources must be distributed among competing programs. Further, program analysis as distinguished from simple program measurement is advocated as providing a more thorough perspective on existing programs, proposed program revisions, and proposals for new programs. This focus upon program information and analysis is found in both state and local government budgeting literature (Botner, 1985; Cook, 1986; Cope, 1986, 1989). Judging from this major strain in budgetary literature, then, one can speculate that states significantly increased their use of program information and analysis between 1970 and 1990.

While consensus may largely exist about the need to use program information, the field is in a state of modest disarray regarding terminology. Commonly used terms include efficiency, effectiveness, impact, outcome, output, productivity, workload, and the like. In order to avoid some of this confusion, the survey used only two terms—effectiveness and productivity—and provided operational definitions of these terms along with definitions of program effectiveness analysis and program productivity analysis:

Effectiveness measures define and quantify the ultimate effects of government activities on society or the environment.

Productivity measures define and quantify the goods or services being produced.

Program effectiveness analysis determines the relationship between governmental activities and the effects of those activities on society or the environment.

Program productivity analysis determines the relationship between program resources (costs) and program goods and services.

The term "effectiveness" as used here equates to some definitions of "impacts," with the emphasis being upon how governmental programs affect people's lives as distinguished from simply the provision of services (Brown, 1988; Nagel, 1986; O'Toole, 1988; Poister, 1984, 1989; Sallack, 1987; Scioli, 1986). "Productivity," as used here, is akin to terms such as "output" and "workload" and when work measurement is associated with costs, a measure of "efficiency" is derived (Burstein, 1987; Downs, 1986; Holzer, 1984; Kelly, 1988; McGowan, 1985; Rabin, 1987; Ramsey, 1982).

Collecting effectiveness information is more complicated and therefore more costly than collecting productivity information. Productivity data can be gathered within a government. Procedures can be readily established to record such information as the number of clients served or the number of miles of highway resurfaced. In contrast, effectiveness measures typically require external collection procedures. What is the employment rate of state university graduates? Do people released from state prisons obtain well paid employment and avoid returning to criminal behavior? An additional problem with effectiveness measurement and analysis is that results may be more difficult to verify. A central budget office, for example, may be suspicious of information reported from the prison system that claimed impressive results in rehabilitating criminals or from a state economic development agency that claimed its programs created thousands of well paying jobs. Given that effectiveness is more difficult to gauge and that results may be suspect, one can speculate that states are more likely to use productivity information and analysis.

B. Budget Requests and Revisions

States were asked in the survey about the kind of documentation required in budget requests. Specifically, were agencies required to submit effectiveness and productivity information when requesting revisions in existing programs or authorization to create new programs? The results are reported in Table

8.1. While in 1970 only about a quarter of the states expected agencies to supply such information, today the vast majority require estimates of effectiveness and productivity for proposed new or revised programs (95 percent in the case of effectiveness and 86 percent for productivity).

Of course, proposed changes in programs are seldom approved initially or at least in their initial form. The result is that revisions in program information need to be made to reflect revisions in funding levels from what was proposed by agencies to what was approved for inclusion in the budget document. In 1970, few states provided for revising program measures to reflect central executive budget decisions, whereas as of 1990 about half made these revisions (see Table 8.1). In those states that make these revisions, about half of the states reported sharing responsibility for this task between the budget office and the agencies (54 percent) and the balance divided between the agencies, themselves (28 percent), and the central budget office (18 percent).

C. Budget Document Inclusion of Program Information

Budget documents can reflect the use of program information in several respects. Effectiveness and productivity can be discussed in narrative discussions of programs throughout the budget document. Effectiveness and productivity measures may be included throughout the document. The budget may also include future year projections of program effectiveness and productivity. Table 8.2 presents survey results on these subjects.

Table 8.1 Budget Requests and Revisions (In Percent)

	1970	1975	1980	1985	1990
New or revised programs in budget requests estimate program effectiveness					
yes	24	78	79	95	95
no	76	22	21	5	5
New or revised programs in budget requests estimate productivity					
yes	29	73	74	79	86
no	71	27	26	21	14
Effectiveness measures revised when funding levels changed					
yes	13	46	49	57	49
no	87	54	51	43	51
Productivity measures revised when funding levels changed					
yes	22	56	52	61	51
no	78	44	48	40	49

Table 8.2   Budget Document Inclusion of Program Information (In Percent)

	1970	1975	1980	1985	1990
Effectiveness discussed in budget narrative					
yes	10	38	42	51	50
no	90	62	58	49	50
Productivity discussed in budget narrative					
yes	24	58	63	67	73
no	76	42	38	33	27
Effectiveness measures included in budget document					
most agencies	2	24	28	26	24
some agencies	27	40	43	49	41
none	71	36	30	26	35
Productivity measures included in budget document					
most agencies	8	26	28	24	33
some agencies	37	48	49	52	44
none	55	26	23	24	24
Future year projections of effectiveness measures included in budget document					
yes	2	18	19	13	26
no	98	82	81	88	74
Future year projections of productivity measures included in budget document					
yes	8	20	19	18	37
no	92	80	81	83	63

While the inclusion of both effectiveness and productivity information in budget narratives has increased over the past two decades, many state budgets still do not provide such coverage. Productivity is more likely to be covered in the narrative than effectiveness (73 percent of the states compared with 50 percent respectively).

Program measures also have increased in popularity. As of 1990, one-third of the budget offices reported productivity measures being included for most agencies (33 percent) and another 44 percent reported that productivity was reported for some agencies, for a total of 77 percent of the states reporting some inclusion of productivity measures in the budget document. Effectiveness measures were somewhat less common, with a total of 65 percent of the states indicating this information was included in the budget document for some or most agencies.

Reflecting on these findings, one can conclude that the rhetoric found in budget literature about the need for inclusion of program information in budgeting seemingly has had little influence on some states. Eleven states indicated that program productivity measures were not included in their budgets, and 16 states indicated effectiveness measures were not included.

Future year projections of effectiveness and productivity were uncommon in 1970 and remained largely uncommon in 1990. Only about a third of the states make projections of productivity and about a quarter make projections of effectiveness. Since effectiveness is more difficult to gauge than productivity, it should not be surprising that projections into the future about effectiveness are less common than projections of productivity. A plausible explanation for the limited use of future year projections is that uncertainty abounds in state budgeting and precludes providing numeric projections of future program effects, productivity, or costs. States have doubts about their own abilities to fund programs and are unsure about their commitments to their local governments and about whether the federal government is firm in its support of state and local programs.

D. The Executive Branch and Program Analysis

Much has been written about analysis of governmental programs. Authors have been concerned about the types of analysis that can be conducted, how analysis can be institutionalized and thereby become an ongoing process, and how analysis can be incorporated into decision making processes (Davis, 1990; Fuchs, 1987; Rossi, 1989; Trumbull, 1990; Wholey, 1989).

Table 8.3 presents survey results on whether various components of the executive branch conduct effectiveness and productivity analysis, whether the central budget office assists agencies in conducting analyses, and the extent to which analyses are part of executive budgetary decision making. Analyses can be conducted by the central budget office, itself, by other central staff units, and by line agencies.

Between 1970 and 1990, the number of budget offices engaging in program analysis grew substantially. While only a third of the state budget offices reported conducting productivity analysis in 1970, some 94 percent now report they conduct these analyses. Effectiveness analysis, on the other hand, grew less overall and was more or less unchanged since 1975. The percent of state budget offices conducting effectiveness analysis rose from 18 percent in 1970 to 65 percent in 1975, and there has been no increase since then.

Similarly, other central staff organizations have increased in their use of program analysis, but the increase has not been dramatic and little growth has been seen since 1975 or 1980. Although most budget offices reported that they conduct analysis, they also indicated that they were largely alone in this endeavor at least in terms of other central units. If effectiveness or productivity analysis is being done, it is most likely to be found in the budget office of a state and not in other central units that presumably report to the governor.

Table 8.3   Executive Branch Conduct and Use of Analysis (In Percent)

	1970	1975	1980	1985	1990
Central budget office conducts effectiveness analysis					
yes	18	65	53	63	66
no	82	35	47	37	34
Central budget office conducts productivity analysis					
yes	31	65	75	81	94
no	69	35	26	19	6
Other central staff organizations conduct effectiveness analysis					
yes	2	18	28	22	28
no	98	82	72	78	72
Other central staff organizations conduct productivity analysis					
yes	8	22	26	22	30
no	92	78	75	78	70
Most major agencies conduct effectiveness analysis					
yes	14	32	44	42	45
no	86	68	57	59	55
Most major agencies conduct productivity analysis					
yes	20	38	41	44	49
no	80	62	59	56	51
Central budget office assists departments regarding program analyses					
substantial	4	21	10	7	9
some	38	50	56	68	75
practically none	58	29	33	24	17
Executive budget decisions based on effectiveness analysis					
substantial degree	15	20	11	21	26
some degree	23	59	70	64	64
rarely	62	20	20	14	11
Executive budget decisions based on productivity analysis					
substantial degree	19	27	21	29	45
some degree	32	54	64	67	55
rarely	49	19	15	5	0

Analysis has increased in popularity among state line agencies, but in about half of the states, these agencies conduct neither effectiveness nor productivity analysis. These survey findings together suggest that the perceived value of conducting program analysis has extensively penetrated budget offices but has met with only limited success with state agencies. The survey results do not suggest reasons for this limited penetration. In some states, the budget office may have jealously guarded against other central units having responsibility for program analysis. Some state agency executives most likely place little value on conducting analysis either for improving their own management capabilities or for providing an "edge" in competing for scarce funds. Other agency executives may have sought funding for establishing their own analytic units but have been turned away because of tight overall state budgets or because their respective central budget offices thought analysis was better situated centrally than in line agencies.

Where analyses are conducted by major agencies, central budget offices commonly provide some assistance. Among the budget offices providing assistance, most said they helped agencies select program areas for analysis (86 percent), helped develop hypotheses for the analysis (83 percent), and assisted in the analytic design of studies (81 percent). Only 31 percent provided analytic training to agency personnel.

Conducting analysis and using analysis in decision making, of course, are two different matters. It is quite possible for a government to have a unit that produces numerous studies each year and have these studies largely ignored (Rossi, 1985). On the other hand, it is possible for a state not to be a major producer of analytic studies but to use studies from whatever sources to aid in decision making.

Several factors come into play in limiting the use of analysis in decision making. Analyses may have limited or nonexistent roles in decision making because participants place little credibility in the studies or because the studies lack clarity (Lauth, 1985; Leviton, 1981; Tarschys, 1986). Organizational structure, such as administrative barriers erected between analytic units and decision makers, can impede the use of analysis (Springer, 1985). If studies are based on premises other than those supported by decision makers, the studies will not be widely used. In other words, decision makers have their own perceptions of what constitutes the public interest, the interests of constituent groups, and the like, and unless these values are part of studies, the results may be ignored (Long, 1990; Osigweh, 1986).

The remaining variables reported in Table 8.3 indicate executive usage of effectiveness and productivity analysis in decision making. All states reported using productivity analysis in executive decision making, with 45 percent reporting substantial use compared with 55 percent reporting only some use. The comparable combined figure for effectiveness analysis was 90 percent, also a high figure. The productivity variable is the only one in this portion of the survey in which the states were unanimous, namely that all reported using productivity analysis. The 1990 finding compares with only about half of the states in 1970 saying they used productivity analysis when the executive made difficult budget choices. States seem to have heeded the advice of many budget reformers that analysis can improve the quality of decisions.

E. The Legislature, Post-Auditor, and Analysis

Since separation of powers is fundamental to American state government, there is no inherent linkage between the executive and legislative branches of governments regarding the methods by which they act on the budget. Given differences in the constituencies served by legislators and governors, one should not be surprised if they demonstrate differing patterns in the conduct and use of analysis. Historically, legislatures had a reputation for being bastions of smoke filled room politics and not for their prowess in analytic capabilities. In more recent times, state legislatures were seen as continuing to meet their representational responsibilities of district interests while becoming more attuned to concepts of effectiveness and productivity (Abney, 1987; Brown, 1984a and 1984b; Funkhouser, 1984; Green, 1984; Lauth, 1985; Robinson, 1989; Webber, 1985).

Budget offices were asked in the survey about their perceptions of state legislatures in the conduct and use of program analysis. Other studies have asked legislative units about the executive and have found considerable congruence in how the two branches view each other (Abney, 1987). The fact that respondents were speaking for their budget offices and not as individuals probably increased the likelihood of congruency in that a budget office would most likely prefer avoiding making comments about the legislature that would be widely challenged by legislators, themselves. Survey findings are reported in Table 8.4 pertaining to legislative conduct and use of analysis.

Since 1970 there is a pattern of increasing conduct of both effectiveness and productivity analysis by state legislatures. However, as of 1990, only about half of the state legislatures engage in such analysis, compared with 94 percent of budget offices engaging in productivity analysis (66 percent in regard to executive effectiveness analysis). Moreover, state post-auditors are not extensively engaged in analysis; according to the budget offices, two-thirds (62 percent) of the state auditors engage in neither effectiveness nor productivity analysis.

Although extensive involvement in preparing analyses outside of the executive branch may not be particularly common, legislatures are perceived to be major consumers of analyses in decision making. The overwhelming majority of states (94 percent) indicated the legislature used productivity analysis to

Table 8.4   The Legislature, Post-Auditor, and Analysis (In Percent)

	1970	1975	1980	1985	1990
Legislature conducts effectiveness analysis					
yes	14	34	42	50	51
no	86	66	58	50	49
Legislature conducts productivity analysis					
yes	16	28	39	50	51
no	84	72	61	50	49
Post-Auditor conducts program analysis					
yes	4	35	42	39	38
no	96	65	58	61	62
Legislative decisions based on effectiveness analysis					
substantial degree	25	20	12	12	9
some degree	19	48	66	73	74
practically none are used	56	32	22	15	17
Legislative decisions based on productivity analysis					
substantial degree	19	20	10	15	13
some degree	25	32	56	76	81
practically none are used	56	48	34	10	6

some degree in decision making, including 13 percent who used it to a substantial degree. "Consumption" of effectiveness analysis was somewhat lower (82 percent).

III.   DISCUSSION

A.   Linkages Between and Among Components of the Budget Process

The conduct of analysis and its use in decision making may be related to the functioning of various units in the executive branch and to the operations of the legislative branch. Executive branch units, for example, may cooperate or compete with one another in conducting analysis.

In states where the central budget office conducts analysis, one might expect other central administrative units and major line agencies to do the same. In a sense, does analysis breed further analysis? However, an equally plausible line of reasoning is that if the central budget office does not conduct analysis, then other state agencies and central administrative units will. When a budget office does not conduct analysis, is a vacuum for analysis created and is that vacuum filled by either other central units or major line agencies?

Table 8.5 compares budget office conduct of effectiveness analysis with that of other central agencies, and the outcome is that there is no statistical relationship. Central administrative units are not more likely to conduct effectiveness analysis in states where budget offices conduct analysis than in states where budget offices do not conduct effectiveness analysis. The opposite relationship also was not confirmed by the data. When budget offices do not conduct analysis, other central units are not likely to meet any perceived need for analysis.

Table 8.6 compares budget office conduct of effectiveness analysis with that of major agencies. The table indicates that at a 5 percent significance level, there is basically no statistical support for the hypothesis that if the central budget office conducts effectiveness analysis, major state agencies will be more likely to conduct such analysis themselves. At a significance level of 10 percent, this hypothesis would be supported.

In the interest of conserving space, comparable data for productivity analysis are not reported here in tabular form. However, one should note that all but one state reported that productivity analysis was conducted by the budget office or other central units. All 47 states reported that the budget office or major agencies conducted productivity analysis.

Table 8.7 compares the conduct of effectiveness analysis by the budget office with its use in decision making. As can be seen from the table, when the budget office conducts effectiveness analysis, executive decision making is more likely to be based on this type of analysis than when the budget office

Table 8.5 States Reporting Conduct of Effectiveness Analysis in Budget Office Compared with Other Central Units

		Other central units conduct effectiveness analysis	
		Yes	No
Budget office conducts effectiveness analysis	Yes	8 (17%)	22 (48%)
	No	5 (11%)	11 (24%)

Missing = 1
Chi square: (DF = 1) 0.108, prob. = 0.742.
Pearson's $R = -0.0488$, prob. = 0.7490.

Table 8.6 States Reporting Conduct of Effectiveness Analysis in Budget Office Compared with Major Agencies

| | | Major agencies conduct effectiveness analysis | |
		Yes	No
Budget offfice conducts effectiveness analysis	Yes	17 (36%)	14 (30%)
	No	4 (9%)	12 (26%)

Missing = 1.
Chi square: (DF = 1) 3.801, prob. = 0.051.
Pearson's R = 0.2844, prob. = 0.0527.

Table 8.7 Conduct of Effectiveness Analysis in Budget Office Compared with Executive Decision Making

| | | Executive decisions based on effectiveness analysis | | |
		Substantial degree	Some degree	Rarely
Budget office conducts effectiveness analysis	Yes	11 (23%)	19 (40%)	1 (2%)
	No	1 (2%)	11 (23%)	4 (9%)

Chi square = (DF = 2) 8.328, prob. = 0.016.
Pearson's R = 0.415, prob. = 0.0037.

does not conduct analysis. A similar pattern exists when comparing legislative decision making with whether or not the legislative staff conducts effectiveness analysis (see Table 8.8).

What, then, are the linkages between the executive and legislative branches of government? In states that have budget offices engaged in analysis, are the legislatures likely to conduct analysis? Is there a relationship between state executive decision making and legislative decision making in their respective reliance on analysis? As can be seen from Table 8.9, a relationship exists between the two branches of government in the conduct of effectiveness analysis. States with budget offices that conduct analysis are likely to have legislatures also engaged in analysis. Conversely, when a budget office does not conduct analysis, the legislature is unlikely to conduct analysis.

Table 8.8 Conduct of Effectiveness Analysis in Legislature Compared with Legislative Decision Making

		Legislative decisions based on effectiveness analysis		
		Substantial degree	Some degree	Rarely
Legislature conducts effectiveness analysis	Yes	4 (9%)	18 (39%)	2 (4%)
	No	0 (0%)	16 (35%)	6 (13%)

Chi square = (DF = 2) 6.042, prob. = 0.049.
Pearson's R = 0.353, prob. = 0.016.

Table 8.9 Comparison Between Executive and Legislative Conduct of Effectiveness Analysis

		Legislature conducts effectiveness analysis	
		Yes	No
Budget office conducts effectiveness analysis	Yes	20 (43%)	11 (23%)
	No	4 (9%)	12 (26%)

Chi square: (DF = 1) 6.595, prob. = 0.010.
Pearson's R = 0.375, prob. = 0.0095.

Table 8.10 indicates a linkage between the executive and legislative branches in the reliance on effectiveness analysis in budgetary decision making. In 24 of the 47 responding states, effectiveness analysis was reported to be used to "some degree" in both branches of the government.

B. State Characteristics and the Use of Program Information and Analysis

While each state is by definition unique, the question arises whether characteristics of states are predictors of the use of program information and analysis. To examine this question, three indexes were derived using information from the 1990 survey. The first is an index of program information being used by the executive branch and is based on the ten variables presented in Tables 8.1 and 8.2. The index compiles results from variables pertaining to effectiveness and productivity information in the budget request process and

Table 8.10 Comparison Between the Use of Analysis in Executive and Legislative Decision Making

| | | Legislative decisions based on effectiveness analysis | | |
		Substantial degree	Some degree	Rarely
Executive decisions based on effectivness analysis	Substantial degree	3 (7%)	8 (17%)	1 (2%)
	Some degree	1 (2%)	24 (52%)	5 (11%)
	Rarely	0 (0%)	2 (4%)	2 (4%)

Chi square = (DF = 4) 8.574, prob. = 0.073.
Pearson's R = 0.360, prob. = 0.014.

the inclusion of such information in budget documents. A state received a score of one for each affirmative response to the variables with a possible range of zero to ten. Five states scored zero, and three states scored ten. Nineteen states were in the mid-range of four to six on the index.

The second index was constructed from the variables pertaining to executive conduct and use of program analysis as shown in Table 8.3. As in the first index, a score of one was recorded for each affirmative response. In regard to the variables dealing with the use of analysis in decision making, a score of one was assigned when a state indicated use to a "substantial degree." While the maximum possible score on the index was nine, the highest achieved score was seven (three states). Two states scored zero. Of the remaining states, 17 scored between 1 and 3 on the scale, and 25 states scored between 4 and 6.

The third index was developed using the legislative variables relating to analysis as presented in Table 8.4. The range was from 12 states scoring 0 to 3 states receiving the highest possible score (5 on the index). Eleven states scored only a 1 and 14 scored 2.

Five socio-economic variables were initially chosen for the analysis: 1) population, 2) state disbursements or expenditures, 3) per capita income, 4) tax capacity, and 5) tax effort. Population was considered as possibly important in that the greater the number of people in a state, the greater the diversity and the greater the need for information that can assist in allocating scarce resources. The size of state expenditures was thought to be positively linked with program information and analysis; as a state budget grows in size, it also grows in complexity, creating a need for program information and analysis.

The next two variables—per capita income and tax capacity—pertain to the ability of a state to pay for the added expense of using program information and analysis in budgeting. The tax capacity index, devised by the Advisory Commission on Intergovernmental Relations, estimates the potential revenues that state taxes could yield (ACIR, 1990; Cohen, 1990). The last independent variable was tax effort, an index developed by ACIR that measures a state's willingness to tax itself in order to meet public needs. The expectation was that as tax effort increased, a state would be more likely to use program information and analysis.

In analyzing the linkages among these variables, the disbursements variable was found to be closely related to population and possibly to the indexes for tax capacity and effort. As population increases, the total state disbursements tend to increase. If population is controlled by using per capita disbursements, that measure tends to parallel the tax capacity and tax effort measures. Therefore, the disbursements measure was deleted from the analysis, leaving the other four independent variables.

The results of regression models using the four independent variables and the three dependent variables are presented in Table 8.11. The important item to note in the table is that only one independent variable proved statistically significant. Population was positively associated with the use of program analysis in legislative decision making. Other than this one case, the independent variables were not associated with legislative decision making or other

Table 8.11 Regression Models Relating Program Information and Analysis to Socio-Economic Variables[a]

	Program information use by executive	Program analysis in executive decision making	Program analysis in legislative decision making
Population	−0.00011	0.00009	0.00009[b]
	(−1.28)	(1.64)	(2.14)
Per capital income	0.00045	−0.00009	0.00016
	(1.27)	(−0.41)	(1.02)
Tax capacity	−0.00452	0.03133	−0.02397
	(−0.10)	(1.11)	(−1.21)
Tax effort	0.00671	0.00741	0.01619
	(0.21)	(0.36)	(1.11)
R^2	0.045	0.045	0.147

[a] t statistics in parentheses.

[b] Significant at 95% confidence level.

indexes that dealt with the executive—use of program information and the role of analysis in executive decision making.

IV. CONCLUSION

The trends identified through the successive surveys of state budget offices indicate that program information and analysis are increasingly prevalent and that program analysis is used increasingly in executive and legislative decision making. State budgetary practices are becoming congruent with budget reform literature that for decades has championed the use of such information and analysis (Lee, 1989).

Program information is standard for budget request processes in most states. Almost all states require agencies to supply information about effectiveness and productivity when requesting revisions of programs or authorization of new programs. In about half of the states, effectiveness and productivity measures are revised when funding levels change.

The formats of budget documents have been altered to incorporate more program information. In about three-quarters of the states, productivity is discussed in budget narratives and productivity measures are provided for agencies' programs. Effectiveness measures are somewhat less common, although more than half of the states include this type of information in their budget documents. One area where there has been only limited change is in the inclusion of future year projections. Only about a third of the states project future productivity and effectiveness measures.

Both productivity and effectiveness analysis are becoming standard, although productivity analysis is clearly better established. Such analysis tends to be centered in the states' budget offices and to some extent in line agencies. The 1990 survey indicates that about half of the legislatures have units that conduct effectiveness and productivity analysis. Not only is analysis being conducted, but it is being incorporated into the decision-making processes of both the executive and legislative branches. Every state reported that productivity analysis was used to some degree or to a substantial degree in executive decision making, and almost all of the legislatures were said to use productivity analysis as well. This study did not find linkages regarding the conduct of analysis among central budget offices, other central staff units, and line agencies. In other words, whether a central budget office conducts analysis is not linked positively or negatively with whether other executive-branch units conduct analysis.

Associations were found between the conduct of analysis and its use in decision making. When a budget office conducts effectiveness analysis, that analysis is likely to be used in executive decision making. Similarly, when a state legislative unit conducts effectiveness analysis, it tends to be used in legislative decision making.

Executives and legislatures tend to mirror one another in regard to program analysis. If the executive's budget office conducts effectiveness analysis, then the legislature is likely to have a unit or units conducting analysis. Moreover, if one branch uses analysis in decision making, the other branch is likely to do so.

State characteristics were compared with three budgeting indexes that were compiled from numerous specific survey variables. The indexes were for the use of program information by the executive branch, the use of program analysis in executive decision making, and the use of program analysis in legislative decision making. The result was that population, per capita income, tax capacity, and tax effort were generally not found to be related to the three dependent indexes, with the one exception of population being related to legislative use of analysis.

While a researcher may prefer to find relationships between and among variables, the lack of such a finding is important in that it may help dispel some myths. This study indicates that one cannot assume that simply because a state is larger, it is more likely to have a budget system that uses program information and that decision makers are more likely to rely on productivity and effectiveness analysis in their deliberations than in states of smaller size. Similarly, the wealth of a state as measured by per capita income is not a good predictor of usage of program information and analysis nor are measures of a state's ability to raise tax revenues and its willingness to tax itself in order to fund programs.

State governments obviously are complex institutions that act according to their own rhythms and timetables, while at the same time being influenced by national trends. States are in communication with each other through a wide assortment of channels regarding how their budget systems operate. At the same time, each state decides for itself whether to proceed with whatever change is being considered for the budget process and the decision to change is not a function of a state's total population, per capita income, tax capacity, or tax effort.

In conclusion, one can query whether the trends of the 1970s and 1980s will continue through the 1990s. As has been seen, all or almost all states now have adopted some reforms and, if there is to be a change, it will be in the opposite direction. For example, all states reported that productivity analysis is used in executive decision making. One can surmise that given the utility of such analysis that there will be relatively little backsliding in the coming years.

In other instances, there is reason to speculate that plateaus have been reached with those states most likely to change having already done so, leaving few other states likely to adopt that change. Since 1970 approximately a third of the states have chosen not to include effectiveness measures in their budget documents. It is conceivable that these states will continue on their current tracks during the 1990s. Similarly, a majority of the states have chosen not to use future year projections of effectiveness and productivity, and one can speculate that those who were most likely to make the changeover to projections of the future made that conversion by 1990. The answers to these and other questions will need to wait for the next survey, which is scheduled for 1995.

ACKNOWLEDGMENTS

Important advice and assistance was provided by faculty colleagues Anthony Cahill, Thomas Luce, and Syedur Rahman and by research assistants Randall Stoner and Dorrial Zurhellen.

REFERENCES

Abney, Glenn and Lauth, Thomas P. (1987). Perceptions of the impact of governors and legislatures in the state appropriations process. *Western Political Quarterly*. *40*:335–342.

Advisory Commission on Intergovernmental Relations (1990). *1988 State Fiscal Capacity and Effort*. ACIR, Washington, D.C.

Botner, Stanley B. (1985). The use of budgeting/management tools by state governments. *Public Administration Review*. *45*:616–620.

Brown, Judith R., Ed. (1984a). Mini-symposium on legislative program evaluation. *Public Administration Review*. *44*:257–267.

Brown, Judith R. (1984b). Legislative program evaluation: Defining a legislative service and a profession. In Brown (1984a):258–260.

Brown, Richard E. and Pyers, James B. (1988). Putting teeth into the efficiency and effectiveness of public services. *Public Administration Review*. *48*:735–742.

Burstein, Carolyn and Fisk, Donald M. (1987). The federal government productivity improvement program: Status and agenda. *Public Budgeting & Finance*. *7* (Winter):36–47.

Cahill, Anthony G., Stevens, John M., and LaPlante, Josephine M. (1990). The utilization of information systems technology and its impact on organizational decision making. *Knowledge: Creation, Diffusion, Utilization*. *12*:53–79.

Cohen, Carole E. (1990). State fiscal capacity and effort: The 1988 representative tax system estimates. *Intergovernmental Perspective*. *16* (Fall):17–22.

Cook, Thomas J., Ed. (1986). Symposium: Performance measurement in public agencies. *Policy Studies Review*. 6:61–170.

Cope, Glen H. (1986). Municipal budgetary practices, *Baseline Data Report*. 18 (May/June):1–13.

Cope, Glen H. (1989). Municipal budgeting and productivity. *Baseline Data Report.* 21 (March/April):1–13.

Davis, Dwight F. (1990). Do you want a performance audit or a program evaluation? *Public Administration Review.* 50:35–41.

Downs, George W. and Larkey, Patrick D. (1986). *The Search for Government Efficiency.* Random House, New York.

Fuchs, Edward P. and Anderson, James E. (1987). The institutionalization of cost-benefit analysis. *Public Productivity Review.* 42:25–33.

Funkhouser, Mark (1984). Current issues in legislative program evaluation. In Brown (1984a):261–263.

Green, Allan (1984). The role of evaluation in legislative decision making. In Brown (1984a):265–267.

Holzer, Marc and Nagel, Stuart S. (1984). *Productivity and Public Policy.* Sage Publications, Beverly Hills.

Howard, S. Kenneth (1973). *Changing State Budgeting.* Council of State Governments, Lexington.

Kee, James Edwin, Ed. (1987). Symposium: Current issues in state budgeting. *Public Budgeting & Finance.* 7 (Spring):3–82.

Kelly, Rita M. Ed. (1988). *Promoting Productivity in the Public Sector.* St. Martin's Press, New York.

Lauth, Thomas P. (1985). Performance evaluation in the Georgia budgetary process. *Public Budgeting & Finance.* 5 (Spring):67–82.

Lee, Robert D., Jr. (1991). Developments in state budgeting: Trends of two decades. *Public Administration Review.* 51:254–262.

Lee, Robert D., Jr. and Johnson, Ronald W. (1989). *Public Budgeting Systems*, 4th ed. Aspen Publishers, Gaithersburg, MD.

Lee, Robert D., Jr. and Staffeldt, Raymond J. (1976). Educational characteristics of state budget office personnel. *Public Administration Review.* 36:424–428.

Lee, Robert D., Jr. and Staffeldt, Raymond J. (1977). Executive and legislative use of policy analysis in the state budgetary process: Survey results. *Policy Analysis.* 3:394–405.

Leviton, Laura C. and Hughes, Edward F. X. (1981). Research on the utilization of evaluations: A review and synthesis. *Evaluation Review.* 5:525–548.

Long, Norton (1990). Conceptual notes on the public interest for public administration and policy analysts. *Administration and Society.* 22:170–181.

McGowan, Robert P. and Poister, Theodore H. (1985). Impact of productivity measurement systems on municipal performance. *Policy Studies Review.* 4:532–540.

Nagel, Stuart S. (1986). Efficiency, effectiveness, and equity in public policy evaluation. In Cook (1986):99–120.

Osigweh, Chimezie A. B. (1986). Program evaluation and its "political" context. In Cook (1986):90–98.

O'Toole, Daniel E. and Stipak, Brian (1988). Budgeting and productivity revisited. *Public Productivity Review.* 12:1–12.

Poister, Theodore H. and McGowan, Robert P. (1984). The use of management tools in municipal government. *Public Administration Review.* 44:215–223.

Poister, Theodore H. and Streib, Gregory (1989). Management tools in municipal government: Trends over the past decade. *Public Administration Review.* *49*:240–248.

Rabin, Jack, Ed. (1987). Symposium: Budgeting for improving productivity. *Public Productivity Review.* *41*:5–71.

Ramsey, James R. and Hackbart, Merlin M. (1982). Impacts of budget reform: The budget office perspective. *State and Local Government Review.* *14*:10–15.

Robinson, William H., ed. (1989). Symposium: Policy analysis for Congress. *Journal of Policy Analysis and Management.* *8*:1–52.

Rossi, Peter H. and Freeman, Howard E. (1989). *Evaluation: A Systematic Approach*, 4th ed. Sage Publishers, Beverly Hills.

Rubin, Irene S. (1990). Budget theory and budget practice: How good the fit? *Public Administration Review.* *50*:179–189.

Sallack, David and Allen, David N. (1987). From impact to output: Pennsylvania's planning-programming budgeting system in transition. In Kee (1987):38–50.

Schick, Allen (1966). The road to PPB. *Public Administration Review.* *26*:243–258.

Schick, Allen (1971). *Budget Innovation in the States*. Brookings Institution, Washington, D.C.

Scioli, Frank P., Jr. (1986). Problems of controlling the efficiency of bureaucratic behavior. In Cook (1986):71–89.

Springer, J. Fred. (1985). Policy analysis and organizational decisions. *Administration and Society.* *16*:475–508.

Stevens, John M. and LaPlante, Josephine M. (1986). Factors associated with financial-decision support systems in state government: An empirical exploration. In Bozeman, B. and Bretschneider, S. (Eds). (1986). Symposium: Public management information systems. *Public Administration Review.* *46*:522–531.

Stevens, John M. and Lee, Robert D., Jr. (1981). Patterns of policy analysis use for state governments: A contingency and demand perspective. *Public Administration Review.* *41*:636–644.

Straussman, Jeffrey D. (1979). A typology of budgetary environments. *Administration and Society.* *11*: 216–226.

Tarschys, Daniel. (1986). From expansion to restraint: Recent developments in budgeting. *Public Budgeting & Finance.* *6* (Autumn):25–37.

Trumbull, William. N. (1990). Who has standing in cost-benefit analysis? *Journal of Policy Analysis and Management.* *9*:201–218.

Webber, David J. (1985). State legislators' use of policy information: The importance of legislative goals. *State and Local Government Review.* *17*:213–218.

Wholey, Joseph S., Newcomer, Kathryn E. and Associates. (1989). *Improving Government Performance*. Jossey-Bass Publishers, San Francisco, CA.

9

States' Responses to Budget Shortfalls: Cutback Management Techniques

Marvin J. Druker and Betty D. Robinson

Lewiston-Auburn College, University of Southern Maine,
Lewiston, Maine

I. INTRODUCTION

The downsizing trend spreading throughout state and local governments in the United States means that not only are there reductions in programs and expenditures, but that there are also fewer people providing administration and services. The management of public employment during fiscal crises has crucial implications for service delivery, government's future labor market position, and the future of public administration.

The fiscal crisis for state governments is now widespread. Recent newspaper reports indicate that over 30 states faced major budget shortfalls in 1990 (Tye, 1990). More recent reports in 1991 raise the estimate of fiscally troubled states to 38 (Lemov, 1991). The economic recession confronting the United States in the early 1990s is markedly different from prior recessions and is having a more significant effect on state governments than did the recessions of the mid-1970s and early 1980s (Hinds and Eckholm, 1990).

The impact of the 1990s recession on state governments is more dramatic because several political and structural changes are taking place. Federal funding was reduced during the era of "New Federalism" under the Reagan and Bush administrations. State governments have had to pick up more of the costs for various programs mandated by the federal government, most notably Medicaid. Also, citizen demand has grown for costly programs such as education, corrections, and environmental protection making it difficult to eliminate or cut back such programs. The last change involves the courts imposing requirements on the states for funding programs related to prisons and schools (Hinds and Eckholm, 1990).

Additionally, the role of the states has changed since the 1970s—states now play a more significant part in the funding and administration of policies. State taxes have risen proportionately to produce the increased revenues needed, but state governments are increasingly limited by citizen pressures against increasing taxes. With a larger role in providing services, states are also more vulnerable to national economic trends (Rebovich, 1985).

State government officials are searching to find viable solutions and innovative alternatives from a policy, political, and administrative point of view. They have responded to the current financial shortfall with a combination of tax increases, program cuts, restructuring of state administration, "passing the buck" to local units of government, and reducing state employment.

In this chapter the focus is on how state governments are approaching cutbacks in state employment, the sources of ideas for their actions, the extent of innovative responses, and the constraints faced by state officials when implementing reductions in the workforce.

II.   RESPONDING TO CUTBACKS

A.   The Environment

State governments have found a new set of circumstances in recent years that represents a departure from past eras in which governments could generally expect continued growth and expansion. As Clark and Ferguson wrote in their study of urban fiscal stress, "The problem variously labeled cutback management or adapting to retrenchment or budgeting under fiscal stress is today's number one issue for most American governments. But it is so new that little analysis specifically addresses it. Most public management discussions prior to the late 1970s assumed continual government growth" (Clark and Ferguson, 1983:245).

Responding to cutbacks presents serious organizational challenges. Levine points to four major difficulties: 1) change is easiest when people have something to gain, but in periods of shortfalls, rewards are unavailable; 2) public organizations have a unique set of constraints on change including civil service procedures, veteran's preference, affirmative action commitments, and collective bargaining agreements; 3) cutbacks create morale problems which make it difficult to increase productivity to make up for cuts; and 4) cutbacks reduce people's enjoyment of working and managing in an organization and this is likely to lead to diminished creativity, innovation, and risk taking (Levine, 1979).

Another facet of the changing organizational environment for state governments is the evolving nature of the workforce. The "Workforce 2000" report authored by Johnston and Packer in 1987 clearly demonstrates that women and minorities increasingly make up the largest portion of new workers. With this structural shift in the labor market, public employers must join private employers in competing for the best of these new workers. If public employers fail to respond to this change, they will endanger further the ability of state governments to meet the service demands of citizens (Johnston and Packer, 1987; Lewis, 1988; National Commission on the Public Service, 1989).

B. The Responses

In past recessions, state and local governments reacted with short-term solutions to the problems of budget shortfalls. Their solutions reflected an unwillingness to take steps which made a structural difference and might result in political fallout. Most states and local governments responded with incremental and short-run changes including fairly common standard operating procedures such as enacting hiring freezes, layoffs, cutbacks on overtime, wage freezes, and postponing employee raises (Wolman, 1980; Rebovich, 1985).

Earlier attempts to manage retrenchment found that the constraints of union contracts, civil service rules, interest group advocacy for programs, political fallout, bureaucratic resistance, and time limitations make it difficult for administrators to have the opportunity and freedom to explore alternatives to layoffs (Levine, Rubin, and Wolohojian, 1981). Evaluations of these programs are based on cost benefit analyses which have demonstrated that savings from traditional layoffs may be illusory (BNA, 1986; Greenhalgh and McKersie, 1980). A recent report by the Bureau of National Affairs on private sector downsizing indicates that more traditional cutback measures may even harm the long-term productivity and profitability of organizations (BNA, 1991).

Recent research, however, shows evidence of an interest in the development of new strategies for responding to retrenchment needs. In contrast to the standard operating procedures used to respond to major shortfalls in the late 1970s and early 1980s, new models are beginning to receive some attention. These models, primarily private sector initiatives developed to cope with the increased downsizing of private organizations, include job sharing, reduced work weeks, voluntary leaves or reduction in hours, voluntary sporadic days off without pay, extensive retraining, and programs to help the morale of remaining employees (BNA, 1991; Campanella, 1987; Carney, 1987; Kochon et al., 1988). Additionally, recent studies indicate a renewed interest in employee involvement either directly or through their union representatives in developing the procedures involved in cutting back (Robinson and Druker, 1991; Druker and Robinson, 1992).

III. A CASE STUDY OF INNOVATIVE RESPONSES TO BUDGET SHORTFALLS

Facing budget shortfalls in the wake of the economic recession, the state of Maine initiated a downsizing strategy to help realize budgetary savings. This innovative program consisted of a comprehensive six-part plan that included sabbaticals allowing employees to attend school with some reimbursement for tuition, leaves of absence, reduced work weeks, sporadic days off, job sharing, and inducements for those of age to retire. These programs allowed employees to continue to receive fringe benefits while on leave.

The program, implemented in 1990, was innovative in that it involved: 1) a conscious decision to avoid layoffs; 2) informal contacts and discussions with the major state employee union; 3) an attempt to accommodate the concerns and interests of employees; and 4) employee choice of whether they wanted to participate in the program. The Voluntary Savings Program in Maine ultimately involved over 1,600 employees—over 10 percent of the state workforce—and resulted in a savings of over $11 million. Many components of this program were consistent with the direction of downsizing innovations in the private sector, namely avoiding costly layoffs, involving employee organizations in the planning of the program, and offering a series of voluntary leave programs that could aid the quality of working life of state employees. (See Robinson and Druker, 1991 and Druker and Robinson, 1992, for detailed discussion of this case.)

The Maine program provides a positive model for the public sector. It fulfills the expectation of Lewis and Logalbo when they wrote that, "The growing perception of scarce resources presents a climate for creative change" (Lewis and Logalbo, 1980). The plan in Maine saved needed money, it did not involve laying off experienced or even newer workers, and it allowed for the implementation of a positive program that the state could continue into the future to attract and maintain nontraditional workers in public service.

IV. RESEARCH DESIGN

With this objective in mind, we developed a survey instrument that was sent to the 50 state human resource and budget offices asking them to respond to questions about their states' financial situation and their strategies for dealing with possible or actual shortfalls in regard to state employees. We received responses from 47 states. The following discussion is based on an examination of the data collected.

Previous studies of retrenchment management have searched for some pattern of responses to the problems created by fiscal crises. One study drew on the "garbage can" model of decision making which argues that the retrenchment process is confused and difficult to explain (Pammer, 1990). In this study we are interested in examining whether patterns exist in how state governments respond to the problem of cutback management.

V. CUTBACK STRATEGIES

The study data made clear that states are responding to budget shortfalls with multiple strategies. Table 9.1 summarizes the number of states adopting multiple strategies.

Of the 47 states responding to our survey, 37 reported some effort at cutback management; 32 had to go beyond just one program; and most of these states had to resort to several programs in order to save the required amounts of money. A number of states reported that the extent of the crisis has forced them to adopt more cutback programs than originally anticipated. Some confusion is evident in that survey responses indicate that many states added programs as the fiscal crisis developed without a clear plan of action (see Section IX) lending some support to a "garbage can" interpretation.

VI. SOURCES OF IDEAS

A great deal of research has been done on how organizations develop and implement new innovations in policies or administration. Many assume that governmental officials make policy decisions by searching for analogous situations in other states. Walker found that innovations spread through the states by geographical regions (Walker, 1969). When Gray (1973) disaggregated

Table 9.1 Number of States Adopting Cutback Programs

Number of reported cutback programs	Number of states
None	10
One	5
Two	7
Three	10
Four	4
Five	6
Six	2
Seven or more	3

data by policy area and level of federal involvement, however, she found that diffusion patterns differed. The spread of innovation by region theory is further questioned by Chi and Grady's report in the 1990–91 *Book of the States*. They report that when officials name other states as the source of an innovation, 60 percent of the states were in a different region from the respondent (p. 394). Other sources of innovative ideas found in the diffusion studies included coworkers and professional associations (Chi and Grady, 1991).

In our questionnaire, we asked states for the sources of ideas relating to innovations in cutback management. Table 9.2 presents those responses.

Table 9.2 indicates that most states still react to current cutback needs by going back to procedures they have used before in such circumstances. Many states have established a record of managing cutbacks from past national recessions as well as more recent regional recessions. The answers show a continuation of state governments confronting current problems with an incremental decision-making process implementing familiar strategies and local solutions to problems.

Sixteen of the states responding, or 34 percent, looked to other states as sources of new ideas. Anecdotal evidence from the surveys and case study indicates that most states, particularly those with the greatest shortfalls, that did look to other states tended to look for states in similar economic situations rather than using geographic region per se in choosing where to look.

The data also indicated that colleagues' ideas are an important source of innovation. Twenty-four or 51 percent of the responding state officials reported using ideas from other department heads in their state governments. In this case only six states reported using either professional associations or professional publications as the source of ideas for managing through the budget shortfalls, and seven states examined private sector models.

Table 9.2   Reported Source of Ideas for Cutbacks

Source	Number of states
Programs used in state before	34
Department heads	24
Legislative initiatives	19
Other states	16
Executive initiative	7
Private sector	7
State employees	6
Budget staff	5
Professional associations	3
Professional publications	3

Table 9.3 Strategies to Deal with Cutbacks

	Number of states
Reducing the number of workers	
Freeze on filling vacancies	34
Early retirement	18
Voluntary (temporary) leave	15
Mandatory furloughs	12
Reduced hours	10
Job sharing	5
Increasing workweek	1
Layoffs	13
Reducing the costs of employees	
Deferred pay increases	18
Reducing costs of benefits	6
Shut down of state operations	3
Pay cuts	2
Lag payrolls	2
Reorganize state workforce	7

VII. STRATEGIES TO DEAL WITH CUTBACKS

The data displayed in Table 9.3 indicate that states have followed a variety of strategies in implementing human resource cuts.

A. Reducing the Number of Employees

To reduce the actual number of employees, the most popular method was the use of attrition or freezing vacancies which was a familiar technique from earlier recessions. Thirty-four states have implemented freezes in response to current shortfalls or in anticipation of future budget problems. Oregon, for example, reported instituting freezes in anticipation of a massive state replacement of local funds for property tax relief over the next several years resulting in a need to plan for future shortfalls. A freeze in hiring offers some protection for current employees and may, if instituted by itself, signal a state's desire to maintain employment security. It is a convenient short-run strategy to buy time and preserve options. In the short run it hurts no one already employed by the state because "hiring freezes rely on 'natural attrition' through resignations, retirements, and death to diminish the size of an organization's work force" (Levine, 1978;321).

Unfortunately, freezing vacancies prevents hiring newer employees to revitalize the bureaucracy and can result in shortages in job fields where high turnover occurs, thereby paralyzing the department. In the long run, if workloads are not reduced, freezes place new work demands on remaining employees. Hiring freezes also harm minorities and women who are more likely to be the next in line to be hired rather than the next to be retired. Additionally, attrition programs can result in a disproportionate loss of direct service versus supervisory or managerial employees. We asked states if attempts were made to preserve direct service jobs, and only 12 states answered affirmatively. This suggests that many states are not following the private sector model of flattening their organizational structures. Such outcomes point out the need for some procedural flexibility even in applying this relatively conservative alternative.

The second most utilized strategy is offering inducements for retirement. Our study of Maine's Voluntary Savings Plan indicated that retirement incentives saved the most money in the short run. The form of encouragement to retire varies widely; in some cases it is the extension of medical benefits for several years and in others it involves a specific reduction in age or years of service required for retirement. Eighteen states adopted some version of early or induced retirement incentive in order to reduce their workforce. The advantage of this program is that it removes the highest paid employees from the state's payroll and allows younger or newer employees to remain. The disadvantage, however, is that people with the greatest expertise leave the state workforce and place additional burden on a state's retirement fund.

Innovative employment policy involving combinations of optional voluntary leaves was adopted by 15 states. Voluntary programs took the form of sabbaticals to pursue education, unpaid leaves of absence, sporadic days off, and reduced work weeks. In many cases, states have continued fringe benefits at a regular work level as an inducement for employees to take advantage of these programs. Such voluntary programs have the advantage of retaining employees in state service, and at least one prior study suggests that those who find voluntary leave programs the most attractive are women and younger workers, two important segments of the public labor market in the future (Druker and Robinson, 1992).

These programs also provide opportunities to test "pilot" employment policies and practices which make state employment more attractive as a part of a quality of work life effort. In fact, several states indicated interest in retaining voluntary programs beyond the crisis as a benefit for public service. The primary drawback of such voluntary approaches, however, is the failure to realize enough savings as a sole cutback measure and the difficulty of covering for on-leave employees, particularly in high demand service areas.

Two other programs which provide both similar opportunities and limitations are job sharing and reduced work weeks. Five states reported implementing job sharing programs and ten reported shorter work weeks.

Shortened workweeks is a downsizing strategy that avoids the costs of incentive programs or layoffs as well as the service disruptions of full-day shutdowns or furloughs. If implemented across the board in an organization, it is also a strategy that communicates concern about equity and job security.

Those ten states in our survey that reported shortened workweeks all used voluntary systems of workweek reduction in combination with an array of additional strategies. Five of these states also instituted mandatory furloughs and/or full state shutdowns. In this scenario, employees who have already volunteered to give up hours and pay are then forced to sacrifice further along with employees who have volunteered nothing when everyone is furloughed. As a result, managers who may need to use voluntary systems again in the future, may find fewer employees stepping forward if their sacrifices went unrewarded the first time.

Four of the states reporting the usage of voluntary reduced workweeks, also reported this method as the "most successful" option due to its popularity with employees.

Another form of reducing the number of employees involves mandatory furloughs which represents a way of cutting wages and salaries without actually laying off employees and incurring the costs of unemployment compensation or bumping rights. Furloughs provide the state with some greater assurance of saving a required amount of money which is not as certain with voluntary programs. On the other hand, they also damage morale and reduce the service level of the state which creates political problems for administrators, not to mention damaging the state's credibility with its citizenry. Furloughs are also an option that may make for greater difficulties with employee unions that usually oppose them. Contracts in New Jersey, for example, prohibit furloughs, and the state administration has avoided the issue by declaring temporary layoffs which have the same net effect.

One state reported that it increased the workweek without any increase in pay. This response raises questions about the impact of such an action both on productivity and the state's reputation as an employer.

A total of 13 states indicated they had actually laid off workers. While this tactic meets the objective of saving money, it is a highly visible, politically charged act on the part of states to demonstrate an attempt to reduce the workforce and the size of state government.

Laying off employees is clearly the action that may have the most devastating impact on the quality of the state workforce. In fact the state does not immediately save the full salary due to the increase in unemployment compensation costs, possible severance payments, administrative costs of civil service or contract bumping rights, and the costs of hiring and training replacements in the future. The costs of bumping rights may include the need to train new people on a job, reduced productivity, and the costs of litigation over conflicting rule or seniority rights interpretations. Bumping can also result in a reduction of women or minorities throughout state service, since in many states these segments have the lowest seniority. Remaining workers have lowered morale, increased workloads, and reduced loyalty to the state (Greenhalgh and McKersie, 1980). Other studies have identified significant increases in health and dental insurance costs and workers compensation claims as employees hastened to use their benefits prior to an anticipated or real layoff (BNA, 1991).

B. Reducing the Costs of Employees

Another strategic approach to cutbacks involves reducing the costs of employees rather than their numbers. Many states engaged in some form of manipulating workers' pay: 18 states deferred pay increases to some time in the future; 6 states reduced benefits such as eliminating cost- of-living adjustments or increasing employee payments to medical insurance; and 2 states reported using payroll lags, which defer a pay period into the next fiscal year. Three states actually imposed pay cuts on their employees. On the basis of the evidence that we were able to collect, only 10 of the 47 states in our survey have not used any of the programs which reduce employee costs to balance their state budgets.

These programs do not drastically alter the nature of state government policies or workforce. And while their intent is to maintain the workforce and level of services, they may actually injure morale and forego resources that could be used for productivity rewards.

C. Reorganizing State Workforces

Seven states indicated that one reaction to budget shortfalls was a reexamination of the state administrative structure. This usually takes the form of setting up a commission of state administrators, state employees, and citizen groups to make recommendations that will ultimately lead to savings. However, research on reorganization of public sector administrative structures indicates that this strategy is more useful for sending a political message than for actually achieving budgetary savings or greater efficiency (Seidman, 1980).

VIII. CONSTRAINTS

The ability of state decision makers to arrive at and implement solutions depends upon the economic, political, and administrative context in which they find themselves. There are real world constraints which put limits, both fiscal and political, on state government's ability to cut back.

In his study of managing fiscal stress in local governments, William Pammer stated, "It is quite obvious then that managing in a period of nongrowth necessitates change, and if that change is sudden or severe there could be an outcry of resistance from citizens and municipal employees. Such opposition may make it difficult to cope with revenue decline regardless of how sensible certain management policies might be" (Pammer, 1990:xvi).

Others have included civil service rules, court decisions on employment policies, union restrictions, interest group resistance, and agency resistance as constraints (Levine, 1979; Wilburn and Worman, 1980).

We asked state budget and human resource officers to indicate what forces tended to constrain them as they sought to implement cutback programs. Their responses are listed in Table 9.4.

Twenty-three or almost half of the states indicated that a concern over reducing services was a significant force restraining cutback strategies. Also, state officials report that requirements set elsewhere limit their discretion. Several constraints are particular to the public sector when dealing with issues of cutbacks: 19 states mentioned federal mandates; 15 talked about legislative action; and 11 cited court orders as factors constraining cutbacks. Union contracts and civil service rules were each mentioned by 14 states as setting further limitations on what alternatives state decision makers can choose to reduce spending.

IX. PLANNING

A continual management challenge for state government is the adoption of a planning strategy in regard to retrenchment. The dilemma for administration is whether to have a plan in place and stay with it or to continue in a "deny and resist" stage (Levine, 1978) until forced by circumstances to respond. Though many states based their reactions on past practices, it was not clear whether a system of responses was in place in anticipation of current fiscal problems.

In our survey we asked state budget and personnel officials how they developed their state's strategy to deal with cutbacks. The results are displayed in Table 9.5.

Table 9.4 Reported Constraints on Implementing Cutback Strategies

Area of constraint	Number of states
Concern for service level	23
Need to comply with mandate	19
Legislative restrictions	15
Union contracts	14
Civil service rules	14
Court ordered restrictions	11

Table 9.5 State Strategies to Deal with Cutbacks

Strategy	Number of states
No plans	8
Plans as shortfalls developed	25
Long term plan in place	5
Combination of long term plan and short term fine tuning	9

These data clearly show that most states either have no plans or only develop strategies as the shortfall occurs. Only five states reported that they had long-term plans in place. Nine states indicated that even though they had long-term plans in place, they still needed to adapt to a more serious situation by going beyond their existing plans. California officials indicated that layoffs were part of its standard response, but that the extent of the shortfalls in the early 1990s was so great that it had to go to other programs to save enough money without devastating the state workforce and state programs.

X. IMPLICATIONS

As we discover more information about what the states are doing in reaction to the need for cutbacks and examine their patterns of responses, more effective planning can occur for what may be extended periods of resource scarcity. There are a number of short-term and long-term implications for public administrators in the downsizing strategies adopted by the states during this period of financial constraint.

A. Damage to Workforce Diversity

First and foremost, the extensive cutbacks have done damage to the goal of creating a revitalized public workforce for the 21st century. Many younger people who might have been attracted to working for the public sector will have to rethink their career goals in the light of the downsizing taking place in the states where public employment grew over the last ten years. For public administrators, we view this as one of the unfortunate aspects of this wave of cutbacks. The studies of "Workforce 2000" speak of the future makeup of the employment market and the need for employers to begin integrating women and minorities who, according to the study, will make up the largest segment of new workers. Cutbacks that damage the diversity of the current public workforce can have far reaching impact on the future labor market position for public employers.

B. Politically vs. Fiscally Sound Policy

With a growing body of research indicating that traditional downsizing pro-grams, particularly layoffs, actually hurt productivity and fail to realize antici-pated savings, the continued use of these strategies in the public sector—while politically attractive in the short run—may have serious and negative long-term impacts on fiscal soundness.

In our case study of the Maine Voluntary Savings Program and through anecdotal comments in the survey, we find evidence that even states with large shortfalls and major downsizing initiatives are not compiling enough data to enable them to evaluate the true costs of their actions. This raises serious ques-tions about the long-term fiscal soundness of state downsizing activities.

The continuing pressure on governors and their appointed department heads to respond politically to downsizing needs is intense, and if the fiscal crisis occurs near an election year, this pressure becomes predominant. Private sector firms, particularly large ones, have established ongoing teams to moni-tor short- and long-term workforce and skill needs in the organization. The teams are comprised of employees from human resource departments and exe-cutive management (BNA, 1991). If such teams were created and institutional-ized with career employees in public service, some of the political pressures on state downsizing initiatives might be alleviated. Union involvement could mitigate employee concern about the role of such a team and provide manage-ment with another venue to collect ongoing employee input into future work-force and skill needs assessment.

C. Impact on Current Workforce

As cutbacks occur in state government in the face of budget shortfalls, deci-sion makers have to be concerned with the impact of cuts on current public employees and ultimately on constituents. For government to continue to operate and to maintain the allegiance of its constituents, there is a need for a committed, service-oriented workforce. But continued threats to employment have the opposite effects—lowered morale and loss of employees with transfer-able skills, great experience, or extensive training. These effects are also docu-mented in recent private sector studies that indicate lowered productivity and reduced profits following downsizing initiatives with high negative impacts on employee morale. "The firms are not becoming 'lean and mean,' as many in the 1980s thought they were, but 'leaner and weaker' than before they down-sized" (BNA, 1991:30).

Research on employee motivation during periods of retrenchment has indicated the importance of organizations developing and fostering sets of intrinsic reward systems for employees. This is obviously true due to the reduction or elimination of extrinsic rewards such as salary increases. Romzek has indicated that there is not an "interchangeability of intrinsic and extrinsic rewards," but that rewards such as public recognition and additional fringe benefits should be considered by governments to maintain a motivated work-force (Romzek, 1985:288).

Significantly, state responses to one of our survey questions asking whether attempts were made to preserve direct services over middle-management jobs indicated that states have not followed the lead of the private sector in moving toward flatter organizations. By focusing on reduction of middle management positions and communicating that strategy to line employees, private sector organizations have been able to protect production and service and to mitigate the downsizing impact on line employee morale (BNA, 1991).

XI. CONCLUSION

The extent of the current wave of economic difficulties is widespread. With the continuation of the policies of the "New Federalism," help from the Federal government will not be forthcoming. State decision makers are, largely, on their own to find new ways to deal with the crisis. There is some evidence that administrators in several states have tried to save money without implementing large-scale layoffs of state workers. Instead they are searching for alternatives to layoffs and applying new options related to a more flexible and innovative employment policy and practices. State administrators could be more innovative by: 1) decentralizing to department heads; 2) looking to other states; 3) pursuing some form of bottom up management or worker participation; or 4) looking to the private sector to find suggestions to deal with the budget crunch. Times of crises can provide an opportunity to be creative about the nature of the public workforce and the delivery of public services.

The decision makers surveyed for this study face challenging political, economic and bureaucratic pressures that constrain their efforts. These constraints probably explain the relatively low level of innovation or spread of innovative downsizing ideas set in motion during this recession. Nonetheless, structural shifts in public sector employment opportunities and the makeup of the future labor force as well as new research on the impact of old downsizing strategies suggest that innovation in the area of public sector employment policy needs to be supported. Further detailed case study research on those states which exhibit the most innovative programs in the area of employment policy would provide more information to decision makers in other states on how constraints can be overcome.

ACKNOWLEDGMENTS

Support for the research discussed in this chapter was provided by a grant from the University of Southern Maine Faculty Senate Research Fund. We wish to acknowledge the editorial assistance of Rebecca Quinlan.

REFERENCES

Bureau of National Affairs (1986). Layoffs called wrong approach to saving money during hard times. *BNA's Daily Reporter System-Daily Labor Report*, The Bureau of National Affairs, Inc., September 22.

Bureau of National Affairs (1991). Downsizing: Creative approaches to corporate change. Washington: The Bureau of National Affairs, Inc.

Campanella, C. (1987). Developing employment security through alternatives to layoffs. *Employment Relations Today*. Winter:347–353.

Carney, J.D. (1987). Downsizing government: Iowa's challenge. *The Journal of State Government*. 60:183–190.

Chi, K. and Grady, D. (1991). Innovators in state governments: Their organizational and professional environment. In *The Book of the States 1990–91*. Lexington: The Council of State Governments, pp. 382–404.

Clark, T. and Ferguson, L. (1983). *City Money*. New York: Columbia University Press.

Druker, M. and Robinson, B. (1992). Offsetting the downside of downsizing: Implementing QWL options. *The Journal of Health and Human Resource Administration*.

Gray, V. (1973). Innovation in the states: A diffusion study. *American Political Science Review*. 67:1174–1185.

Greenhalgh, L. and McKersie, R. (1980). Cost effectiveness of alternative strategies for cutback management. *Public Administration Review*. 40:575–583.

Hinds, M. and Eckholm, E. (1990). 80's leave states and cities in need. *The New York Times*. December 30, 1990:1,16.

Johnston, W.B. and Packer, A.H. (1987). *Workforce 2000*. Indianapolis, Indiana: Hudson Institute.

Kochan, T.A., MacDuffie, J.P. and Osterman, P. (1988). Employment security at DEC: Sustaining values amid environmental change. *Human Resource Management*. 27:121–143.

Lemov, P. (1991). The axe and its victims. *Governing*. August:26–30.

Levine, C. (1978). Organizational decline and cutback management. *Public Administration Review*. 38:316–325.

Levine, C. (1979). More on cutback management: Hard questions for hard times. *Public Administration Review*. 39:179–183.

Levine, C., Rubin, I, and Wolohojian, G. (1981). *The Politics of Retrenchment*. Beverly Hills: Sage Publications.

Lewis, C. and Logalbo, A. (1980). Cutback principles and practices: A checklist for managers. *Public Administration Review. 40*:184–188.

Lewis, G.B. (1988). The consequences of fiscal stress: Cutback management and municipal employment. *State and Local Government Review*. Spring:64–71.

National Commission on the Public Service. (1989). *Leadership for America: Rebuilding the Public Service*. Washington: National Commission on the Public Service.

Pammer, W. (1990). *Managing Fiscal Strain in Major American Cities*. New York: Greenwood Press.

Rebovich, D. (1985). Fiscal stress in the American states. In *State and Local Government Administration*, J. Rabin and D. Dodd (Eds.). New York: Marcel Dekker, Inc., pp. 161–185.

Robinson, B. and Druker, M. (1991). Innovative approaches to downsizing: The experience in Maine. *Employee Relations Today*. Spring:79–87.

Romzek, B. (1985). The effects of public service recognition, job security and staff reductions on organizational involvement. *Public Administration Review. 45*:282–292.

Seidman, H. (1980). *Politics, Position, and Power*. New York: Oxford University Press.

Tye, L. (1990). Downturn forces deficits in 30 states. *The Boston Globe*. November 11, 1990:39–40.

Walker, J. (1969). The diffusion of innovations among the American states. *American Political Science Review. 63*:880–899.

Wilburn, R. and Worman, M. (1980). Overcoming the limits to personnel cutbacks: Lessons learned in Pennsylvania. *Public Administration Review. 40*:609–612.

Wolman, H. (1980). Local government strategies to cope with fiscal pressure. In *Fiscal Stress and Public Policy*, C. Levine and I. Rubin (Eds.). Beverly Hills: Sage Publications.

Part Three
Subnational Comparative Financial Management

10

Government Purchasing: The State of the Practice

Charles K. Coe

North Carolina State University at Raleigh, Raleigh, North Carolina

I. INTRODUCTION

Governments purchase over $500 billion, which constitutes about 20 percent of the gross national product. Because of the large sums involved, purchasing goods and services is a large part of any government's operations. Professional and progressive purchasing procedures reduce the cost of government; but the converse is equally true, shoddy practices result in waste and excessive costs. The seemingly constant stream of stories about slipshod defense contracting bears witness to this point.

Government purchasing differs from private purchasing in several distinctive ways. First, businesses purchase in secret with only the buyer deciding on the vendor—a choice that can be made on the basis of price, convenience, or on personal considerations such as friendship or family ties. Governments, in sharp contrast, must conduct all of their dealings in the public eye, subject to strict legal guidelines. Secondly, governmental purchasing often is more subject to social and political strictures. For example, states and localities sometimes require that particular goods be bought locally or that preferences be given to minorities or the handicapped. Finally, because of the market mechanism, private sector purchasing is generally more professional. The bottom line, the amount of profit, is sharply reduced by incompetent purchasing such as delays in receiving goods, stock unnecessarily tied up on inventory shelves, and by the absence of vendor competition. Given the increasing pressure of international competition, the private sector has improved its purchasing procedures. Thus, private purchasing managers in general are better trained than public managers. Furthermore, firms are more likely to have state-of-the-art computerized purchasing and inventory control systems.

While private sector purchasing may be better than public purchasing, governmental purchasing has made very significant advancements over its history. Governmental purchasing has gone through four stages (CSG, 1988:101). In the 1800s the emphasis was on contracts for public works. The chief concern was protecting taxpayers against fraud and favoritism. Purchasers were exclusively technicians who needed little educational preparation.

Centralization of purchasing into a single department marked the second stage. The adoption of the income tax and then the outbreak of World War II caused the federal expenditures to grow greatly. Greater control over purchasing was needed. It was highly inefficient to allow agencies to do their own purchasing. Centralized purchasing demanded that purchasing officials be better trained and operations be more sophisticated.

World War II signaled the third stage of purchasing. Huge amounts of supplies had to move throughout the world and vast amounts of military weapons and equipment needed to be built in a short time frame. Consequently, purchasing became more sophisticated. For example, computers were first introduced to make acquisitions and schedule construction projects.

Purchasing is now in its fourth stage. Even greater expertise is now required because governments must make intelligent decisions about purchasing a wide range of technologically sophisticated equipment and systems such as communications systems, computer hardware and software, telephone systems, CATV, and telecommunications networks. Further, governments are faced with other new challenges including a heightened sensitivity to ethical conflicts, the selection of professional services, and decisions about whether to privatize services.

II. THE STATE OF PRACTICE

The challenges now facing governments are indeed great. A cost conscious and tax shy public wants governments to be more efficient, which is a clarion call for more purchasing competition, more innovation, higher ethical standards, and for better trained purchasing officials. What is the state of practice? How well are governments responding to the challenges of the 1990s? The report card is mixed. While marked improvements are being made in some areas, progress is slow in other critical aspects of purchasing management. Let us examine the state of practice of governmental purchasing.

A. Education and Training

Unfortunately, most governmental purchasing officials must learn their craft only on the job through experience, not through any structured education

(CSG, 1988:101). While on the job knowledge is indeed valuable, it should be complemented by formal training and instructional programs; yet relatively few such programs are offered at any level of government. The private sector, driven by the bottom line, recognizes the need; but unfortunately government mostly does not. In 1981, 275 colleges and universities offered courses in purchasing, but these were for industrial purchasing. The opportunity to receive a degree in public purchasing is virtually non-existent (CSG, 1988:101).

Out of the academic environment, however, some progress has been made. In 1978 the National Institute of Government Purchasing (NGIP) joined the National Association of Purchasing Managers (NAPM) to create a Universal Public Purchasing Certification Council and program. The NGIP offers seminars throughout the country to certify purchasing officials as a Certified Public Purchasing Officer (CPPO) or as a Professional Public Buyer (PPB). These programs offer a good, basic understanding of purchasing and buying, but participation in them is generally restricted to larger governments that can afford the tuition and travel cost. As of 1990 there were about 600 CPPOs and 1,000 PPBs, which is commendable, but still only a small fraction of the total number of government purchasing officials in cities, counties, schools, states, and colleges and universities. Furthermore, while both certification programs are very useful, they cannot prepare the purchasing officer for the very specific purchasing laws and regulations of each state. Thus, each state should have a training program to complement the NGIPs. Such a program would emphasize state law and be geared to those smaller local jurisdictions that cannot afford to send people to the NGIP. Ideally, these programs would certify purchasing officials as does the NGIP. Unfortunately, however, North Carolina is the only state to have such a program, which is operated by the Institute of Government at the University of North Carolina at Chapel Hill.

In addition to training by the NGIP or other agencies, governments themselves provide formal training; however, the frequency of such training is very slim. In 1982 state purchasing officials reported that only 12 states provide special training for new employees; moreover, only five states have any training programs for their entire purchasing staff. At the local level, the picture is the same; only nine percent of cities and 13 percent of counties have any training programs (CSG, 1988:102).

When we compare the salaries of private sector purchasing officials to their public sector counterparts, it is therefore not surprising, considering the general lack of professional training by governments, that public officials lag far behind. The General Accounting Office found that the salaries for the federal positions of Buyer I to Buyer IV in the federal government range from 29 percent to 38 percent behind salaries paid to comparable private sector employees (GAO, 1987:19).

Further, the salaries paid to purchasing officials generally are quite low, considering the range of responsibilities and expertise required. For example, a 1989 survey reports that the salaries of 22 percent of purchasing officials are less than $20,000; another 55 percent have salaries less that $28,000 (NIGP, 1989:9). Moreover, this survey significantly underreported smaller jurisdictions of less than 50,000 population which undoubtedly have even lower wages.

The lack of training and low pay at the local level are due in part to organizational reasons. In small cities, counties, and schools purchasing is just one of many responsibilities that the finance director or clerk has. As governments get larger, they create a purchasing office, typically under the supervision of the finance director whose background is in accounting not purchasing. Thus, finance directors sometimes are simply not aware of the cost savings and economies that result from state-of-the-art purchasing. City and county managers and school superintendents need to recognize the importance of the purchasing and inventory functions and ensure that salaries are high enough to attract and retain professionals. To provide for autonomy and professionalism, top managers of large, local jurisdictions should consider splitting purchasing from the finance director and put purchasing under the direct supervision of an assistant manager for operations.

B. Federal Purchasing

The history of federal purchasing reflects a long standing concern on the part of the President and Congress to have economical and efficient operations. In 1792 Congress authorized the Treasury and War Departments to make purchases for the federal government. In 1809 the Procurement Act required that formal advertising be used in purchasing and over the years rules were established for bidding and for military purchases. In 1949 the General Services Administration (GSA) was created to purchase for all agencies except Defense, NASA, Energy, and the Energy Research and Development Agency. GSA sets standards for purchases, issues long-term contracts, and stores supplies.

As the federal government grew in size, maintaining tight accounting control over purchasing became more problematic. Numerous studies and reports have centered on how to improve purchasing. Numerous actions have also been taken by both Congress and the Executive Office to shore up glaring deficiencies. In 1974 the Office of Federal Procurement Policy (OFPP) was set up to coordinate and improve the efficiency of purchasing. In 1976 the Federal Acquisition Institute (FAI) was created to train procurement personnel and conduct research to improve purchasing practices. The Financial Integrity Act of 1982 requires ongoing evaluations of the internal control and accounting systems that protect federal programs against fraud, waste, abuse, and mismanagement. In 1984 the Federal Competition in Contracting Act was passed to increase competition within departments and narrow the justification for sole source contracting. Finally, in 1987 the Director of Office and Management administratively appointed a Chief Financial Officer (CFO) for the federal government and for each department and agency.

Despite the intense interest in improving purchasing and financial management generally, progress generally has been slow. For example, the OFPP encountered widespread resistance from Congress, defense agencies, and other agencies (Walsh and Leighland, 1989:487). Moreover, GAO finds that, while the Financial Integrity Act has resulted in modest progress towards tighter controls over financial transaction, the results are considerably less than what Congress intended (GAO, 1989:3). To back up this assertion, the GAO cites examples of purchasing problems (GAO, 1989:20-21):

In 1988 the Naval Security and Investigative Command reported instances of procurement fraud, conflict of interest, and bribery.
After spending over $30 billion on the B-1 bomber, it does not work as planned.
GSA has serious internal control weaknesses such as its incomplete analysis of the range of alternatives for satisfying federal telecommunication requirements.

GAO also notes considerable shortcomings in the area of property control (GAO, 1989:30-31). The federal government has over $450 billion in property, plant, and equipment, or about 40 percent of the government's total reported assets. Yet GAO repeatedly takes federal agencies to task for their poor control over these valuable assets. For example, the Army has no accounting system to control fraud, waste, and abuse to the $2 billion in government material furnished to contractors. Moreover, the amount of unneeded inventories in stock grew from approximately $10 billion in 1980 to about $29 billion in 1988.

GAO also cites numerous instances of poor inventory control in agencies other than Defense. For example, for over 18 years the GAO has reported inadequate internal controls over personal property located at about 260 foreign posts and 21 domestic cities. This condition exists because the State Department does not follow regulations.

Interestingly, while improvements should indeed be made to Defense contracting, Defense is more competitive than the private sector in one way. In fiscal year 1986 Defense competitively bid 82 percent of its contracts compared to 56 percent by businesses (Williams and Bakhshi, 1988:32). However, because large weapons systems are difficult to bid competitively, only a slightly higher dollar amount of purchases were bid competitively by Defense.

Though Defense receives more bids than the private sector, a great deal of waste and fraud nevertheless exists in federal purchasing and inventory management. What can and should be done to tackle this problem? GAO recommends that OMB develop and implement a long-range, government-wide financial management improvement plan (GAO, 1990:24). The hope is that a plan would result in a coordinated and integrated system and would provide direction and continuity when leadership changes occur. Any real hope for success, however, depends on sufficient resources being available for implementation (GAO, 1990:25).

C. Achieving More Competition

At the heart of purchasing is competition. The goal of any purchasing agency should be to have lively competition, not just in prices, but in the competence of vendors, in the quality of the goods and services bought, and in the ability of vendors to make timely deliveries. Active competition, of course, results in lower prices and higher quality products and services. To this end, most governments stipulate a dollar limit over which competitive, sealed bids must be taken with public notice and opened in public. Most jurisdictions require that bids be awarded to the "lowest responsible bidder." In all but a few cases, this is synonymous with the lowest bidder. The qualification, "responsible," is included to reject vendors with a past history of poor performance or vendors that cannot meet bid requirements.

Below the dollar bid limit, established either by law or policy, statutes usually require that purchases be based on a system of informal bidding or quotes. Usually, the government must receive a specified number of informal bids or quotes before making a purchase. Having a process of informal bidding becomes more important as bid limit amounts are raised, which has been the case in many states (CSG, 1988:24) and local units (NIGP, 1989:18).

Although rules requiring bids and procedures for informal quotes indeed ensures a healthy measure of competition, competition is nonetheless sometimes constrained by laws, by improper purchasing procedures, and by the anticompetitive practices of bidders. Let us examine each.

1. Laws Limiting Competition

Some states and local jurisdictions limit competition by only buying from vendors in their geographic area. As early as 1954, state purchasing officials opposed such in-state preference statutes. Nonetheless, 12 states still have in-state preference laws, requiring that a specific percentage of state contracts be awarded either to bidders located in the state or to firms that produce goods within the state (CSG, 1988:26). The typical level of preference is 5 percent. Research shows that preference laws increase state expenditures by about 3 percent per capita over what would be expected (CSG, 1988:27). Moreover, at least three-quarters of the states have statutes extending some preference to state firms usually in the case of tied bids. States should eliminate any in-state preferences laws.

Many local jurisdictions also limit competition with a "keep the money at home" mentality (NIGP, 1989:13). Ten percent of cities legally require that goods be bought locally, and 37 percent do not have a legal requirement but do so administratively. Nine percent of counties have similar legal restrictions and 33 percent do so administratively. Localities give preference to local vendors because they contribute to the local economy in the form of taxes and outside firms do not. This practice, however, usually results in excessive costs. Instead of a blanket local preference policy, local jurisdictions should determine exactly how much taxes would be lost and only give preference in those few cases where lost taxes are greater than savings gained through competition (for a formula to calculate this difference, see Coe, 1989:100).

Competition is further limited by policies that give preference to small or disadvantaged businesses. In 1961 Congress legislated that "a fair portion" of federal funds be awarded to small businesses. If a firm obtains a federal contract over a certain amount, it must make a "best effort" to place orders with small subcontractors for a specific percentage of the total contract. Fifty-three percent of federal agencies and states either legally or administratively have percentage preferences for small or disadvantaged businesses as do about 32 percent of cities and counties (GIGP, 1989:14). In these instances, legislators have determined that the goals of encouraging small businesses and of promoting social equity are more important than the goal of efficiency through paying the lowest possible cost.

Another way governments limit competition is by requiring purchase of certain goods made only in America. Congress passed the Buy American Act to ensure that the U.S. maintains its ability to produce several "essential" goods. The Act specifies that a contract be awarded to a domestic supplier provided that its price is not over a given percentage greater than that offered by the foreign vendor. A total of 52 percent of federal agencies and states use buy American provisions as do 42 percent of cities and counties. These policies are seen by economists as counterproductive because they, like tariffs, in the long run make American businesses less competitive and ultimately increase prices.

2. *Improper Purchasing Procedures*

Sometimes governments conduct purchasing procedures that limit competition. Often, these actions are simply due to ignorance of more suitable methods. Improper practices are continued because "We have always done it this way." For example, traditionalism sometimes stands in the way of selecting professional services competitively. Historically, professional services—such as those rendered by auditors, fiscal advisors for bond issues, architects and engineers, banks, and lawyers—were not acquired competitively. That is, governments simply negotiated a price and a contract for services with a particular firm and did not inquire of other firms. In the case of consulting

engineers, the charge was a percentage of construction costs based on a formula devised by the American Society for Professional Engineers.

In the last 10 years, however, there has been a notable trend toward more
competition. Governments more often seek from firms competitive proposals
in which price is one factor considered. With respect to the selection of consulting engineers, the Environmental Protection Agency has led the way by
requiring that competitive price proposals be sought by cities and counties that
receive EPA grants to improve their sewage treatment systems. Likewise, the
Government Finance Officers Association (GFOA) calls for competition in the
process of selecting outside auditors to audit financial records.

Experience shows that price competitive procedures can result in lower
prices. Model contracts are available to design Requests for Proposals (RFPs)
and contracts for the services of fiscal advisors (Petersen and Watt, 1986),
banks (Miller, 1986), consulting engineers (Coe, 1979), and auditors (Gauthier, 1989). Nonetheless, some governments are reluctant to seek competition
either for political reasons or because they fear change.

Despite the cost advantages of competition, governments should be careful
when purchasing professional services. Cost should not be the principal factor
considered; instead, most important is the firm's ability to do a professional
job as demonstrated by past experience. The obvious danger, however, is that
elected officials may feel pressured into taking the lowest proposal even
though that firm may be less able to provide a professional product. Because
goods are selected almost always on the basis of the lowest cost, officials may
feel intense pressure to not award a contract for professional services to a
higher costing firm, even though that firm has a demonstrably better track
record. To help governments resist this temptation and to understand the arguments for and against competition, the NIGP has prepared an excellent handbook on the purchasing of professional services (Zemansky, 1987).

Another purchasing practice limiting competition is what is known as
"back door selling" which occurs when vendors cultivate favor among agency
personnel who use their products. Suppliers may try to gain favor by financial
enticements such as gifts, bribes, kickbacks, and expense paid trips to the
vendor's home office. Most often, however, the sales representative simply
gains an edge by being helpful in supplying technical data and by becoming a
close friend. Consequently, agency officials become sold on a particular
vendor's items and design the purchasing specifications so that only the
favored supplier can meet them. Determining the frequency of "back door selling" is not possible, but clearly it does happen. For example, 41 state purchasing officials indicate that they are aware of such practices taking place in
their state (CSG, 1988:158).

Other purchasing practices may limit competition as well. For example,
paying invoices slowly discourages vendor competition and often precludes

participation by small businesses that need a steady cash flow to survive. Moreover, competition is limited when a jurisdiction mutually agrees with a contractor to extend a contract. Finally, most favored customer stipulations restrict competition by requiring that contractors not offer to other clients prices lower than those quoted to the government.

3. Anti-Competitive Practices by Bidders

Though an infrequent occurrence, competition is restricted by vendors themselves in two ways. First, firms may resort to collusive bidding. For example, they may rotate low bids among each other or may allocate business by geographical location or territory. Second, firms may submit identical bids because a manufacturer agrees with his distributors on a set price, or because competitors agree on charging one price within a geographic zone.

Collusive bidding often is especially hard to detect. Unlike governmental decisions that must be made in the public arena, suppliers' decisions to act in restraint to trade are made secretly. Two handbooks that explain how to counter anti-competitive practices are *Government Purchasing and the Antitrust Laws* (1977) and *Impediments to Competitive Bidding* (1963).

III. ADVANCES TO THE FIELD OF PURCHASING

Notwithstanding the need to increase training, to reform federal purchasing, and to achieve greater competition, the field of purchasing has made some very significant strides especially during the 1970s and 1980s. A singular development was the publication of the Model Procurement Code by the American Bar Association (ABA). The NIGP and the National Association of State Purchasing Officials (NASPO) find much to commend the code but have some reservations about parts that do not reflect accurately state and local experience (CSG, 1988:12). All parties agree, however, that the code has increased the public's awareness and interest in improving governmental purchasing.

The code recommends that purchasing policy be separated from purchasing operations. The policy functions should be carried out by a central policy office, located preferably as a separate entity in the executive branch. The policy office can be headed by an official under the chief executive or by a board. The policy office should issue purchasing regulations and conduct research and training.

On the other hand, actual day to day purchasing should be headed by a chief procurement officer with at least eight years purchasing experience.

The code is used as a guide. States and local jurisdictions adapt it to their own local conditions. By 1988, 13 states had passed bills based on the model code. Some states, like Georgia, adopted only parts of the code. Bills were also being drafted or are under consideration in six other states (Lemov, 1988:97). At the local level, a survey of larger local jurisdictions indicates that 29 percent have adopted the model code (NIGP, 1989:4).

Only a few of the 13 states that have adopted the model code have mandated that their local jurisdictions adopt the code. New Mexico requires that all but home rule cities adopt the law, and South Carolina and Virginia mandate that local jurisdictions enact procurement ordinances consistent with the state code.

A. An Increased Ethical Awareness

Purchasing is potentially an ethical minefield because large sums of moneys are involved. At one extreme, bribery, kickbacks, and fraud can occur. Such instances are relatively uncommon but do occur. For example, in a recent New York scandal, 106 municipal officials were offered bribes and 105 accepted them (Lemov, 1988:96). Furthermore, scandals in Defense contracting are an unfortunate occurrence.

Governments have taken various actions to curb such abuses. Reaction has been especially intense at the federal level. In 1986 Congress enacted the Anti-Kickback Act, which provides civil and criminal penalties for kickbacks between subcontractors and contractors. The law also spells out the fine points on bribery, illegal gratuities, outside income, kickbacks, conflicts of interest, and 47 different forms of contract fraud. The law is a maze, and as a consequence, the General Services Administration teaches a course on ethics to federal purchasing officials (Johnston, 1989).

At the state level, various actions have been taken as well. Codes of ethics have existed in states since the early 1900s. However, not until the 1970s did conflict of interest laws become common due to numerous scandals. Between 1974 and 1984, 45 states enacted new conflict of interest provisions or revised existing ones (Walsh and Leighland, 1989). Additionally, states have adopted the model code or use it as a guide. The code eliminates any possible errors of judgment due to vague or non-existent policies and procedures. The code prescribes very specific and comprehensive rules for organizing procurement offices, for soliciting and handling bids, and for dealing with protests about contracts. The code also has very specific ethical prohibitions against purchasing agents accepting any gifts, favors, or meals.

The publication, *Ethics and Quality Purchasing* (Zemansky, 1988), is helpful to those looking for guidance in the area of purchasing ethics. This handbook contains the *NIGP Code of Ethics*, samples of model city ordinances on ethics, and typical ethical dilemmas faced by purchasing agents and other managers. Without clear and specific guidelines, what constitutes ethical behavior is murky. For example, can a purchasing agent accept insignificant items from suppliers like a desk calendar? Can an employee accept a lunch from a supplier when business is discussed? Should managers be able to resign and use their expertise to help businesses that contract heavily with the government? The answers to these and other such ticklish questions should be clearly spelled out in the law or in a written procedures manual.

B. Innovative Purchasing Techniques

The field of purchasing is becoming more sophisticated on two fronts. First, smaller local units are adopting professional procedures that larger jurisdictions have used for some time. In this vein, smaller jurisdictions are making real progress with respect to inventory management and to cooperative purchasing. Second, governments of all sizes are adopting new and advanced techniques such as value engineering, computerization, total cost purchasing, faxing, commodity coding, and life-cycle costing. Let us discuss each of these improvement areas.

1. *Inventory Management*

Inventory control has long been a deficient area of governmental purchasing. For example, the typical governmental inventory only turns over three times per year (NIGP, 1989:8). That is, the inventory's annual sales divided by the average monthly inventory on hand is three times. Inventory turns in the private sector vary with the industry but generally are seven or higher. This means that governments are tying up in their inventories excessive amounts of cash that could be invested or used for other purposes. One empirical study documents this fact (Reid et al., 1984). Moreover, even with such sizable inventories on hand, sometimes critical parts or supplies are not available when needed.

One reason for this problem is that the inventory function often is performed by operating departments not by central purchasing. Central purchasing has more expertise in inventory management, and it makes sense to centralize all purchasing functions. This is the trend at the state level. Twenty-three states report that inventory and property disposal are now more often a function of central purchasing (CSG, 1988:169).

A second reason why inventory control has been slack is that, until the 1980s, inexpensive software was not available to manage inventories. To order the optimal amount and minimize stock on shelf, the economic order quantity (EOQ) method must be used. EOQ is based on the relationship between the cost of placing an order, an item's annual usage, and the cost of carrying the item in the inventory. Furthermore, this method calculates the optimal reorder point and a safety margin for each item of stock. Considering that a typical inventory has a large number of items in stock, these formulae must be automated.

Historically, large governments have had the programming staff to develop inventory management software to make such calculations; however, small local jurisdictions did not have programmers. However, since the mid-1970s a wide variety of off the shelf inventory management software has been written. It is available at an inexpensive price and can be operated on personal and mini-computers. Consequently, many small local jurisdictions are now implementing inventory control systems and this trend will continue.

2. *Cooperative Purchasing*

Governments can cooperatively purchase with each other in three ways. First, two or more jurisdictions can combine their requirements into a single request for bids either for goods or for services. Second, one government may operate a warehouse and allow one or many governments to buy from the warehouse. For example, schools buy and stock large inventories of office and maintenance supplies. Schools can allow cities and counties to take advantage of the lower unit costs of these goods by permitting them to buy out of the school inventory. Finally, cooperative purchasing most commonly happens when local jurisdictions buy goods on state contracts. States buy large amounts and commonly obtain significantly lower unit prices than local jurisdictions. Only five states (Florida, Hawaii, Kansas, North Dakota, and Vermont) do not permit local jurisdictions to purchase on state contract (CSG, 1989:167–168). Further, 45 states formally or informally help local units with mailing lists, specifications, and similar information.

Cooperative purchasing results in substantial savings. Savings of at least 10 percent are reported by 80 percent of cities and counties (NIGP, 1989:7). Moreover, 43 percent of federal and state agencies report savings of more than 15 percent. And in the case of some goods, the savings are greater than 30 percent.

Despite the obvious cost advantages of cooperative purchasing, about a third of larger local governments do not do it (NIGP, 1989:7). The percentage of nonuse is undoubtedly higher in small sized local units. Why? The biggest constraint is a "keep the money at home" attitude on the part of local elected officials. Local jurisdictions do not purchase on state contract because they think that goods and services bought from suppliers in their jurisdiction will contribute to the tax base. This is true. The empirical question, however, is how much taxes are gained versus dollars lost on purchases not made cooperatively? A method is available to make such a determination (Coe, 1989) and to work out the often delicate political aspects of implementation (Singer, 1988). However, despite these aids and the obvious economic advantage, key business officials sometimes place such intense political pressure on local elected officials to buy locally so that the "money is kept at home."

In addition to buying on state contract, there is a growing trend toward local jurisdictions co-purchasing (Lemov, 1988:96). For example, 27 towns in Connecticut jointly accept bids on 12 items, such as chlorine, gasoline, paint, and fertilizer. Moreover, local jurisdictions band together to purchase services cooperatively. For example, 40 cities in Allegheny County, Pennsylvania share six street sweeping machines and three catch basin cleaning machines; ten cities in Georgia jointly employ someone to test their wastewater treatment plants; and three cities in Maryland jointly purchase computer hardware and software.

Cooperative purchasing is also being considered between states. In-state preference policies complicate this arrangement; nonetheless, a number of possibilities are being examined. For example, Florida, Georgia, and Alabama are considering joining to buy long-distance telephone services at cheaper rates.

3. *Performance Purchasing*

A growing trend exists to purchase based on overall performance not just on lowest price. Performance purchasing looks at factors other than just price. Compared to 5 years ago, 44 states report that they are taking more into account the cost of supplies, energy, parts, warranties, maintenance, and other costs of owning and operating a product in determining the low bidder (CSG, 1988:144).

Performance purchasing requires that performance specifications be used. The specifications aim at purchasing goods that are both economical and efficient. Performance purchasing looks at whether prospective products have characteristics that will result in more efficient operations. The efficiency of each brand can be determined from technical data required to be submitted as part of the bid process. Sometimes central purchasing must use outside expert knowledge to assess technical data.

An aspect of performance purchasing is Life Cycle Costing (LCC), which considers the total cost of ownership of a commodity or building. In addition to the initial acquisition cost, LCC accounts for the cost of using and of disposing of commodities. The rationale behind LCC is that, while the initial cost of a product may be greater than a competing good, the cost of ownership may be less because, over its useful life, it is less expensive to operate or maintain. LCC is used for such energy consuming items as any motorized vehicle, air conditioners, water heaters, pumps, typewriters, lamps, and copying machines. LCC is also used to decide what types of buildings to construct based on a building's energy usage over its useful life.

Because of the oil shortage of the early 1970s, LCC and other energy preserving practices were very common. However, as the energy crisis abated, LCC became less frequent, which is unfortunate because LCC is such an effective cost-saving measure.

Historically, governments have not made full use of LCC because of the political problem sometimes caused when awarding bids that are not the lowest. Another reason for nonuse is that smaller governments are not able to develop the very technical specifications needed to purchase energy consuming goods. Top managers should address the political obstacle by clearly documenting to elected officials and to the citizenry the substantial savings that result from LCC. Regarding specifications, in the 1970s the federal government subsidized several states' development of LCC specifications. Government wishing to use LCC should acquire specifications from the states of North Carolina and Connecticut, which have specifications for over 40 items.

4. *Value Engineering*

Value engineering is a method of analyzing a product or service so that its function can be performed at the lowest possible overall cost without sacrificing quality. Achieving the lowest cost may require redesigning or eliminating components by using different, new, or more efficient technology. Value engineering can be used during a project's design phase or during its construction. The federal government conducts value engineering on defense projects, highway construction, and water resource projects. Moreover, the Environmental Protection Agency (EPA) requires that value engineering be done during the design phase of wastewater treatment projects costing more than $10 million. An explanation of the EPA approach illustrates both the process and benefits of value engineering.

During the design phase, a local jurisdiction that has received an EPA grant over $10 million must form an independent team of professionals. EPA guidelines recommend that these professionals have expertise in design, sanitary, structural, electrical, and mechanical engineering. Next, the local jurisdiction briefs the team on the project's purposes, requirements, capacities, cost, and other specifics. The value engineering team then studies the project's plans and specifications to identify and evaluate alternatives that will accomplish the project at less cost or more efficiently. The local jurisdiction then reviews and assesses proposed changes and incorporates them into the final design. EPA reports that from 1977–1983, value engineering has resulted in net savings of $400 million on 273 projects (GAO, 1985:13).

After the project is designed, value engineering during construction takes advantage of a contractor's expertise. An incentive clause is included in the bid package and the subsequent contract. If the contractor proposes cost savings measures, and the owner agrees to the proposal, a contract change order is processed specifying the revised construction measure, the reduction in contract price, and the contractor's share of any savings. EPA does not require value engineering during construction; thus, it is much less prevalent. Nonetheless, where performed, value engineering during construction results in very large cost savings (GAO, 1985:7).

The use of value engineering will increase. The General Accounting Office (GAO) strongly urges that value engineering be conducted on EPA-funded wastewater treatment projects costing $10 million or less and that EPA funds be able to be used to pay for the cost of the value engineering team (GAO, 1985:13). Furthermore, GAO strongly promotes the use of value engineering in all federal agencies that have construction projects.

5. *Computerization*

When asked to cite the single change or improvement most benefiting their department, state purchasing agents most often referred to computerization (CSG, 1988:171). Computers are used for a wide variety of functions. We have already referred to the inventory system. Another very useful purpose is to maintain an inventory of how much, how often, and from whom commodities have been bought. Data on usage patterns, current and future market conditions, warehouse capacities, and inventory levels are used to determine whether particular items can be bought more advantageously either as an individual purchase or in great volume. Moreover, automation is used to maintain vendor history files, generate bid lists, and track purchase orders.

The NIGP has developed purchasing software that will operate on personal computers. One valuable aspect of this package is its commodity coding system. Governments buy thousands of different items. Large governments have names of bidders frequently numbering more than 8,000. To ensure a good response from bidders, the bidders list needs to be coded into major commodity classifications. The extent to which major commodity classes are subdivided depends on the nature of the item and the responses received to bid solicitations. The NIGP software has a classification coding system that increases the likelihood of an excellent bidder response.

A total of 23 percent of governments use the NIGP commodity code; 37 percent use some other coding system; and 40 percent do not have a bid classification system (NIGP, 1989:5).

6. *Other Purchasing Enhancements*

According to purchasing officials, the most significant productivity improvement available to the purchasing unit since the advent of the personal computer and the creation of the NIGP software is the use of facsimile machines (NIGP, 1989:19). Facsimile machines are used for a variety of functions:

Use by facsimile machines	Percent of use
Accept request for quotations	77
Accept sealed bids	18
Accept bid bonds	12
Keep bids confidential	71

Apparently, purchasing departments are encountering few problems using facsimile machines for these purposes. Only 6 percent of the respondents say it has created any purchasing problems. Only 7 percent indicated that "junk" messages are a problem. More governments (21 percent), however, have requested a legal opinion on the use of it for bidding, and 14 percent have established a written policy on the use of facsimile machines.

Another trend that will certainly continue to increase is the use of operational recycling programs. Many states and local units are passing mandatory recycling legislation. Governmental jurisdictions buy recycled products, collect materials for recycling, and operated drop off centers and pick up recycled materials. A total of 43 percent of governments operate such a recycling program (NIGP, 1989:20). Purchasing departments often take the lead in awarding recycling contracts and in purchasing recycled goods.

IV. SUMMARY

Governmental purchasing is both an opportunity and a challenge. Strengthening purchasing and inventory management will reduce the cost of government while ensuring that the most appropriate goods and services are available to operating departments. For this to become a reality, however, government must provide more training to purchasing officials and must pay wages that attract professionals.

The future can only bring increased demands on the purchasing profession. New and heightened standards of ethical behavior exist for all public managers. The seemingly harmless, insignificant gift from a thankful vendor now is a risky offering. Moreover, the public should increase its demand for better and more cost efficient services. And yet resistance to new taxes will increase as international business competition squeezes American industry. At the heart of any government is the purchasing function. Sophisticated technology—including computers, new software, and facsimile machines—now aids the purchasing manager. The ultimate challenge is to use this technology to its fullest while ensuring as much competition as possible and efficient procedures and policies.

REFERENCES

Coe, Charles. (1989). *Public Financial Management*, Prentice-Hall, Inc., Englewood Cliffs, New Jersey.

Coe, Charles. (1979). *Getting the Most from Professional Services: Consulting Engineer*, Institute of Government, University of Georgia, Athens, Georgia.

(CSG) The Council of State Governments (1989). *State and Local Government Purchasing* (3rd ed.), Iron Works, Pike, Kentucky.

(GAO) U.S. General Accounting Office (1990). *Financial Management*, Washington, D.C.

(GAO) U.S. General Accounting Office (1989). *Financial Integrity Act*, Washington, D.C.

(GAO) U.S. General Accounting Office (1987). *Procurement Personnel: Information on the Procurement Workforce*, Washington, D.C.

(GAO) U.S. General Accounting Office (1985). *Greater Use of Value Engineering*, Washington, D.C.

(GAO) U.S. General Accounting Office (1977). *Government Purchasing and the Antitrust Laws*, National Association of Attorneys General, Washington, D.C.

(GAO) U.S. General Accounting Office (1963). *Impediments to Competitive Bidding*, Council of State Governments, Iron Works, Pike, Kentucky.

Gauthier, Steven J. (1989). *Audit Management Handbook*, Government Finance Officers Association, Chicago, Illinois.

Johnston, David (1989). Boning up on new ethics of procurement. *New York Times*, May 23.

Lemov, Penelope (1988). Purchasing officials push new techniques to get more for their money. *Governing*:40–43, 45–47.

Miller, Girard (1986). *Investing Public Funds*, Government Finance Officers Association, Chicago, Illinois.

(NIGP) The National Institute of Governmental Purchasing (1989). *Results of the 1989 Procurement Research Survey*, Falls Church, Virginia.

Petersen, John E. and Watt, Pat (1986). *The Price of Advice*, Government Finance Officers Association, Chicago, Illinois.

Reid, Richard A., Huth, Case, and Bryson, Donald N. (1984). Inventory cost determination: A public sector challenge. *Journal of Purchasing and Materials Management*. 20:27–31.

Singer, Jerry (1988). *Purchasing Management*, International City Management Association, Washington, D.C.

Walsh, Annette H. and Leighland, James (1989). Designing and managing the procurement process. In *Handbook of Public Administration*, J. L. Perry (Ed.). Jossey-Bass, San Francisco, pp. 483–498.

Williams, Robert F. and Bakhshi, V. Sagor (1988). Competitive bidding: Department of Defense and private sector practices. *Journal of Purchasing and Materials Management*. 24:29–35.

Zemansky, Stanley D. (1987). *Contracting Professional Services*, National Institute of Governmental Purchasing, Falls Church, Virginia.

Zemansky, Stanley D. (1988). *Ethics and Quality Public Purchasing*, National Institute of Governmental Purchasing, Falls Church, Virginia.

11

Contracting Out: A Comparative Analysis of Local Government Practices

Lawrence L. Martin

Florida Atlantic University, Fort Lauderdale, Florida

I. INTRODUCTION

The adoption of privatization techniques as an integral component of the financial management practices of government has been called one of the most important public administration developments of the 1980s (Moe, 1987; Seidman, 1990). As Kolderie (1986) has observed, once government realized that a decision to *provide* a service need not be ipso facto a decision to *produce* that service in-house with government employees, whole new ways of thinking about government service delivery came into being.

The privatization of public services has become so much a part of the fabric of government today that the National Academy of Public Administration suggests that the tools of privatization should be part of every public administrator's repertoire of financial management skills (Salamon et al., 1989). Of all the various privatization approaches, contracting out is by far the most popular (Touche Ross and Company, 1987). Looking toward the 1990s, government interest in privatization in general, and contracting out in particular, continues to be strong (Clark, 1989; Naisbitt and Aburdene, 1990; Levine, Peters, and Thompson, 1990.)

This chapter explores the use of contracting out by local municipal and county governments. Municipal government is taken to mean: cities, towns, and villages. Counties include parishes and boroughs in states where these units of local government perform traditional county government functions. The chapter begins by defining exactly what the term contracting out connotes in order to differentiate it from other privatization and government financial management techniques. The extent of contracting out by local government is then described. The results of a major study comparing the relative efficiency and effectiveness of contracting out versus direct government delivery of services is then discussed. Finally, the chapter concludes with some speculation concerning the future of local government use of contracting out in the decade of the 1990s.

The data describing the extent of contracting out by local government are derived from a secondary data analysis of three national studies of privatization techniques—including contracting out. Two of the studies were conducted under the auspices of the International City Management Association (ICMA) with the resulting data reported by Shulman (1982); Hatry and Valente (1983); Valente and Manchester (1984), Morley (1989), and Farr (1989). The third study was conducted and reported by Touche Ross and Company (1987).

The two ICMA studies were conducted in 1982 and 1988; both were based on mail surveys. The 1982 survey was sent to 4,700 municipal and county governments nationwide and achieved a response rate of 38 percent (Hatry and Valente, 1983:200). The 1988 survey was sent to 4,870 municipal and county governments and achieved a response rate of 35 percent (Farr, 1989:ix). The Touche Ross and Company study was conducted in 1987 and consisted of a mail questionnaire sent to all municipalities over 5,000 population and all counties over 25,000 population; a 19 percent response rate was achieved (Touche Ross and Company, 1987:1).

The combined timing and use of the ICMA and Touche Ross and Company studies adds significantly to our general understanding of local government involvement with contracting out because they permit both cross sectional and longitudinal comparisons to be made. The two ICMA studies are particularly useful because the 1988 survey was modeled after the 1982 survey and focused on essentially the same service areas.

The Touche Ross and Company study also asked local governments to comment on their future privatization plans, with particular attention being paid to contracting out. The Touch Ross and Company study thus provides us with the ability to peer into the future of local government contracting in the 1990s.

II. CONTRACTING OUT DEFINED

As originally conceptualized by Hatry (1983), the term "contracting out" is defined as a legally binding agreement between government and a private entity where the government pays the private contractor to provide some service. Thusly defined, contracting out excludes both intergovernmental contracts and franchising. Because intergovernmental contracts do not involve private sector entities, this administrative practice is generally not considered a form of contracting out nor even a form of privatization.

Contracting out also excludes franchise agreements which are considered a separate and distinct privatization approach. Under the franchise approach, government grants a private sector organization the exclusive right to provide a service in a specifically defined geographical area with the citizen or user directly paying the franchisee (Hatry, 1983:5). The major difference then between contracting out and franchising is who pays, despite the fact that both practices involve the use of contracts. If government pays the service provider, the practice is considered contracting out. If consumers or users directly pay the service provider, the practice is considered franchising. The distinction between contracting out and franchising may seem artificial to some. Nevertheless, it is important in correctly interpreting the data presented in this chapter because the definition of contracting out used in the two ICMA studies was based upon Hatry's definition and excluded franchise agreements (Hatry and Valente, 1983; Farr, 1989).

III. THE EXTENT OF LOCAL GOVERNMENT CONTRACTING OUT

As a framework for analysis, the two ICMA studies selected five major local government service areas for study: 1) public works, transportation, and utilities, 2) public safety, 3) health and human services, 4) parks and recreation services, and 5) general government support services. These same five local government service areas are consequently used to organize the following discussion of local government contracting out activity.

In interpreting the data in the tables that follow, a note of caution is urged when making comparisons between the 1982 and 1988 study data. In the 1982 ICMA survey, local government respondents were asked to indicate if they contracted out with a private profit making firm, a private neighborhood organization, or a private nonprofit organization. In the 1988 study, local government respondents were asked only to indicate if they contracted out with a private organization.

The actual effect that the differing response categories may have on the reported incidence of contracting out activity in the 1988 study is unclear. At least one researcher suggests that the different response categories may have led to an underreporting of contracting out in the 1988 survey (Morley, 1989:38). This conclusion is based upon the contention that in such areas as health and human services, some local government respondents may not have included nonprofit contractors in the response category "private organizations."

In the following tables, two figures appear for some services under the heading "1982 Survey." The first figure represents the percentage of local government respondents who reported contracting out with a private for-profit organization; the second figure represents the proportion that reported contracting out for the same service with a private nonprofit organization. The second figure is included when, in the opinion of the author, the reported contracting out activity with nonprofit organizations was significant enough to warrant inclusion. The 1982 data regarding contracting out activity with private neighborhood organizations is not reported in the following tables due to the infrequency and insignificance of this mode. As a final caution, the reader is reminded that where data for contracting out activity with both for profits and nonprofits is presented, the figures contain some double counts (i.e., some local government respondents reported contracting out the same service with both for profit and nonprofit organizations). Consequently, the two figures for extent of nonprofit and for profit activity cannot be combined.

With the above cautions in mind, the discussion of the extent of local government contracting out activity begins with the service area of public works, transportation, and utility services.

A. Public Works, Transportation, and Utility Services

Table 11.1 presents the data from the 1982 and 1988 ICMA studies on the use of contracting out in the area of public works, transportation, and utility services. The percentages represent the proportion of local government respondents reporting that their jurisdictions contracted out for each of the identified services.

Two major observations can be made about the data in Table 11.1. First, public works, transportation, and utility services constitute a service area where considerable local government contracting out activity is taking place. The most popular contracted services include: solid waste collection (both commercial and residential), street repair, street light operation, tree trimming and planting, and hazardous waste disposal.

The second major observation that can be made about Table 11.1 is that the level of contracting out activity in this service area appears to have remained relatively stable between 1982 and 1988. Between the two time periods, 1982 and 1988, no service demonstrates any major decline in contracting activity and only one service, utility billing, demonstrates a major increase. In 1982, only 13 percent of local government respondents indicated they contracted out utility billing services. In the 1988 survey, however, 32 percent indicated that their jurisdictions contracted out for this service.

The 1988 survey indicates that hazardous materials disposal has become one of the major contracted services in this service area with 44 percent of

Table 11.1 Local Government Use of Contracting Out in the Area of Public
Works, Transportation and Utility Services, 1982 and 1988

Service	1982 Survey[a] %	1988 Survey %
Residential solid waste collection	35	36
Commercial solid waste collection	44	38
Solid waste disposal	28	25
Street repair	27	36
Street and parking lot cleaning	9	15
Traffic sign installation and maintenance	26	27
Street light operation	39	46
Meter maintenance and collection	7	7
Tree trimming and planting	31	36
Cemetery administration and maintenance	11/8	11
Parking lot and garage operations	12	14
Bus system operation and maintenance	24/9	26
Airport operations	24/4	30
Utility meter reading	10	7
Utility billing	13	32
Hazardous materials disposal	X	44

X = missing data or question not asked.

[a] Where two figures appear, the first reflects contracting out activity with for-profits, the second
with non-profits.
Sources: Adapted from Valente and Manchester, 1984:96; Shulman, 1983:8; and Farr, 1989:xii.

local government respondents indicating they contract out for this service.
Missing data preclude a determination of the extent of hazardous waste collection contracting out in 1982.

B. Public Safety

Local government contracting out activity in the service area of public safety
is shown in Table 11.2. The most prominent feature of Table 11.2 is the relatively minor amount of contracting out activity that appears to be taking place
in this service area. Except for vehicle towing and storage—and to a
significantly lesser extent—emergency medical services, local government
appears disinclined toward contracting out for public safety services. The
operation of prisons and jails and the operation of parole programs, two services included in the 1988 study for the first time, also show only minor contracting out activity.

Table 11.2 Local Government Use of Contracting Out in the Area of Public Safety, 1982 and 1988

Service	1982 Survey[a] (%)	1988 Survey (%)
Crime prevention and patrol	3/2	4
Police/fire communications	1/3	1
Fire preventions and suppression	1/3	1
Emergency medical services	13/10	18
Traffic control/parking enforcement	1	1
Vehicle towing and storage	78	80
Operation of prisons and jails	X	1
Operation of parole programs	X	3

X = no data or question not asked.

[a] Where two figures appear, the first reflects contracting out activity with for-profits, the second with non-profits.

Sources: Adapted from Shulman, 1982:8; Farr, 1989:6; and Morley, 1989:38.

With a few notable exceptions, such as San Francisco, California's long standing practice of contracting out patrol services and Scottsdale, Arizona's contract for fire suppression services with the private firm Rural Metro (Fitzgerald, 1989), the contracting out of public safety services appears to be an idea whose time has not yet come. A possible explanation for the apparent absence of local government interest in contracting out public safety services may be ongoing reservations concerning constitutional and civil rights issues associated with the practice—particularly when the powers of arrest and incarceration are involved (Mullen, Chabotar, and Carrow, 1985; Hackett, 1987).

C. Health and Human Services

In Table 11.3, the extent of local government involvement with contracting out for health and human services is presented.

When it comes to health and human services, government at all levels has a long history of involving the private sector in service delivery (Benton, Field, and Millar, 1978; Hatry and Durman, 1985; Kettner and Martin, 1987). In 1978, the Urban Institute estimated that nationally more public financed human services were provided under contract with the private sector than were provided directly by government (Benton, Field and Millar, 1978).

In interpreting the data in Table 11.3, the problem with the differing response categories between the 1982 and 1988 surveys becomes apparent. As can been seen from the 1982 data, local government is significantly involved

Table 11.3   Local Government Use of Contracting Out in the Areas of Health and Human Services, 1982 and 1988

Service	1982 Survey[a] (%)	1988 Survey (%)
Sanitary inspections	1/5	3
Animal control	6/8	11
Animal shelter	13/17	17
Management and operation of hospitals	25/24	24
Public health programs	7/25	19
Drug and alcohol treatment programs	6/38	34
Mental health and retardation programs	6/38	35
Child day care	33/34	34
Child welfare	5/22	17
Programs for the elderly	4/28	19
Management and operation of public housing	12/17	14
Para-Transit operations	22/20	30
Operation of homeless shelters	X	43
Food programs for the homeless	X	26

X = no data or question not asked.

[a] Where two figures appear, the first reflects contracting out activity with for-profits, the second with non-profits.

Sources: Adapted from Shulman, 1982: 8–9; Hatry and Valente, 1983:203; Morley, 1989:37; and Farr, 1989: xiii.

in contracting out for health and human services with both profit and nonprofit organizations. For several services identified in the 1982 study, such as drug and alcohol treatment and mental health and retardation programs, local government respondents reported contracting with more nonprofits (38 percent) than they did with for profits (6 percent). As stated earlier, the use of the single response category "private organization" in the 1988 study may have led to an underreporting of contracting out activity with nonprofits.

The potential problem of underreporting in the 1988 study notwithstanding, a couple of major observations can be made about the data in Table 11.3. First, local government appears to be continuing its historic, and significant, involvement with contracting out for health and human services. Second, most services show either little change or a slight decrease in contracting out activity between the 1982 and 1988 studies although contracting out activity for 1988 may be understated somewhat.

If indeed contracting out for health and human services declined slightly during the 1980s, the most likely explanation would be that this service area represents a mature market for contracting out and thus one would not expect to find much of an increase—and perhaps even expect some decrease—in overall contracting out activity.

Two human service programs, operation of homeless shelters and food programs for the homeless, not reported on the 1982 study, show significant contracting activity in the 1988 study. Some 43 percent of local government respondents reported they contracted out for the operation of homeless shelters.

D. Parks and Recreation Services

Table 11.4 presents the level of local government contracting out activity involving parks and recreation services. Except for the operation of arts programs, local government is not significantly involved in contracting out in this service area. Fluctuations between the 1982 and 1988 data show significant decreases in contracting out activity involving the operation of libraries, museums, and arts programs. This decrease in activity involving the operation of libraries, museums, and arts programs could be real, or again it could simply be an artifact of the problem of differing response categories between the 1982 and 1988 surveys.

E. General Government Support Services

One might well assume that the area of general government support services would be one where a great deal of contracting out activity would be taking place. As Table 11.5 illustrates, local government contracting out in this ser-

Table 11.4   Local Government Use of Contracting Out in the Area of Parks and Recreation, 1982 and 1988

Service	1982 Survey[a] (%)	1988 Survey (%)
Recreation services	4/12	8
Management and operation of recreation facility	8/9	12
Park landscaping and maintenance	9/2	13
Operation of convention centers and auditoriums	5/6	11
Operation of libraries	1/10	1
Operation of museums	3/30	8

[a] Where two figures appear, the first reflects contracting out activity with for-profits, the second with non-profits.
Sources: Adapted from Hatry and Valente, 1983:206; Shulman, 1982:9; and Farr, 1989:xiii.

Table 11.5 Local Government Use of Contracting Out in the Area of General Government Support Services, 1982 and 1988

Service	1982 Survey[a] (%)	1988 Survey (%)
Building and grounds maintenance	19	27
Building security	7	13
Fleet management/vehicle repair:		
heavy equipment	31	41
emergency vehicles	30	41
all other vehicles	28	38
Data processing	22	17
Legal services	48	55
Payroll	10	7
Tax bill processing	22	9
Tax assessing	6/4	10
Delinquent tax collection	10/3	14
Secretarial services	4	7
Personnel services	5	8
Labor relations	23	33
Public relations and information	7/2	10

[a] Where two figures appear, the first reflects contracting out activity with for-profits, the second with non-profits.
Sources: Hatry and Valente, 1983:217; Morley, 1989:37; and Farr, 1989; xiii.

vice area is quite mixed. Some services, such as tax assessing and personnel services, show little contracting out activity, while other services, like fleet management/ vehicle repair, building and ground maintenance, labor relations and legal services demonstrate significant contracting out activity. Overall, however, four times as many services show an increase in contracting out activity between 1982 and 1988 than show a decrease. The area of legal services is particularly noteworthy in that 55 percent of the local government respondents to the 1988 survey reported contracting out for this services.

F. Summing Up Local Government Contracting Out Activity

Based upon the above analysis of the two ICMA national studies, what general inferences can be drawn about the extent of local government contracting out activity? First, local government contracting out activity is broad based. All five of the service areas reviewed demonstrate at least some contracting out activity.

Second, contracting out is more pronounced in certain service areas than others. Considerably more contracting out activity is taking place in the service areas of public works, transportation, utility services, and general government support services. Less contracting out is occurring in the areas of public safety and parks and recreation services. Health and human services appears to represent a mixed bag. The potential problem of underreporting contracting out activity with nonprofit organizations in the 1988 study may be confounding the data here.

Third, the service area of public works, transportation, and utility services, as well as the area of general government support services, evidence a clear upward trend in contracting out activity between 1982 and 1988.

IV. CONTRACTING OUT AND COST SAVINGS

One of the most frequently cited reasons for contracting out is to constrain or reduce service costs. Does local government really constrain or reduce service costs when it contracts out? Does the reality of contracting out live up to its promise? The most definitive answer to this question currently available is provided by a comparative study of contract service delivery and direct government service delivery involving the 121 municipalities that comprise the Los Angeles (California) Standard Consolidated Statistical Area. The study was conducted by Ecodata, Inc. in 1983 under the auspices of the U.S. Department of Housing and Urban Development (Stephens, 1984).

From a list of 138 candidate services, the Ecodata study selected eight services for detailed examination: street cleaning, janitorial services, residential refuse collection, payroll, traffic sign maintenance, asphalt overlay construction, turf maintenance, and street tree maintenance. For each of the eight services, the Ecodata study compared the 121 municipalities on as many variables as possible including service levels and scale of output. Ten contract service delivery cities were eventually matched with ten direct government service delivery cities for each of the eight services. Detailed data were then gathered on the cost of contract service delivery and the cost of direct government service delivery.

Table 11.6 presents the final Ecodata cost comparisons between contract service delivery and direct government service delivery holding constant for scale, level of service, and service quality. For each service a common efficiency measure of unit of service was used for comparison purposes. For example, refuse collection comparisons are based on the cost of collecting one ton of garbage, curbside, one time per week for one year (Stephens, 1984:14).

The costs of administering and monitoring contracted service delivery is also included in computing the total cost of contract service delivery. These costs are frequently overlooked in comparing contract versus direct govern-

Table 11.6   A Cost Comparison Between Contract Service Delivery and Direct
Government Service Delivery

Service	Direct delivery cost ($)	Contract delivery cost ($)	Percent difference
Street cleaning	14.17	9.93	43
Janitorial	6.49	3.74	73
Refuse collection	29.97	21.16	42
Payroll preparation	5.93	6.13	N.S.
Traffic sign maintenance	2,039.44	1,303.38	56
Asphalt overlay	83.99	42.85	95
Turf management	81.09	57.92	40
Street tree maintenance	50.80	37.08	37

N.S. = not significant.
Source: Adapted from Stephens 1984:14.

ment service delivery (Kelly, 1984). Surprisingly, the Ecodata study discovered that on the average, contract administration and monitoring costs represented some 25 percent of the total cost of contract service delivery (Stephens, 1984:6). The overall study findings presented in Table 11.6 are equally surprising.

For seven of the eight study services, the exception being payroll preparation, contract service delivery was less expensive—orders of magnitude less expensive—than direct government service delivery. For example, direct government delivery of asphalt overlay construction was found to be nearly twice (95 percent) as expensive as contract service delivery, while direct government delivery of janitorial service delivery was found to be some 73 percent more expensive than contract service delivery. The cost advantage of contracting out over direct government service delivery is equally pronounced for all the other services excepting payroll preparation.

The Ecodata study broke new ground by also attempting to identify the specific reasons why contract service delivery was less expensive than direct government service delivery. The immediate conclusion that one might jump to is that contractors simply pay their employees lower salaries. This turns out not to be the case. For the eight study services, government on average paid its workers a monthly salary of $1,442.00, while contractors paid their employees a monthly salary of $1,521.00. Additionally, the fringe benefit packages of contractor employees totaled $551.00 per month, while the fringe benefit packages of government workers averaged $524.00 per month (Stephens, 1984:15).

What then does account for the comparative cost advantage that contract service delivery appears to have over direct government delivery? The Eco-data study reached three major conclusions. First, the study contends that private sector contractors tend to get more work out of their employees than does government. The study discovered that contractors' employees worked an average of 237 days per year compared to only 226 days for government workers. The difference is accounted for by the greater number of paid holi-days and vacation days granted government workers.

The second major conclusion reached by the Ecodata study is that private sector contractors make more effective use of part time workers than does government. According to the study, private sector contractors make more and better use of part time workers to flatten out seasonal peaks and valleys in their workload. The third major conclusion reached by the Ecodata study is that private sector contractor managers have more authority than their govern-ment counterparts. The study found that in general, contractors' managers had greater authority over their subordinates in terms of hiring, firing, promotion, and incentives. Unlike government managers, the Ecodata study also found that contractors' managers were also more likely to have overall responsibility for the maintenance of all equipment essential to their work. Unlike govern-ment managers who can point an accusing finger at the equipment services department when mechanical things go wrong, private sector contractor managers can only point a finger at themselves. Consequently, private sector managers are considered to be more accountable and responsible for their overall work.

V. THE FUTURE OF LOCAL GOVERNMENT CONTRACTING OUT

What does the future hold in store for local government use of contracting out? Is contracting gaining or decreasing in popularity with local government? Some light can be shed on these questions by consulting the national study of privatization and contracting out conducted by Touche Ross and Company (TRC) in 1987.

The TRC study asked local governments about their future contracting out plans for certain services. Specifically, the TRC study wanted to know whether local government had specific plans to contract out any services within the next two years. The time horizon is 1989. Table 11.7 presents the resulting data.

As Table 11.7 indicates, local government interest in contracting out is still quite pronounced. However, the types of services local government is

Table 11.7   Local Government Plans for Future Contracting Out Activity

Service	Percent responding
Solid waste collection or disposal	56
Buildings or grounds	47
Vehicle towing or storage	37
Administration (e.g. legal, accounting, payroll, collections, etc.)	30
Traffic signals or street lighting	27
Fleet or vehicle maintenance	27
Data processing	22
Recreation, parks, convention halls, stadiums, or cultural activities	21
Airports	10

Source: Adapted from Touche Ross and Company, 1987:10.

interested in contracting for appear to be more focused than in the past. Solid waste collection and disposal heads the list in Table 11.7, with 56 percent of local government respondents not already contracting out for this service indicating that they had plans to do so prior to the end of 1990. The next most frequently cited services include: building and grounds maintenance (47 percent), vehicle storage and towing (37 percent), administrative activities (30 percent), traffic signal and street lighting (27 percent), and fleet/vehicle maintenance. Also interesting is the finding that 10 percent of local government respondents indicated their jurisdictions were considering contracting out the operation of their airports.

VI.   SUMMARY AND CONCLUSION

In this chapter, the extent of local government contracting out activity across the county was explored. The evidence suggests that examples of contracting out can be found for virtually every type and kind of local government program, service and activity. However, contracting out appears to be more popular in the service areas of health and human services, general government administration, and public works, transportation, and utility services. Contracting out is less popular in the service area of parks and recreation services and is the least popular in the area of public safety.

The available evidence suggests that contracting out can and frequently does result in helping local government to constrain or reduce service costs. Contract service delivery appears to have a clear competitive advantage over direct government delivery due to the ability of private contractors: to get more work out of their employees, make better use of part time employees, and hold their managers more accountable.

In terms of future popularity, local government interest in contracting out shows little evidence of decreasing. The most popular services targeted by local government for contracting out in the 1990s are residential waste collection and disposal, building and grounds maintenance, vehicle towing and storage, and general government administration.

All in all, the use of contracting out as a local government financial management technique only shows signs of becoming more important in the future.

REFERENCES

Benton, Bill, Field, Tracy, and Millar, Rhona (1978). *Social Services—Federal Legislation vs. State Implementation*, The Urban Institute, Washington, D.C.

Clark, Francis P. (1989). Privatization in the United States. *Indiana University School of Public and Environmental Affairs Review. 10*:74–87.

Farr, Cheryl (1989). *Service Delivery in the 90s: Alternative Approaches for Local Governments*. International City Management Association, Washington, D.C.

Fitzgerald, Randall (1988). *When Government Goes Private*. Universe Books, New York.

Hackett, J. (1987). Contracting for the operation of prisons and jails. *Research in Brief.* National Institute of Justice, Washington, D.C.

Hatry, Harry (1983). *A Review of Private Approaches for Delivery of Public Services*. Washington, D.C.: The Urban Institute Press.

Hatry, Harry and Durman, Eugene (1985). *Issues In Competitive Contracting for Social Services*. The National Institute of Government Purchasing, Washington, D.C.

Hatry, Harry and Valente, Carl (1983). Alternative service delivery approaches involving increased use of the private sector. *The Municipal Year Book—1983*. International City Management Association, Washington, D.C. pp. 199–217.

Kelly, Joseph (1986). *Costing Government Services: A Guide for Decision Making*. Government Finance Officers Association, Washington, D.C.

Kettner, Peter and Martin, Lawrence (1987). *Purchase of Service Contracting*. Sage, Newbury Park.

Kolderie, Ted (1986). Two different concepts of privatization. *Public Administration Review. 46*:285–291.

Levine, Charles, Peters, Guy, and Thompson, Frank (1990). *Public Administration: Challenges, Choices, Consequences*. Scott, Foresman and Company, Glenville.

Moe, Ronald C. (1987). Exploring the limits of privatization. *Public Administration Review. 47*:453–460.

Morley, Elaine (1989). Patterns in the use of alternative service delivery approaches. *The Municipal Year Book—1989*. International City Management Association, Washington, D.C., pp. 33–44.

Mullen, Joan, Chabotar, Kent, and Deborah Carrow (1985). *The Privatization of Corrections.* National Institute of Justice, Washington, D.C.

Naisbitt, John and Aburdene, Patricia (1990). *Megatrends 2000.* William Morrow and Co., New York, pp. 154–177.

Salamon, Lestor, Campbell, Alan, Korb, Lawrence, Lourdan, John, Miller, Gerald, Moe, Ronald, O'Connell, Brian, Seidman, Harold, and Waldo, Dwight (1989). *Privatization: The Challenge To Public Management.* National Academy of Public Administration, Washington, D.C.

Seidman, Harold (1990). Public enterprise versus privatization in the United States. *International Review of Administrative Sciences. 56*:15–28.

Shulman, Martha (1982). Alternative approaches for delivering public services. *Urban Data Service Report. 14*, International City Management Association, Washington, D.C.

Stephens, Barbara J. (1984). *Delivering Municipal Services Efficiently: A Comparison of Municipal and Private Service Delivery.* U.S. Department of Housing and Urban Development, Washington, D.C.

Touche Ross and Company (1987). *Privatization in America.* Touche Ross and Co., Washington.

Valente, Carl and Manchester, Lydia (1984). *Rethinking Local Services: Examining Alternative Service Delivery Approaches—Management Information Services Special Report. 12.* International City Management Association, Washington, D.C.

12

Managing State Debt: Issues and Challenges

James R. Ramsey

Western Kentucky University, Bowling Green, Kentucky

Merl M. Hackbart

University of Kentucky, Lexington, Kentucky

I. INTRODUCTION

An aging infrastructure, the changing fiscal federalism of the 1980s, and growing demand for public services in a slow growth economy placed increased financial pressure on the states to seek new solutions to their overall financial management problems in the 1980s.[1] In seeking such solutions, the states have increasingly turned to the credit markets for assistance in meeting their responsibilities for the maintenance of an economically competitive infrastructure system. In addition to providing a readily available financial supplement to their fiscal resources for financing infrastructure, the issuance of bonds is often perceived, both politically and financially, as a relatively "painless" method for providing new capital financing. As a result of the states' increased use of debt financing, the amount of outstanding long-term state bonds increased from $87 billion in 1977 to $264 billion in 1987, an increase of over 300 percent (Hackbart, 1990).

This increasing tendency for state governments to utilize debt financing as a major capital and infrastructure funding source raises several financial management questions including 1) what are the theoretical issues associated with the use of debt to finance state government capital acquisitions, 2) what is the role of debt financing in the capital budgeting process of the states, 3) are there guidelines which can assist a state to determine how much debt it can afford as it contemplates new debt issues, and 4) what are the debt management policy issues which a state should focus on as it evolves an overall debt management/financial management plan for the 1990s and beyond?

241

All of these questions provide significant challenges to the states as they attempt to plan to meet their capital improvement and infrastructure needs. The purpose of this chapter is to consider these questions and review the contributions of recent literature as a means of focusing on these crucial financial management policy issues. In considering these questions, the issuance of bonds to finance capital projects can be an effective and theoretically justifiable tool in the financial management of a state. Moreover, there is an emerging set of principles and analytical techniques to utilize when developing and implementing an effective debt management system. Among the tools and concepts available to states to assist in resolving some of these issues are cost benefit models to aid the capital budgeting process and debt capacity models and concepts to assist state government managers and policy makers to focus on critical debt level issues. Recent research on overall state debt management policy also provides new focus on critical debt issuance, marketing, and management issues. Each of these areas is covered in sections of this chapter.

II. THEORY OF DEBT FINANCE FOR STATE GOVERNMENTS

The conventional wisdom of public finance is that state governments finance current operating expenses (personnel, utilities, rent, travel, and the like) with current revenue sources (taxes, user fees, and recurring governmental transfers)[2] and that capital projects (those expenditures with an extended asset life) may be financed with long-term bonds (Oates, 1972). The rationale for the conventional wisdom is based upon the benefit principle of taxation which states that those consumers who benefit from the consumption of a public good are the taxpayers who should pay for the good. Since capital projects have a multiyear life, the benefit principle suggests that future users of capital projects pay their share of the cost of projects financed with bonds since they are required to pay taxes or user fees to amortize the bonds. Therefore, the conventional wisdom of public finance suggests that financing capital projects with bonds allows some of the project cost to be shifted to future beneficiaries.

This conventional wisdom of public finance has been challenged by those who assume the existence of perfect capital markets and the existence of a "Tiebout world" (Oates, 1972). This challenge to the conventional wisdom suggests that it is impossible to shift costs of government services financed by bonds to future taxpayers. The existence of perfect capital markets implies that all participants in the debt markets have the opportunity to borrow at the same costs. Therefore, an individual would be able to access funds at the same interest rate as would state government. The "Tiebout" world concept is the notion that taxpayers vote with their feet. That is, an individual taxpayer selects the state in which to reside based on the total package of public services offered and the tax payments used to support those services. If a particular state changed its mix of services or taxes, an individual in a "Tiebout world" would move to another state which offered the basket of services and taxes more compatible with his or her tastes and preferences.

Therefore, the challenge to the conventional wisdom of public finance argues that if an individual lives in State A and State A elects to finance a public project through the issuance of bonds, and the individual prefers that the project be paid out of current revenues instead of borrowing, the individual can go to the capital market and purchase a security which will yield a stream of payments equal to their future tax liability. Alternatively, in a Tiebout world, the individual can move to another state that does not use debt finance. In this manner, an individual can avoid paying for debt financed capital projects in the future.

While a full discussion of the challenge to the conventional wisdom is not presented here, it is worthwhile to consider briefly the market for state bonds since an understanding of this market supports the conventional wisdom and refutes the assumptions upon which the challenges to it relies. Governmental bonds, as defined by the Tax Reform Act of 1986, retain their total tax exemption for individual purchasers of the bonds.[3] This tax exemption is the most important and distinctive characteristic of municipal bonds since municipal issuers are able to borrow funds at interest rates which are below the rates at which individuals or businesses can borrow. Therefore, credit markets are not perfect. The interest rate differentials in the taxable and tax exempt markets impact a governmental issuer's decision to pay for capital projects from available revenues or the issuance of long-term debt. Conceptionally, a municipal issuer that has funds available to pay for a long-term capital asset can invest those funds in the taxable securities market and the investment earnings will exceed the debt service cost on long-term bonds issued to finance the project in the tax exempt securities market. Again, this supports the conventional wisdom that the use of debt financing by municipal issuers is often appropriate.

If a state government decides to build a park that has an asset life of many years and the state government seeks to have those individuals who will benefit from the park pay for the park, the governmental unit may issue long-term bonds (say 30 years) to finance the facility. If the park is a general purpose facility that potentially can be used by everyone in the state, general obligation bonds would be issued so that all future taxpayers of the community would share in the cost of the park by making tax payments to the state, a portion of which would be used to retire the bonds used to finance the park. If the facility has a specific purpose (golf, tennis, fishing, and the like), the state would issue revenue bonds and user fees would be imposed so that the consumers of the park would pay a fee, a portion of which would be used for ongoing operating expenses and a portion of which would be used for future debt service payments. In either case, consumers of the good, both now and in the future, would share in the cost of the good over the life of the bonds. Therefore, bond financing of long-term capital projects allows for the cost of projects to be shifted to the beneficiaries of the project.

Borrowing by state governments is appropriate for several practical reasons. First, many public projects (buildings, road projects, prisons) are extremely expensive and debt financing is the only practical means of paying for needed projects. By analogy, most individuals who try to accumulate the funds necessary to pay for a house would never own a house. Second, debt financing avoids tax friction, or the constant changing of tax rates up and down, to provide the revenue needed to finance expensive capital projects on a pay as you go basis.

Therefore, debt financing by state governments is an appropriate means of financing capital projects. This is not to say, however, that all capital projects should be financed through borrowing or that there is not a limit on the amount of debt financing which a state can afford given its revenue sources. For example, as noted earlier, individual consumers often finance home purchases through the use of borrowing. However, the individual has revenue constraints that determine the monthly mortgage payments he or she can make. In like manner, while a number of capital projects may be economically viable and justified, the revenue constraints of a state, along with other factors, define a debt affordability level for that state. The following sections of this chapter deal with the capital budgeting process and this affordability issue.

III. THE CAPTIAL BUDGETING PROCESS AND DEBT FINANCING

As noted earlier, the focus of this chapter is the use of debt financing by state governments in their overall financial management process. It is implicit in this discussion that an issuer has implemented a capital budgeting process and has identified those projects that are candidates for debt financing (Mikesell, 1986). While there is significant variation among the states in the approach taken, a recent study indicated that at least 40 states engage in some form of capital budgeting (Thomassen, 1990). In minimum form, a capital budget exists when "capital and noncapital amounts are reported separately either within an overall budget or as separate budgets" (U.S. General Accounting Office, 1986). Of the states utilizing capital budgets, approximately 20 charge their capital and/or operating budgets with debt service payments associated with their capital debt. Therefore, debt service affordability becomes a critical budgeting decision. Moreover, the calculation and analysis of such project debt service requirements are an integral component of the capital budgeting process. Such assessments include, among other factors, whether the proposed projects are affordable given overall budgetary constraints.

For example, as part of the budget preparation phase of the budget cycle, assume that the capital projects listed in Table 12.1 are all candidates for debt financing, since each project has a net discounted present value of benefits greater than the net discounted present value of costs or, as indicated on Table 12.1, each project has a discounted benefit to cost ratio which is greater than one (see Appendix A for a fuller discussion of these issues). In other words, each project listed in Table 12.1 is economically viable because the residents of the region contemplating the projects would clearly benefit from their completion. Table 12.1 also lists the estimated annual debt service for each project, assuming the projects are financed by fixed-rate long-term bonds. While, as noted, all six projects listed in Table 12.1 are economically viable, a key budgetary decision which must be considered is whether or not all six projects are affordable. If sufficient state revenues are currently available, the budget office could recommend all of the projects for funding; if resources are limited, the budget office could establish a target benefit to cost ratio, discount rate, or internal rate of return and elect to fund only those projects that exceed the target rate. However, from a more practical budgetary perspective, the question is how many of these projects can be afforded for debt financing with current and future revenues given competing uses for such funds? Or, more fundamentally, a state must decide, as part of the budgetary process, the level of available resources it can or should commit to debt service on capital projects given other competing needs (operating programs) for available state resources.

As shown on Table 12.1, if bonds are sold to finance the projects, the total annual debt service is estimated to be $2,000,000. Now, let us assume that the issuer has defined its affordable level of debt so that debt service should not exceed 5 percent of its available revenues so as to limit the displacement of operating programs which higher debt service to total budget ratios would

Table 12.1 Capital Budgeting Process

Project	Ratio of present value of benefits to present value costs	Debt service associated with 20 year bond issue to finance project ($)
1	2.5	200,000
2	2.0	1,000,000
3	1.6	50,000
4	1.6	250,000
5	1.3	400,000
6	1.1	100,000
		2,000,000

require. In this instance, the projected growth in new revenue in the year being budgeted for must be $40,000,000 for all six economically viable projects to be affordable.[4] If the upcoming budget year revenue estimate indicates revenue growth of only $30,000,000, the new affordable level of debt or the debt capacity, given this approach, are those projects which will not cost more than $1,500,000 in annual debt service. Therefore, on a purely financial basis, only the first four projects would be financed if the ratio of present value benefits to present value costs were utilized as the capital allocating criterion. [5]

IV. MANAGING THE LEVEL OF STATE DEBT

The issuance of state bonds represents a long-term fixed commitment of state resources and, consequently, has direct implications regarding a state's ability to provide other critical state services. Although the exact impact of debt issuance on a state's ability to meet other expenditure obligations is frequently unclear, some "crowding out" of other programs is inevitable. Moreover, the ultimate crowding out impact of state bond issuance is difficult to estimate at any point in time, due to the growing use of moral obligation bonds (potential resource liabilities) and the use of lease back financing (such as certificates of participation), which may be used to avoid constitutionally specified debt limitations that constrain new debt issuance. With such arrangements, future state appropriations are, potentially, being committed to debt service, although such commitments may be indirect.

Consequently, the possibility of crowding out effects resulting from excessive debt service obligations (whether general obligation, revenue, or moral obligation) is increasingly a concern of state policy makers and the rating agencies as they attempt to assess the relative credit worthiness of new debt issues. Such concern is typically raised by the credit rating agencies through the rating process. In turn, state policy makers often tend to relate debt policy management guidelines to ratings, because a general rating downgrade is often perceived by the public as an indication of excessive increases in state debt holdings, ineffective financial management, or a combination of these factors. Any of these perceptions can have serious financial and political implications. Moreover, a credit rating downgrade increases the cost of debt financed capital, which can induce further crowding out and the displacement of other operating programs. Therefore, states often, formally or informally, impose stable credit rating requirements as a precondition of the issuance of new debt. (See Appendix B for representation of theoretical issues involved here.)

As noted earlier, just as there are guidelines for the use of consumer mortgage financing and limits to how much an individual can afford for mortgage payments, car payments, and other debt payments, one would expect that there are limits to the amounts state governments may borrow, without crowding out current operating expenses and programs from their budgets. The budgetary relationships between operating expenses and the debt service required to support capital projects is of particular concern during periods of revenue shortfalls (Ramsey, 1987). The debt service on bonds issued to finance capital projects becomes a nondiscretionary expenditure item in the budget. If budget reductions are required to accommodate revenue shortfalls, it is the discretionary items in the budget that must be cut. Moreover, what may be an acceptable or affordable level of debt today, could become an "unaffordable" level of debt in the future should a revenue shortfall occur. For example, as shown in Table 12.2, suppose a state with projected revenues of $1,000,000 defines its affordable level of debt service as 5 percent or $50,000 of projected revenues and approves capital projects for bond financing accordingly. If, in fact, actual revenues are $900,000, then the actual ratio of debt service to revenue is 5.5 percent, a level that may be considered unaffordable. Once bonds are sold, debt service is fixed. Therefore, normally, any future budget balancing expenditure adjustments to meet unanticipated shortfalls would fall proportionately on operating programs. If such operating cuts are substantial, policy makers might have to choose between "high priority" operating programs and meeting debt service. Thus, a state government's assessment of debt capacity must focus upon both the current and future ability to pay. As a consequence, state bond rating agencies attempt to assess an issuer's ability to meet future debt service obligations (including periods of revenue shortfalls) when assigning credit ratings (Lamb, 1989).

Thus, a key component of an effective infrastructure financing and debt management program for state governments must include an estimate of the amount of new debt that a state can incur without overextending its commitment of future revenues to meet debt service. If such an estimate can be developed, policy makers will have better information regarding the amount of new debt that can be issued without significantly displacing other state government expenditures and thus maintain its current and future financial integrity. Oftentimes, state policy makers assume that creit ratings indirectly reflect (at least as perceived by the rating agency) a state's ability to meet future debt ser-

Table 12.2 Impact on Ratio of Debt Service to Revenue of a Revenue Shortfall

	Original Budget Projections ($)	Actual Budget ($)
Revenues	1,000,000	900,000
Debt service	50,000	50,000
Debt service/revenue	0.05%	0.055%

vice and attempt to avoid rating downgrades which might suggest that a state is overextending itself and thus limiting its ability to meet other state priority needs.

Rating differentials can often result in significantly different borrowing costs to issuers. The spread between bonds with the highest and lowest investment grade credit ratings has averaged between 80 and 100 basis points in recent years (Willson, 1986). Therefore, credit rating assignments influence borrowing rates for issuers, future debt service payments, and thus, indirectly, future debt capacity. At the same time, the level of debt of a governmental unit is one of the key financial variables reviewed by the rating agencies when assigning a rating. Thus, Figure 12.1 depicts the relationship between the rating process and an issuer's debt capacity. As shown, current debt levels influence ratings which, in turn, influence capital costs, debt service payments, debt capacity, and/or debt levels. Since the rating assigned to state and local

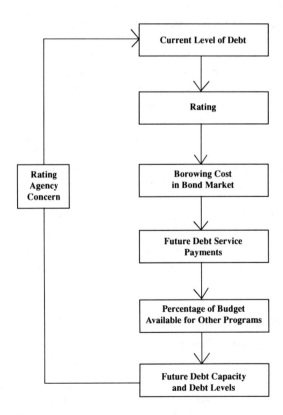

Figure 12.1   Relationship between rating and debt capacity.

debt is a key variable influencing the issuer's borrowing cost and level of debt holdings, it is useful to briefly discuss the rating process.

A difficulty with the rating process is that neither issuers of bonds nor the users of ratings assigned by the major rating agencies are fully informed about either the variables used to determine rating assignments or the weight assignment to these variables (Carleton, 1969; Horton, 1969; and Rubinfield, 1978). Although Standard & Poor's Corporation publishes a useful manual that discusses the key factors influencing a rating, a detailed checklist of factors and weights for each different rating assignment is not provided (Standard & Poor's Corporation, 1989). Several studies have been designed to determine a surrogate set of credit rating variables that statistically relate to rating assignments. One such study identified the following surrogate variables for state issuers: 1) debt, 2) revenues, 3) personal income of residents, 4) population, 5) expenditures, 6) agricultural activity, 7) mineral extraction activities, 8) manufacturing, and 9) general demographic information (Osteryoung, 1978). Another study concluded that for local governments, only economic variables show any real discriminating ability in their determination of rating assignments. One authoritative text on municipal bonds identifies "red flags" or trends which would pose potential problems in the fiscal stability of state and municipalities. The categories of "red flags" include 1) revenue based indicators; 2) expenditure based indicators; 3) cash management indicators; and 4) debt indicators (Lamb, 1980).

To determine various approaches to calculating debt capacity, a survey of state issuers was carried out to identify "guideposts" for calculating optimal or maximum debt levels (Ramsey, 1988). To focus upon debt capacity "guideposts" used by state issuers, discussions were held with representatives of the National Association of State Treasurers, the Government Finance Officers' Association, various investment banking firms, and the two major rating agencies to determine those states which have developed procedures for identifying debt capacity levels. Twelve states were identified and studied (Ramsey, 1988). A summary of the debt level "guideposts" used in each of these states is provided below:

Alaska: Credit ratio analysis is based on the ratio of debt service to revenues. State policy has been to keep debt service at or below 5 percent of unrestricted revenues. State officials in Alaska believe that states with "AA" credit ratings like Alaska, rarely exceed the 5 percent level and Alaska officials believe that holding debt service within the limit will preserve the state's rating.

Maryland: Limits debt service on General Obligation (G.O.) debt to 8 percent of general fund and state property tax revenues, and 3.2 percent of state personal income. In addition, Maryland's Capital Debt Affordability Committee recommends G.O. debt to personal income ratio targets based on continuing standards set in 1982 that are calculated to "strengthen" the state's "AAA" credit rating.

South Carolina: Debt service cannot exceed 7 percent of general fund receipts.

Connecticut: Debt service cannot exceed 7 percent of general fund receipts.

Tennessee: Debt service must be less than 15 percent of general fund receipts.

New York: Projects personal income, tax receipts, and population growth for five years. The resulting figures are then used to predict future debt ratios based on borrowing needs set forth in the state's Five Year Capital Plan. These predicted ratios are compared to national norms.

Oregon: Has constitutionally mandated debt ceilings for each category of authorized debt. These ceilings limit debt to specified percentages of the true cash value of all taxable property in the state. Officials in the State Treasurer's office accept these ceilings as total debt capacity and compare the amount of outstanding bonded indebtedness to these figures. Forty-eight percent of this capacity was in use as of June 30, 1986.

Wisconsin: Ties debt capacity to the aggregate value of all taxable property and sets, as upper limits, the lesser of three- fourths or 1 percent of the aggregate value of all taxable property or 5 percent of the value of all taxable property minus indebtedness.

Vermont: Limits new debt issues to 90 percent of the amount of debt retired during the previous year.

Virginia: Compares its Moody's ratios to the national medians.

New Hampshire: Uses Moody's Investors Service ratios as a gauge of appropriate debt levels.

California: Analyzes per capita debt service, debt service per $1,000 personal income, per capita bonded indebtedness, and bonded indebtedness per $1,000 personal income in relation to national averages.

Table 12.3 summarizes the variable(s) identified by the 12 study states as most important in calculating their debt capacities. As can be seen, the most frequently cited factor is revenue (6 of the 12 states). The other factors identified as determinants of debt capacity are: personal income (three states), population/population growth (three states), assessed value of real property (two states), and historical debt levels within the state (two states) (Ramsey, 1988).

V.   DEBT CAPACITY ASSESSMENT

In addition to the rule of thumb and overall guideline approaches utilized by a number of states to manage debt levels, efforts have been undertaken to estimate debt or debt service capacities more precisely based upon statistical

Table 12.3 Independent Variables as Used by States in Calculating Debt Capacity

Revenue	Personal income	Population/ population growth	Assessed property value	Historical debt
Alaska	Maryland	California	Oregon	Vermont
Maryland	California	Wisconsin	Wisconsin	California
South Carolina	New York	New York		
Tennessee				
New York				
Connecticut				

Source: Survey conducted by authors, 1987.

models which focus on economic, demographic, and financial variables which have been identified by the rating agencies and others as affecting or being closely associated with the estimation of state debt capacity.

Such efforts by Ramsey and Hackbart (Ramsey, 1990) utilized multiple regression estimating techniques (ordinary least squares) to estimate a stable credit rating debt expenditure model for various states. In their model, a state's ability to present evidence of ability to sustain a given level of debt represents a proxy for the state's debt capacity for that debt or credit rating level. The following variables were utilized in their model:

1. Per capita income;
2. State revenues;
3. Population; and
4. Assessed value of real property.

While recognizing that many factors, both qualitative and quantitative, affect a state's ability to support a given level of debt and/or retain its credit rating, these variables have been identified as ones for which data are available for the states to utilize in empirically estimating levels of debt which are sustainable and thus warrant stable credit ratings. Also, these variables represent measures of the income or wealth of an issuer and thus represent proxies of a state's fiscal constraint or ability to repay its debt obligation. This modelling approach also assumes that states typically attempt to maintain a stable credit rating. Therefore, by predicting a level of debt which will maintain a stable debt rating, a sustainable level of debt (or debt capacity for the state) can be estimated.

Their model is structured as follows:

$$Y = a + b_1x_1 + b_2x_2 + b_3x_3 + b_4x_4 \tag{1}$$

where Y = a state's debt outstanding, x_1 = a state's per capita income, x_2 =

a state's revenue, x_3 = a state's population, and x_4 = a state's full value of assessed real property.

Theoretically, they assume a positive relationship should exist between debt outstanding and each of the independent variables. That is, the greater the per capita income in a state, the greater the state's fiscal capacity and the more debt and other expenditures the state can afford. In this context, a state's revenues include taxes, agency or user fees, and recurring intergovernmental grants. State population is a proxy for the demographic characteristics of a state, and it is expected that the larger a state's population, the more taxpayers and the greater the ability to pay for debt service and other purchases. The full value of assessed real property is a proxy for a state's wealth base, which would have similar implications.

In their research, data were collected for the 50 states for the time period 1972–1984 and a multiple regression estimating technique (ordinary least squares) was used to estimate their stable credit rating debt level equation. The results of this estimation were:

$$Y = -4450.00 + .5317x_1 + 240.599x_2 + .0528x_3 - .0352x_4$$
$$(58416.512) \quad (.0466) \quad (23.997) \quad (.008856) \quad (.002215)$$
$$ADJ\ R^2 = 0.8454$$

The values in parenthesis below the coefficients represent the standard errors. The independent variables taken as a whole were statistically significant (F test) and each of the independent variables tested alone proved to be statistically significant (t test.). Therefore, their equation appeared to represent a good model or statistical approach for explaining past debt levels and predicting future debt capacity.

For statistical estimating reasons (the possible existence of multicollinearity), several further statistical analysis of the results were undertaken (Ramsey, 1990). While a detailed discussion of this analysis is not presented here, their analysis suggested that the use of the above equation to estimate debt capacity levels may 1) result in biased estimates due to specification problems, and 2) a simpler statistical model could be developed that would produce statistically significant estimates of debt capacity. Therefore, a stepwise regression was performed for each individual state to determine if, for a given state, any of the independent variables could be dropped from this equation without reducing the statistical significance of the equation. That is, the authors suggest that some of the dependent variables in the equation may not help define a state's sustainable credit rating debt level.

Performing a stepwise regression approach to the equation for each of the 50 states, they found that for the states listed in Table 12.4 the revenue variable alone best explains past debt levels and can be used to predict future debt

(Ramsey, 1990). Table 12.5 lists those states for which the personal income variable best explains past debt levels. Table 12.6 lists those states for which the assessed value of real property variable best explains past debt levels. Table 12.7 lists those states for which the population variable alone best explains past debt levels. Table 12.8 lists those states for which none of the independent variables in equation 1 were statistically significant in explaining those states past levels of debt.

Table 12.4 States for Which State Revenue Best Explains Past Debt Levels

Connecticut	Montana
Idaho	New Hampshire
Illinois	Ohio
Indiana	South Carolina
Kentucky	Utah
Michigan	Washington

Table 12.5 States for Which Personal Income Best Explains Past Debt Levels

Missouri	Oklahoma
North Carolina	Wyoming

Table 12.6 States for Which Assessed Value of Real Property Best Explains Past Debt Levels

Delaware	Nevada
Louisiana	New Jersey
Massachusetts	Rhode Island

Table 12.7 States for Which Population Best Explains Past Debt Levels

Georgia	New Mexico
Hawaii	New York
Maine	Tennessee
Minnesota	Texas
Mississippi	Wisconsin

Table 12.8   Those States for Which None of the
Variables in Equation 1 Explain Past Debt Levels

Alabama	Maryland
Alaska	Nebraska
Arizona	North Dakota
Arkansas	Oregon
California	Pennsylvania
Colorado	South Dakota
Florida	Vermont
Iowa	Virginia
Kansas	West Virginia

To estimate future debt capacity levels for an individual state using this conceptual approach, it is necessary to determine from Tables 12.4–12.7 which factor or variable best explains past debt levels for a particular state (Ramsey, 1990). For example, revenue was found to be statistically significant in explaining past debt levels for the state of Kentucky. Future revenues for Kentucky must be estimated (this is done as a prerequisite to the preparation of Kentucky's biennial budget) and "plugged" into the appropriate statistical equation for Kentucky. The official revenue estimates for Kentucky for 1988–1989 and 1989–1990 (1988–1990 biennium) were utilized to predict the state's debt capacity for the next two-year budget period. Kentucky's debt capacity was estimated to be approximately $390 million in new debt financed projects in the next biennium (1988–1990 biennium). Table 12.9 compares this capacity with the authorized debt amounts of the Kentucky General Assembly for the previous four biennial budgets. Table 12.10 shows the historical ratios of state debt to revenue ratios for the same period. These data indicate debt service to revenue ratios, previously reviewed, within guidelines utilized by several states.

Table 12.9   Debt Authorized by Recent Sessions of the General Assembly and 1988–1990 Estimate

BIENNIAL budget periods	PRINCIPAL debt authorized ($)
1980–1982	689,312,400
1982–1984	534,024,000
1984–1986	535,929,000
1986–1988	494,721,100
1988–1990	390,000,000

Table 12.10 Debt Service to Revenue Ratios for Kentucky, 1980–1990

Year	Total revenue (000)	Debt service (000)	Debt service as a percent of revenue
1980	2,895,178	156,751	5.4
1981	3,099,448	165,539	5.3
1982	3,242,716	170,667	5.3
1983	3,452,400	184,887	5.4
1984	3,738,248	201,024	5.4
1985	3,959,214	209,671	5.3
1986	4,248,081	247,384	5.8
1987	4,934,001	247,419	5.0
1988	5,464,858[a]	275,711	5.1
1989	5,783,459[a]	335,441[a]	5.8
1990	6,037,309[a]	350,164[a]	5.8

[a] Estimated

The projected amount of new debt estimated with this statistical technique is a function of projected growth in the variable identified as the most important factor for explaining debt in an individual state (Ramsey, 1990). For example, in the case of Kentucky, if revenue growth is more or less than the amount estimated, the amount of new debt that can be supported will vary accordingly. In addition, the projected amount of new debt service assumes that the proportion of revenues spent for debt service that has existed for approximately the last 20 years should continue in the future. This, of course, is a policy decision which could be changed in the future. Finally, as previously noted, rating agencies analyze many more factors than those identified in this statistical analysis in the determination of a rating. Consequently, an issuer's debt capacity may be impacted, positively or negatively, by nonquantitative factors that cannot be estimated statistically.

VI. STATE DEBT MANAGEMENT POLICY

The task of managing the issuance and repayment of state debt has grown in size and complexity over the last decade. This growth is evident in the amount of debt outstanding (noted earlier as increasing 300 percent from 1977 to 1987), the level of issuing activity (up from $12.4 billion in 1977 to $50 billion in 1987), and the number of separate issuing entities (up 58 percent from 1977 to 1987) (Hackbart, Leigland, Riherd, and Reid, 1990).

Despite growing state use of debt financing, relatively little is known regarding current state debt management policies and practices including the planning of new debt issues, authorization of issues, and structuring, marketing, and repayment practices for outstanding debt issues. A recent study sponsored by the National Association of State Treasurers (NAST) and others (Hackbart, Leigland, Riherd, and Reid, 1990) considered several state debt management policies and practices in an effort to provide a base line perspective regarding these critical financial management issues. The study involved a survey of the 50 states and focused on comparative state practices in the debt management area.

The study found that there are two overriding constraints which influence state debt management practices and options. First, constitutional restrictions on borrowing are common among the states and vary considerably. Second, restrictions imposed on state issuance of state tax exempt bonds by the Tax Reform Act of 1986 (TRA86) has had a significant impact on state debt issuance and management policies. Such restrictions include adjustments to record keeping, requirements for annual reports to be filed with the U.S. Treasury regarding every transaction involving tax-exempt interest, and new rules regarding arbitrage and advance refunding record keeping.

Some 40 states indicated a variety of limitations on state debt issuance and approval procedures existent as a result of constitutional requirements. Among such limitations are specific dollar limits on outstanding debt, approval of issues including referenda and/or extraordinary legislative majorities, and flexible debt limits tied to revenue collection, property values, and the like. Such requirements have strongly influenced the debt issuance and management practices of the states. For example, 8 of the 11 states which currently do not issue full faith and credit bonds have some kind of dollar limit on debt, suggesting that this type of debt limit may severely constrain state borrowing behavior. States may, however, circumvent constitutional limits by foregoing full faith and credit debt completely and, instead, issue nonguaranteed or revenue backed debt, as does Arizona or Colorado. States may also create semiautonomous government corporations to issue such nonguaranteed debt, as in the cases of Indiana and Kentucky. Finally, states may simply change their constitutions periodically to enhance their debt issuance options. For example, Texas is restricted to casual borrowing, a $200,000 ceiling, with no constitutionally detailed avenues authorizing additional debt; each state bond issue is, consequently, authorized via a constitutional amendment.

The sale of state debt involves a series of processes, including decisions regarding the use of bond proceeds (e.g., as part of the capital budgeting process), the authorization of specific proposals to issue debt, the assembly of a team of expert advisors (e.g., bond counsel, financial advisor, other legal advisors, accountants, auditors, and other experts), the design and structuring of the bond issue (decisions regarding size, timing, nature of the debt instrument used, and the like), selection of underwriter or underwriting syndicate (via negotiation or formal competition), arrangements for credit ratings and the like. The study found significant variation among the states regarding the degree of centralization and decentralization and degree of autonomy of issuing entities in carrying out these functions. Centralization and control were more pronounced among the states in the issuance of full faith and credit bonds (27 of 39 states issuing such debt do so through a "central" finance office) and state revenue debt (27 of 34 states issuing such debt) than in the issuance of special purpose or special authority debt. Only a handful of states maintain control over the structuring and sale of debt for special purpose governments or special authorities even though, as indicated, such entities constitute the major growth area for new state bond issues in the decade of the 1980s.

With the emergence of increased state government concern with debt ratings, debt levels, and related issues, debt oversight has emerged as a critical state management issue. Included here are periodic calculations of outstanding debt levels, ongoing and direct review, approval of capital construction plans, and debt issuance supervision and control. The issuance of state G.O. and revenue debt is typically subjected to oversight by a variety of elected and appointed officials of state government. Most debt issuing state special authorities appear to be relatively free from oversight, other than that exercised by their boards of directors.

The principal means of overseeing the activities of these entities is through appointments to the boards of trustees (bodies that also authorize specific bond issues in 32 states, as noted above). Typically, such appointments are made by the governor. In California, Maine, Massachusetts, Pennsylvania and Vermont, for example, the State Treasurer sits on the boards of all special purpose governments issuing debt. In Maine, Missouri, New York and many other states, the governor appoints the trustees of each state's authority. A second means of oversight for special authorities involves formal requirements for regular reporting by these entities. For example, Arizona's Salt River Power District sets its own debt limits and structures its own bond issues, but is required to report amounts of its outstanding debt to the Department of Revenue. Authorities in Hawaii must report on a regular basis to the State Director of Finance, the legislature, and the governor regarding their bond market activity. Authorities in Rhode Island must report all bond issuing activities on a regular basis to the State Public Finance Board. A third means of oversight involves direct controls over special authority actions in the form of specific review and approval powers exercised by officials of regular state governments. For example, the State Treasurers in Delaware, Oregon, and North Carolina must approve capital plans of issuing authorities in those states. The Kentucky Office of Investment and Debt Management reviews and approves all authority capital projects, and manages debt service payments. The governors of New York and New Jersey may veto the board minutes (and thus any and all board actions) of certain authorities in those states, thus affording them a powerful, but rarely used, form of oversight.

As indicated, however, most state authorities, commissions, districts, and the like appear to be relatively free from oversight. For example, the Arkansas Development Finance Authority maintains its own information on debt issues, and is not required to report information to state officials. Similarly, Colorado's authorities are not subject to formal reporting requirements, and are not supervised by any state office. The same is true of special purpose governments in Idaho, Connecticut, Delaware, Montana, Nebraska, Ohio, and a number of other states.

VII. SUMMARY

The issuance of bonds by state governments can play an integral part of their financial management programs. Long- term capital projects for which the present value of benefits exceeds the present value of costs are economically viable and are candidates for bond funding. Conceptually, there is a limit to the amount of debt a state can incur and not crowd operating programs from the budget either presently or in the future. In the determination of an issuer's rating, the rating agency attempts to quantify that issuer's ability to pay the debt service incurred for the life of the issue. Many issuers have formulated their own "guideposts" or rules of thumb to identify appropriate debt limits or ability to pay. A review of the literature and a survey of states indicated that while the rating agencies and states attempt to identify their debt capacity, there have been few efforts to statistically estimate models for calculating an issuer's debt capacity. Efforts of some researchers have, however, begun to focus on approaches to deal with this critical state financial management issue. Likewise, only recently have efforts been undertaken to assess and analyze overall state debt management policies and practices. Such analysis indicates great diversity in state debt management and oversight. Clearly, state debt management policies and practices are emerging as a critical financial management issue. As states assume more responsibility for infrastructure finances, the importance of these issues will be further magnified.

VIII. APPENDIX A

A critical component of the capital budgeting process is the calculation of the present value of capital project benefits and costs. The concept of present value is important since a dollar today has a greater value than a dollar tomorrow. Thus, the calculation of the present value of capital project benefits and costs allows state policy makers to compare "apples to apples" when making the budget decision.

To understand the concept of present value it is easier to start with the concept of future value. If the market interest rate is i, we can invest R_0 today to receive $(1 + i)R_0$ next year; or

$$R_1 = (1 + i)R_0$$

Where R_1 = next year's income.

In two years we would have

$$R_2 = (1 + i)R_i = (1 + i)^2 R_0$$

assuming the interest rate is constant over time. In general, the income we would earn in future years can be written as:

$$R_n = (1 + i)^n R_0$$

Where n = time periods.

Now, we can reverse our thought pattern and ask "how much is R_1 income next year equivalent to today?" That is, what is the present value of a future income of R_1? This could simply be found by:

$$R_0 = \frac{R_1}{1 + i}$$

or dividing each side of the original equation by $(1 + i)$. In general then, the present value of receiving R_n, n years from now is:

$$R_0 = \frac{R_n}{(1 + i)^n}$$

If we have a stream of future income or benefit payments, we can find the present value of this income stream by summing the present value of the income to be received in each year. For example:

$$PV(R) = \frac{R_1}{1 + i} + \frac{R_2}{(1 + i)^2} + \cdots + \frac{R_n}{(1 + i)^n} = \sum_{j=1}^{n} \frac{R_j}{(1 + i)^j}$$

The significance of present value is that it tells us how large an amount of money we would have to invest at the market interest rate in order to generate a stream of returns R.

For example, suppose that a government investment project is expected to generate a financial payment of $1,000.00 per year for 40 years. Suppose further that we can define the market rate of interest to be 6 percent. The present value of this repayment scheme would be:

$$PV(R) = \frac{1000}{1.06} + \frac{1000}{(1.06)^2} + \cdots \frac{1000}{(1.06)^{40}} = \sum_{j=1}^{n} \frac{1000}{(1.06)^j}$$

$$= 1000 \sum_{j=1}^{n} \frac{1}{(1.06)^j} = \$15,046$$

Now, suppose that the entire cost of the project were to be incurred in year 1 (so that the present value of the costs are in fact the cost of the project). If the project cost \$10,000, would it be a worthwhile investment? If the project cost \$15,000, would it be worthwhile? We would tend to think so, but to say for sure we would have to examine the opportunity costs of investing \$10,000 or \$15,000 in some other projects. That is, we may be able to generate a revenue stream of more than \$1,000 by investing \$10,000 or \$15,000 in some other project.

Thus far, the discounting process seems fairly easy and straightforward and it is obvious how discounting can assist in the budgetary decision making process. However, when discounting public investments we encounter several problems, the foremost of which is determining the appropriate discount rate. Previously, market interest rates were discussed as if only one such rate existed. However, in fact there are almost an infinite number of rates which can be utilized.

Until recently, government decision makers believed that the appropriate rate of discount to apply to public expenditures was the cost of borrowing money, which for the government has been low relative to other interest rates due to the perceived credit quality of treasury securities (the lower the discount rate the higher the present value of a project).

It can be argued that government should recognize that its investments withdraw resources from the private sector of the economy and that the correct discount rate for government expenditures is the opportunity cost of capital, i.e., the rate of return in the private sector. That is to say, if the rate of return on private investment projects is 10–15 percent (say this is what GM or IBM earns on their capital investments), then any use of resources by the government which yields less than 10–15 percent is inefficient. Therefore, if we have efficient capital markets, the appropriate discount rate is the rate of return on private investment projects.

It can still be argued that government often uses resources that would not otherwise have been made available for private investment, therefore, the private opportunity cost is irrelevant. Accordingly, the source of government's investable funds determines the appropriate discount rate. In other words, we could construct an average of the private opportunity costs, weighted by the proportions of total government investment financed from each source of funds. This is shown in the illustration on p. 261.

| | Interest weight | | |
Source of Capital	i	w	w × i
foregone investment	10%	½	5%
foregone consumption	6%	½	3%

$$Wa = \frac{Wi}{W} = \frac{8\%}{1} = 8\%$$

In general, the sources of funds rule yields a lower discount rate for public investments than the private opportunity cost rule (again, this is due to the existence of market imperfections).

A final argument regarding the appropriate rate of discount to be used is based upon the notion that public investments are qualitatively different from private investments and that the private motivations leading to a determination of the market interest rate should not be allowed to influence government investments. In other words, there are many expenditures or investments that will not be undertaken in the private market. Therefore, individual consumers and producers cannot be relied upon to express society's preferences for future capital goods because the time horizon of individuals is much shorter than that of society. Thus, government should make the decision as to the rate of time preference of society and this rate of social time preference is then the appropriate rate of discount for government expenditures.

Another argument to support the use of the rate of social time preference as the discount rate is that since we cannot quantify all of the benefits of public expenditures, they tend to be underevaluated. Therefore, we can compensate for this undervaluation by discounting future outputs at a lower discount rate.

This approach is not entirely satisfactory, however, because such rates understate the costs of government investment projects. Therefore, there continues to be some question as to what is the appropriate discount rate to use to calculate the present value of benefits arising from government expenditures.

IX. APPENDIX B: DEFINING DEBT LEVELS

The appropriate allocation of state revenues between operating programs and debt service is a concern of rating agencies, legislators, and executive branch financial managers, and is emerging as a critical financial management policy concern. Unfortunately, significant differences may exist between a theoretically defined debt expenditure model and one that is operationally feasible for state budgetary decision making. From a theoretical point of view, the concept of the appropriate level of debt expenditure may be represented as the level of state resources committed to debt that maximizes the utility of the residents of the state. The commitment of resources to debt financed capital (i.e., debt service) then simply represents one of a set of public goods expenditures available to the residents of the state.

The equilibrium allocation of public resources to debt financed capital is defined in equation A1 as those values of G_1, G_2, and R that maximize the state utility function, subject to its budget or fiscal constrain as specified in Equation A2.

Maximize: $U = F(G_1, G_2, R)$ (A1)

Subject to: $FC = P_2(G_2) + [P_1(G_1) + P_3(R)]$ (A2)

Where:

U = Utility function of goods and services consumed by the residents of a state

G_1 = Quantity of operating goods provided by the state for the public

G_2 = Quantity of capital goods provided by the state and financed with bonds

R = Quantity of private goods consumed by the public

FC = Aggregate fiscal constraint (budget of the state (including all publicized or private resources available to utilize in the acquisition of G_1, G_2, or R by individuals or by public decision makers)

P_1 = Price of operating goods provided by the state

P_2 = Debt-financed capital costs

P_3 = Price of private goods

Given this budget constraint and utility function, one could assume that 1) the historical equilibrating behavior of the political process regarding the selection of debt-financed capital goods vis-a-vis other public and private goods, given state preference patterns, is observable; and 2) the financial market's perception of that behavior, given the risk and uncertainty regarding future economic and demographic conditions of the state, are reflected in the current credit rating of each state. As discussed below, if an "overallocation" of state appropriated funds is made to debt service, a lower bond credit rating might result, increasing P_2 in equation 2. As shown in Exhibit 12.1, a higher price of debt financed capital projects (P'_2) would cause the budget constraint (FC) to rotate counterclockwise to FC_1, resulting in a new point of utility maximum (E'): a point that is lower than the original level of maximum utility (E) that existed prior to the overallocation of debt capacity. Therefore, in this framework, there is a level of debt that exceeds a defined appropriate level for the state and thereby reduces a state's point of maximum utility.

It follows, then, that a state would pursue a policy of maintaining an acceptable credit rating on its bonds and that this credit rating defines, in part, the state's target appropriate level of debt. By maintaining a constant rating,

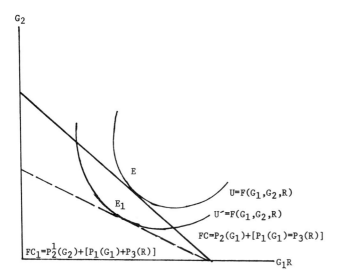

Exhibit 12.1 Equilibrium model for public and private goods given increased cost of debt-financed capital.

the cost of debt would be maintained in approximate equilibrium with alternative uses of the state's resources (assuming constant consumer preferences).

NOTES

1. For example, the Water Quality Act of 1987 phases out federal grants for local wastewater treatment projects. Instead the federal government is now providing "seed money" for states to establish State Revolving Funds for which loans will be made to local governments for these projects. States must pick up twenty percent of the costs of the State Revolving Funds. Most states will use the bond market to finance this cost.
2. Many local governments used revenue sharing funds to finance recurring expenses. The elimination of revenue sharing then created a fiscal strain for these governments as they sought alternative funding sources.
3. The Tax Reform Act of 1986 defined two general types of municipal bonds: governmental bonds and private activity bonds (PAB). The latter are bonds which are issued for the benefit of an individual (student loan bonds and mortgage revenue bonds) or businesses (industrial revenue bonds). PAB are subject to the Alternative Minimum Tax for individuals. Thus, for the first time municipal bonds are not totally tax exempt. Governmental bonds are used for public purpose projects such as governmental office buildings, roads, parks, jails, and the like. These bonds retain their tax exemption for individuals.
4. ($2,000,000 × .05 = $40,000,000)
5. Total debt service for projects 1, 2, 3 and 4 would be $1,500,000.

REFERENCES

Carleton and Lerner (1969). Statistical Credit Scoring of Municipal Bonds. *Journal of Money, Credit and Banking*. November, pp. 750–764.

Hackbart, Merl and Leigland, James L. (1990). State Debt Policy: A National Survey. *Public Budgeting and Finance*. Vol. 10, No. 2, Spring.

Hackbart, Merl, Leigland, James, Riherd, Rhonda, and Reid, Marasia (1990). *Debt and Duty: Accountability and Efficiency in State Debt Management*. The Council of State Governments, Lexington, Kentucky.

Horton, Joseph (1969). A Statistical Rating Index for Municipal Bonds. *Financial Analysts Journal*. March/April, pp. 72–75.

Lamb, Robert and Rappaport, Stephen P. (1980). *Municipal Bonds, The Comprehensive Review of Tax Exempt Securities and Public Finance*. New York: McGraw-Hill Book Company, pp. 98–114.

Mikesell, John L. (1986). *Fiscal Administration: Analysis and Application in the Public Sector*. Chicago: Dorsey Press, Chapter 5.

Oates, Wallace E. (1972). *Fiscal Federalism*. New York: Harcourt Brace Jovanovich, Inc., pp. 153–161.

Osteryoung, J.S. and Blevins, D.R. (1978). State General Obligation Bond Credit Ratings. *Growth and Change*. July, pp. 29–35.

Ramsey, James (1987). Government Finance. *Kentucky 1987 Annual Economic Report*. Lexington, Kentucky: University of Kentucky Center for Business and Economic Research, p. 14.

Ramsey, James and Hackbart, Merl (1988, 1990). State and Local Debt Capacity: An Index Measure. *Municipal Finance Journal*. Vol. 9, No. 1, and Vol. 11, No. 1.

Ramsey, James R., Gritz, Tanya, and Hackbart, Merl M. (1988). State Approaches to Debt Capacity Assessment: A Further Evaluation. *International Journal of Public Administration*. Vol. 11, No. 2.

Rubinfield (1978). Credit Ratings and the Market for General Obligation Municipal Bonds. *National Tax Journal*. March, pp. 17–21.

Standard & Poor's Corporation (1989). *S&P's Municipal Finance Criteria*. New York, NY.

Thomassen, Heinz (1990). Capital Budgeting for a State. *Public Budgeting and Finance*. Vol. 10, No. 4, Winter, p. 72.

U.S. General Accounting Office (1986). *Budget Issues: Capital Budgeting Practices in the States*. Washington, D.C., GAO, p. 2.

Willson, Stephen (1986). Credit Ratings and General Obligation Bonds: A Statistical Alternative. *Government Finance Review*. Vol. 2, No. 3, June, p. 21.

13

Capital Budgeting Practices

C. Bradley Doss, Jr.

Georgia State University, Atlanta, Georgia

I. INTRODUCTION

During the 1980s the fashion in government circles was to emphasize business-like approaches to various types of public services. At the state and local levels in particular, there was much talk about concepts such as economic development and privatization. Efficiency emerged as a major driving force for governmental decision making and officials at all levels of government found themselves becoming more concerned with the "bottom line" than ever before.

Several explanations have been discussed by scholars and practitioners for this new found interest in economy. Obviously, the demise of federal programs such as General Revenue Sharing plus curtailed block grants and categorical spending were primary factors. In addition, the taxpayer revolt and the federal 1986 tax reform legislation greatly diminished the amount of funds available for both public works projects and social programs. At the federal level, concern about the deficit plus a conservative Republican administration in the White House meant that the city federal linkage of the previous two decades was no longer viewed as the solution to local ills (Sequerth, 1988).

Thus, the old city-federal relationship was becoming obsolete and a new framework which emphasized state and local government responsibility, fiscal conservatism, and economically rational behavior began to emerge. Within this environment of financial restraint and analysis, there is at least one area where many state and local governments have historically been concerned with quantification and long-range planning. The degree of sophistication among many of the governmental entities involved in this area is on a par with, and actually exceeds, similar practice among private enterprises. The area is the field of capital budgeting.

In this chapter, the practice of capital budgeting in the private sector is briefly reviewed and compared to a general description of capital budgeting techniques among local governments. Recent research providing insight into what actually transpires among local financial planners and elected decision makers is then presented. The chapter concludes with a discussion of the likely status of capital budgeting practices among local governments in the future.

II. CAPITAL BUDGETING IN THE PRIVATE SECTOR

The object of planning for capital expenditures is to increase the wealth of the corporation. In dealing with the corporate concept of capital budgeting, the major considerations are to maximize the return on the capital invested and to minimize the amount of risk incurred (Boness, 1972). Unlike government, which must provide certain services to its constituents regardless of per capita costs, the biggest decision facing corporations is what to do with their capital. Since the company has limited resources and investment possibilities are relatively unlimited, the determination of which decision to make is crucial to the future success of the enterprise (Abdelsamad, 1973).

Corporate capital outlays fall into two major categories: 1) those that are required to maintain the present level of operation, and 2) projects which require large sums of capital for expansion, cost reduction, and/or replacement of worn out facilities and equipment (Singhvi, 1981). As opposed to recurring costs, capital costs are considered to be expenditures which exceed a certain dollar volume for items that will provide the corporation with service for a period of more than one year (Mayer, 1978). Unlike fixed assets such as land, capital investments carry maintenance and replacement obligations which the corporation must consider in all future budgetary decisions (Murdick and Deming, 1968).

Consequently, capital spending decisions essentially become a statement of goals and objectives for the future operation of the company. The future economic vitality of the company to a large extent depends on the success it attains in developing a systematic administrative mechanism to insure that future capital spending decisions fit into the company's established long-term strategy and goals (Edge and Irvine, 1981). Reduced to its lowest level, this means that once you decide to erect the "golden arches," you better plan on selling a few hamburgers.

What methods do corporations use to make their capital spending decisions? While it might be logical to assume that the investment that provides the maximum return is the one that corporate leaders will make, other factors tend to hold considerable influence. In particular, the interpretation of what is the best rate of return is dependent on a number of considerations. First, there is no guarantee that the division of a corporation that argues for a certain capital expenditure can be counted on to supply objective data about the demand for the project (Boness, 1972). While outright deception is not likely to be the intent, it would be highly speculative to assume that all project proposals within the corporate apparatus are free from bias. For example, the cookie division may want to make more cookies in spite of the fact that people don't seem to be buying as many as they did in the past. Therefore, demand figures produced by the cookie management may be based on "best case" scenarios.

Secondly, all capital spending decisions carry a certain amount of administrative and overhead expenses which may essentially be considered a sunk cost in the proposed project(s) (Abdelsamad, 1973). While these sunk costs should not be allowed to unduly influence the final determination, there is likely to be managerial pressure to fund a project which has already cost the corporation a great deal of money in engineering, planning, and legal expenses. Nevertheless, there are four major decision models which corporate leaders typically use to guide their capital spending decisions (Gaertner, 1982). They are briefly described below:

1. BOP—Decision makers look at a particular capital expenditure in terms of a three-part scenario. First they estimate the "Best" outcome; next the most "Optimistic"; and finally, the most "Pessimistic." Probabilities are assigned to each outcome and the results are calculated. The sum is compared to the sums of other projects and a project ranking is thereby determined.

2. Payback—The original investment is divided by the anticipated cash flow in order to determine how long it will take to recoup the original investment. This method tends to ignore the useful life of the project and does not consider the opportunity costs of the money invested.

3. ROAI—The Return on Average Investment method includes not only payback, but depreciation and salvage value of the project. It still ignores, however, the time value of money.

4. DCF—The Discounted Cash Flow method is perhaps the most sophisticated of the methods listed here. It assumes that a dollar received today is worth more than a dollar received in the future. By focusing on the time value of funds invested, DFC provides the most realistic true cost of a given project.

Two additional versions of the DCF model are frequently utilized at the corporate level. The Net Present Value (NPV) method and the Internal Rate of Return (IRR) both allow the time value of the investment to be considered in substantial detail (Wiggins, 1980). While methods which consider the time value of money are both sophisticated and popular with corporate decision makers, a tendency exists for these techniques to give undue emphasis to projects that have benefits which can be easily quantified (Vogt, 1983). Consequently, projects with the potential to produce beneficial outcomes may not rank well if their outputs do not lend themselves to concise measurement. As discussed later, this is a major problem with public sector projects.

In spite of the elaborate probabilistic models designed to estimate the future benefit of capital projects, no organization can predict the future with certainty. Thus, investment decisions are typically based on incomplete information and past experience which may contain errors in estimation. This may lead to the selection of less than optimum, or simply wrong, alternatives. In this type of environment where managers and decision makers can predict immediate costs better and more accurately than they can estimate future benefits, there is a tendency to select capital projects which have the greatest impact on immediate needs.

Uncertainty cannot be quantified. However, risks can be determined by assigning probabilities to certain outcomes. Decision tree models are frequently utilized to assign levels of probability to specific outcomes. In spite of these models, there is no guarantee that making a good decision will lead to a good outcome. Often the fear of making a bad choice leads to inaction and this can be the most negative consequence of an over reliance on analytic models.

Corporations are frequently assumed to base their decisions solely on rational inputs. However, there is sometimes an incentive on the part of certain elements of the company to present biased information to higher management. There are also some additional corporate motivations which may not appear to be economically rational.

Corporations may be reluctant to abandon low profit or even unprofitable product lines because of tradition, personnel upheaval, and other factors which can best be described as sentimental. For example, if corporate headquarters are located in small or midsized cities where the corporate hierarchy has strong ties to the community, there may be great reluctance to consider moving to a more cost efficient location. In a similar vein, if a company got its start making "green widgets," the production of widgets may continue long after the market for widgets has declined. The company may even keep the original plant in operation many years after the economic life of the plant has been exhausted because "that is what the founder would want us to do."

Although corporations are frequently on the cutting edge of innovation, the need to maximize profit, enhance cash flow, and avoid upheaval frequently plays a major role in capital spending decisionmaking. In many corporate environments, failure is punished more than success is rewarded. As a result, management is often reluctant to speculate on future product lines or capital investments if current activities are producing a reasonable rate of return. Of course, changes in technology coupled with market innovation may force corporations to embark on major capital spending programs to insure their very survival. The desire for stability, however, is often a decisive factor in determining capital spending priorities in the corporate sector.

The argument is sometimes made that much of governments' capital spending is influenced by mandates from higher levels of government and by the court system. City and county officials complain that the demands of state and federal programs in areas such as water treatment and solid waste, coupled with court orders regarding school facilities and correctional institutions, essentially dominate capital spending decision making. However, corporations also are affected by the same types of mandates.

Many corporations spend a great deal of their revenue trying to comply with pollution control stipulations, health and safety regulations, and waste disposal requirements. As a result, a certain percentage of corporate capital spending may end up being designated for compliance activities and may not contribute to profit. Mandates have the same sort of impact on corporate capital budgets that they do on government capital budgets.

As stated previously, the marketplace plays a major role in corporate capital spending decisions. There are two major types of market influences. One deals with the impact of technology and innovation. When new technologies are created, businesses are forced to adopt them in order to remain viable. An obvious example is the transition from vacuum tubes and wires to printed circuits in electronic products. Companies that failed to adopt this new technology suffered severe downturns or went out of business. On a more mundane level, if the grocery store at one end of a shopping mall expands and adds new product lines, the grocery at the other end of the mall must either do likewise or face the economic consequences of an eroding customer base.

III. CAPITAL BUDGETING IN THE PUBLIC SECTOR

While the preceding discussion may be mildly interesting, the reader might well be wondering what it has to do with the practice of capital budgeting at the local government level. The point is, an assessment of the degree to which government has implemented a private sector financial management tool such as capital budgeting, is somewhat dependent upon an examination of how business, per se, implements the procedure. The corporate world does not always make purely rational decisions and a host of ancillary issues may play a key role in the determination of outcomes.

In a similar vein, a set of competitive factors much like those which affect business influence governmental capital-decision making. Although we do not frequently think of governments as competitors, in reality they are. While junkets of state and local officials to Japan and Europe seeking commitments for factories and industrial plants may receive the most attention from the media, competition among counties, cities and towns for new businesses is also intense. Much of this competition is manifested in the form of tax incentive packages, economic development projects (in town industrial parks, etc.) and/or increased capital spending for infrastructure expansion (water and sewer lines, new streets, etc.).

In general, capital budgeting has often been thought of as a means of allocating scarce resources among competing projects (Pritchard and Hindelang, 1981). For reasons just explained, capital spending decisions have a long-term impact on both private and public organizations. In fact, some students of capital budgeting argue that the setting of spending priorities is the most difficult single element of the process (McClain, 1966; Hillhouse and Howard, 1961; Corwin and Getzels, 1981). In the final analysis, no matter how much an organization tries to rely on quantification, at some point all capital spending decisions involve value judgments.

The political process is the means whereby priorities are established in the public sector. In spite of reformers' demands that government be more "businesslike" (economically rational), pluralist political interaction is likely to have much to do with setting goals and objectives. Yet, corporate political problems are remarkably similar to conflicts within governmental organizations. Projects may be undertaken because of the perceived enhanced image or prestige they will bring to management (Wiggins, 1980); corporate managers may fear and distrust their own computer technicians and withhold information from them; and managers may engage in "gamesmanship" with managers from other divisions to try to influence the outcome of capital spending decisions by manipulating financial and market data.

Yet, there is one major difference in the decision-making process of the two sectors. While corporate spending decisions are frequently influenced by the factors cited above, they are not as likely as government to be affected by changes in priorities that are in direct conflict with ongoing activities. The corporate hierarchy does change its makeup from time to time and, on occasion, corporate managers are brought in specifically to change policy and establish new goals. In the governmental environment, however, policy may change as often as elections are held. Thus, there is a much higher likelihood that a new regime will bring with it a set of capital spending priorities that is in direct conflict with existing projects. Very few capital projects are free standing or independent (Steiner, 1980). They are almost always interconnected to other projects and when there is a change in political priorities, the impact on the capital spending program can be devastating.

We have already seen that there are similarities between the practice of capital budgeting in the corporate sector and in the public sector. Although corporate leaders sometimes boast about the sophistication of their decision-making process with regard to capital spending, "politics" frequently plays a role in the final selection of the corporate projects that do get funded. Still, the fundamental mission of most corporations is to make a profit. There is very little incentive to invest in capital projects that do not directly enhance net income to the company. Government in general and local government in particular must provide services and fund projects that do not make rational economic sense. Local governments may benefit by applying some of the cost benefit and other decision-making models we have discussed to capital budgeting. Quantification alone, however, is typically not viewed as an acceptable selection criterion among most local government officials. At the local government level, capital project decision making may not even be recognizable as a systematic process when viewed by corporate practitioners.

As our discussion focuses on capital budgeting among city and county governments, the first problem that captures our attention is definitional. What exactly is a capital expenditure? According to the Government Finance Officers Association (GFOA), capital expenditures include those made for land, buildings, and major equipment which have significant value and a useful life of several years (Rosenberg and Stallings, 1978). Capital investments are commitments of resources made with the expectation of realizing future benefits over a reasonably long period of time (Wacht, 1980). Frequently cited examples of capital expenditures include the construction of buildings and infrastructure components, purchase of land, and the purchase of both major pieces of fixed equipment (turbines, mainframes, etc.) and of moveable equipment (fire engines, earth moving machinery, etc.).

As a practical matter, however, these definitions may require modification and refinement before capital expenditures can be clearly separated from routine expenditures. A typical example is the purchase of automobiles and light trucks. For small units of government, periodic purchase of police vehicles may be considered major capital expenditures. Midsized and larger units of government may routinely purchase several or even dozens of automobiles from the general operating budget each year. Although the object of the expenditure—an automotive vehicle—fits the letter of the definitions of capital expenditures cited above, different governmental entities have their own operational definitions of what is a capital expenditure and what is routine. Thus, in addition to having a prolonged useful life (more than one year), the variable that best defines capital stock is the dollar amount of the expenditure. Units of government that demarcate between routine expenditures and capital expenditures tend to utilize a dollar threshold to separate the two categories.

Because of the importance of capital outlays on the fiscal health of the community, it is frequently suggested that a separate capital budget be adopted. The central purpose of the capital budget should be to guide overall allocation of the unit of government's capital expenditures (Devoy, Wise, and Towles, 1979). The capital budgeting process includes: 1) preparation of revenue and expenditure estimates for the work to be done; 2) submission of the budget plan for approval; 3) approval by the executive and legislative body; and 4) execution (McClain, 1966). Therefore, the capital budget can be viewed as a method of linking functional programmatic categories to the availability of resources and subjecting them to political and managerial approval (Moak and Gordon, 1965).

The advantages of the capital budget to the community are many. As previously stated, it is a major planning tool which enables community leaders to relate isolated projects to overall community needs and priorities. Also, by treating capital expenditures separately, the impact on the operating budget to fund unanticipated capital programs is minimized. This leads to less budgetary uncertainty and tends to have a stabilizing effect on the tax rate. Therefore, communities which allocate a certain percentage of their total revenues each year to a set of prioritized capital projects and are thereby able to maintain somewhat stable tax rates may be very attractive to new households, investors, and new businesses.

IV. THE CAPITAL IMPROVEMENT PROGRAM (CIP)

Ideally, a capital budget is simply one major component of an overall Capital Improvement Plan/Program (CIP). A CIP is a comprehensive document which allows the city to not only budget for immediate capital projects, but to evaluate the condition of existing projects and determine future capital needs for both expansion/new construction and for major renovation or replacement of existing capital stock. Thus, the CIP should also include a linkage to land use plans, transportation plans, and other growth-oriented strategies (Levitan and Byrne, 1983). It should also list the realistic economic life of both existing and proposed capital purchases and it should encompass a routine inspection program of existing capital stock (Rabin, Hildreth, and Miller, 1983).

Perhaps the most useful component of the CIP, however, is the linkage of physical needs with fiscal needs. Engineers, department heads, and public works experts may have sound arguments about the need for various projects, but ultimately it may be a financial decision that determines the priority of project implementation. Ultimately, the word "need" as it applies to capital spending decisions is a value judgment (Kamensky, 1984). Therefore, using the CIP as a guideline for decision making, it may be logical to give priority to projects: 1) that are already under construction; 2) that have sequential relationships to other projects (e.g., new sewer line to a new housing project); 3) that complement programmatic priorities (e.g., new park to support expanded recreation programs); 4) that are based on urgency (e.g., anticipated failure of water treatment facility or equipment); and 5) that are required by higher levels of government (Hillhouse and Howard, 1961).

The suggested length for a CIP is six years. This includes one planning year and five one-year increments (Levitan and Byrne, 1983). Although some CIP proponents recommend slightly shorter or longer time spans, there is general agreement among both practitioners and academicians that shorter plans do not allow enough time for implementation and longer plans are too future oriented to be politically meaningful (Devoy, Wise, and Towles, 1979; Vogt, 1983). Given that most local government elected officials hold offices with either two- or four-year terms, the adoption of a five- or six-year CIP makes it somewhat vulnerable to possible change in political priorities.

No matter how elaborate the CIP, however, local government officials cannot make meaningful decisions about capital projects unless they have some idea about the flow of future revenues. The ability to estimate initial project outlays for purchase and/or construction and to accurately estimate operating revenue needs is the key to successful implementation of the CIP. There are, of course, certain pitfalls which influence the formulation of revenue forecasts. They range from too much reliance on past budgets as predictors of the future to exaggeration of potential revenues and understatement of likely costs (Aronson and Schwartz, 1982).

In a way the CIP is very similar to some of the corporate approaches to capital budgeting mentioned previously. CIPs combine the setting of priorities with estimates of costs and predictions of cash flow and revenue impact. To the extent that local governments adopt and implement CIPs, they are following economically rational practices with regard to capital expenditures. In reality, however, there are numerous political and economic forces which may affect the design and implementation of the CIP just as with the business model. For example, there may be actors in the budgetary process who are disinclined to be completely objective in their compilation of cost figures or in their estimates of the number of people served by the project. Or, a newly elected mayor might believe he/she has a mandate to make certain changes regardless of the current set of capital spending priorities.

So, in reality, capital budgeting may not always follow the prescribed format. Not all local governments will choose to adopt separate capital budgets, others will appear to be concerned about the long-term impact of capital project decisions but will not have adopted a CIP. Still other localities may have very formal CIPs, but fail to follow them. The point is, while the literature may tell us something about how capital budgeting should be practiced at the local government level, what actually occurs in this area may not follow the prescribed format.

V. THE STATE OF THE ART

Research conducted during the 1980s provides additional insight into the actual capital budgeting practices of municipal governments. For example, in 1982 the National League of Cities and the United States Conference of Mayors (NLC/USCM) surveyed 1,400 U.S. cities about both infrastructure and capital budgeting practices (Urban Data Services, 1984:1–10). In a related study, the International City Management Association conducted a membership survey in 1985 dealing with city and county capital financing methods (Valente, 1986:3–16). The author conducted a survey of 1,430 U.S. cities in 1985 specifically aimed at identifying and assessing capital budgeting practices among cities over 10,000 in population (Doss, 1986:101–108; 1987:57–69). A 1987 survey of 200 municipal governments with populations of 50,000 or more dealt with capital techniques and finance methods (Kee, Robbins, and Apostolou, 1987:16–22). In somewhat of a departure from the trend to study city governments, the federal Office of Management and Budget conducted an assessment of capital budgeting practices among state governments in 1986 (Hush and Peroff, 1988:67–72).

The author's survey was designed to both replicate certain parts and to add to the NLC/USCM study. The NLC/USCM study will be used as a basis for many of the tables in this chapter and appropriate comparisons will be made to the other studies as noted.

Perhaps the first question to answer about capital budgeting among U.S. cities is the extent to which it is being practiced. In Table 13.1, methods of dealing with capital budgeting are outlined.

The data indicate a direct relationship between city size and the existence of a separate capital budget. Smaller cities are less likely to have a separate capital budget than larger cities. Smaller cities are also more likely to account for capital spending through a separate line item, either one year or multiyear, than are larger cities. Evidence of a CIP appears to follow the same pattern: the larger the city, the more likely it is to have a CIP. However, only about 5

Table 13.1 Method of Dealing with Capital Budgeting and Evidence of Capital Improvement Program (CIP) Expressed as a Percent of N

City size	N	Separate cap. bud.	Separate one-yr.	Line-item: multi-yr.	No. cap.	Other	Have CIP[a]
10–25	316	48	55	20	8	7	59
25–50	257	53	54	20	4	10	65
50–100	150	63	51	13	4	13	74
100+	128	73	31	9	2	14	92
All	851	56	50	17	5	10	68

[a] The N upon which the CIP percentages are based is 839 rather than 851 due to missing data in some survey instruments.

percent of the total respondents indicate that they are not dealing with capital budgeting at all.

According to the literature, a separate capital budget is simply an element of a CIP. In theory, a city can have a capital budget without having a CIP, but it cannot have a CIP without having a separate capital budget. In Table 13.2, evidence is presented that theory and practice do not exactly coincide. Of the total number of respondents, the data indicate that about 55 percent (475) claim to have a separate capital budget, but only 85 percent have a CIP. According to the literature, that is not inconsistent with recommended budgeting practices. However, of the 42 percent of the respondents (376) indicating that they do not have a separate capital budget, 44 percent (166) state that they do have a CIP. Thus, we have a divergence from the prescriptive literature about what local governments should do in this area. A sizeable number of the respondents appear to believe that it is important to have a CIP whether they have a separate capital budget or not. Thus, many municipalities which account for capital budgeting by line item or by some other means claim to have implemented a CIP.

One of the fundamental problems with survey research is that it is often difficult to measure the effectiveness or efficacy of a particular management or budgetary tool. Students of government know that it is not unusual for agencies, bureaus, and departments to claim to have implemented a particular recommended or mandated practice when, in fact, they have done little more than adopt it in "name only." There was some interest in trying to determine if

Table 13.2 Existence of CIP According to Evidence of a Separate Capital Budget (SCB)

Population strata	N	Existence of SCB	Percent with CIP
10–25	152	Yes	80
	166	No	38
25–50	135	Yes	83
	124	No	42
50–100	94	Yes	84
	57	No	55
100+	94	Yes	97
	29	No	69
All cities	475	Yes	85
	376	No	44

Gamma = 0.75835

this was the case with regard to the implementation of CIPs among respondent cities. The respondents that indicated that they had a CIP were asked to rate the formality of their CIP according to a 5-point scale. Using this approach, a low numeric rating indicates that the CIP is not considered very important and a high numeric rating indicates that the municipality views the CIP as an important, formal document. The results are depicted in Table 13.3.

Once again, city size appears to be linked to outcome. In this case, the degree of indicated formality of the CIP increases as population increases. Over all, about half of the respondents (48 percent) stated that their CIP was either a formal or a very formal document. Although not presented in tabular form, the data also indicate that respondent cities in the three smaller population strata which possess a separate capital budget tend to be much more likely to attribute a high degree of formality to the document. There was little difference in degree of formality between cities that possess a separate capital budget and those that do not in the largest population stratum (over 100,000).

About 85 percent of the total respondents from cities with CIPs indicated that the CIP covers a five- to six-year period, and 93 percent indicated that it is updated annually. There is also evidence that the respondent cities are engaged in some sort of routine inspection of capital stock. Approximately 64 percent (304) of the cities with separate capital budgets and 48 percent (180) of the cities without separate capital budgets claim to conduct annual inspections to determine the condition of existing capital stock and to anticipate maintenance needs. The degree of sophistication of the inspection programs was not assessed by the survey instrument. Again, referring to the time frame and update procedures recommended by the literature on capital budgeting, the practice follows the prescribed format fairly well.

One other issue needs to be discussed with regard to capital budgeting in general and the CIP in particular. There is some evidence in the public

Table 13.3 Perceived Degree of Formality of CIP Among Cities Which Have a CIP

Population strata	N	Very informal + informal (%)	Average (%)	Very formal + formal (%)
10–25	184	24	33	35
25–50	164	26	22	50
50–100	110	23	25	52
100+	111	14	22	59
All cities	569	23	26	48

administration literature suggesting that professionally managed cities are somewhat more likely than cities managed solely by elected leaders to adopt and implement various "good government" management tools and procedures. A fairly extensive study in 1983 of cities over 25,000 in population indicated little difference in the use of general purpose management tools such as productivity improvement, management by objectives, and performance monitoring between mayoral and council manager respondents; however, there was evidence of increased implementation of more technical tools such as program budgeting and management information systems (Poister and McGowan, 1984). With regard to capital budgeting, per se, Doss found that cities with council manager governments were more likely than mayoral cities to engage in capital budgeting; to have a CIP; to indicate a high degree of CIP formality; and to implement a routine inspection program of capital stock (Doss, 1986).

The data in the tables cited above tend to indicate that the majority of cities above 10,000 population are cognizant of the distinction between routine and capital expenditures; that they have some means of budgeting for capital expenditures; that they are generally supportive of both the need to adopt a CIP and to keep it current; and that they tend to view the CIP as a rather formal document. Two additional issues remain to be discussed, the degree to which mandates affect capital spending decisions and methods of financing capital projects.

As previously noted, local governments and corporations are both affected by two types of mandates: those dictated by government and those dictated by the marketplace. Local officials frequently argue that their spending decisions are too heavily influenced by federal and state requirements that a certain level of regulatory compliance be attained within a prescribed time frame. For example, requirements that cities upgrade their wastewater treatment facilities or implement more rigorous solid waste management techniques are examples of this type of mandate. A second group of mandates is those exacted by the courts such as classroom size/availability and prison overcrowding. Evidence of the degree to which mandates influence capital spending decisions is presented in Table 13.4.

Prior to discussing these data, there is one other area regarding mandates that has not received a great deal of attention in the literature, but may have a profound impact on capital spending. To some extent, it can be argued that the financial rating services such as Moody's Investment Service and Standard and Poor's Corporation are influencing what type of capital projects local governments undertake based on their tendency to give higher ratings to projects which have dedicated revenues (user fees), high salvage value (office buildings, etc.), or are tied to economic growth and development. Projects dealing with somewhat vague "quality of life" issues such as park expansion and recreational facilities, improved traffic management, or general infrastructure

Table 13.4 Impact of State and Federal Program Priorities on Local Capital
Project Selection/Prioritization

Population strata	N	State/federal impact	Expressed as degree of influence based on 5 point Likert scale					
			Very low (%)	Low (%)	Avg. (%)	High (%)	Very high (%)	Missing (%)
10–20	314	State	20	11	33	21	14	5
	312	Federal	22	13	28	20	18	8
25–50	255	State	20	11	34	20	16	3
	255	Federal	20	11	32	16	21	3
50–100	148	State	18	20	37	14	12	4
	149	Federal	20	15	33	14	18	2
100+	120	State	18	15	38	20	10	2
	121	Federal	15	10	35	28	12	1
All cities	837	State	19	13	35	20	14	14
	837	Federal	20	12	31	19	18	14

repair/renovation may end up with lower bond ratings and, thereby, receive a lower priority among decision makers. This issue will be dealt with in more detail in the section on capital financing.

For the total number of respondents (837), the data indicate that, at the highest point on the scale, federal priorities are slightly more likely than state priorities to be thought of as having an impact on capital spending decision. In general, however, for both state and federal programs, the response was rather evenly divided: about one-third combined low and very low; one-third in the average category; and one-third combined high and very high. Among this group of respondents, intergovernmental priorities did not appear to have as much impact on capital spending decisions as might be imagined.

The respondents were also asked to rank order a list of six specific reasons for setting capital spending priorities. Three reasons—to ensure public health and safety, to provide basic residential services, to foster economic development—were ranked one, two, three. Health received a cumulative 96 percent affirmation, residential services received 89 percent affirmation, and economic development received 65 percent affirmation. The remaining three reasons received lower scores: to meet federal requirements, 21 percent affirmation; to meet state requirements, 13 percent affirmation; and to provide more jobs, 5 percent affirmation. This apparent low ranking of state and federal requirements lends credence to the data presentation in Table 13.4.

In a survey of 97 finance officers of cities with populations greater than 50,000, Kee, Robbins, and Apostolou (1987:16-22) specifically asked about the role of federal and state government in influencing capital spending decision. They found that about 55 percent of respondents listed compliance with federal and state regulations as being of major importance in selecting capital projects. Another 40 percent of the respondents attributed minor importance to these factors. A majority, 66 percent, of respondents indicated the availability of federal funds was a major factor in determining whether or not to approve capital spending projects and 50 percent indicated that state funding availability was a major factor.

Central to the discussion of capital budgeting is the issue of how capital projects are financed. As stated previously, since businesses exist for the primary purpose of making a profit, they are free to invest in any venture that has an acceptable degree of risk and an adequate rate of return. Traditionally, organizations invest in areas in which they already have expertise, but there is nothing to prevent them from investing in completely unfamiliar ventures if permission is granted by the corporate board of directors.

Typically, local governments do not have this luxury. Not only do they have to undertake many projects which do not make rational economic sense, they are also limited by federal and state regulations which affect their ability to raise revenues and enter into contractual agreements. In addition, governmental decision makers must often consider certain philosophic issues, such as fairness and equity, which may never occur to corporate directors.

For example, Kee, Robbins, and Apostolou (1987:16-22) found that about a third of the respondents to their study did not use any quantitative method of assessing capital projects. Another 40 percent used benefit cost analysis as the primary method of analysis and another 17 percent indicate that it is a secondary method.[1] Approximately 13 percent used payback as the primary method of analysis and 24 percent use it as a secondary method. Only 2 percent of the respondents used internal rate of return (IRR) or net present value (NPV) and none of the respondents used the accounting rate of return (ARR) method. The percentage using these last three methods as a secondary method ranges from 4 to 14 percent. Political factors and difficulty in quantifying outputs were the primary reasons listed by the respondents for not utilizing the two most sophisticated methods of assessment—IRR and NPV.

In the past, local governments tended to view capital spending according to a simple dichotomy: capital stock could only be acquired through expenditure or debt (Boness, 1972). A third option was to transfer the responsibility to another level of government. For example, in 1970 about half of state and local capital expenditures was financed by debt and about 22 percent by the federal government. By 1977, borrowing was down to 32 percent and the federal contribution had increased to 43 percent (Sbragia, 1983:67-111). The demise of General Revenue Sharing, the curtailment of major block grant programs, and privatization have tended to cause the formula to revert to the ratios of the past. Although Rosenfeld notes that the federal contribution to state and local capital spending increased somewhat in 1983 and 1984 after its demise at the end of the Carter Administration and the beginning of the Reagan Administration, by 1985 the trend was once again downward (Rosenfeld, 1989:74–84). In 1986, about 65 percent of state and local capital spending was financed by current revenue or debt and only about 35 percent was contributed by the federal level (Petersen, 1988).

During the 1980s, local governments began to experiment with a variety of new approaches to capital financing. For example, Industrial Development Bonds (IDB's) became increasingly popular. IDB's were issued to construct office parks, supplement housing development costs, and finance economic development projects. Also, a variety of unusual types of cooperative agreements with the private sector were implemented and new forms of debt instruments were issued. The combined range of both standard and innovative capital financing options may be viewed according to three broad categories as outlined by M. G. Valente (1986):

Traditional methods—includes current revenues, general obligation (G.O.) bonds, revenue bonds, special assessments, and tax increment financing
Public-private approaches—tax exempt lease purchases, sales leaseback, exactions, privatization.
Creative bond approaches—deep discount/zero coupon bonds, variable rate bonds, put option bonds, bonds with warrants, minibonds and mininotes.[2]

When exploring the use of various capital financing options by local governments, the majority of activity appears to be in the traditional methods. To a large extent this may be due to the considerations of administrative ease, political acceptance, and availability just cited. It may also be due to the fact that, among smaller local governments, creative methods may simply be too far fetched to make sense to the individuals involved. First, in Table 13.5, data are presented from the Doss study regarding ten methods of capital financing which fall into the traditional and public private categories.

These data indicate that, in spite of the criticisms of pay as you go financing cited in the budgeting literature, there is still a reliance on methods of financing that are pay as you go in nature. According to these respondents, current revenues are the most frequently used means of financing capital projects, followed by three federally financed methods: block grants, revenue sharing, and categorical grants. General obligation bonds rank fifth and revenue bonds rank ninth among the methods listed. Revenue bonds which, according to some authors, have become increasingly popular since they frequently do not require voter approval and are not backed by the full faith and

Table 13.5 Percentage of All Cities Using Ten Methods of Financing Capital
Projects in Rank-Order of Frequency of Use ($N = 851$)

Name of method	Frequently (%)	Fairly often (%)	Occasionally (%)	Very seldom (%)	Never used (%)	Missing (N)
Current rev.	48	21	17	9	3	24
Block grants	27	26	23	11	10	29
Gen. rev. shr.	37	15	11	11	23	20
Fed. categoricals	15	25	30	18	8	32
G.O. bonds	24	15	24	20	15	24
State grants	13	25	38	16	5	28
Reserve funds	15	16	22	20	23	47
Special assmts.	15	14	22	23	22	29
Revenue bonds	10	15	22	20	30	31
Lease purchase	5	10	21	29	34	25
Other	3	1	2	1	5	742

Source: Doss, 1986:101–108

credit of the municipality, rank well below general obligation bonds in frequency of use. Also, notice that reserve funds, i.e., savings, are the seventh
most popular method of payment.

Some students of local government finance may choose to argue that
reserve funds are essentially the same as current revenues. While the two
methods have been separated by the survey design utilized in the cited study,
the author acknowledges that there is merit to this argument. Readers may
wish to add the two together, thereby further strengthening the notion that
current revenues are the most popular method of payment among this group of
respondents.

One other comment needs to be mentioned at this point. Both the ICMA
and the Doss studies were conducted prior to the passage of the 1986 Tax
Reform Act. The Act contained numerous provisions which might have an
impact on local government financial operations. In particular, it redefined tax
exempt status for some types of bonds—especially those involving public
private partnerships—and this might be expected to affect local government
capital spending (Petersen, 1988). A study of 234 cities with populations
greater than 50,000 was initiated on behalf of the National League of Cities in
June, 1987 (Pagano, 1987:1–20). Among other things, changes in capital
spending after one year of operating under the provisions of the Act were
found to have resulted in reductions in capital spending by almost half of the
respondent cities (45 percent). Moreover, Pagano found that over three-fourths

of the respondent cities had made some type of alteration in capital and debt policies because of the Tax Reform Act. Thus, the long range impact of the Act on capital spending bears further scrutiny (Pagano, 1987:1-20).

The ICMA study cited above assessed the popularity of additional means of financing projects and data were collected from county as well as city governments. In Tables 13.6 and 13.7 a summary of the results is presented according to the three types of methods examined by ICMA: traditional, public private, and creative bond options.

The data in Table 13.6 indicate that traditional methods are by far the most frequently utilized capital finance tools. In descending order, current revenues, general obligation bonds, assessments/betterments, revenue bonds, and tax increments are the most popular traditional methods. When county respondents are separated from the group, only current revenues and general obligation bonds are mentioned by as many as half of the respondents.

While the data in Table 13.7 indicate that there is some support for certain public private arrangements among respondents in the 100,000+ population strata, the data indicate little utilization of so-called creative options overall. It might be useful, however, to recall the previous discussion about both availability and knowledge when assessing the impact of some of the creative methods. Possibly there is considerable interest in some of these options, but many localities simply lack the wherewithal to implement them.

The size of the governmental entity was also found to influence the means of financing capital projects among the ICMA respondents. With regard to traditional methods, localities in the largest strata were especially reliant on current revenues and G.O. bonds and somewhat more reliant on revenue bonds than were respondents from smaller strata. In the other two groups of options, a population progression was apparent with regard to lease/purchase arrange-

Table 13.6 Percentage of Cities and Counties Using Traditional Methods of Financing Capital Projects ($N = 718$)

Population strata	N	Current revenues (%)	G.O. bonds (%)	Rev. bonds (%)	Assmts./ btrmts. (%)	Tax incrmt. (%)
10–25	160	71	51	26	28	4
25–50	259	73	56	28	36	14
50–100	146	68	52	35	43	16
100+	153	78	80	41	39	20
Cities only (all)	527	76	59	36	44	17
Counties only (all)	191	63	59	19	16	3

Source: Valente, ICMA, 1986:3–16

Table 13.7 Percentage of Cities and Counties Using Public-Private Arrangements and Creative Bond Methods of Financing Capital Projects (N = 718)

A. Public-private arrangements:

Population strata	N	Lease/ purchase (%)	Sale/ leaseback (%)	Developer exactions (%)	Privatization (%)
10–25	160	9	0	12	2
25–50	259	15	2	14	3
50–100	146	16	1	18	2
100+	153	33	10	31	5
Cities	527	20	3	21	3
Counties	191	13	2	10	2

B. Creative bond methods:

Population strata	N	Zero coupon	Var. rate	Put option	Bond/ warrants
10–25	160	1	2	0	1
25–50	259	0	3	1	0
50–100	146	1	4	2	0
100+	153	5	14	5	0.5
Cities	527	2	5	2	0
Counties	191	2	5	1	1

Source: Valente, ICMA, 1986:3–16

ments and developer exactions. Respondents from the 100+ strata were also more likely to be involved with sale/leaseback agreements and variable rate bonds than other respondents, although no progression according to population strata was apparent, per se.

Unfortunately, variations in survey population, the inclusion of county governments in the ICMA study, and other factors make it difficult to directly compare responses between the two groups of respondents. Only five specific financing methods are included in both of the studies. A comparison is presented in Table 13.8. Keep in mind, however, the previous comments about the way current revenues were treated in the author's study and also pay close attention to the table notes.

In spite of the possible influence of the county respondents in the ICMA study, there is still a great deal of variation in reported use of some of the tools within certain population strata among the two groups of respondents. The most obvious differences are for lease/purchase methods and for certain population categories regarding assessments and revenue bonds.

Table 13.8 Comparison of Results of Two Studies Regarding Percentage of Usage of Selected Methods of Financing Capital Projects by Population Strata

Method	Strata/study (%/%)			
	10–25 ICMA/Doss N: (160)/(316)	25–50 ICMA/Doss (259)/(252)	50–100 ICMA/Doss (146)/(150)	100+ ICMA/Doss (153)/(128)
Current rev.	71/84[a]	73/91	68/80	78/80
G.O. bonds	51/60	56/62	52/62	80/70
Revenue bonds	26/39	28/50	35/50	41/62
Assessments	28/41	36/57	43/55	39/57
Lease/purchase	4/31	14/40	16/36	20/35

[a] ICMA study asked respondent to "report their use of various capital financing arrangements over the past four years." Apparently it did not differentiate among degrees of use. Doss study used five point ordinal scale to measure use. Percentages cited above are based on sum of three positions on scale: frequently, fairly often, and occasionally. Positions labeled "very seldom" and "never used" not included in Doss percentage totals. Also, ICMA data indicate that counties tended to use finance tools less frequently than cities. Responses for cities only not reported in the ICMA article by population strata, thus counties are included in ICMA data reported in this table which may account for the across the board diminution of reported usage by combined city and county ICMA respondents.

The surveys by ICMA and the author are two of the major investigations of capital budgeting practices among local governments in recent years. The survey by Kee et al. is somewhat more limited in scope, although it does offer useful insight into certain aspects of the practice of capital budgeting. The three studies primarily represent two different perspectives. The ICMA survey instrument was addressed to the manager or chief elected official and the author's instrument and the Kee instrument were addressed to the chief finance officer. As is the case with all mailed surveys, there is no guarantee that the addressee will complete the questionnaire. In the case of the author's study, about 70 percent of the returned instruments were completed by the addressee or by finance staff. The point is, although it can never be said with certainty that survey data accurately represent the reality of a given situation, these studies, and others, indicate that capital budgeting is apparently a topic of considerable importance and interest among local government administrators. A great deal of time and effort is apparently being expended on decisions about capital projects and the means of financing them.

Finally, although some mention has been made of capital budgeting at the state level, in reality, the disparity among the states makes meaningful comparison extremely difficult. For instance, OMB staff conducted a survey of all 50 states with regard to capital budgeting and found that 42 states report having capital budgets and 41 states (including 4 that do not have a capital budget) generally borrow money to finance capital projects (Hush and Peroff, 1988:67–79). Only 9 of the 42 states indicate that all capital spending is included in the capital budget. Four states which do not have a separate capital budget account for capital spending as a separate line item. Transportation projects are frequently excluded from the capital budgeting process (Hush and Peroff, 1988). Thus, additional research is needed to determine to what degree similarity exists among the states with regard to the actual practice of capital budgeting.

VI. CONCLUSION

The summary of research findings about how local government officials currently engage in the practice of capital budgeting is of considerable importance to students and practitioners of public finance. Although more than one interpretation of the presented data may be possible, certain conclusions are rather apparent.

First, city size is important in estimating the scope and breadth of capital budgeting practices. This makes intuitive sense—larger cities are likely to spend more money on capital projects than small cities and are, by necessity, likely to adopt sophisticated methods of tracking and analyzing their expenditures. Yet, although there may be evidence of trends according to size among the population strata discussed in this chapter, it cannot be inferred from the data that governments in the smaller two strata (10–25,000 and 25–50,000) are uninvolved or unconcerned about capital budgeting. Indeed, the data indicate considerable interest in sophisticated capital budgeting procedures such as adoption of CIPs among smaller governments.

Second, the data appear to indicate that the definition of the Capital Improvement Program/Plan (CIP) as discussed in prescriptive budgeting literature may be too limited to reflect current practice. Over 40 percent of the respondent cities that claim to have a CIP indicate that they do not have a separate capital budget—the key ingredient of a CIP (according to the literature). Thus, capital budgets and CIPs may be modified or hybridized to reflect local concerns and issues.

Third, although there is a great deal of attention paid to novel, innovative means of financing capital projects, the data indicate that traditional methods—current revenues, G.O. and revenue bonds, assessments and increments—are still the preferred means of funding. In spite of the Reagan Administration's emphasis on privatization, there is no evidence by the presented data of a major move in that direction. In particular, there appears to be very little interest in creative bond methods as a means of acquiring funds for capital projects.

Fourth, local governments are affected by many of the same considerations and constraints which affect corporations in the decision-making process regarding capital spending. Although there may be less emphasis on quantitative analytic techniques among local governments, the literature indicates that there may be less pure rational thinking within the private sector than many governmental administrators might imagine. To some extent, political considerations play a major role in both sectors in the selection of capital projects. Local government officials might find this to be useful information when next they are accused of making irrational decisions by individuals from the private sector.

In conclusion, capital budgeting has begun to emerge in recent years as a topic of importance to students of budgeting and governmental finance. While the basic concept of capital budgeting appears to cross public private boundaries, there are considerable differences in the implementation of the practice both between the sectors and within population strata of the public sector. Yet, in spite of what we have learned about capital budgeting, there is a great deal we do not know. We still have not carefully assessed capital budgeting practices among small local governments (under 10,000), and county governments have been somewhat neglected as well.

Also, there is an emerging body of public works and public administration literature about the nation's infrastructure. Numerous authors argue that the infrastructure of many of our major cities is at the point of catastrophic breakdown. Obviously, to the extent that these arguments are correct and to the extent that public policy reacts to them in future years, even greater emphasis may be placed on the subject of capital budgeting.

NOTES

1. The term, "benefit cost," has a variety of meanings ranging from highly developed quantitative models to simplistic "do the numbers" schemes. It is not clear from the findings as reported by Kee et al. (1987) if benefit cost was defined by the survey instrument. Consequently, the degree of sophistication of the technique cannot be assessed from the findings as presented.
2. For a full definition and discussion of these financial tools, see Valente's article in the *1986 Municipal Year Book*. In addition to a host of other worthwhile information, Valente also describes three considerations, other than equity, which affect local government decisions about the type of financing method to undertake:
   1. Administrative ease—does the unit of government have the expertise to implement the option?;
   2. Political acceptance—do private citizens and the business community find the option acceptable?; and,
   3. Availability—is the financing tool available and does state law permit it?

REFERENCES

Abdelsamad, Moustafa H. (1973). *A Guide to Capital Expenditure Analysis.* AMACOM, New York.

Aronson, J. Richard and Schwartz, Eli (1982). *Management Policies in Local Government Finance.* MFOA/ICMA, Washington, D.C.

Boness, A. James (1972). *Capital Budgeting: The Public and Private Sectors.* Praeger Publishers, New York.

Burchell, Robert W. and Listokin, David (Eds.) (1981). *Cities Under Stress.* Center for Urban Policy Research, Rutgers, New Jersey.

Connors, Tracy D. and Callaghan, Christopher T. (Eds.) (1982). *Financial Management for Nonprofit Organizations.* American Management Association, New York.

Corwin, Margaret A. and Getzels, Judith (1981). Capital expenditures: Causes and controls. In Burchell and Listokin (1981):387–401.

DeVoy, Robert and Wise, Harold, with Towles, Joan (1979). *The Capital Budget.* Council of State Planning Agencies, Washington, D.C.

Doss, C. Bradley (1986). An Assessment of the Capital Budgeting Practice of Municipal Governments in the United States. Dissertation, University of Georgia, Athens.

Doss, C. Bradley (1986). The role of capital budgeting and related fiscal management tools in municipal governments. *State & Local Government Review. 18* (Fall):101–108.

Doss, C. Bradley (1987). The use of capital budgeting procedures in U. S. cities. *Public Budgeting and Finance. 7.* Autumn:57–69.

Edge, C. Geoffrey and Irvine, V. Bruce (1981). *A Practical Approach to the Appraisal of Capital Expenditure.* The Society of Management Accountants of Canada, Hamilton, Ontario.

Gaertner, James (1982). Capital expenditure budgets. In Connors and Callaghan (1982):45–57.

Hillhouse, Albert M. and Howard, Kenneth (1961). *State Capital Budgeting.* Council of State Governments, Chicago.

Hush, Lawrence W. and Peroff, Kathleen (1988). State capital budgets. *Public Budgeting and Finance. 8* (Summer):67–79.

Kamensky, John M. (1984). Budgeting for state and local infrastructure: Developing a strategy. *Public Budgeting and Finance. 4* (Autumn):3–17.

Kee, Robert, Robbins, Walter, and Apostolou, Nicholas (1987). Capital budgeting practices of U. S. cities: a survey. *The Government Accountants Journal. 36*:16–22.

Levitan, Donald and Byrne, Michael J. (1983). Capital improvement programming. In Rabin and Lynch (1983):585–599.

Mayer, Raymond R. (1978). *Capital Expenditure Analysis.* Waveland Press, Prospect Heights, Illinois.

McClain, Jackson M. (1966). *Capital Budgeting in Selected States.* University of Kentucky, Lexington.

Moak, Lennox L. and Gordon, Kathryn K. (1965). *Budgeting for Smaller Governmental Units.* Municipal Finance Officers Association, Chicago.

Murdick, Robert G. and Deming, Donald D. (1968). *The Management of Capital Expenditure*. Mcgraw-Hill, New York.

Pagano, Michael A. (1987). *The Effects of the 1986 Tax Reform Act on City Finances*. National League of Cities, Washington, D.C.:1–20.

Petersen, John E. (1988). Infrastructure financing: Examining the record and considering the options. In Stein (1988):94–116.

Poister, Theodore H. and McGowan, Robert P. (1984). The use of management tools in municipal government: A national survey. *Public Administration Review*. *44*:215–228.

Pritchard, Robert E. and Hindelang, Thomas J. (1981). *The Strategic Evaluation and Management of Capital Budgeting*. AMACOM, New York.

Rabin, Jack, Hildreth, W. Bartlet, and Miller, Girard J. (Eds.) (1983). *Budget Management: A Reader in Local Government Financial Management*. University of Georgia, Athens.

Rabin, Jack and Lynch, Thomas D. (Eds.) (1983). *Handbook on Public Budgeting and Financial Management,* Marcel Dekker, Inc., New York.

Rosenberg, Phillip and Stallings, C. Wayne (1978). *A Guidebook to Improved Financial Management for Small Cities and Other Governmental Units*. Government Finance Officers Association, Chicago.

Rosenfeld, Raymond A. (1989). Federal grants and local capital improvements. *Public Budgeting and Finance. 9*:74–84.

Sbragia, Alberta M. (Ed.) (1983). *The Municipal Money Chase: The Politics of Local Government Finance*. Westview Press, Boulder, Colorado.

Sbragia, Alberta M. (1983). Politics, local government, and the municipal bond market. In Sbragia (1983):67–111.

Sequerth, John. (1988). Coping with cutbacks. *American City and County. 103*: pf4–pf5.

Singhvi, Surendra (1981). The capital investment budgeting process. In Sweeny and Rachlin (1981):345–372.

Stein, Jay M. (Ed.) (1988). *Public Infrastructure Planning and Management*. Sage Publications, Newbury Park, California.

Steiner, Henry M. (1980). *Public and Private Investments: Socioeconomic Analysis*. John Wiley and Sons, New York.

Sweeny, W. Allen and Rachlin, Robert (Eds.) (1981). *Handbook of Budgeting*. John Wiley and Sons, New York.

Urban Data Services (1984). *Infrastructure*, vol. 16, International City Management Association, Washington, D.C.

Valente, Maureen G. (1986). Local government capital financing: Options and decisions. *Municipal Year Book*. International City Management Association, Washington, D.C.

Vogt, A. John (1983). Budgeting capital outlays and improvements. In Rabin, Hildreth and Miller (1983):128–143.

Wacht, Richard F. (1980). *A New Approach to Capital Budgeting for City and County Governments*. Georgia State University, Atlanta.

Wiggins, C. Don (1980). A case study in governmental capital budgeting. *Governmental Finance. 9*:19–22.

14

Public Cash Management: Issues and Practices

Merl M. Hackbart

University of Kentucky, Lexington, Kentucky

James R. Ramsey

Western Kentucky University, Bowling Green, Kentucky

I. INTRODUCTION

Historically, state and local governments have often been slow to adopt new cash management practices, frequently due to statutory and/or constitutional limitations which prescribed investment alternatives and maturities for safety reasons (see ACIR, 1977). However, during the last decade, the cash management philosophy of state and local government policymakers has changed significantly. This changing philosophy has resulted from a number of factors including:

State and local government officials began to realize that safety and cash management efficiency are not mutually exclusive.

State and local government managers and policymakers understood that the prevailing higher interest rates of the past decade represented opportunities to earn significant income on investable funds.

State and local government policymakers began to understand that income from efficient cash management could offset the need for additional tax revenue to finance critical public services during periods of severe fiscal stress as have been experienced in the last decade.

The purpose of this chapter is to identify and discuss the components of a state and local cash management program. The concept of cash management has often been used to refer strictly to the investment of public funds. However, this chapter will define a cash management program more broadly to include the receipt and deposit of funds, cash forecasting and banking relationships, and the investment of funds. Such a comprehensively defined cash management program ensures that a public organization deposits its funds in a timely fashion and pays its bills on time and that the availability of funds for investment purposes is maximized.

II. CASH MANAGEMENT: THE BASIC ELEMENTS

The goal of a cash management program is to "reduce the amount of cash that is being used within the firm so as to increase organizational profitability, but without lessening business activity or exposing the firm to undue risk in meeting its financial obligations" (Smith, 1979). While this cash management goal was developed for the private sector, it is equally applicable to the public sector. This cash management goal suggests that an organization should maintain an objective of minimizing cash holdings in order to maximize investment return, or "profitability."

A cash management program consists of four distinct components. These are 1) cash mobilization, 2) cash forecasting, 3) banking relationships, and 4) investment management. Each of these components is discussed in greater detail below. The "bottom line" for a comprehensive cash management program is a basic common sense tenet: one cannot invest funds that one does not have. Therefore, a cash management program's goal is to ensure that funds are deposited as quickly as possible and that bills are paid on time so that funds may be invested consistent with the defined objectives to maximize return consistent with safety and liquidity constraints.

III. CASH MOBILIZATION

The cash mobilization component of a cash management program involves the maximization of cash available for investment. This includes two fundamental processes: 1) accelerating the receipt of revenues, and 2) controlling the disbursement of funds. The processes and activities involved in carrying out these functions will depend on the fund being managed (including its source and use) and the organizational and geographical characteristics of the state and local governmental unit including its degree of autonomy and policy emphasis. In this section, emphasis is given to describing and analyzing alternative cash mobilization procedures available for use by the state and local government cash manager.

A. Revenue Acceleration

State and local government receipts come from four principal sources as indicated by Figure 14.1. The receipt date for tax collections may be specified in

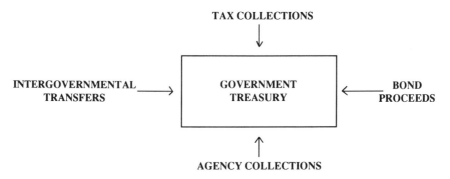

Figure 14.1

the enabling statute or ordinance and, therefore, may be beyond the policy or operational influence of the cash manager. In other cases, state and local governments may find that by requiring taxes to be remitted more rapidly by taxpayers (e.g., sales, corporate tax, severance tax) and perhaps, more often, allows funds to be invested for longer periods, thus increasing investment income. The date for the closing of a bond sale is typically included in the official statement for the bond sale and is normally subject to the discretion of the financial manager given the condition of the financial markets, processing times, and the need for funds.

Intergovernmental transfer receipt dates have historically tended to be flexible and subject to negotiation when federal and state laws are silent as to the transfer date and when "ownership" of funds is transferred between levels of government. Ownership patterns among federal agencies were typically guided by the generic type of transfer which might be involved including cost reimbursement (followed for years by the U.S. Department of Transportation) to the "delayed drawdown" procedures (followed by the U.S. Department of Health and Human Resources). However, the recently enacted Cash Management Improvement Act of 1990[1] defines uniform and consistent procedures for the receipt and disbursement of funds between the federal government and state and local governments. States have until 1992 to comply with this new legislation and its impact on state and local governments will be significant.

Agency fund collections include both "earmarked" tax revenues and agency receipts including enterprise funds (e.g., user fees at parks departments). Enterprise funds mirror cash acceleration options available to the private sector while other earmarked taxes and agency receipts such as tuition payments tend to follow statutory requirements or policies promulgated by special authorities. Therefore, acceleration options available to the cash manager tend to be limited. By contrast, government enterprise activities have the option of following normal private sector speed up processes including 1) modifying the paying behavior of the enterprise's customers or (2) improving the delivery system for such payments (Smith, 1979).

Since state and local government cash managers often have little control over time receipt technicalities of tax and other revenues, cash mobilization emphasis is typically directed toward expediting the collection and deposit of tax and other revenues within their depository institutions. Such activities are referred to as the "minimization of the negative float" associated with the receipt of funds. "Negative float" is the time delay between the disbursement of tax receipts by an individual or corporation and the receipt of those funds by the state treasurer or appropriate finance official.

Negative float can be divided into three subcategories (Smith, 1979). These categories of float are as follows:

"Mail float"—the lag between the time the taxpayer or other revenue source mails his payment and the moment at which the state or local government unit receives the payment.

"Processing float"—the time lapse between the receipt of the tax payment or revenue source and the deposit of such funds in the appropriate banking institution. This float category, essentially, represents the time required to appropriately record and process the payment by the Treasurer, Comptroller, or appropriate finance official.

"Clearing float"—the time lapse which may occur between the deposit of the check in the bank and time at which the bank recognizes the check as a legitimate source of funds. This float arises due to the processing time required to clear funds through the various banking institutions and the central bank—the Federal Reserve System.

The various categories of float are further depicted in Figure 14.2. Mail float is represented by the time lapse between taxpayer disbursement Point A and collection Point B; processing float occurs between Point B and Point C and involves tax processing activities; and clearing float is represented by the time lapse between the time of deposit by the Treasurer and the recognition of "good funds" by the bank at Point D.

Efforts to minimize negative float include the use of 1) lock box systems, 2) cash concentration accounts, and 3) electronic funds transfers. Lock box systems are designed to reduce mail float while concentration accounts are utilized to mitigate processing float. Electronic funds transfer processes influence both mail float and clearing float for banking institutions.

With a lock box system, taxpayers, user fee payers, and others mail payments directly to preselected post office boxes. The lock boxes are typically checked several times each day by a bank in the region who, in turn, records and deposits the checks for the appropriate agency or government. Deposited

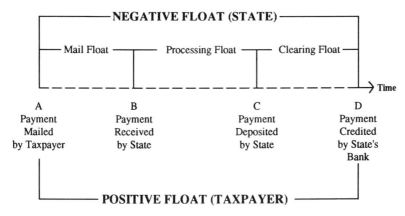

Figure 14.2   Float representation.

funds are then, normally, electronically transferred to the principal depository bank for the state or local government unit. A lock box system is represented by Figure 14.3.

The full implementation of a lock box system for a state would involve the strategic location of lock boxes throughout the state and/or nation in cities where there is sufficient volume to offset the costs of operation. In a typical

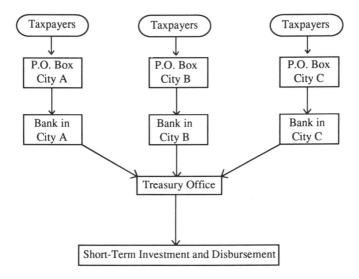

Figure 14.3   Lock box system (from Mikesell, 1986).

system, a regional bank would provide the collection and processing services for a fee or would be reimbursed by a compensatory balance agreement.

The use of lock box systems has had mixed reactions by state governments. For example, in one state, a lock box system has been used in combination with check encoding and sorting machines to transmit revenue receipts to regional banks for clearance (Bretschneider, 1982). Both mail and processing float have been reduced as a result of the innovation. In other states, concerns have been raised, however, by various state officials regarding the taxpayer's right to privacy of tax receipt information. If returns are handled with the same degree of concern for confidentiality and security as those processed by state agencies, no adverse taxpayer's right to privacy problems should occur (Bretschneider, 1982). Moreover, when used in combination with wire transfers, lock box systems can significantly reduce negative float from tax and other revenue receipts.

Like lock box systems, the use of concentration accounts is more applicable to state governments than to local governments and municipalities. The concentration account is a regional account which is utilized by multiple funds for initial deposits. Subsequently, funds are dispersed to the centralized depository account for investment or disbursement to payees. In addition, funds are typically wire transferred to the central depository bank/account to reduce mail float. Processing float may also be reduced by turning processing activities over to commercial banks which might have more efficient, cost-effective processing techniques than do state agencies.

The concentration account is represented by Figure 14.4. As shown, funds arrive from multiple sources and are processed into the concentration account by the Treasurer's office or by a commercial bank and become available for immediate investment or wire transfer to a centralized depository bank. In the absence of such an account, individual agencies and proprietary units across the state may operate small depository accounts which may be less efficient and can generate significant negative float.

To facilitate funds movement from the original receipt bank to the concentration bank are several paper and wire transfer funds systems such as Depository Transfer Checks (paper movement of funds) and the Automatic Clearing House (wire transfer of funds). In addition, funds can be moved by the use of wire transfers using the Federal Reserve System. A full discussion of the costs and benefits of each of these is beyond the scope of this presentation; however, each of these different methods for moving funds has different associated costs and availability of funds. The cash manager must evaluate these cash movement methodologies to determine which is most cost effective for his/her cash management program (Summers, 1986).

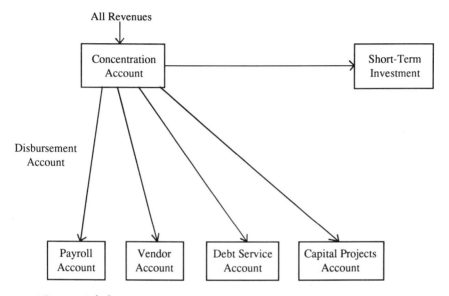

Figure 14.4   Concentration account representation (from Mikesell, 1986).

B.   Disbursement Management

As noted by one cash management expert, "cash mobilization is as dependent on a government's disbursement policies as it is on practices designed to accelerate the deposit of revenue" (Kiley, 1981). Characterized as positive float, there is value associated with the difference between the time a check is written to pay bills and the time the check is actually paid by the bank. Management of the time difference along with the timing of the initial disbursement authorization to take into account discounts while not paying debts prior to a due date if a discount is not available constitute the key features of an effective disbursement management system.

The importance of a properly managed disbursement system has been shown to be significant. For example, if a payment due in 30 days carries a 1 percent discount when paid in full in 10 days (20 days in advance), the savings are equivalent to an annual rate of return of 18 percent (Legislative Research Commission, 1982). The equivalent rates for full payment 30 days in advance would be 12 percent. Such rates would, of course, be compared to the "opportunity interest foregone" to determine the optimal disbursement pattern.

In addition to timing of disbursements, the means of disbursement is also an important consideration. Disbursement float can be eliminated via a zero balance account. With such an account, a single general account is maintained along with single clearing accounts for different agencies or funds (Advisory Commission on Intergovernmental Relations, 1977). The special clearing accounts are maintained with zero balances until checks are presented for payment. At that time, funds are transferred from the general account to cover the payment or payments scheduled for that time period. The funds in the general account are, of course, invested in relatively liquid securities which can be converted to cash as the need arises to cover the clearing demands of the separate clearing accounts.

IV. CASH FORECASTING

The principal reason for cash forecasting is to provide the investment or portfolio manager with reliable information regarding patterns of revenue receipts and expenditures by investment fund. Such information permits the funds to be invested in longer term, higher yielding assets. As shown in Figure 14.5, different funds tend to demonstrate different receipt and expenditure patterns. At the same time, different assets have different yield curve patterns as displayed in Figure 14.6. The matching of investable funds against receipt and expenditure patterns to maximize yield becomes the challenge of the cash forecasting process. Obviously, in making cash forecasts, accuracy is of utmost importance. If an asset is prematurely liquidated due to unanticipated cash flow needs, income from that investment may be severely reduced. Therefore, forecasting precision is critical to effective cash management.

Forecasts may be made by 1) judgment given past patterns of receipts and expenditures, 2) by time series analysis which utilizes statistical equations to predict the future flows based upon the supposition that past patterns best predict the future, and 3) by economic analysis which explains past cash flow relationships including tax and other revenues and expenditures and economic performance to predict future cash flows through mathematical and statistical equations. Such cash forecasts can be short term involving daily, weekly, or monthly assessments of cash flow patterns. Short-term forecasts are vital for the management of the portfolio within the fiscal year period as the investment manager may want to realize all investment income within the fiscal year if the government unit is operating on a cash or a quasi-cash accounting system. Longer term forecasts (beyond the fiscal year) provide the cash manager with early indications of potential cash flow problems in the out years. Long-run forecasts can also assist the investment manager in selecting higher yielding long-term assets when appropriate. An example would be a capital construction fund or agency revolving fund which does not have to be managed so as to realize investment income within a single fiscal year period (Bretschneider, 1982).

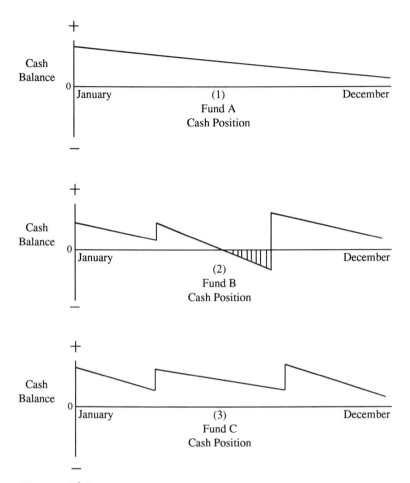

Figure 14.5   Revenue and expenditure patterns by fund (from ACIR, 1977).

Regardless of the cash forecasting approach (judgment, time series, or economic/time series), the essence of cash forecasting involves a process of segregating financial transactions into flow patterns. For example, as shown in Figure 14.7, revenue inflows which might come from agency receipts, taxes, user fees, or intergovernmental transfers can be expended, held, or invested. Likewise, funds which are invested can be reinvested, liquidated and made available for expenditures, or held in cash or "cash equivalents" for contingency purposes. The indicated key decision points require that the investment manager be knowledgeable regarding revenue inflows and expenditure outflows as well as the level of funds to be held as cash or cash equivalents to account for potential errors in the cash flow estimates. With such data and

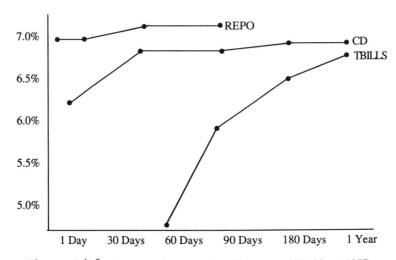

Figure 14.6   Asset yield curves (from Ramsey and Hackbart, 1987).

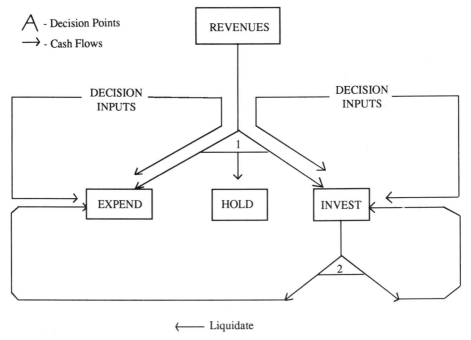

Figure 14.7   Decision making process cash flow (from Bretschneider et al., 1982).

information, the manager is in a better position to estimate the funds to be invested, their duration as well as the quantity of funds which might be reinvested as assets reach maturity. The flows could also be represented to reflect greater cash flow precision (see Appendix A).

The forecasting process as it relates to the total cash management cycle is shown in Figure 14.8. With a judgment model, the analyst would simply review past cash flow and forecast future patterns to make investment decisions. With time series forecasting, attempts would be made to project cash flows given past patterns. Decisions regarding new investments and reinvestments would be based upon the existing portfolio as well as allowable limits on cash held for precautionary purposes. With an economic/time series fore-

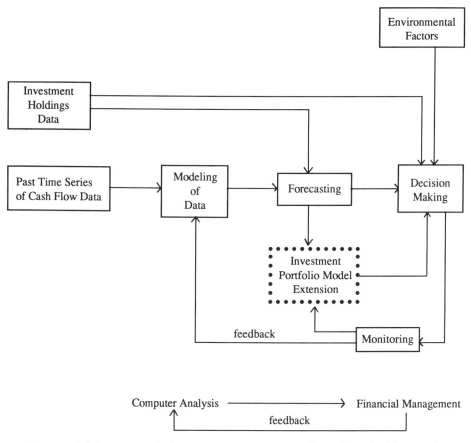

Figure 14.8 The cash flow management process (from Bretschneider et al., 1982).

casting approach, greater emphasis would be directed toward modelling past time series data regarding cash flow and the current investment portfolio yield or cash flow. Computer data bases are, of course, critical to all forecasting techniques as they form the basis for carrying out the analysis of previous patterns of receipts and expenditures and making judgments regarding the degree of reliability which can be placed on such patterns (Bretschneider, 1982).

V. BANK RELATIONSHIPS

Banking relationships are another element of a complete cash management system. As suppliers of services to state and local governments (including operating and maintaining depository accounts, lock box systems, processing checks, and providing other financial services), banking institutions provide an integral component of the cash management process. In addition to providing transaction services, banks facilitate investment activities and may provide an investment option for public fund managers as a provider of certificates of deposit or repurchase agreements.

Banking policy issues for state and local governments include 1) whether single or multiple depository accounts should be maintained, 2) whether banking services will be paid for with fees for services provided or whether a "compensating" balance will be maintained with the selected depository bank or banks, and (3) whether contract banking services will be secured via bid or negotiated.

Issues surrounding single or multiple depository accounts have both efficiency and structural implications. A single depository bank provides an opportunity to locate all fund balances or investable funds in a single banking institution. In such a situation, zero balance accounts and/or concentration accounts may be facilitated. The state's banking structure also impacts the decision process regarding a single or multiple depository banking choice. With cross state or branch banking, one major banking institution may be able to provide a complete set of cash management services including lock boxes, concentration accounts, zero balance accounts, and other routine banking services. In such a situation, the use of a single statewide bank as a depository may be an efficient model. In other states with more limiting banking laws, different combinations of depository and banking service arrangements may be more desirable.

As noted, the method of paying for banking services involves a choice between paying fees for individual banking services such as check clearing and the like vis-a-vis maintaining a compensating balance. With the fee for service approach, bidding or negotiation determines the fee structure for each service performed. The compensating balance approach involves an "estimate" of the aggregate services or an actual account of services performed and the concomitant determination of the appropriate balance of funds which, if invested by the bank at the current market rate, will yield a comparable total compensation package. Some states and localities are statutorily forbidden from making direct payments for banking services. In such cases, the compensating balance approach becomes the preferred method by default. In less restrictive settings, state or local governments may select the preferred bank compensation method.

VI. INVESTMENT MANAGEMENT

The final component of a comprehensive cash management program is the actual investment of the available funds. The investment of public funds is usually carried out pursuant to the achievement of three objectives: 1) safety of the public funds involved, 2) liquidity, and 3) maximization of the return on investment funds. The relative weighing of the three objectives varies depending upon the fund and its cash flow characteristics, the willingness of the governmental unit to trade off risk for return, and staff expertise and capability to manage the portfolio.

A. Investment Goals

1. *Safety*

Like the trade off between maturity and rate of return, trade offs also exist between rate of return and risk. In other words, certain investment assets contain a credit risk premium to reflect the probability that the original cash value may not be realized at the maturity of the investment asset.[2] For active cash management, safety also refers to the degree to which an asset's cash value may be determined at any point in time or its predictability. Figure 14.9 indicates, in relative terms, the predictability associated with several categories of investable assets. Cash, of course, is perfectly predictable, while certificates of deposit, U. S. securities, and commercial paper are partially predictable. By comparison, stocks and private bonds are unpredictable.

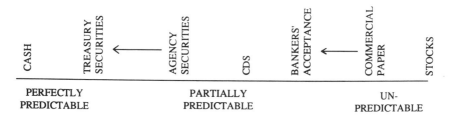

Figure 14.9 Predictability of portfolio assets.

Two issues arise for the investment manager as a result of concern over safety. First, the manager must determine the degree to which the government unit will accept risk in return for potentially higher investment returns. Often such risk acceptance will be specified by statute or ordinance in the form of a listing of permissible assets—assets in which the governmental unit can legally invest. The second issue facing the investment manager involves the identification of means of predicting cash flow requirements so as to reduce the need to convert assets prior to maturity to cash to meet expenditures since the portfolio manager is exposed to market risk if forced to liquidate assets prior to maturity.

As indicated by the hypothetical yield curve shown by Figure 14.10, longer term investments tend to yield higher rates of return. To the degree that a governmental unit can effectively predict net cash flow requirements, the investment manager can achieve higher rates of return by extending investment periods within a portfolio. In doing so, return is further maximized without impacting the safety or predictability needs of the organization.

2. *Liquidity Considerations*

Liquidity refers to the speed and ease with which an investment asset can be converted to cash. Liquidity is measured in the credit markets by the activity of the secondary market for the asset (the bid ask spread). For example, there

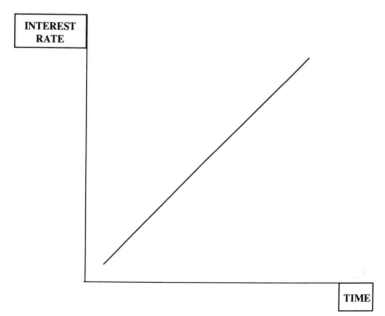

Figure 14.10 Yield curve.

is a very active secondary market for Treasury securities with very small differences between the price at which a Treasury security can be bought or sold at a point in time. Therefore Treasuries are considered to be very liquid. Real estate, on the other hand, often has a less active secondary market and is therefore considered less liquid. Liquidity is an important investment consideration for the previously discussed reasons.

3. *Yield Maximization*

The maximization of return on a state or local government's portfolio requires careful, effective management of a series of interrelated activities. Information which the portfolio manager must have to make effective return maximizing decisions include the following items:

Information regarding the cash flow patterns for the various funds that he/she will be managing.

Information regarding the set of assets in which funds can be invested by the portfolio manager.

Information regarding the nature and characteristics of the assets in which can be invested, including the security's maturity, its denomination, its marketability, and yield.

Information regarding investment strategies available and how they can be implemented given the cash flow requirements of the government unit/ fund, permissible assets and the knowledge and capability of the investment office's staff and scope of investment operations.

The interaction of multiple objectives becomes obvious upon reviewing the list of factors which must be considered in the investment management process. Certainly, liquidity needs present an overriding consideration in the investment policy decision-making process. Likewise, the specification of permissible assets is directly tied to safety goals of the organization. In fact, most states legislate permissible assets because, as noted earlier, concern for safety of investments tends to override other investment goals. For that matter, it has been argued that the permissible assets for most state and local governments are inherently safe. Therefore, only liquidity and yield remain as concerns of the state investment manager (Kiley, 1981). In the next section of this chapter, other investment concepts are discussed in more detail. These form the essence of a state or local government's investment policy as they represent the parameters within which a "prudent man rule" to investment management might generally apply (Bretschneider, 1982).

B. Permissible Assets

Given cash flow characteristics, the cash manager attempts to select a set of assets which will maximize returns of the portfolio. The public investment manager is, however, typically constrained regarding the specific assets which can be used in the portfolio. As noted, such constraints emerge from an over-riding concern for portfolio security and may involve statutory or regulatory restrictions. Such restrictions generally fall into three categories including 1) eligibility standards, 2) interest rate setting, and 3) special depository financial institution restrictions which vary from permissive to very specific (Hackbart, 1975).

As noted, the first category of state laws affecting portfolio management policy involves eligibility standards for the investment of surplus funds. State statutes specifying types of assets, maturity of assets, and number of assets which can be held are commonplace among the states. Asset holdings are typi-cally limited to securities of the highest credit quality such as U.S. Govern-ment obligations (Treasury bills, notes, agency obligations) or commercial bank deposits, bankers' acceptances, and collateralized repurchase agreements (Hackbart, 1975; also see Bretschneider, 1982). Appendix B provides a detailed list of the assets most frequently utilized by public funds managers and their characteristics.

The second category of laws affecting investment options includes re-strictions on the interest rate to be paid on state and/or local government investments. For example, often legal requirements specify that the State Treasurer set the rate on state time deposits at a rate equal to the available rate on U.S. Government securities for comparable maturities. Other states require bidding of rates for state bank deposits (Bretschneider, 1982).

The third group of state statutes circumscribing state investment practices tends to constrain the depository relationships with financial institutions. Included are specifications regarding the type of financial institution which can hold state deposits (commercial banks vis-a-vis thrifts) so as to ensure that funds placed with financial institutions can be collateralized. Such collater-alization requirements prescribe that a financial institution holding state funds match such holdings with high quality securities (typically U.S. Government securities) to guard against default. The impact of collateralization might be a slightly reduced asset yield but enhanced security. The investment manager must continually revalue collateral to ensure the collateral's value meets statu-tory specifications, such specifications are generally 100 percent of asset value or some greater collateralization requirement.

C. Investment Strategies

In general, one of three investment strategies are pursued by public funds managers: 1) passive investment strategies; 2) active investment strategies; or 3) hybrid investment strategies (Fong, 1985). The manager utilizing passive strategies assumes that the credit markets are efficient (Walton, 1981). That is, a passive portfolio manager assumes that perfect information is transmitted instantaneously to an infinite number of buyers and sellers in the credit markets so that the opportunity to realize price appreciation from the existence of temporary price disequilibriums in the markets will not exist. In addition, the passive portfolio manager does not formulate a market expectation that either interest rates will go up or down in an effort to achieve price appreciation. Thus, the passive manager seeks to maximize only coupon income and does this with a buy and hold approach whereby securities are bought and held to maturity (Fong, 1985).

The active portfolio manager, on the other hand, assumes that the credit markets are not efficient. The active manager assumes that temporary price disequilibriums do occur in the markets and that by taking advantage of these trading opportunities, the public funds manager can increase portfolio yield through asset price appreciation. The active manager is willing to make a market call, or forecast of future interest rates, in an effort to structure the portfolio to take advantage of price movements (Fong, 1985). While the passive manager is risk averse and attempts to ignore interest rate risk, the active manager is willing to take a predetermined amount of risk in order to achieve a greater portfolio return (Fong, 1985). An active manager for example may have cash to invest for 90 days. The active manager may expect interest rates to fall and security prices to rise. Therefore, this manager may buy a two-year Treasury Note with the expectation that in 90 days the security can be sold for a capital gain.

The final portfolio strategy is the category of hybrid approaches which contain elements of both the passive and active strategies. The portfolio manager following a hybrid strategy attempts to create a portfolio with an assured return for a specific time horizon regardless of interest rate movements. Unlike the active manager, the hybrid approach does not attempt to maximize overall portfolio return but rather seeks a target portfolio return. Unlike the passive manager, the hybrid approach does not accept interest rate volatility and the price movements which accompany it but rather, through continual restructuring of the portfolio, attempts to smooth out the impacts of interest rate movements. As with an active approach, this requires the recognition of the total yield or return of the portfolio.

A common hybrid approach is the Treasury roll (Fong, 1985). For example, the portfolio manager may buy a two year Treasury Note. The next month, the portfolio manager sells this security and the "new" two-year Treasury being sold by the United States Treasury is purchased. The process continues every month. If interest rates go up while the security is held in the portfolio, the value of the security goes down and the portfolio realizes a capital loss when the security is sold. However, if the new interest rate is higher, more interest income will be earned to offset the capital loss. Conversely, if interest rates fall while the security is held in the portfolio, a capital gain is realized but the funds will be reinvested at a lower interest rate. This "rolling" strategy allows for the achievement of a target rate of return; it has been said that the manager who uses the hybrid approach does not strike out or hit a home run but rather consistently hits singles.

The actual set of strategies utilized by a portfolio manager will be a function of the specific goals adopted for the portfolio. In addition, since active and hybrid strategies require greater management time and expertise, very practical considerations often are important in the selection of an investment strategy. Also, within a portfolio, one strategy may be appropriate for one governmental fund or set of accounts and another strategy may be more appropriate for other funds or sets of accounts. The same portfolio may use a combination of strategies.

VII. SUMMARY

The management of state and local government cash reserves has emerged as a major financial management issue in the 1980s. State and local governments have begun to realize more fully that effective cash management can be a significant source of additional nontax revenue. Therefore, a growing need exists to identify the most efficient and effective techniques and processes to improve the cash management process.

As noted, there are four major components of the cash management process, including cash mobilization, cash forecasting, banking relationships, and investment management. Each of these cash management system components involves a series of steps or activities which can enhance investment earnings. Cash mobilization activities as well as cash investment management processes of state and local governments can be significantly improved by drawing on private sector practices and procedures. Activities such as lock boxes, concentration accounts, zero balance accounts, and cash forecasting practices described in this chapter are among the adoptable practices.

As state and local governments continue to increase their cash management capability, portfolio management, cash forecasting, and mobilization procedures will be enhanced. The financial sector is changing rapidly as a result of changing regulations, technology, and approaches to financial management. The challenge to the public sector is to continue to identify and adopt new practices so that financial resources are optimized. To do less would be to breach the public trust.

VIII. APPENDIX A: CASH FLOW AND FORECASTING
(Bretschneider, 1982)

Modelling cash flows can simplify a complex system of revenue and expenditure patterns for state and local governments. By such simplification, the cash manager can develop insights regarding the cash flows of a government unit and more effectively visualize and anticipate the consequences of alternative actions and policies. In the same sense, the elements of a cash forecasting system can be modelled to focus on the data and statistical issues associated with a cash forecasting system. In the equations which follow, cash flow equations and a representation of the basic elements of a cash forecasting system are represented.

State cash flows may be stated as follows:

$$B_t = R_t - E_t \tag{1}$$

Simply put, this means that for any period, t, the net change in cash balance (B_t) is equal to the difference between new revenue inflows (R_t) and new expenditure outflows (E_t) for that period. B_t, therefore, represents the new cash surplus (or shortage) to be added to (or subtracted from) existing asset holdings.

The new cash balance represents only one part of the cash flow important to investment decision making. Also of concern are the flows that occur when investments mature. As securities held in a portfolio mature, they represent cash in addition to net inflows that are available for investment purposes. Therefore, cash holdings may be expressed in the following manner:

$$C_t = B_t + I_t \tag{2}$$

In this case, for any period, t, cash holdings (C_t) available for investment are equal to the net change in cash to balance (B_t) plus any investments maturing in that period (I_t).

A state and local government's investment portfolio consists of securities that vary greatly in type, size, and maturity. Consequently, on any given day, several different investments may mature. In reality then, I_t represents the sum of all securities (n) being liquidated in period t, or:

$$I_t = I_{1t} + I_{2t} + \cdots I_{it} \tag{3}$$

or

$$I_t = \sum_{i=1}^{n} I_{it} \tag{4}$$

By definition, I_{it} is the amount held in investment i maturing in period t.

By combining equations 1, 2 and 4, the model of state cash flows for any given period, t, becomes:

$$C_t = (R_t - E_t) + \sum_{i=1}^{n} I_{it} \tag{5}$$

One source of funds purposefully left out of this model is the cash held in the form of compensatory balances. As noted in the text, governments often maintain idle bank balances as compensation for services rendered by financial institutions. Since these balances represent funds not available for investment or disbursement, and should never exceed minimum requirements except for the brief period in which they are being disbursed, they are not of real concern to the cash manager. Therefore, they are not incorporated in the cash flow model.

In a typical state or local government, fund account records provide all the information required regarding revenue and expenditure flows (R_t and E_t of the model, respectively). Depending on the structure or the accounting system, account records may require additional filtering to isolate the appropriate transactions. In other words, individual transactions are reduced to "real" cash flows and aggregated by day, week, and month by account.

Given the cash flow transaction equations, the amount of cash on hand to invest should be determined. However, in order to make investment decisions, the cash manager must also be cognizant of future cash flows. For example, information regarding how long those funds will be available for investment and what future shortages and surpluses can be anticipated is required. Cash forecasting is needed to fill those information gaps.

The data available for use in the construction of a forecasting procedure for state cash flows are in the form of a time series. By definition, a time series is any sequence of measurements taken on a variable over time at equally spaced intervals. The cash flow data base provides revenue and expenditure data in this form. Consequently, forecasting methodologies include a variety of time series analyses.

In predicting future values of a particular variable, time series analysis assumes that the future is a function of the past. Future cash flows, in other words, are no more than an extrapolation of historical revenue and expenditure patterns. In mathematical terms, time series methods can be generalized to the following model (SAS/ETS User's Guide-Econometric and Time-Series Library, 1980):

$$X_t = b_0 + b_1 X_{t-1} + b_2 X_{t-2} + \cdots b_i X_{t-i} + e_t \tag{6}$$

This means that the dependent variable at time t (X_t), is a function of its recent history (values for a finite number of periods equal to i), plus an error term.

Applying this model to state or local government cash flows, one comes up with the following:

$$R_t = b_0 + b_1 R_{t-1} + b_2 R_{t-2} + \cdots b_i R_{t-1} + e_i \tag{7}$$

Simply stated, revenue in time r (R_t) is a function of past revenue flows, plus an unspecified error term (e_t). Similarly, expenditures can be stated as follows:

$$E_t = b_0 + b_1 E_{t-1} + b_2 E_{t-2} + \cdots b_i E_{t-1} + e_t \qquad (8)$$

This indicates that expenditure flows in time t (E_t), are a function of historical outflows, plus an error term (e_t).

Accuracy is of the utmost importance to forecasting the future. Therefore, the assessment of the performance of different forecasting methodologies given a post sample experimental design approach is appropriate. Such an approach entails five steps. First, historical data are divided into two samples, one to be used to estimate the forecast model, and the other to be used in validating forecast performance. Second, the forecast model based on estimation sample data is used to forecast future values. Third, these forecasts are compared to the actual values in the validation sample and accuracy measures are calculated. Fourth, this process is done for all forecast methods being considered and the accuracy measures for each are compared. Fifth, and finally, the best forecast model is selected and used. This process is repeated when new data is obtained. Among the methods which might be employed in this matter are 1) stepwise autoregressive methods, or 2) exponential smoothing methods.

IX. APPENDIX B: MARKET INSTRUMENTS

Security	Minimum Denomination	Form	Guarantee	Interest Payment Schedule and Day Basis for Computation	Original Maturity Range
Tresury Notes and Bonds	$1,000, $5,000 and $10,000	Book entry, registered or bearer	Full faith and credit of U.S. Gov't.	Semiannually; actual # of days ÷ # of days in cpn. period	12 months to 30 years
Treasury Bills	$10,000	Book entry	Full Faith and credit of U.S. Gov't.	Treasury bills are issued at a discount; actual # of days ÷ 360 days	3 months to 1 year
Bankers' Acceptances	$100,000	Bearer	Guaranteed by accepting bank	Discount basis; actual # of days ÷ 360 days	30 days to 270 days
Certificates of Deposit	Round lot $100,000	Bearer	Guaranteed by issuing bank	Semiannually, quarterly and annually at maturity; actual # of days 360 days	30 days to 1 year and over 4 years

Security	Minimum Denomination	Form	Guarantee	Interest Payment Schedule and Day Basis for Computation	Original Maturity Range
Farm Credit Discount Notes	$50,000	Bearer	No expressed liability assumed by U.S. Gov't.	Discount obligation; actual # of days ÷ 360 days	Up to 9 months
Farmers Home Administration Insured Notes	Varies $25,000 $100,000 $500,000 $1,000,000	Older issues registered only; recent issues, bearer or registered	Full faith and credit of U. S. Gov't.	Actual ÷ 365 days	5 years to 15 years
Federal Home Loan Bank Bonds	Older issues $5,000; new issues $10,000	Bearer; book entry for all new issues as of Nov. 25, 1977	No expressed liability assumed by U.S. Gov't.	Semiannually; 30-day month ÷ 360 days	1 year to 20 years
FHLMC Capital Debentures	$10,000	Book entry only	Federal Home Loan Mortgage Corporation	Semiannually 30-day month ÷ 360 days	10 years
Commercial Paper	Round lot $100,000; minimum $25,000	Bearer	Guaranteed by issuing corporation	Discount basis; actual # of days ÷ 360 days	3 days to 270 days
Asian Development Bank Notes and Bonds	$1,000	Registered as to principal only	No Guarantee by U.S. Gov't.	Semiannually; 30-day month ÷ 360 days	5 years to 25 years
Banks for Co-Operatives Bonds	$5,000	Bearer on older issues; book entry on all new issues as of Jan. 1, 1978	No expressed liability assumed by U.S Gov't.	At maturity of 6 - months issues. Otherwise, semi-annually; 30-day month ÷ 360 days	6 months to 3 1/2 years
Farm Credit Banks Consolidated System-Wide Bonds	Varies $1,000 $5,000	Book entry only	Guaranteed by 37 banks of the Farm Credit System	At maturity for 6-month and 9-month issues; otherwise semi-annually; 30-day month ÷ 360 days	6 months to 11 years
Export Import Bank Debentures and Participation	$5,000	Registered or bearer, eligible for book entry	Full faith and credit of U.S. Gov't.	Semiannually; 30-day month ÷ 360 days	3 years to 15 years

Security	Minimum Denomination	Form	Guarantee	Interest Payment Schedule and Day Basis for Computation	Original Maturity Range
Federal Land Bank Bonds	$1,000	Bearer except for older registered issues; book entry for all new issues as of Jan. 1, 1978	No expressed liability assumed by U.S. Gov't.	Semiannually; ÷ 360 days	18 months to 15 years
FNMA Capital Debentures	$10,000	Registered or bearer, eligible for book entry	No expressed liability assumed by U.S. Gov't.	Semiannually; 30-day month 360 days	5 years to 25 years
FNMA Debentures	$10,000	Bearer; book entry for all new issues as of March 10, 1978	No expressed liability assumed by U.S. Gov't.	Semiannually; 30-day month ÷ 360 days	13 months to 25 years
FNMA Discount Notes	$5,000	Bearer	No liability assumed by U.S. Gov't.	Discount obligation; actual # of days ÷ 360 days	30 days to 270 days
Federal Home Loan Mortgage Participation Certificates	$100,000	Registered	Guaranteed by the Federal Home Mortgage Corporation	Monthly payment of principal and interest; 30-day month ÷ 360 days	30 years, 12 years prepaid life
Federal Home Loan Bank Consolidated Notes	$100,000	Bearer	No expressed liability assumed by U.S. Gov't.	Discount notes; actual # of days ÷ 360 days	Up to one year
Federal Home Loan Corporation Guaranteed Mortgage Certificates	$100,000 $500,000 $1,000,000	Registered	Federal Home Loan Mortgage Corporation	Semiannually; 30-day month ÷ 360 days	18 years to 31 years
Federal Intermediate Credit Bank Bonds	$5,000	Bearer on older issues; book entry on all new issues as of Jan, 1, 1978	No expressed liability assumed by U.S. Gov't.	At maturity for 9-month issues. Otherwise semi-annually; 30-day month ÷ 360 days	9 months to 4 years

Security	Minimum Denomination	Form	Guarantee	Interest Payment Schedule and Day Basis for Computation	Original Maturity Range
Inter-American Development Bank Bonds	$1,000	Registered	No expressed liability assumed by U.S. Gov't.	Semiannually; 30-day month ÷ 360 days	20 years to 30 years
International Bank for Reconstruction and Development (World Bank) Bonds	$1,000	Registered or bearer	No expressed liability assumed by U.S. Gov't.	Semiannually; 30-day month ÷ 360 days	5 years to 25 years
Penn Central Transportation Certificates (Gov't. G'td.)	$10,000	Registered	Guaranteed by Secretary of Transportation; general obligations of U.S. Gov't.	Semiannually; 30-day month ÷360 days	5 years to 15 years
Postal Service Bonds	$10,00C	Registered of bearer, eligible for book entry	No expressed liability assumed by U.S. Gov't.	Semiannually; 30-day month ÷ 360 days	25 years
General Services Administration Participation Certificates	$5,000	Registered	Full faith and credit of U.S. Gov't.	Semiannually; 30-day month ÷ 360 days	30 years
GNMA Federal Home Loan Mortgage Corporation	$25,000;	Registered or bearer	Full faith and credit of U.S. Gov't.	Semiannually; 30-day month ÷ 360 days	2 years to 25 years
GNMA, FNMA Bonds	$25,000	Registered or bearer	Full Faith and credit of U.S. Gov't.	Semiannually; 30-day month ÷ 360 days	5 years to 20 years
GNMA Participation Certificates	Some $5,000; most $10,000	Registered or bearer; check specific issues	Full faith and credit of U.S. Gov't.	Semiannually; 30-day month ÷ 360 days	8 years to 20 years
GNMA Pass Throughs	Minimum denomination $25,000; multiples of $5,000 thereafter	Registered	Full faith and credit of U.S. Gov't.	Monthly payment of principal and interest; 30-day month ÷ 360 days	30 years; 12 years prepaid life assumed

Security	Minimum Denomination	Form	Guarantee	Interest Payment Schedule and Day Basis for Computation	Original Maturity Range
Private Export Funding Corporation	$5,000 on older ossues	Registered	Interest guaranteed by Ex-Im Bank	Semiannually; 30-day month ÷ 360 days	4 years to 11 years
Small Business Administration Debentures	$10,000	Registered	Guaranteed by SBA; general obligation of U.S. Gov't.	Semiannually; ÷ 360 days	10 years
Tenessee Valley Authority Bonds	$1,000	Registered or bearer	No expressed liability assumed by U.S. Gov't.	Semiannually; 30-day month ÷ 360 days	5 years to 25 years
Washington metropolitan Transit Authority Bonds	$5,000	Registered or bearer	Guaranteed by Secretary of Transportation; general obligations of U.S. Gov't.	Semiannually; 30-day month ÷ 360 days	40 years

NOTES

1. Due to different cash management procedures utilized by different federal agencies, the State/Federal Cash Management Reform Task Force was formed with representation from the Office for Management and Budget, the Department of Treasury, the National Association of State Auditors, Comptrollers and Treasurers (NASACT), and the National Association of State Budget Officers (NASBO) to develop one comprehensive set of cash management procedures to be used by federal, state, and local governments. This joint cooperative effort resulted in the passage of the Cash Management Improvement Act of 1990.
2. The discussion here focuses upon credit risk instead of market risk. The credit risk for a U.S. Treasury security is considered minimal; however, its value at any time prior to maturity is a function of interest rates. Therefore, even a U.S. Treasury security that has minimal credit risk does have some market risk prior to maturity.

REFERENCES

Advisory Commission on Intergovernmental Relations (1977). *Understanding State and Local Cash Management*. Advisory Commission on Intergovernmental Relations, Washington, D.C., pp. 11–14.

Bretschneider, S., Hackbart, M., and Ward, B. (1982). *State Cash Flow Management: The Kentucky System.* Martin Center for Public Administration, University of Kentucky, Lexington, Kentucky.

Fong, H. Gifford and Fabozzi, Frank J. (1985). *Fixed Income Portfolio Management.* Dow-Jones-Irwin, Homewood, Illinois, pp. 93–228.

Hackbart, M. and Johnson, R. (1975). *State Cash Balance Management Policy.* The Council of State Governments, Lexington, Kentucky, pp. 2, 7.

Kiley, J. (1981). A Perspective on Public Cash Management in the 1980s. *Government Finance.* December, pp. 5, 6.

Legislative Research Commission (1982). *Program Evaluation: Commonwealth Cash Management*, No. 124. Legislative Research Commission, Frankfort, Kentucky, p. 18.

Ramsey, J.R. and Hackbart, M.M. (1987). *Introduction to Cash Management.* Government Finance Officers Association, State of New Hampshire, Concord, New Hampshire.

SAS/ETS User's Guide—Econometric and Time-Series Library (1980). ASA Institute, Cary, North Carolina, p. 3.3.

Smith, K.V. (1979). *Guide to Working Capital Management.* McGraw-Hill, Inc., New York, N.Y., pp. 71, 72.

Summers, B.J. (1986). Dr. Frankenstein and the ACH. *Economic Review.* April, pp. 5–8.

Walton, Edwin J. and Gruber, Martin J. (1981). *Modern Portfolio Theory and Investment Analysis.* John Wiley and Sons, New York, N.Y., pp. 358–388.

Index

315